Education, Reform and the State

Over the past twenty-five years, education has been transformed as it has moved to the centre of the political stage. There has been intense public and political interest in educational issues and there have been major changes in the ways in which schools, FE colleges and universities are organised and controlled. *Education, Reform and the State* provides the definitive contemporary history of education policy. The book brings together leading scholars to reflect on the major legislative and structural changes in education. Chapters include:

- Education, the state and the politics of reform: the historical context
- Creating a mass system of higher education
- The reinvention of teacher professionalism
- Empowerment or performativity?
- Gender and education policy

Education, Reform and the State combines contemporary history and policy analysis in a unique way, providing students of education policy, academics and researchers with important reference material.

Contributors: Jim Campbell, Geoffrey Walford, Martin Jephcote, Prue Huddleston, Gareth Rees, Dean Stroud, Richard Daugherty, Gary McCulloch, Patricia Broadfoot, Peter Tymms, Carol Fitz-Gibbon, Alan Dyson, Roger Slee, Sally Tomlinson, Madeleine Arnot, Miriam David, Gaby Weiner, Susan Robertson, Hugh Lauder, Tony Edwards.

Robert Phillips is Senior Lecturer in Education at the University of Wales Swansea. **John Furlong** works in the School of Social Sciences, Cardiff University. His previous publications include *Mentoring Student Teachers: The Growth of Professional Knowledge* (1995), co-authored with Tricia Maynard and published by Routledge.

Education, Reform and the State

Twenty-five years of politics, policy and practice

Edited by Robert Phillips and John Furlong

ROUTLEDGE / FALMER
Taylor & Francis Group

London and New York

First published 2001
by RoutledgeFalmer
11 New Fetter Lane, London EC4P 4EE

Simultaneously published in the USA and Canada
by RoutledgeFalmer
29 West 35th Street, New York, NY 10001

RoutledgeFalmer is an imprint of the Taylor & Francis Group

Typeset in Baskerville by Taylor & Francis Books Ltd
Printed and bound in Great Britain by St Edmundsbury Press,
Bury St Edmunds, Suffolk

British Library Cataloguing in Publication Data
A catalogue record for this book is available from the British Library

Library of Congress Cataloging in Publication Data
Education, reform and the state : twenty-five years of politics, policy and
practice /edited by Robert Phillips and John Furlong.
Includes bibliographical references and index.
1. Education and state–England. 2. Education and state–Wales.
3. Educational change–England. 4. Educational change–Wales.
I. Phillips, Robert, 1959– II. Furlong, John, 1947–
LC93.G7 E3755 2001
379.42–dc21   00-047060

ISBN 0–415–23764–5

Contents

Contents

Illustrations

Tables

Figures

Contributors

Madeleine Arnot is a Fellow of Jesus College and University Lecturer in the School of Education at the University of Cambridge. She has published extensively on the sociology of gender and education and on equality and citizenship issues in educational policy. Her recent publications include *Feminism and Social Justice in Education* (Falmer, 1993, co-edited with K. Weiler), *Review of Recent Research on Gender and Educational Performance* (Stationery Office/Office for Standards in Education, 1998, with J. Gray, M. James and J. Rudduck), *Closing the Gender Gap: Postwar Educational and Social Change* (Polity Press, 1999, with M. David and G. Weiner), *Challenging Democracy: International Perspectives on Gender, Education and Citizenship* (RoutledgeFalmer, 2000, co-edited with J.A. Dillabough) and the forthcoming *Reproducing Gender? Selected Critical Essays on Educational Politics and Practice*.

Patricia Broadfoot is Dean of Social Science and Professor of Education at the University of Bristol. She is well known for her work in assessment and comparative education and is editor of two international journals in these fields – *Assessment in Education* and *Comparative Education*. She co-directed the three phases of the PACE project, a major ESRC-funded study of the impact of the National Curriculum and National Assessment on primary school pupils and teachers.

Jim Campbell is Director of the Institute of Education, Warwick University. His main research interests are curriculum development and curriculum policy in primary education. His publications include *Developing the Primary Curriculum* (Holt, Rhinehart & Winston, 1985), *Breadth and Balance in the Primary Curriculum* (Falmer, 1993), *Primary Teachers at Work* (Routledge, 1994), *The Meaning of Infant Teachers' Work* (Routledge, 1994) and *Curriculum Reform at Key Stage 1: Teacher Commitment and Policy Failure* (Longman, 1994). The last three books reported the findings of a longitudinal study of the impact of curriculum reform on teachers' work.

Richard Daugherty is Professor of Education and Head of the Department of Education at the University of Wales Aberystwyth. His research interests are in the fields of assessment, education policy and geography education. His publications include *National Curriculum Assessment: A Review of Policy 1988–1994* (Falmer, 1995). He has recently completed an edited book (with R. Phillips and G. Rees) entitled *Education Policy in Wales: Explorations in Devolved Governance* (University of Wales Press, forthcoming).

Miriam David is Professor of Policy Studies in the Department of Education at the University of Keele. She has an international reputation for her research on families, gender and education. Her recent publications include *Parents, Gender and Educational Reform* (Polity, 1993), *Mother's Intuition? Choosing Secondary Schools* (Falmer, 1994, with A. West and J. Ribbens), *Negotiating the Glass Ceiling: Careers of Senior Women in the Academic World* (Falmer, 1998, co-edited with D. Woodward) and *Closing the Gender Gap: Postwar Educational and Social Change* (Polity Press, 1999, with M. Arnot and G. Weiner). She is currently completing research projects on children's understandings of parental involvement in education and student choice of higher education, and a book on a feminist sociology of family life (2000, Polity Press).

Alan Dyson is Professor of Special Needs Education and Co-Director of the Special Needs Research Centre in the Department of Education, University of Newcastle upon Tyne. His research interests are in special needs education and in the relationship between social and educational inclusion. He is a member of the government's National Advisory Group on Special Educational Needs and of the National Education Research Forum. Recent books include *Theorising Special Education*, with C. Clark and A. Millward (Routledge, 1998), *New Directions in Special Needs*, with C. Clark, A. Millward and D. Skidmore (Cassell, 1997), *Towards Inclusive Schools?*, with C. Clark and A. Millward (Fulton, 1995) and *Schools and Special Needs: Issues of Innovation and Inclusion*, with A. Millward (Paul Chapman, in press). He has been at Newcastle University since 1988. Prior to that, he spent thirteen years as a teacher, mainly in urban comprehensive schools.

Tony Edwards is Emeritus Professor of Education at Newcastle University, having retired in 1997. His research interests are reflected in several co-authored books, including *The State and Private Education* (Falmer, 1989, with J. Fitz and G. Whitty), *Specialisation and Choice in Urban Education* (Routledge, 1993, with G. Whitty and S. Gewirtz) and *Separate but Equal? A Levels and GNVQs* (Routledge, 1997, with C. Fitz-Gibbon, F. Hardman, R. Haywood and N. Meagher). He was Chair of the Education Research Assessment Exercise in 1996.

Carol Fitz-Gibbon is Professor of Education and Director of the Curriculum Evaluation and Management Centre at the University of Durham. Her work on monitoring was described in *Monitoring Education: Indicators, Quality and Effectiveness* (Cassell 1996) which won the Standing Conference on Studies in Education 1997 prize for the best book by an established author. Other interests include evidence-based education.

John Furlong is Professor in the University of Cardiff School of Social Sciences. During the last fifteen years he has researched and written extensively on initial teacher education. His publications include *Initial Teacher Education and the Role of the School* (OUP, 1988), *Initial Teacher Training and the Role of Higher Education* (Kogan Page, 1996), *Mentoring Student Teachers: The Growth of Professional Knowledge* (Routledge, 1995) and *Teacher Education in Transition: Reforming Teacher Professionalism* (OUP, 1999).

Prue Huddleston is Principal Research Fellow and the Director of the Centre for Education and Industry at the University of Warwick. She has a particular interest in post-16 curriculum and vocational qualifications; recent publications include *Teaching and Learning in Higher Education: Diversity and Change* (Routledge, 1997, with L. Unwin).

Martin Jephcote is Lecturer in Education, Director of the PGCE (Further Education) and Director of Teaching and Learning at the University of Cardiff School of Social Sciences. His research interests are in the policy-making and implementation process in post-compulsory education and training and the governance of further education. Recent publications include *Teaching Economics and Business* (Heinemann, 1996, with S. Hodkinson).

Hugh Lauder is Professor of Education in the Department of Education, University of Bath. He has written and researched for many years on the relationship between educational outcomes and social class, and has recently published (with A.H. Halsey, P. Brown and A.S. Wells) *Education, Economy and Society* (Oxford, 1998).

Gary McCulloch is Professor of Education at the University of Sheffield. His principal research interests are in the social history of education, curriculum, teachers and education policy. His recent publications include *Teachers and the National Curriculum* (Cassell, 1997, edited with Gill Helsby), *Failing the Ordinary Child? The Theory and Practice of Working Class Secondary Education* (OUP, 1998), *The Politics of Professionalism* (Continuum, 2000) and *Historical Research in Educational Settings* (Open University Press, 2000, with W. Richardson). He is currently preparing full-length discussions of teacher professionalism and the secondary school curriculum, and of historical research in educational settings. He is currently editor of the international journal *History of Education*.

Robert Phillips is Senior Lecturer in Education at the University of Wales Swansea. He has written extensively on history education and education policy. His *History Teaching, Nationhood and the State: A Study in Educational Politics* (Cassell, 1998) won the Standing Conference for Studies in Education (SCSE) prize for the best academic book published on education in 1998. He has recently completed another edited book (with R. Daugherty and G. Rees) entitled *Education Policy in Wales: Explorations in Devolved Governance* (University of Wales Press, 2000). He is currently Project Director of the ESRC-funded *British Island Stories: History, Identity and Nationhood* (BRISHIN).

Gareth Rees is a Professor in the Cardiff University School of Social Sciences, where he is also Deputy Director. He has researched and published widely in the areas of participation in lifelong learning, the role of education and training in regional economic development, and the governance of education policy. He has recently completed ESRC-funded projects on participation in lifelong learning and on the impacts of devolution on the governance of economic development. He has also been a senior consultant to an OECD study of 'learning regions'.

Susan Robertson is Reader in Sociology of Education at the University of Bristol. Susan has written on and taught in the areas of sociology, political sociology and policy studies in education in Australia, Canada and New Zealand before taking up a position at Bristol in 1999. Her particular interests are theorising state formation, social class, teachers' labour and globalisation. Susan's recent books include *Teachers' Political Activism* (James Lorimar, 1997, with Harry Smaller) and *A Class Act: Changing Teachers' Work, Globalization and the State* (Falmer, 2000).

Roger Slee is Chair of Teaching and Learning and Dean of the Faculty of Education at the University of Western Australia. He has published widely on the theory and practice of special education and is editor of the international journal *Inclusive Education*.

Dean Stroud completed B.Sc. (Econ.) and M.Sc. degrees at Cardiff University. He is currently finishing his Ph.D., which examines how university students socially construct the 'graduate labour market' and their relationships to it, in the context of the radical restructuring of British higher education.

Sally Tomlinson is Emeritus Professor at Goldsmiths' College, University of London, and a Research Associate in the Department of Educational Studies at Oxford. She has researched and written extensively on the education of ethnic minorities and on education policy. She has co-edited (with Maurice Craft) *Ethnic Relations in Schools: Policy and Practice in the 1990s* (Athlone, 1995) and (with M. O'Connor, E. Hales and J. Davies) *Hackney Downs: The School that Dared to Fight* (Cassell, 1999). She has recently completed *Education in a Post-Welfare Society* for the Open University Press (2000).

Peter Tymms taught in a wide variety of schools from central Africa to Easington before starting an academic career. He is presently a Reader in Education in the School of Education, University of Durham, and is Director of the PIPS project, which involves monitoring the achievement, progress and attitudes of pupils aged 4–11 in over 4,000 primary schools. His main research interests are monitoring, school effectiveness and research methodology.

Geoffrey Walford is Professor in Education Policy and a Fellow of Green College at the University of Oxford. His books include *Educational Politics: Pressure Groups and Faith-Based Schools* (Avebury, 1995), *Affirming the Comprehensive Ideal* (co-editor, Falmer, 1997, with R. Pring) and *Doing Research about Education* (editor, Falmer, 1998). He is Director of a Spencer-funded project on faith-based schools: a comparative study of England and the Netherlands.

Gaby Weiner is Professor of Teacher Education and Research at Umeå University in Sweden. She has written and edited a number of books and reports on social justice, equal opportunities and gender. These include *Feminisms in Education: An Introduction* (Open University Press, 1994); *Equal Opportunities in Colleges and Universities* (Open University Press, 1995, with M. Farish, J. McPake and J. Powney), *School Effectiveness for Whom? Challenges to the School Effectiveness and School Improvement Movement* (Falmer, 1998, co-edited with R. Slee and S. Tomlinson) and *Closing the Gender Gap: Postwar Educational and Social Change* (Polity Press, 1999, with M. Arnot and M. David). She is currently co-editor (with L. Yates and K. Weiler) of the Open University Press series 'Feminist Educational Thinking'.

Part I

Introduction and historical overview

1 Introduction and rationale

John Furlong and Robert Phillips

Setting the scene: Ruskin and beyond

The last quarter of the twentieth century, specifically the period 1976–2001, was profoundly important in the history of education. It witnessed a transformation in the ways in which education in England and Wales was organised, controlled and managed. As with other spheres of social policy, few aspects of education remained unchanged: the period saw fundamental changes in the structure and nature of educational institutions, in the organisation of the curriculum, in the nature of teachers' work and professionalism, and in the aims and purposes of assessment. It was a period which was characterised by profound and often confrontational debates over the nature and purposes of education in society, particularly those between education, the economy and the nation. The changes initiated during the period altered the power relationships which had underpinned the education system, since the 1944 Education Act, which itself had shaped the post-war educational world.

Our starting point is Callaghan's speech on education given at Ruskin College, Oxford, on 18 October 1976, and we conclude exactly twenty-five years later, near the end of New Labour's first administration. Although there had already been some well-publicised debates over aspects of education in the 1970s, Callaghan's speech was significant because it signalled direct interest in education by central government at the highest level. At the beginning of the twenty-first century, we are now very familiar with well-publicised direct interventions in education by prime ministers and other senior ministers, yet in 1976 this was regarded as something of a novelty. This changing context for the conduct of educational policy discourse reveals much about the shifting power structures relating to education itself. The Ruskin speech and the so-called 'Great Debate' which followed represented a symbolic indication of central government's desire to influence the nation's education in certain ways. A dominant and recurring theme throughout most of the period under investigation is therefore the growth of central influence over educational politics, policy and practice.

There is considerable consensus and agreement amongst contemporary historians of education that 1976 should be regarded as a significant turning point in the history of education. Aldrich (1996: 4) suggests that after 1976, the year 1944 would no longer be seen as the 'dividing line between past and present' in education policy. This is because, as Brooks (1991: 4) stresses, not only did it represent a 'stage in the assertion by central government of its stake in the nation's education system', but it also marked the transition between the expansionist period of the 1960s and the retrenchment of the 1980s. The connection here between education and nationhood needs to be stressed, for, as we shall see in Chapter 2, Callaghan made explicit the relationship between education and the nation's well-being, particularly its economic prosperity. As we shall also see in the other chapters which follow, this was to dominate much governmental thinking on education throughout our period and, at the time of writing, is central to the 'modernising' priorities of the present government. Thus, as Esland (1996: 47) suggests:

> Even at the time, the 1976 speech was seen as a defining moment; but in retro-spect its significance if anything seems greater. For the first time in the history of mass education in Britain, the state set out a clear priority for the economic purpose of education, thereby establishing an explicit connection between education and economic nationalism.

Rationale for the book

The observation above provides a useful justification for this volume; it seems appo-site on the twenty-fifth anniversary of Ruskin to publish a book documenting the history of the period which focuses upon the connection between education, reform and the state. Yet the book is not merely a straightforward contemporary history, as it draws upon the rich and wide-ranging literature which also emerged during this period in response to the reforms. This includes scholarly work which analysed education reform at the macro (state) level, and the analytical work which described the impact of reform on, for example, curriculum and assessment, primary and secondary schools, post-compulsory and higher education, educational administra-tion and governance and teacher education and professionalism. It also utilises work which has sought to describe the conceptual ideas which underpinned these reforms, such as equity, 'choice', marketisation and accountability.

Each of the contributors to the volume reflects on the major legislative and struc-tural changes in their designated fields over the past twenty-five years. Although the contributors have identified their own specific questions and themes (see below), over-arching ones such as the following are appropriate to all the chapters:

- What have been the major legislative reforms and structural changes which have influenced education policies over the past twenty-five years?
- What were the major ideological, political and educational factors which accounted for these changes?
- In what ways have certain areas of education been 'transformed' during this period?
- To what extent is there continuity with regard to education policy over the period as a whole?
- What have been the merits and demerits of these changes?

In essence, the book is a contemporary history of education policy, drawing upon some of the 'illuminative' approaches associated with that analytical tradition commonly associated with policy sociology. The work of Stephen Ball has been pre-eminent in this respect, particularly the seminal *Politics and Policy Making in Education: Explorations in Policy Sociology* (Ball 1990), which did so much to alert us to the ideological context of reform in the late 1980s and early 1990s. It is therefore appropriate that we use a quotation from the historian Barraclough, chosen by Ball himself, to provide a useful rationale and justification for this volume:

> In the long run contemporary history can only justify its claim to be a serious intellectual discipline and more than a desultory and superficial review of the contemporary scene if it sets out to clarify the basic structural changes which have shaped the modern world.
>
> (Barraclough 1967: 16, quoted by Ball 1990: 1)

Structure and outline of chapters

Following the above, we very much hope, therefore, that the book will be of utility to students, academics, education professionals and policy makers alike, who wish to understand more clearly the factors which have shaped the contemporary education scene in England and Wales and who wish to 'continue the debate' (see Williams *et al.* 1992) over the nature of educational provision in England and Wales. The book is divided into five sections. Section 1 provides an introductory historical overview; Section 2 analyses the changing institutional contexts for reform; Section 3 focuses upon three key themes which dominated not only the Ruskin speech but most of the subsequent twenty-five years, namely professionalism, accountability and standards; Section 4 evaluates issues relating to equality in education; Section 5 offers an analytical conclusion to the period and also contemplates the future.

In Chapter 2, Robert Phillips provides a retrospective evaluation of the impact of Callaghan's Ruskin speech by considering continuity and change in educational reform in England and Wales over the whole of the last twenty-five-year period. He suggests that Callaghan did not anticipate the scale and pace of education reform that would be initiated after 1976 and that it would be misconceived to suggest that all subsequent policy reforms had their origins in that particular moment. However, Phillips argues that although each of the subsequent periods had a set of characteristic dynamics of its own, Callaghan's intervention was profoundly important in that it helped shape the 'discursive framework' within which subsequent debates over education policy would take place. This influence, Phillips argues, has been just as apparent under the post-1997 New Labour administration as it was throughout the Conservative administrations of the 1980s and 1990s.

Perhaps the most highly contested area of education during this period was the primary sector, and in Chapter 3 Jim Campbell describes what he calls the 'colonisation' of the primary school curriculum over the last twenty-five years with regard to its aims, nature, assessment and modes of delivery. In 1976, he suggests that the metaphor of the curriculum as a secret garden, despite its over-use, did have some resonance with reality as individual teachers were able to experiment with aspects of their curriculum according to local and individual interests. Today, the scene is very different because, according to Campbell, successive governments have sought to take control or, to use Campbell's term, attempted to 'colonise' the curriculum. He describes three strategies that have been utilised in different periods. The first phase, from 1976 to 1986, was characterised by gentle persuasion; the second phase, from 1987 to 1996, involved the imposition of standards and accountability measures by statute; the third phase, which began in 1992/3 and came into full force after the election of the New Labour government of 1997, involves the imposition of a performance culture on primary schools, a concentration on raising standards of literacy and numeracy, and the development of officially sponsored pedagogies.

Geoffrey Walford looks at secondary schools over the same period and considers the changing fate of the 'comprehensive ideal'. That ideal, he suggests, affirms that children's education should not be disadvantaged by their background and that the state should provide free, high-quality education for all in comprehensive schools. Walford begins by briefly outlining the development of the comprehensive system which became the dominant model of secondary education in England and Wales during 1970s. He then outlines interlinked policies introduced after 1979 to support and encourage the selection of particular children for unequally funded schools. The development of the Assisted Places Scheme in 1980, grant-maintained schools in 1988 and specialist schools after 1993, all served progressively to undermine the comprehensive principle. As a result of all of these moves, Walford suggests that by 1996 it was estimated that only 40 per cent of all secondary schools were LEA maintained and fully comprehensive. Moreover, he argues that in contrast to what might be expected from a Labour government, many of their polices since 1997 appear to be designed to generate an even greater challenge to the comprehensive ideal, with fragmentation into different types of school, more selection according to a range of different criteria and greater inequality in what schools offer.

As already stated, a fundamental theme of Callaghan's speech was the notion that the education system was not providing industry and the economy with what it required in terms of a skilled and well-educated work force, a theme which has dominated educational discourse throughout our period. Martin Jephcote and Prue Huddleston analyse a crucial sector of education in this respect, namely further education (FE). They argue that in many respects FE has been blighted by the governmental view that education and training should be seen as an investment in human capital and as a means to economic growth and wealth creation, and also the belief that the prolonged decline of the UK was the result of poor education and training. Consequently, from the 1980s onwards, they argue, post-16 education and training was increasingly regarded by politicians as a key means of responding to the demands of economic restructuring. They conclude by suggesting that despite the often dramatic changes in FE, the challenges facing the sector are not fully resolved.

Gareth Rees and Dean Stroud consider changes in the field of higher education. As they note, during the latter decades of the twentieth century, the place of higher education in British society has been transformed. Until the 1960s, the universities and other higher education institutions impinged relatively little on the lives of most people. The expansion of higher education since then has enormously widened its range of influence. This transition to a mass system of higher education, they argue, embodies a profound – if not generally much noticed – educational and social transformation. However, there are, suggest Rees and Stroud, important caveats to be noted to this largely positive story, most significantly in the move away from the notion of higher education as a 'right of citizenship' to one of 'market/individual consumer'. Moreover, this social transformation has entailed a fundamental restructuring of the organisation of higher education itself, most crucially the basis upon which universities are funded. These changes, in turn, have required the reformulation of the relationships between central government and the higher education sector. The principal rationale for the expansion of higher education has been the contribution of an enlarged sector to fulfilling the ambitions of successive governments to bring about a long-term improvement in the competitiveness and growth of the British economy. In this regard, the changes which have taken place echo the school reforms in the last twenty-five years.

Robert Phillips and Richard Daugherty explore what has perhaps been one of the unintended consequences of greatly increased centralisation of control over education in the last twenty-five years, namely the move towards educational devolution in Wales. As they say, it is both ironic and remarkable to reflect that, during the period between 1988 and 1998, a time of increasing policy centralisation by Conservative governments, Wales was able to develop a distinctive educational and institutional framework that preceded political and legislative devolution in 1999. The main engine of this restructuring, they suggest, was the Education Reform Act of 1988 that revolutionised the role of the state in education, thereby inadvertently raising questions about the relationship between the Welsh nation and the British state in a new context. Phillips and Daugherty trace the origins of these developments, particularly in relation to the school curriculum; they argue that this period of educational history in Wales provides an opportunity to analyse the ways in which educational reform, cultural politics and political nationalism are interrelated.

Gary McCulloch considers the changing nature of teacher professionalism over the last twenty-five years. In 1976, he argues, the prevailing image of teacher professionalism in England and Wales revolved around an ideal of teachers individually and collectively possessing a high degree of autonomy and control in the curriculum domain. Within this sphere, he suggests that it was widely assumed that their role included the freedom to decide not only how to teach but also what to teach, and that they had a primary responsibility for curriculum development and innovation. As he says, this prerogative was not subject to the fickle demands of parents and the community, still less to the interests of the state or political parties. Rather, it was to be carefully preserved and the province of teachers' experience, judgement and expertise, which would ensure the gradual evolution of content and methods in line with social and cultural change. In fact, McCulloch suggests that this ideal did not entirely accord with reality. Nevertheless, the desire to challenge teacher autonomy (interpreted by many of those close to government as no more than vested interests) has been a key feature of educational policy in the last twenty-five years, so much so, McCulloch argues, that today teacher autonomy has been fundamentally redefined. What replaced it in the 1990s was first a pragmatic adjustment in the balance between teachers' rights and responsibilities in the class-room and public accountability. More recently, under New Labour there has been a wholesale recasting of the ideal of teacher professionalism characterised as the 'New Professionalism'.

John Furlong also considers changes to the nature of teacher professionalism, but within the context of initial teacher education and training. He argues that over the last twenty-five years there has been a recognition on the part of successive governments that, if the wide range of reforms being introduced were to be a success in the longer term, then it was essential to win the hearts and minds of teachers themselves, especially new teachers entering the profession. As a result, initial teacher education has become an increasingly important area of educational policy development. He suggests that there have been two different sorts of changes that have influenced the structure and content of initial teacher education and training in England and Wales during this period. The first, directly following from Callaghan's Ruskin speech, has been the growing insistence on increased account-ability within the system. The second has been varying and sometimes competing definitions about what the outcomes of initial education and training should be. Visions of professionalism implicit in initial education and training policies have therefore changed substantially over the last twenty-five years; what has not changed, Furlong argues, has been the determination of successive governments to re-establish accountability within the system so that it is they, rather than those in higher education, who can take the lead in defining what professionalism should be.

Patricia Broadfoot, in her chapter, discusses changes in what she sees as the defining principle of English education in the late twentieth century – assessment. In the first part of her chapter she sets out some of the key assessment policy devel-opments in English education which have taken place during the last twenty-five years; then she moves on to locate those developments in terms of the powerful assumptions that have dominated the thinking that informed them. Those assump-tions, she argues, derive from a very particular assessment discourse – that of 'performativity'. Rooted in a rationalistic assumption that it is possible and indeed desirable to 'measure' performance – whether this be of the individual pupil or of the institution as a whole – the concept of performativity, Broadfoot suggests, repre-sents one of the clearest expressions of modernist thinking typical of the post-Enlightenment era. However, Broadfoot argues, assessment of this sort is an imperfect tool. While it is superficially credible, it is deeply flawed, serving to rein-force existing social divisions and causing a great deal of unnecessary pain for both individuals and institutions. Moreover, it is of doubtful validity as a representation of what individuals can do, and inhibits the effective learning of many. Above all, she argues, this form of assessment is ineffective in preparing individuals to meet the challenges of tomorrow.

Peter Tymms and Carol Fitz-Gibbon remind us of Callaghan's main concern, and the concern of virtually all of the reforms since his intervention, namely the need to raise national standards of achievement in schools. As they point out, the reforms themselves have been accompanied by the development of a national system of testing of children's achievement, and the results are starting to generate an extensive longitudinal database. In principle, therefore, we are now in a position to ask whether standards have indeed risen over the last twenty-five years. Tymms and Fitz-Gibbon consider whether the reforms actually helped to raise achievement among the nation's pupils. What the figures demonstrate, at least at first glance, is a considerable rise in achievement at the ages of 11, 16 and 18 – indeed, some rises seem to have been dramatic. But should the national figures be taken at face value? Tymms and Fitz-Gibbon provide a detailed critique of current assessment and measurement procedures and draw on a range of other forms of longitudinal evidence to question some of the results. There are, they suggest, many difficulties to be overcome before we have a national assessment system with which we can confidently answer the all-important question about whether standards are indeed rising.

Alan Dyson and Roger Slee examine special education policy, asking to what extent the current Labour government's endorsement of the principle of inclusion of children with special educational needs into mainstream provision can be seen as the triumph of liberalism during the last twenty-five years. As they argue, children who do not 'fit in', who resist schooling, who have a language other than the language(s) of instruction or who have disabilities and difficulties, present a set of challenges for the education authorities; somehow, those educational authorities must respond. They argue that in England and Wales, those responses have drawn heavily upon a liberal, perhaps even progressive tradition, in that they have been marked by a concern for the well-being of the disadvantaged or disabled individual; they have been concerned with values of equity in terms, for instance, of resource distribution, opportunities and outcomes and participation. However, Dyson and Slee suggest that those responses, precisely because of their liberal tendencies, have failed to challenge the structural features of the English and Welsh education systems which produce disadvantage and disability, and have, moreover, been marked by deep ambiguity in terms of the very values which they appear to embody.

Sally Tomlinson looks at the issue of ethnicity and race in education. She argues that in a post-industrial, post-colonial society, such as Britain, education has two key contributions to make in ensuring that racial and ethnic minorities are given equal treatment, opportunities and respect. The first is to ensure that the education system supports racial and ethnic minorities in the achievement of the educational qualifications that provide employment opportunities and the chance of occupational and social mobility. Education is also, she argues, the key institution in persuading the white majority that they now live in a diverse multicultural society, that minority cultures can be accorded recognition and respect without threatening national identity, and that post-imperial racist attitudes and beliefs are outdated and counterproductive. To what extent have policies and practice in education over the last twenty-five years achieved these two aims? Tomlinson concludes that there has been some success but that the system as a whole could have done better. She documents how the educational achievements of ethnic and racial minorities improved considerably, especially during the 1990s. But despite the rhetoric of social inclusion and a plethora of government policies to alleviate disadvantage, there are, she argues, still structural barriers to race equality, many of them created by policies associated with the development of the educational market. There has also, she argues, been a failure to develop a National Curriculum that is appropriate for a diverse society in the twenty-first century.

Susan Robertson and Hugh Lauder consider the issue of social class and education. In the past twenty-five years, they argue, there has been a fundamental restructuring of the economy and the labour market as well as of education. In these circumstances, they ask, is the concept of social class still of relevance for an understanding of education? If so, in what ways has such economic and educational change led to a recasting of the social class structure in England and Wales? In the first section of their chapter, Robertson and Lauder document the changes that have taken place in education and the economy; they then examine the nature of social class and its relevance to contemporary social and educational analysis. In the third and final section of their chapter, they examine evidence for the claim that, rather than social class related issues disappearing, the recent changes in education, the economy and society have led to a reconfiguration of social class structures which have had profound implications for people's lives in England and Wales.

Madeleine Arnot, Miriam David and Gabby Weiner focus on gender and educational policy, arguing that changes in the schooling of boys and girls in England and Wales created one of the most significant educational transformations of the late twentieth century. It was this period, they argue, that saw the culmination of attempts to break the hold of Victorian family values over the education of schoolboys and schoolgirls. Until then, the culture and curriculum provision of state schools was designed to sustain a sexual division of labour which presumed a wage-earning male head of household and a female dependent housewife. The challenge to such values, they argue, was not the immediate goal of either post-war social democratic governments or the New Right governments under Margaret Thatcher and John Major. Nevertheless, economic and social policy changes (particularly in family policy and values) and the women's movement all helped to release female education from women's domestic lives, and had a major effect in reshaping male and female pupils' aspirations and identities.

Finally, Tony Edwards both provides a retrospective analysis of the period and raises questions about the future direction of education policy. He suggests that the period 1976–2001 was dominated by three main issues, namely educational performance, markets and the changing nature of state provision of education. Edwards shows that the reforms of the period simply cannot be understood without a full appreciation of the economic imperative behind them, particularly the need to meet the demands of international competition. This, says Edwards, has raised all sorts of issues about the nature and purpose of state provision of education. Almost inevitably, the period witnessed a parallel undermining of traditional notions of education as a public service by a belief in the greater effectiveness of market provision and a growing uncertainty about the scope and direction of state intervention in public education – and this during a period in which government control, aspects of institutional autonomy and consumer choice all markedly increased. Edwards speculates about future directions and patterns of education, focusing particularly upon the relationship between the market and publicly funded education.

References

Aldrich, R. (1996) *Education for the Nation*, London: Cassell.

Ball, S. (1990) *Politics and Policy Making in Education: Explorations in Policy Sociology*, London: Routledge.

Barraclough, G. (1967) *An Introduction to Contemporary History*, Harmondsworth: Penguin.

Brooks, R. (1991) *Contemporary Debates in Education: An Historical Perspective*, London: Longman.

Esland, G. (1996) 'Education, training and nation-state capitalism', in J. Avis, M. Bloomer, G. Esland, D. Gleeson and P. Hodkinson (eds) *Knowledge and Nationhood: Education, Politics and Work*, London: Cassell.

Williams, M., Daugherty, R. and Banks, F. (eds) (1992) *Continuing the Education Debate*, London: Cassell.

2 Education, the state and the politics of reform

The historical context, 1976–2001

Robert Phillips

Introduction

This chapter offers a retrospective evaluation of the Ruskin speech and considers its significance twenty-five years on within the context of the subsequent politics of education during the period. One of its major aims is to consider how far the speech provided the discursive political framework within which debates over education policy and practice were framed between 1976 and 2001. An attempt is made, therefore, to assess continuity and change with regard to educational reform during the period as a whole. Labour's victory at the 1997 election is particularly important in this respect, in that it provides an opportunity in this chapter and at various points throughout the book to analyse the extent to which 'New' Labour either continued or departed from many of the ideas initiated at Ruskin and from policies initiated by Conservative administrations between 1979 and 1997.

Ruskin and the 'Great Debate': framing the agenda?

During the period 1976–2001, education became an issue of enormous public interest, an interest that was fuelled considerably by the media. It is therefore perhaps rather apt to consider that news of the fact that the prime minister was intending to make a speech on education had been leaked to the press in July 1976, some time before he actually delivered it (Chitty 1989). Spinning, it seems, has a long history in Labour politics. Thus, by the time Callaghan stood up at Ruskin College, Oxford, on 18 October 1976, speculation was already high that the speech was to be an important one. Yet the speech was not entirely original: Callaghan drew heavily upon the ideas in the Department of Education and Science *Yellow Book* (DES 1976) and the Downing Street Policy Unit (see Donoghue 1987). The full significance of the speech, in fact, lies in the wider context of the 1970s out of which it was born, and the long-term impact it had in terms of framing debates over education in the following decades.

The 1970s had witnessed a series of economic, political and social crises, including the world oil crisis, economic dislocation, inflation and the breakdown of industrial relations, and political uncertainty. By wishing to focus upon education so explicitly in 1976, Callaghan linked the wider crisis in society, politics and the economy to a perceived 'crisis' in education (Bolton 1987). There seemed to be ample evidence to suggest that aspects of the education system were in difficulties, as represented on British television screens by the infamous William Tyndale affair (apparently demonstrating that primary education was out of control), and by the growth of youth unemployment (see Dale 1989). As we shall see, the link made by Callaghan in the speech between education and 'crisis' was profoundly important for the subsequent history of educational politics between 1976 and 2001. In this sense, Callaghan 'established the discursive boundaries within which all subsequent curriculum debate and policy making at government level have been framed' (Davies and Edwards 1999: 265).

At various points in the speech, Callaghan made it clear that he was conscious of the symbolic importance and sensitivity of a prime minister involving himself directly in debates over education (Callaghan 1976). The context of educational politics – specifically, the historical relationship between education and the state – is important here. As Lawton (1980) and others have made clear, a tradition of relative autonomy had been cultivated by educational institutions and organisations during the (so-called) period of educational 'consensus' that had built up between government, local authorities and teachers after the 1944 Education Act, based upon the concomitant social democratic commitment to equality of opportunity (Ranson 1990). Yet by suggesting that two crucial partners in education, namely parents and industry, had been excluded from this partnership, one of the most significant aspects of Callaghan's speech lies in the way it demonstrated that there was, in reality, at best only partial 'consensus' over education. As he made clear:

> I take it that no one claims exclusive rights in this field. Public interest is strong and legitimate and will be satisfied. We spend £6 billion a year on education. So there will be discussion … parents, teachers, learned and professional bodies, representatives of higher education and both sides of industry, together with the Government, all have an important part to play in formulating and expressing the purpose of education and the standards that we need.
>
> (Callaghan 1976)

Here, then, was the central core of the speech: state education was funded by government, parents and industry and therefore there could be no question of these parties being excluded from the debate over educational standards. After all, 'with the complexity of modern life we cannot be satisfied with maintaining existing standards, let alone observe any decline. We must aim for something better.' Again showing his sensitivity towards the views of teachers, Callaghan stressed that he had been very 'impressed' by what he had seen in schools and that teachers would always have a very 'special place' in any discussions about education reform because of their 'real sense of professionalism and vocation'. Yet there were aspects of education, particularly the curriculum, that 'concerned' him. First was that the education system was not providing industry with pupils who were numerate and skilful in science and technology. Second, he shared the 'unease' felt by 'parents and others' with 'the new informal methods of teaching'.

As far as potential policy solutions to these problems were concerned, Callaghan, again respectful of the sensitivity of his position, did not announce definite legislative intentions. On the other hand, by providing an insight into his thinking, he also pre-empted debates over the curriculum that were to dominate in the subsequent decade and beyond. He was thus 'inclined' to favour a 'basic curriculum with universal standards' which would not only 'equip children to the best of their ability for a lively, constructive place in society' but which also prepared them 'to do a job of work'. He claimed the balance in this respect was wrong; there was little merit in producing 'socially well adjusted members of society' when they lacked the 'basic purposes' of education, which he defined as 'basic literacy, basic numeracy, the understanding of how to live and work together, respect for others, respect for the individual'. Finally, Callaghan claimed that the examination system needed to be reviewed. In summarising the major points of his own speech, Callaghan laid out the framework that would dominate much of the educational discourse for the next twenty-five years:

> Let me repeat some of the fields that need study because they cause concern. These are the methods and aims of informal instruction; the strong case for the so-called 'core curriculum' of basic knowledge; next what is the proper way of monitoring the use of resources in order to maintain a proper national standard of performance; then there is the role of the inspectorate in relation to national standards; and there is the need to improve relations between industry and education.

Scholars on the Left have been highly critical of Callaghan and the Ruskin speech. Simon (1991), for example, argues that the speech 'paved the way' for the New Right assault on education and the Thatcherite reforms of education in the 1980s and 1990s. Yet Callaghan himself did not anticipate the scale and pace of education reform that would be initiated after 1976 (Callaghan 1987, 1992) and it would be misconceived to argue that all or even most subsequent policy reforms had their origins in 1976, flowing onwards (Whig-like) in some unbreakable chain to the present day. As Lawton (1992) and others have reminded us (and this is often forgotten or overlooked by the Left) Callaghan was raising legitimate concerns about the state of education in 1976. Similarly, Batteson (1997) argues that although the William Tyndale affair may well have been an isolated (extreme) example, concerns over the effectiveness of comprehensive schools, standards, progressive education and accountability were already valid areas for debate in 1976. For Batteson, the real significance of 'the moment of 1976' was that Callaghan's warnings were on the whole dismissed by the Left, thus allowing the New Right to grasp the political initiative over education in the decades that followed.

Like Davies and Edwards (1999), my own view is that although each of the sub-periods as a whole (see below) had a set of characteristic dynamics of its own, 1976 was profoundly important for the subsequent shaping of the discursive framework within which debates over education policy would take place. Specifically, the speech was important for five main reasons:

1   It represented a lack of confidence by elements within Labour in the comprehensive school movement and a public severing of any link between Labour and 'progressive' curricular reform.

2.　Callaghan's speech signalled a greater propensity for the central state to influence what was taught in schools; this included the prospect of central government playing a significant role in the shaping of curriculum policy. Thus, 1976 was a turning point in the sense that, from Ruskin onwards, there was the view among government, the civil service and, to a far lesser extent, the inspectorate that 'there had to be greater control of education in general in order to ensure a marked improvement in standards'. It was after 1976 'that partnership was replaced by accountability as the dominant metaphor in discussions about the distribution of power in the education system' (Chitty 1989: 136).

3　The speech initiated the perception both within political circles and within public minds that there was a close relationship between the economy and the education system. By linking the perceived shortcomings of the education system with economic and industrial crisis, Callaghan placed 'the issue of school and work at the centre of the political agenda' (Bash and Coulby 1989: 8).

4　The speech marked a particular style of educational politics after 1976: Callaghan's use of praise at various points in the speech could not hide the veiled criticism of teachers. This critique of teacher autonomy and teaching methods would be transformed in the decade following 1976 into a full-scale assault against the education system. Moreover, by linking developments in education to the wider crisis in the economy and society, Callaghan unwittingly enabled the New Right and their allies in the media to develop this critique in different ways over the subsequent two decades.

5　The implication that parents would have a great say in education policy making after 1976 represented something of a reconstitution of the traditional framework of post-war control of education, based upon central government, local education authorities (LEAs) and teacher organisations. Ultimately, as we shall see, the 'parental interest' would be elevated to new heights within educational policy discourse in the decades following 1976.

The politics of 'reversing the ratchet': the New Right and education, 1979–97

Yet little seemed to change immediately as far as the relationship between central government and the education profession was concerned. Moreover, compared to the often frantic, volatile and very public nature of debates over education which became familiar in the later twentieth century, the so-called 'Great Debate' which followed the speech appears relatively tame (Williams 1992). In retrospect, the 'Great Debate' does not seem 'Great' at all. Meetings were held between the Secretary of State for Education and various industrial and educational organisations, followed by eight regional conferences. Policy documents were then produced both by the DES and Her Majesty's Inspectorate (HMI) in the period after 1976 which placed emphasis upon the need for greater accountability in the education system and advocated a more direct role for the Secretary of State for Education in debates over education. On the other hand, equal emphasis was placed upon the need for central government to develop 'broad agreement' with local authorities (DES 1977) or 'shared responsibility' with teachers over education policy (DES 1980, 1981).

Even the Conservative election victory in 1979 under Margaret Thatcher seemed at first to signal 'business as usual', symbolised by the appointment as Thatcher's first Secretary of State for Education of Mark Carlisle, generally known as a moderate 'wet'. Yet there were three significant policy shifts under his administration. First, Labour's Circular 10/65, which asked all LEAs to adopt a policy of comprehensive schooling, was abolished. Second, the Education Act 1980 provided greater opportunities for parental choice over schools, although LEAs were still given the upper hand. The third significant initiative was the announcement of the Assisted Places Scheme, which for some time had been advocated by elements within the Conservative Party (Edwards *et al.* 1989).

The appointment of Keith Joseph as Secretary of State for Education in 1981 seemed to signal a clear shift to the Right. Joseph was renowned as the ideological driving force behind Thatcherism, and the appointment of the former Secretary of State for Industry would suggest that this was a symbolic appointment, an indication of things to come. Yet there is considerable consensus among scholars of the history of education policy in the late twentieth century that Joseph's period in office (1981–6) promised far more than it delivered, illustrated, for example, by Morris and Griggs' (1988) reference to much of this period as the 'wasted years'. Interestingly, Joseph at the end of his life also expressed disappointment with his term in office at education (Ribbins and Sherratt 1997).

Much of this can be explained by Joseph's ideological complexity. As a committed neo-liberal, in a speech in the 1970s he had coined the metaphor of 'reversing the ratchet' to describe the need by the Tories to overhaul the post-war welfare state in favour of a new consensus, based upon privatisation and market individualism. Yet when in office as Secretary of State for Education, he found himself in something of a political straitjacket. Committed to an ideology that shunned state control, Joseph realised in practice that 'reversing the ratchet' as far as educational reform was concerned could only really be achieved through state intervention (see Salter and Tapper 1988). It was a dilemma that would not be resolved until much later in the Thatcher years.

Some initiatives during the early 1980s seemed to signal a continuation of the Ruskin theme of greater central accountability. In 1982, it was announced that the Schools Council would be abolished. The government also took greater control of teacher education through the introduction of the Council for the Accreditation of Teacher Education (CATE: see Furlong's chapter). In 1985 the GCSE was introduced, and in the same year the document *Better Schools* (DES 1985) advocated a more common curriculum framework in schools, with the reassurance, however, that schools would have the biggest say in curriculum planning.

Yet a more significant piece of legislation during this early period was the announcement of the Technical and Vocational Education Initiative (TVEI) in 1983. Its significance lies in the ways in which it was conceived and what it revealed about the shifting power structures within the central state itself. As Dale (1989) has pointed out, none of the important bodies associated with education – DES, LEAs, teacher groups or HMI – were consulted about the initiative, which seemed to be a brain-child of David (later Lord) Young of the Manpower Services Committee (MSC). This seemed to signal a shift in the direction of power in education away from the DES and LEAs and towards new branches of government, more closely associated with industry, employment and enterprise, and quangos which increasingly became part of a third tier of governance in the 1980s and 1990s. The subsequent history of TVEI is just as interesting for the light it sheds upon the circumscribed ability of the central state at this time to influence what actually occurred in schools. As a number of studies of TVEI demonstrated (see McCulloch's chapter), as the initiative was implemented, schools and LEAs shaped the policy in ways which perhaps had not been intended by its authors.

There were many, both within and outside the Tory Party, who realised (like Joseph) that reform of the education system could only really come about – as Callaghan had hinted – through more direct forms of central control. As Knight (1990) and others have shown, in this respect the appointment of Kenneth Baker as Secretary of State in 1986 proved a turning point in the 'making' of Tory education policy. Unfettered by the ideological baggage that seemed to constrain his predecessor, Baker was motivated by a combination of political ambition and probably a genuinely held belief that 'ratchet reversing' in education could only be effectively achieved through radical state-centred and state-driven reform (Lawton 1994).

Crucially, Baker's appointment also coincided with the run-up to the 1987 election and, as Thatcher made clear in a series of media interviews, education reform would become a far great priority for the Tories after 1987. This period was also characterised by a spate of publications from New Right pressure groups such as the Institute of Economic Affairs, the Adam Smith Institute and the Hillgate Group (see Quicke 1988). Buoyed by the subsequent electoral success of 1987, over the next five years the Tories embarked upon the biggest programme of legislation in the history of education, which, in varying forms, bore very close resemblance to the proposals set out by the New Right groups, particularly the Hillgate Group's *Whose Schools?* (1986), which provided something of a blueprint for the government's programme.

The 1988 Education Reform Act (ERA) has rightly attracted enormous interest among academics. As a number of commentators have pointed out (Ball 1990; Chitty 1992; Deem 1988; Lawton 1989a, 1989b), with its 238 sections the Act was one of the biggest single pieces of legislation passed by the Tories in their time in office, and gave the Secretary of State for Education more powers than any of his/her cabinet colleagues. By establishing a National Curriculum, it symbolised an unprecedented move by the central state to control education. However, by also encouraging the establishment of grant-maintained status (GMS) schools and City Technology Colleges (CTCs) independent of local education authorities, at the same time it encouraged greater competition within the education system. This combination of 'competition and control' (Bash and Coulby 1989) was one of the many apparently contradictory elements of the Act. As Whitty (1989) has demonstrated, these were the product of tensions between the neo-liberal and neo-conservative strands within New Right ideology which produced the Act. Nevertheless, as others have demonstrated, the fusion of market individualism and the strong state is what gave Thatcherism such broad populist appeal and durability (Gamble 1988).

If 1976 and 1988 (along with 1944) are rightly seen to be turning points in the history of post-war education, 1992 was in many ways equally significant. That year saw John Major win the election; one could have expected that the tide of reform would slow down. However, following the election there was speculation in the press that Major made a deal with the New Right that, in return for getting off his back over Europe, they could 'have' education. Evidence for this may be seen not only in the appointment of prominent New Right activists within the education policy framework itself (see Ball 1993) but also in significant legislation after 1992, represented in the publication of *Choice and Diversity: A New Framework for Schools* (DfE 1992), in which the government summarised its education policies around five principal themes – quality, diversity, parental choice, autonomy and accountability.

Quality in education was to be achieved primarily through the National Curriculum, backed up by a rigorous system of external assessment at 7, 11, 14 and 16, producing a whole series of performance indicators (what Broadfoot in her chapter calls 'performativity') that would give the 'consumers' of education (i.e. parents) the essential information in order to make informed 'choices' about schools. Diversity was to be achieved through the extension of GMS schools and CTCs which were to be free from local authority control. Parental choice was to be ensured through a Parents' Charter and open enrolment, thus encouraging parents to make preferences for schools that were perceived to be performing well and in the process promoting the educational 'market'. As well as those measures mentioned above, greater school autonomy was ensured through delegated powers of financial management in order to make them more conducive to the needs and requirements of their 'consumers'. LEA representation on school governing bodies was reduced, with parent governors given greater influence. Finally, greater accountability was achieved not only through educational markets and performance indicators but also through reforms to teacher training; above all, accountability was to be achieved through a rigorous system of inspection, with HMI being replaced by the Office for Standards in Education (Ofsted).

The Conservative years between 1979 and 1997 were thus monumental in the history of education policy. A total of over twenty pieces of education-related legislation changed fundamentally the ways in which schools were organised, managed and controlled (Tomlinson 1993a). The legislation 'altered the basic power structure of the education system (Maclure 1989: v). Thus, what Gipps (1994) has referred to as an 'explosion of developments' since 1979 also initiated intense activity among academics to 'voice concerns' (Arnot and Barton 1992) about the New Right 'project' in education, particularly the values that underpinned the reforms. Thus, the National Curriculum was criticised not only for being bureaucratic and assessment-led; by undermining teacher autonomy and being so explicitly political, it was argued by some that it was essentially undemocratic (Jones 1989; Kelly 1995; Carr and Hartnett 1996). Other work pointed to the negative impact of inspections, upon not only teacher morale but also even the school standards that they were supposed to ensure (Cullingford 1999; Dunford 1998).

Yet it was the notion of educational 'choice', markets and diversity which came under closest scrutiny. As Ranson (1990: 15) pointed out, the market philosophy which underpinned the reforms reproduced 'the inequalities which consumers bring to the market place'. Moreover, as Robertson and Lauder point out in their

chapter, because of the limited amount of access to 'good' schools, the system operated only in the form of a quasi-market, which compounded inequality further. As
quasi-market policies began to take hold in education, the work of Bowe and Ball
(1992) and Gewirtz *et al.* (1995) suggested that the notion of parental 'choice' was
heavily circumscribed: for example, not only by geography but also by social class
factors (for an analytical discussion of this debate, see the chapters in this volume by
Walford *et al.* and Edwards). Other work pointed to the injustices of the preferential
financial treatment given to GMS schools and CTCs over comprehensive schools.

These debates can only be properly understood, of course, when we consider
what 'reversing the ratchet' meant in practice for the New Right. The reforms of
the period 1979–97 represented an attempt to change the political and social landscape, and education, particularly because of its perceived importance to the
national economy (a point made explicit by Callaghan in 1976), was to be a central
focus for the New Right's reform of the post-war welfare state. The period 1979–97
thus marked a fundamental and radical break from the past, particularly in relation
to social justice. Muschamp *et al.* summarise this as follows:

> Inherent in the concept of social justice was the view that schools would
> produce equality of opportunity for children to achieve their educational
> potential regardless of their social grouping. During the 1980s and 1990s a
> crisis in confidence in the comprehensive system appears to have led the
> Conservative government to redefine equality of opportunity. *Equality in educational
> achievement* has given way to *equality of access to provision* with the development of
> the concept of 'equity' by the New Right.
>
> (1999: 101, my emphasis)

There is, then, a world of difference between the cautious 'questioning' of the
post-war education settlement articulated by Callaghan in 1976, and the full-scale
assault on it mainly from 1988 onwards. On each of the five points raised by
Callaghan, the 'ratchet reversing' of the period 1979–97 resulted in an education
system changed to an extent that was unrecognisable from the one that existed in
1976. Specifically, these changes included the following:

1   As was indicated above, the 'comprehensive ideal' (see also Walford's chapter)
    had been fundamentally challenged, progressivism had been attacked and there
    had been a return to more traditional curricular forms via the National
    Curriculum.
2   Although Ruskin had been a turning point in the central state's interest in what
    was actually taught in schools, the Tory reforms took this to new levels of
    centralised control. By 1997, all aspects of education were closely controlled by
    government.
3   A fundamental and irrevocable link had been established both in the political
    and the public mind that education should exist primarily to serve the interests
    of the national economy. Moreover, as Edwards suggests in his chapter, the
    discursive emphasis upon educational 'failure' during the period provided a
    convenient excuse for failures in managing the economy.

4   Whereas Callaghan's carefully phrased questioning of aspects of the teaching profession had been at the core of the 'Great Debate', the New Right's 'discourse of derision' (Ball 1990; Wallace 1993) in the 1980s and 1990s against teachers meant that the relationship between teachers and the state was at best strained and at worst, confrontational.

5   Callaghan had stressed the importance of the role of parents in the control of education; by 1997, in theory at least, they had become the dominant partner within educational policy discourse (see Brown 1997). These changes combined meant that, to use Chitty's (1989) phrase, the education system (as with other elements within the welfare state) had been 'transformed'.

The third way or the same way? 'New' Labour and education, 1997–2001

Given the turbulent educational politics outlined above, it is hardly surprising that, reflecting the general optimism felt by many in the country at large, many professionals working within state education viewed the extraordinary landslide victory achieved by Tony Blair's 'New' Labour party in 1997 with 'new hope' (Halpin 1997). Although recognising that it was both unrealistic and in many ways undesirable to return to the pre-1976 'consensus' (did it exist anyway?), many within education fervently hoped that New Labour would reform many of the perceived worst excesses of New Right policies. Yet an analysis of education policies since 1997 suggests that 'New Labour appears intent on following a similar policy-line on education to that of the Conservatives when they were in office' (Demaine 1999: 5). How and why has this situation come about?

New Labour's first few years in office witnessed an enormous amount of legislative activity that gave merit to Blair's claim that 'education, education, education' would be the major priority for the new government. It immediately fulfilled its electoral commitment by abolishing the nursery vouchers system established by the Tories, and its first Education Act, only a month after the election, abolished the Assisted Places Scheme. In June, the government set up a Standards Task Force to advise it on education policy. By July, it had published its important White Paper *Excellence in Schools* (DfEE 1997a), which set out in detail its aims and objectives for education. Within a year, it had published Green Papers on special needs (DfEE 1997b), on lifelong learning (DfEE 1998a) and, more controversially, on the future of the teaching profession (DfEE 1998b). Within only a year it had also passed three Education Acts, and in 1999 there was a further White Paper on post-16 education (DfEE 1999a). By 2000, the new government had established rigorous literacy and numeracy strategies, set up homework clubs and other measures to facilitate 'out of hours' learning, and had initiated important policies such as the 'Sure Start' programme for pre-school children, Education Action Zones, and Beacon Schools to spread good practice. It had also reformed the National Curriculum through the Review 2000.

As Ball (1999: 195) aptly comments, 'Whatever else one would want to say about Labour's education policies there is certainly no shortage of them!' This frantic activity is even more interesting when it is placed within the broader historical context of Labour's educational politics: there had been nothing remotely similar in terms of legislative activity with regard to education in the previous periods of post-war Labour governments in 1945–51, 1964–70 or 1974–9.

Like Demaine (1999), however, the overwhelming perception of scholars is that New Labour's period in office represents far more continuity with 'New Right' than with 'Old Labour' (Powell 1999; Power and Whitty 1999). Hartnett (1998) argues that, despite adopting a new political style, New Labour simply represents continuity with the ideas and policies that were prevalent between 1979 and 1997 and which had been initiated in 1976. Similarly, Ball (1999: 196) suggests that 'we need to attend as much to the continuities as to the differences between Labour and the Conservatives'. Apart from a number of notable exceptions, citing the abolition of the Assisted Places Scheme, the 'compromise' over GMS schools (by re-naming them 'foundation' schools) and the abandonment of nursery vouchers, Ball points in particular to the continuity of personnel in key posts after 1997 to support his thesis: Tate at the Qualifications and Curriculum Authority (QCA), Millett at the Teacher Training Agency (TTA) and above all Woodhead at Ofsted.

Likewise, in a close analysis of New Labour's record in office, Docking (2000: 32) suggests that to a large extent 'for all the rhetoric, the present Government's policies for schools are fundamentally the Conservatives' dressed up in New Labour's clothes'. Indeed, according to Docking, New Labour has taken many New Right approaches further. For example, the government has made 'prescriptive and detailed interventions about how to teach and organise classrooms, challenging the professional competence of teachers and their right to make their own professional judgements as never before' (ibid.: 33). In addition, it has not been afraid to promote setting over and above mixed ability teaching (DfEE 1997a, 1999b). On the other hand, New Labour has advocated the need for a research-based profession, one of a number of seemingly contradictory elements within New Labour's education policy agenda (see Furlong's chapter for a more extensive discussion of this complex vision of a 'new professionalism').

Yet it is on the fundamental question of social justice that most debate and analysis has centred. Muschamp *et al.* (1999) for the most part concur with the continuity thesis, citing the New Labour commitment to the central tenets of education policy discourse of the earlier period: namely, 'standards', 'choice' and 'accountability'. However, they also see social democratic elements within New Labour's policies, for example in its commitment to combating social exclusion, in its championing of the inclusion of children with special needs into mainstream schools and, above all, in its support for lifelong learning. Similarly, it is for this reason that Hodgson and Spours (1999) describe New Labour education policies as 'Radical Centre' rather than 'Radical Centre-Left', based upon three main principles. First, they argue, New Labour clearly adopts a 'traditionalist interventionist' approach to school standards, with an emphasis upon basic skills. Second, there is a 'voluntarist framework partnership' within the New Labour project, represented by the support of lifelong learning based upon individual responsibility, information technology and the development of a system of qualifications which recognises a wider range of knowledge and skills. Third, Hodgson and Spours argue that New Labour has adopted a more 'egalitarian approach' to social and educational inclusion which aims to focus more attention upon marginal groups, particularly through the widening of participation in education and training.

It is perhaps this third point that is the most difficult to sustain. It receives only qualified support from Docking (2000: 34), who argues that one of the few 'new' features of Labour's approach to education is the way in which it is pursuing 'social democratic policies in its attempts to reach two parts of the child population that the Conservatives failed to reach effectively'. These are, namely, early years children (witnessed by a far more comprehensive programme within this sector) and children from low-income families in inner cities (via Education Action Zones and the *Excellence in Cities* initiative). This latter observation concurs with Power and Whitty's (1999) analysis; they argue that the only substantially 'new' aspect of the so-called 'third way' as applied to education is indeed the Education Action Zone initiative.

Yet other aspects of education policy seem to have very little to do with traditional social democratic principles. One of the most important, of course, relates to New Labour's policies on selection. As Webster and Parsons (1999) have shown, although New Labour are rhetorically committed to ending selection (witnessed by Blunkett's now infamous 'read my lips' speech at the Labour Party Conference in 1995, in which he seemed to pledge to abolish all forms of selection), its compromise over GMS/foundation schools, as well as its reluctance to end selection via direct legislation, represents a significant retreat from the social democratic commitment to comprehensive education and ending selection. New Labour's commitment instead to 'standards not structures' (DfEE 1997a), and more particularly its decision to allow parents to vote on the future of local grammar schools, signifies the party's betrayal of the comprehensive ideal (see Walford's chapter, and also Edwards *et al.* 1999). This was given empirical justification when, following a vote over grammar schools in Ripon in 2000, Blunkett seemed to give support to the parents' decision not to end selection.

One of the most interesting aspects, then, of the educational politics of the period 1976–2001 concerned the ways in which New Labour has responded to the education policy agenda of the New Right and the Tories. Little wonder that for those on the Left, New Labour represents a 'retreat from social democracy' (Sullivan 2000; see also Gewirtz 1999 for an excellent critique) in relation not only to education but to social policy more generally. Like the New Right, it is clear that New Labour represents a variety of ideological traditions which explains its seemingly contradictory policy outcomes. New Labour's application of the so-called 'third way' can be defined rather flatteringly as a combination of neo-liberalism and state socialism (Giddens 1998) – a sort of market socialism – or, alternatively, merely as 'a pragmatic, ideology-free response to the realities of pleasing a middle-class electorate and the severe fiscal restraints presented by the Treasury' (Daugherty *et al.* 2000).

Overwhelmingly, political theorists, sociologists and historians alike – including the author of this chapter – take the latter view. One of the major reasons for this pragmatic imperative within New Labour lies, of course, in the successive electoral calamities suffered between 1979 and 1997, which had an enormous impact upon the party. Moreover, Labour's transformation during the period was a reflection of a more widespread structural political/cultural shift and a hegemonic move

Rightwards within society and politics generally (Hall and Jacques 1983; see also Robertson and Lauder's chapter). Faced with a fundamentally changed political/social landscape, in all aspects of social policy Labour began to discard many of the post-war Keynesian tenets which were regarded as fundamental to the welfare state – 'ratchet reversal' was not, therefore, confined to Conservatives in the late twentieth century. Moreover, hegemonic shifts, monetarism and fiscal restraints went hand in hand with political pragmatism and electoral success. With regard to education policy, Demaine (1999: 17) articulates this well when he claims that:

> Labour's education policies involve an overriding pragmatism which takes advantage of the prevailing political conditions. If Blair's way is neither old left nor new right, and proves acceptable to such a wide range of voters, this is at least in part due to the effects of the policies of previous governments.

It is tempting to view Blair's appointment as leader in 1994 as the turning point in this process (Hartnett 1998), but fundamental shifts in Labour's ideas on education can be traced back to the 1980s (Inglis 1991). The Labour document *Meet the Challenge, Make the Change* (Labour Party 1989) advocated the abolition of the Assisted Places Scheme and bringing GMS schools and CTCs back into local authority control. On the other hand, there was a portent of things to come in the belief that comprehensive schools should be allowed to develop their own 'distinctive character' and be allowed to specialise in teaching certain subjects. This found its logical conclusion when Labour gained office in 1997 in the 'shift of policy of choice based on school status (grammar and GMS schools *v.* general comprehensives) to one based more on curricular diversity (specialist *v.* general comprehensives)' (Docking 2000: 33). Similarly, in the early 1990s, Labour was at least vague about whether it supported the principle of a National Curriculum, with Jack Straw admitting that the party would probably keep it, despite the conflict and controversy surrounding it in the 1980s and 1990s (see Campbell's chapter). Yet again, when it came to office, New Labour was not only deeply committed to the National Curriculum but also, by strengthening the commitment to literacy and numeracy, appeared to be even more 'traditionalist' than the Tories.

If there were some indications of a significant shift in thinking in the 1980s and 1990s, the transformation of Labour certainly became manifest and transparent after Blair became leader in 1994. A central core of the Blairite project is to stress the reality of the process of modernisation and the need for society to respond to it in 'new' ways. The onset of globalisation makes this an imperative: what is needed is change, competition and innovation. As Ball (1999) and Cole (1998) emphasise, the discourses of globalisation and modernisation are thus particularly important for explaining the nature of New Labour's education agenda (Edwards also makes this point eloquently in his chapter). Nevertheless, in order to make itself appear distinctive from the New Right, it has had to appear to offer more. According to Jones (1996: 19), the challenge for Blair and New Labour is that education 'must provide at one and the same time both a means of increasing the competitiveness of a re-skilled British economy, and a way of reconciling, through the provision of equal opportunity, the objectives of competitiveness and social justice'.

In many ways, then, the key principles articulated by Callaghan at Ruskin sit very closely alongside the New Labour project:

1   New Labour's policies on school choice represent the fruition of Callaghan's apparent lack of confidence in the ability of comprehensive schools to deliver educational standards.
2   New Labour's enthusiasm for attempting to influence not only what is taught but also how it is taught, its support of rigorous inspection, assessment and target setting, signifies that the 'accountability metaphor' dominates educational discourse at the beginning of the twenty-first century.
3   Not only does New Labour see the need to ensure a close correlation between school aims and the economy's needs, but this is given the added imperative of international competition and globalisation.
4   In order to realise these goals, New Labour recognises that teachers' work has to be more regulated than ever before, but also modernised into a 'new professionalism'.
5   For New Labour, it is parents – particularly those in middle-class marginal constituencies – who will be key to determining educational policy priorities now and in the future.

Conclusion

Although I began this chapter with the warning against over-emphasising the continuity of education policy during the period as a whole, I end it by suggesting that New Labour's educational agenda represents something of a natural fruition of Ruskin. This is not as contradictory as it first appears when one considers that, as with all historical periods, events and circumstances could have worked out fundamentally different between 1976 and 2001. What if, for example, John Major had lost the 1992 election to Neil Kinnock?

At the time of writing, disappointment is well established among those on the Left that the three years after the electoral victory of 1997 represent a betrayal of traditional cherished principles. Yet as Batteson (1997: 372) has emphasised, it was the Left's own 'obsession with structures' in 1976 that prevented it from responding effectively to Callaghan's warnings. In addition, it failed to recognise that Ruskin 'and the reconnection of education with the world outside was a necessary and valuable process' (Tomlinson 1993b: 140). Viewed in this way, 'the moment of 1976' can be interpreted as a missed opportunity by the Left which concomitantly allowed the New Right to grasp the ideological initiative in the educational politics of the 1980s and 1990s. Within this thesis, the key reference in *Excellence in Schools* to 'standards not structures' can be interpreted not merely as a rhetorical slogan, but as a symbolic recognition within Labour not only of the political realities of the early twenty-first century but also of the missed opportunities of 1976.

Acknowledgement

I am grateful to Tony Edwards and John Furlong for comments on an earlier draft of this chapter.

References

Arnot, M. and Barton, L. (eds) (1992) *Voicing Concerns: Sociological Perspectives on Contemporary Education Reforms*, Wallingford: Triangle.

Ball, S. (1990) *Politics and Policy Making in Education: Explorations in Policy Sociology*, London: Routledge.

——(1993) 'Education, Majorism and the curriculum of the dead', *Curriculum Studies*, 1(2): 195–214.

——(1999) 'Labour, learning and the economy: a "policy sociology" perspective', *Cambridge Journal of Education*, 29(2): 195–205.

Bash, L. and Coulby, D. (1989) *The Education Reform Act: Competition and Control*, London: Cassell.

Batteson, C. (1997) 'A review of politics of education in the "Moment of 1976" ', *British Journal of Educational Studies*, 45(4): 363–77.

Bolton, E. (1987) *The Control of the Curriculum*, Occasional Paper 3, Durham: School of Education, University of Durham.

Bowe, R. and Ball, S., with Gold, A. (1992) *Reforming Education and Changing Schools: Case Studies in Policy Sociology*, London: Routledge.

Brown, P. (1997) 'The "Third Wave": education and the ideology of parentocracy', in A.H. Halsey, H. Lauder and A. Wells (eds) *Education, Culture, Economy and Society*, Oxford: Oxford University Press.

Callaghan, J. (1976) 'Towards a national debate', reprinted in *Education*, 22 October: 332–3.

——(1987) *Time and Chance*, London: Collins.

——(1992) 'The education debate', in M. Williams, R. Daugherty and F. Banks (eds) *Continuing the Education Debate*, London: Cassell.

Carr, W. and Hartnett, A. (1996) *Education and the Struggle for Democracy: The Politics of Educational Ideas*, Buckingham: Open University Press.

Chitty, C. (1989) *Towards a New Education System: The Victory of the New Right?* London: Falmer.

——(1992) *The Education System Transformed*, Manchester: Baseline Books.

Cole, M. (1998) 'Globalisation, modernisation and competitiveness: a critique of the New Labour project in education', *International Studies in Sociology of Education*, 8(5): 315–22.

Cullingford, C. (ed.) (1999) *An Inspector Calls: Ofsted and Its Effect on School Standards*, London: Kogan Page.

Dale, R. (1989) *The State and Education Policy*, Milton Keynes: Open University Press.

Daugherty, R., Phillips, R. and Rees, G. (eds) (2000) *Education Policy in Wales: Explorations in Devolved Governance*, Cardiff: University of Wales Press.

Davies, M. and Edwards, G. (1999) 'Will the curriculum caterpillar ever learn to fly?' *Cambridge Journal of Education*, 29(2): 265–75.

Deem, R. (1988) 'The Great Education Reform Bill, 1988 – some issues and implications', *Journal of Education Policy*, 3(2): 181–9.

Demaine, J. (ed.) (1999) *Education Policy and Contemporary Politics*, London: Macmillan.

DES (1976) *School Education in England: Problems and Initiatives (The Yellow Book)*, London: HMSO.

——(1977) *Curriculum 11–16 (HMI Red Book)*, London: HMSO.

——(1980) *A Framework for the School Curriculum*, London: HMSO.

——(1981)*The School Curriculum*, London: HMSO.

——(1985) *Better Schools*, London: HMSO.

DfE (1992) *Choice and Diversity: A New Framework for Schools*, London: HMSO.

DfEE (1997a) *Excellence in Schools*, London: Stationery Office.

——(1997b) *Excellence for All Children*, London: Stationery Office.

——(1998a) *The Learning Age: A Renaissance for a New Britain*, London: Stationery Office.

——(1998b) *Teachers: Meeting the Challenge of Change*, London: Stationery Office.

——(1999a) *Learning to Succeed: A New Framework for Post-16 Learning*, London: Stationery Office.

——(1999b) *Excellence in Cities*, London: Stationery Office.

Docking, J. (ed.) (2000) *New Labour's Policies for Schools: Raising the Standard?* London: David Fulton.

Donoghue, B. (1987) *Prime Minister: The Conduct of Policy under Harold Wilson and James Callaghan*, London: Jonathan Cape.

Dunford, J. (1998) *Her Majesty's Inspectorate of Schools since 1944: Standard Bearers or Turbulent Priests?* London: Woburn.

Edwards, T., Fitz, J. and Whitty, G. (1989) *The State and Private Education: A Study of the Assisted Places Scheme*, Lewes: Falmer.

Edwards, T., Whitty, G. and Power, S. (1999) 'Moving back from comprehensive education?' in J. Demaine (ed.) *Education Policy and Contemporary Politics*, London: Macmillan.

Gamble, A. (1988) *The Free Economy and the Strong State*, London: Macmillan.

Gewirtz, S. (1999) 'Bringing the politics back in: a critical analysis of quality discourses in education', paper presented at the Standing Conference on Studies in Education Annual Conference: Assuring Quality in Education: Public and Private?, Royal Institute of Architects, London, 10 November.

Gewirtz, S., Ball, S. and Bowe, R. (1995) *Markets, Choice and Equity in Education*, Buckingham: Open University Press.

Giddens, A. (1998) *The Third Way: The Renewal of Social Democracy*, Cambridge: Polity Press.

Gipps, C. (1994) *Beyond Testing: Towards a Theory of Educational Assessment*, London: Falmer.

Hall, S. and Jacques, M (eds) (1983) *The Politics of Thatcherism*, London: Lawrence & Wishart.

Halpin, D. (1997) 'Editorial: New Labour: new hope for education policy?' *British Journal of Educational Studies*, 45(3): 231–4.

Hartnett, A. (1998) 'Spinning, shaming and winning: New Right into New Labour – the metamorphosis of educational policy in England and Wales, 1976–1997', *Curriculum Studies*, 6(3): 341–56.

Hatcher, R. and Jones, K. (eds) (1996) *Education after the Conservatives: The Response to the New Agenda for Reform*, Stoke: Trentham.

Hillgate Group (1986) *Whose Schools? A Radical Manifesto*, London: Hillgate Group.

Hodgson, A. and Spours, K. (1999) *New Labour's Educational Agenda: Issues and Policies for Education and Training from 14+*, London: Kogan Page.

Inglis, B (1991) 'The Labour Party's policy on primary and secondary education, 1979–89', *British Journal of Educational Studies*, 39(1): 4–16.

Jones, K. (1989) *Right Turn: The Conservative Revolution in Education*, London: Hutchinson.

——(1996) 'Cultural politics and education in the 1990s', in R. Hatcher and K. Jones (eds) *Education after the Conservatives: The Response to the New Agenda of Reform*, Stoke: Trentham.

Kelly, A. (1995) *Education and Democracy: Principles and Practices*, London: Paul Chapman.

Knight, C. (1990) *The Making of Tory Education Policy in Post-War Britain, 1950–1986*, London: Falmer.

Labour Party (1989) *Meeting the Challenge, Make the Change*, London: Labour Party.

Lawton, D. (1980) *The Politics of the School Curriculum*, London: Routledge & Kegan Paul.

——(1989a) *Education, Culture and the National Curriculum*, London: Hodder & Stoughton.

——(1989b) *The Education Reform Act: Choice and Control*, London: Hodder & Stoughton.

——(1992) *Education and Politics in the 1990s: Conflict or Consensus?* London: Falmer.

——(1994) *The Tory Mind on Education, 1979–1994*, London: Falmer.

Maclure, S. (1989) *Education Re-Formed*, London: Hodder & Stoughton.

Morris, M. and Griggs, C. (eds) (1988) *Education – the Wasted Years? 1973–1986*, London, Falmer.

Muschamp, Y., Jamieson, I. and Lauder, H. (1999) 'Education, education, education', in M. Powell (ed.) *New Labour, New Welfare State? The 'Third Way' in British Social Policy*, Bristol: Policy Press.

Powell, M. (ed.) (1999) *New Labour, New Welfare State? The 'Third Way' in British Social Policy*, Bristol: Policy Press.

Power, S. and Whitty, G. (1999) 'New Labour's education policy: first, second or third way?' *Journal of Education Policy*, 14(5): 535–46.

Quicke, J. (1988) 'The "New Right" and education', *British Journal of Educational Studies*, 26(1): 5–20.

Ranson, S. (1990) 'From 1944 to 1988: education, citizenship and democracy', in M. Flude and M. Hammer (eds) *The Education Reform Act, 1988: Its Origins and Implications*, London: Falmer.

Ribbins, P. and Sherratt, B. (1997) *Radical Educational Policies and Conservative Secretaries of State*, London: Cassell.

Salter, B. and Tapper, T. (1988) 'The politics of reversing the ratchet in secondary education, 1969–1986', *Journal of Educational Administration and History*, 20(2): 57–69.

Simon, B. (1991) *Education and the Social Order, 1940–1990*, London: Lawrence & Wishart.

Sullivan, M. (2000) 'Labour, citizenship and social policy: a retreat from democracy?' University of Wales Swansea Inaugural Professorial Lecture, 20 March.

Tomlinson, J. (1993a) *The Control of Education*, London: Cassell.

——(1993b) 'Education for capability: a review of the eighties and prospects for the nineties', in A. Cashdan and J. Harris (eds) *Education in the 1990s*, Sheffield: Sheffield Hallam University Press.

Wallace, M. (1993) 'Discourse of derision: the role of the mass media within the education policy process', *Journal of Education Policy*, 8(4): 321–37.

Webster, D. and Parsons, K. (1999) 'British Labour Party policy on educational selection 1996–8: a sociological analysis', *Journal of Education Policy*, 14(5): 547–59.

Whitty, G. (1989) 'The New Right and the National Curriculum: state control or market forces?' *Journal of Education Policy*, 4(4): 329–41.

Williams, M. (1992) 'Ruskin in context', in M. Williams, R. Daugherty and F. Banks (eds) *Continuing the Education Debate*, London: Cassell.

Part II
The changing institutional context

3 The colonisation of the primary curriculum

Jim Campbell

Introduction

The time between the 'Great Debate', started by Prime Minister James Callaghan's speech at Ruskin College in 1976, and the publication of national tests results for 11-year-olds in 2002 has one defining characteristic: the colonisation by the government of the primary school curriculum, with regard to its aims, nature, assessment and modes of delivery. By colonisation I mean, metaphorically, the 'settlement in a hostile or newly conquered country' (*Shorter Oxford English Dictionary*) so as to control and administer it according to purposes set by the colonising authority. No metaphor is perfect, but in this attempt to colonise the primary curriculum, the natives proved more unruly than the colonisers expected and the colonisers consistently misread the context in which they were working, although in the end they succeeded. The central conceptual problem in the period under review is how substantial and substantive change to the curriculum has been brought about by the government. I argue below that there were three phases in the attempt to solve this problem, but the curriculum was only defined as a problem when the questions being asked about education started to change, when economic difficulties undermined the optimism about social institutions, and especially educational institutions, in the mid 1970s. When this happened, colonisation of the primary curriculum became inevitable, and was able to be construed in the public and professional discourse as desirable to bring about improvements in accountability and performance.

In 1976, the metaphor of the curriculum as a secret garden, though already being over-used, had some resonance with reality. In the early to mid 1980s, it was still possible to produce case studies of primary classrooms where teachers experimented in their curriculum simply because it took their fancy or it followed a recently acquired interest (Campbell 1985: 13–14). By the late 1990s, however, the DfEE confirmed that no primary school had been allowed to experiment with its curriculum since 1989 (Campbell 1998: 99).

It is dangerous to romanticise the value of primary teachers' autonomy or to demonise state intervention. In the 1970s, curricular autonomy was not much in evidence in primary mathematics, where a national survey by HMI found over-dependency on commercial schemes and low levels of innovation in primary science (DES: 1978). As for state intervention, Pollard *et al.* (1994) found a range of responses to government-imposed reforms among their sample of primary schoolteachers, including 'compliance', but they also reported, as the majority response, 'incorporation' – appearing to change, but incorporating changes into existing practices and thereby lessening the impact. Among a minority, they reported 'resistance' – simply not implementing the reforms. More recently, Richards found small primary schools 'domesticating' the highly prescriptive National Curriculum (Richards 1999: 91).

On the basis of the evidence available, it is possible to construct the colonisation process as falling into three phases, although there are overlaps, not clean breaks, between them. The first phase was from 1976 to about 1986, and was characterised by *gentle persuasion* exercised by HMI, which successfully moved the system towards consensus over broad curricular frameworks (Campbell 1989). The second phase was from 1987 to 1996, when a detailed statutory prescription of the curriculum and a set of accountability mechanisms were imposed on every school (Tomlinson 1993). It was a phase characterised by an unsuccessfully contested attempt to impose *standards and accountability by statute*, and although the accountability measures were effectively secured, improvement in standards proved elusive. The third phase started about 1992/3, and came into full force after the election of the New Labour government in 1997. The phase, as yet incomplete, is characterised by the imposition of a *performance culture* on primary schools, a concentration on raising standards in literacy and numeracy, an officially sponsored pedagogy, and the successful domination by HMCI Chris Woodhead over matters of primary curriculum policy.

Gentle persuasion: 1976–86

At the time of the 'Great Debate', Bennett's ground-breaking and controversial study of teaching styles (Bennett 1976) triggered a moral panic about primary pedagogy. Bennett's findings, that teaching styles he called 'informal' were less effective than others at enabling children to learn the basics, mirrored the widely publicised concerns of the Black Papers that preceded Bennett's study. In retrospect, however, a more pervasive, less melodramatically received influence was embodied in an empirical survey of classroom practice, *Primary Education in England*, conducted by HMI (DES 1978). There has been no dispute about the representativeness of the sample of classrooms surveyed. Although HMI agreed with Bennett about the limited extent of informal practice, some of the findings were dynamite politically. HMI reported that more able pupils were consistently, across all ages and all subjects, set work poorly matched to their abilities, and that there were low expectations held for pupil performance by teachers, especially in inner cities. The curriculum was not generally planned to incorporate progression, and was narrowly focused on the basics of mathematics and English, with poor or patchy provision in most other subjects.

The findings of the *Primary Education in England* survey could have been used publicly to attack primary teachers for incompetence and the failure to provide an entitlement curriculum. However, there was little press interest in the survey, and HMI did not seek publicity for it. Instead of stimulating public opprobrium, HMI, having incorporated a normative reform agenda into the survey's empirical base, set about implementing it by gently persuading the profession, the civil service and ministers that there were real problems in primary education which needed to be addressed. This agenda included the need to broaden the primary curriculum from its undue concentration on English and mathematics, to raise standards of cognitive attainment, especially for the able pupils, to match work set to pupils' different capacities, and to create more consistency and progression in the curriculum. The seeds of the National Curriculum, with its four linked concepts of 'breadth and balance', 'standards', 'differentiation' and 'entitlement', were sown in the survey and came to fruit in a series of documents, most notably the DES national framework proposal *The School Curriculum* (DES 1981), *The School Curriculum 5–16* (DES 1985a) and the Third Report of the Education Select Committee (House of Commons 1986). The latter report proposed a national framework for the primary school curriculum, giving pupil entitlement as its principal justification. Through these documents, not all of them formally written by HMI, gentle persuasion delivered a professional consensus about the broad objectives for the primary curriculum. At this time, when policy making was focused very much on implementing changes of organisational structure and curriculum for comprehensive secondary education, HMI had in effect been given, or had seized, free rein to work on the primary curriculum (Campbell 1989).

The official government position on primary education came in the forcefully articulated White Paper *Better Schools* (DES 1985b), where the arguments advanced by Sir Keith Joseph to the 1984 North of England Conference for the establishment of a 'broad agreement about the objectives and the content of the school curriculum' were codified. In paragraph 31, the White Paper linked curriculum reform to accountability quite directly. Clarity about curricular objectives would enable schools' performance to be 'more fairly judged against agreed expectations', and was 'a prerequisite for monitoring progress over time in the achievement of higher standards of performance'.

On primary standards, the White Paper was critical:

> Many teachers' judgements of pupils' potential and of their learning needs tend to reflect preconceptions about the different categories of pupils ... As a result, expectations of pupils are insufficiently demanding at all levels of ability.
>
> (para. 21)

> The Government believes that, not least in the light of what is being achieved in other countries, the standards now generally attained by our pupils are neither as good as they can be, nor as good as they need to be if young people are to be equipped for the world of the twenty-first century.
>
> (para. 9)

Nonetheless, in keeping with gentle persuasion, *Better Schools* did not advocate a prescriptive national curriculum; it proposed agreement about a broad framework only and ruled out anything more detailed:

> It would not be appropriate for either the Secretaries of State or the LEA to deter-
> mine the detailed organisation and content of the programme of the pupils of any
> particular school ... It would not in the view of the Government be right for the
> Secretaries of State's policy for the range and pattern of the 5–16 curriculum
> to amount to the determination of national syllabuses for that period.
>
> (paras 35–6)

The political recognition of substantial problems in the curriculum was
supported by two major research studies into primary practice. Most directly, the
ORACLE project (Galton and Simon 1980; Galton *et al.* 1980) had demonstrated
that a 'class enquiry' pedagogy, in which teachers spent greater proportions of time
engaging pupils in whole class interaction, was associated with higher cognitive
performance by pupils, but was practised by a minority of teachers. Moreover,
Bennett and Desforges (1984) had shown that even the most highly regarded
teachers had difficulty in differentiating effectively in primary classrooms.

The period of gentle persuasion was probably unsustainable; gentle persuasion
was unable to generate rapid or substantial change, particularly important for
policy making, as evidence accumulated of the scale of problems in the primary
curriculum. It ended with the Second International Mathematics Study (SIMS),
reporting comparative performance in school mathematics. This study's findings
were interpreted as showing the performance of English 13-year-olds to be
mediocre compared to our economic competitors, some one to two years behind on
average, and, most unnervingly, to have declined relative to other countries since
the First International Mathematics Study (FIMS) some twenty years previously.
The detailed analyses of these data are explored by Travers and Westbury (1989)
and reviewed by Reynolds and Farrell (1996), but it is the political consequences
that are most relevant here. The SIMS results appeared to confirm, in respect of
mathematics, all the messages about poor standards coming from HMI since 1978,
and they thereby became available to legitimise more direct intervention by the
government. As Brown (1996: 211) put it: 'The SIMS league tables undoubtedly
hastened the political imposition of the English national curriculum.'

Standards and accountability by statute: 1987–96

The Education Reform Act of 1988, preceded by a consultation paper in 1987,
reflected a major policy change on the school curriculum; it introduced a statutory
and highly detailed curriculum comprising ten subjects, statutory assessment and
testing at ages 7 and 11, and the publication of test results. The Acts that followed
provided for statutory inspection of schools, with the responsibility for the conduct
of inspections being given to an unusual non-ministerial government department,
the Office for Standards in Education (Ofsted). There were, however, important
inhibitors, of special salience for primary schools, built into the 1988 Act, designed
to restrict the extent of government penetration into classroom practice. The state
was prohibited from prescribing curriculum organisation or textbooks, teaching
methods and time allocations for particular subjects. These were all left to individual schools.

There are many narratives, including from some of those closely involved in implementing policy (e.g. Baker 1993; Black 1993; Graham with Tytler 1993; Ribbins and Sherratt 1997), attempting to explain how education policy moved sharply away from the 1985 White Paper position on the curriculum to the detailed prescription that followed. Although there have been substantial academic analyses of the consequences of the reforms, the origins of the dramatic policy volte-face are less clearly established. There are anecdotes of Mrs Thatcher's hairdresser inventing the curriculum while giving her a perm; there is the public record of Sir Keith Joseph's opposition in the House of Lords to the excessive detail proposed, on neo-liberal and pragmatic grounds. There is the claim that Kenneth Baker saw a way of leaving a lasting mark on political history by bringing in massive and far-reaching reforms, which he linked historically in importance to the Balfour and Butler Acts.

Against these explanations, which rely on personal style, beliefs or ambitions of senior politicians, there was, according to Graham (Graham with Tytler 1993: 13) the fact that the civil service seized the opportunity to intervene directly:

> There was also a marked change in the attitudes of civil servants after the introduction of the 1988 Education Reform Act, which they rightly saw as their first chance of having real power over state education. There was a volatile mixture of palpable fear of failing to deliver what was expected of them and a determination to run the whole programme. This was the first time ever that the DES had control of the curriculum and it was the beginning of the demise of HMI, although that was barely appreciated at the time.

Graham makes a convincing case that a big part of the bureaucratisation of the curriculum arose from the obsession in the civil service to control it and ensure its effective delivery at the school level. The explanations from personal ambition and civil service opportunism are not contradictory, but mutually reinforcing, if it is assumed that Baker's ambition could be realised most effectively by harnessing the service to it.

Despite the fear of failure, the attempt to raise standards in primary schools by statute was characterised by a profound misunderstanding of everyday practice in state primary schools, where a curriculum largely modelled on conventional secondary school practice of separate subjects was unfamiliar. The policy failure arose from an unwillingness at the centre of government to establish curricular priorities on the one hand, or give attention to pragmatic implementation details on the other. The best illustration of these twin failures concerned policy on the teaching of English, including literacy. At the level of priorities, even teachers in the most disadvantaged areas, who wanted to concentrate almost exclusively on teaching literacy and numeracy, were required to implement a ten-subject curriculum, which forced them to reduce the time they had previously spent teaching children to read (see Campbell and Neill 1994a). At the pragmatic level, there was palpable ignorance about, or neglect of, research on time allocations for different areas of the curriculum. Guidance to the working parties writing the syllabuses (see *Education* 1993: 3) proposed that about 20 per cent of curriculum time should be spent on English. This is about 10 per cent less than teachers anywhere in the world give to teaching the national language (Meyer *et al.* 1992), and 10 per cent less than teachers in this country typically gave to English according to every relevant study in the post-war period, including some conducted for the DES (Campbell 1993). The 'reform' of the primary curriculum, designed to raise standards of pupil attainment, was pressurising infant teachers to spend less, not more, time on teaching literacy, and the curriculum model underlying the reforms was reinforcing that pressure. The consequence was immense stress among teachers trying conscientiously to make the reforms work but finding that they were unable to do so. A metaphor of a 'running commentary' captured the sense of frustration among most primary teachers at the time:

> Well, what is frightening now is that we are being blinkered now into the national curriculum ... I am noticing it far more now that I never complete what I hope to achieve. There is always, like, a carry-forward so that you never get the feeling at the end of a session or day, 'Great, I've done this that I hoped that we would do' ... there is this running commentary, really, in the background saying that 'You haven't done this, or you haven't done that' which I find very annoying considering that you work so hard.
>
> (Infant teacher quoted in Campbell and Neill 1994b: 67)

Four years after the reformed primary curriculum was introduced, official sources acknowledged that it had led to superficiality in pupil learning and was undeliverable even by the most able teachers (DES 1993; NCC 1993). A review designed to slim down the statutory curriculum (Dearing 1993) proposed 'discretionary time' equivalent to a day a week, free of national prescription, but was able to do so only by introducing an unconvincing set of 'curricular arithmetic', pretending that English and mathematics could take less time than they needed. The reality was that under the time allocations in the Dearing report, adequate time could be given to English and mathematics only if schools allocated all the so-called discretionary time to these two subjects.

The emerging evidence about the impact of the National Curriculum on practice in primary schools was ambiguous. Pollard *et al.* (1994) reported change in curriculum and teaching methods in line with government policy, while most other empirical studies (e.g. Alexander 1997; Campbell and Neill 1994a, 1994b) emphasised continuity with previous practice. By 1996 the results of the Third International Mathematics and Science Study (TIMSS) were showing continued relative decline in mathematics performance by English pupils, and some reviews (Campbell 1996; Brooks 1998; Foxman 1998) began to conclude that the National Curriculum had failed to raise standards in primary schools some seven years after its introduction. The TIMSS study provided once again, as had its predecessor, the evidential legitimation for further and more invasive occupation by the government of curriculum territory.

There is a slightly different perspective, focused less on the detail of the curriculum and more on accountability to consumers. It reflects much of the neo-liberal thinking provided to the government as the National Curriculum proposals were out for consultation, and is best embodied in an address by the Permanent Secretary in the DfEE (Bichard 1999). Bichard, echoing the views of the New Right, argued that the Education Acts of the late 1980s and early 1990s were good examples of the need 'to confront vested interests': that is, that they were fundamentally about breaking the producer dominance in the education service in order to render it more consumer-led. Given the easy and now uncontested establishment of the National Curriculum and testing, the weakening of LEA control, the imposition of inspection by Ofsted and the direction over professional training and development by the Teacher Training Agency (TTA) and the DfEE, on Bichard's criterion the post-1987 policies, far from being failures, should by 1996 be judged to have been outstandingly successful. Curriculum reform was less important an objective, despite the rhetoric attached to it, than levering in mechanisms for accountability. The broadly based ten-subject curriculum was still in place, though teaching methods and curriculum time allocation remained matters for the schools.

Imposing a performance culture on primary schools: 1996 to the present day

There has been a long line of critical analysis focusing on the influence of the professional culture in primary schools into which any reformed curriculum has to embed itself. It is: 'cosy, insulated ... quite cut off from the complexities of politics' (White 1982: 49); generalist rather than specialist (Alexander 1984); nurturant, caring and self-sacrificing (Steedman undated); and it values the affective relationships with pupils (Evetts 1990). It is a 'collaborative culture' (Nias 1989), collegial, not competitive, and there is a commitment to differentiated learning, with individualised and small group pedagogy (Webb and Vulliamy 1996). It celebrates vocationally oriented motivation and an ethic of care (Acker 1990; Evetts 1990). Although there are important achievements in respect of pastoral care and moral education in this culture, as was recognised in the Primary Survey (DES 1978), there is little in any of these analyses to suggest that the professional culture values high cognitive performance, and there has been a long trend in the research evidence that it too unquestioningly embodies low expectations (e.g. DES 1978). The cultural critique has a long history, but it was re-invigorated in 1992 with the DES discussion paper *Curriculum Organisation and Classroom Practice in Primary Schools* (Alexander et al. 1992), in which the authors reflected a critique of the culture of primary education, emphasising the ineffectivenesss of the pedagogical practices it supported.

The discussion paper generated controversy among academics in primary education, mostly because of its palpable authority. Of the three authors, two – Alexander and Rose, respectively a professor specialising in primary education and the most senior primary specialist HMI – were leading experts in the field, and the paper had been based on a trawl of most of the relevant research. For this reason, the attack on primary culture was deeply resented in the profession (see Richards 1999: 105–8). Much critical comment from academics (e.g. Dadds 1992; Carr 1994) was focused on Alexander, the one independent academic among the wise men, who has since provided an insider's account of the writing and the reception of the paper (Alexander 1997).

This somewhat personalised focus diverted academics' attention away from the more sustained attack on the culture of primary education which was to intensify from 1996 onwards. The attack was based on three assumptions about primary education:

- it was continuing to under-perform in literacy and numeracy;
- too much time was spent by pupils on creative activities lacking intellectual challenge; and,
- the problem was culturally systemic and embodied in teaching methods insufficiently focused on direct instruction.

These assumptions became associated with HMCI Chris Woodhead, the third author of the 1992 discussion paper, who had recognised that the weakness of the statute-based reforms (having been largely instrumental in attempting to implement them) was that they had been merely technical – changing components of the curriculum, altering the nature of tests, but treating the professional culture as unproblematic. By 1998, he made explicit his view that the problem lay holistically in the professional culture:

> The lesson of the last ten years is as bleak as it is clear. The government of the day can reform each and every element in the educational enterprise, but if these reforms do not challenge the orthodoxies which have dominated classroom life in too many schools for the past forty years, then they will do nothing to raise standards.
>
> (Woodhead 1998: 1)

The status of the attack on primary education had already been raised in 1996 through a series of public statements about the poor performance of primary schools from a powerful trinity – HMCI Woodhead, the Labour leader Tony Blair, and Prince Charles. Prince Charles, on the day his divorce settlement was made public – when he might reasonably be expected to have other things on his mind – announced that there was 'dishearteningly widespread evidence of underperformance in schools, particularly in the primary sector' (*Guardian*, 12 July 1996). And Blair, as Labour leader, at what one might once have thought of as the other end of the social spectrum from royalty, promised

> a radical improvement in primary school standards. We do not share the view that primary school standards are adequate. They aren't. Fifty per cent of children are failing to reach appropriate levels in numeracy and literacy tests at age eleven. That is unacceptable.
>
> (Labour Party 1996: 1)

HMCI Woodhead's annual report (Ofsted 1996: 8) noted 'overall standards need to be raised in about half of primary schools'. Which was the father and which the son in this trinity was unclear, but Woodhead, who the previous year had claimed that 15,000 teachers were incompetent, was the moving, though not necessarily the holy, spirit in it.

The election of the Labour government brought in a continuation, and an intensification, of the focus on literacy and numeracy established under the Conservatives in 1996. In January 1998, Secretary of State Blunkett relaxed the statutory requirement to cover all the non-core foundation subjects in full for the next two years, shrugging off the uncomfortable fact that the curriculum was already being reviewed by the Qualifications and Curriculum Authority (QCA); he extended the National Literacy and Numeracy projects into 'strategies' for daily literacy and numeracy hours in all schools, and required schools to set targets for improvement in the percentage of 11-year-old pupils reaching Level Four in national tests in English and mathematics by 2002. This prioritisation of reform effort was very significant in winning over the hearts and minds of an overworked teaching profession; giving teachers a small number of targets to focus on contrasted dramatically with the multiple initiatives in 1988. This was significant because the literacy and numeracy strategies specified teaching methods, including the amounts of time to be devoted to whole class interactions, individual or group work and a closing plenary session, and weekly time allocations. They also drew heavily for implementation on texts and other learning material. Since governing bodies of primary schools were expected, but not required, to introduce these lessons, the prohibition on prescribing teaching methods or time allocations in the 1988 Act was not actually broken in the letter. But the almost universal adoption of the national strategies broke into the culture embodied most powerfully in pedagogical practice. The over-riding purpose – to change the professional culture – had been signalled by Barber, anticipating – or influencing – Woodhead:

> Let us imagine that an incoming government chooses to give top priority to raising standards of literacy ... What in practice does it mean to give something priority? *Statute would have little or nothing to do with it. The central challenge would be to change teachers' behaviour in classrooms.*
>
> (Barber 1996: 33, my emphasis)

The speed of implementation was very fast, and largely uncontested. The literacy and numeracy hours, in any case, were widely welcomed by most primary teachers according to Ofsted (1999a), not least because they de-limited the range of reform objectives that were imposed on them. In three short years the professional culture appeared to have been transformed: significant increases in the amount of direct instruction in lessons planned with clearly delimited and achievable objectives defined nationally; reduced amounts of time on creative activities; almost uniform teaching methods; and the acceptance of performance targets for literacy and numeracy that would have been thought unrealisable ten years previously. The target setting in particular challenged complacency across the system in all types of schools, whether in the leafy suburbs or the inner cities, since targets for improvement were benchmarked, admittedly crudely, against the performance in schools with similar intakes.

Criticism of the apparent destruction of the 'broad and balanced' curriculum was scathingly dismissed by Woodhead (1998), and the Secretary of State made it clear that whatever the outcomes of the review by QCA, the emphasis on mathematics and English would remain in place in primary schools beyond 2000. He could find support in HMCI's annual report for 1998 (Ofsted 1999b), in which significant improvements in the quality of teaching and in standards of pupil attainment were drawn to his attention. When the 1998 Green Paper *Teachers: Meeting the Challenge of Change* (DfEE 1998) was published, laying out provision for performance-related pay, fast-tracking and holding back salary increments for the poor performers, a system for reinforcing the performance culture in primary schools became available. By September 1999, largely through the influence of Barber at the Standards and Effectiveness Unit in the DfEE and Woodhead as HMCI, the state had effectively taken over the three areas previously seen as the high ground of professional independence: the broad and balanced curriculum had been re-balanced through increased priority for literacy and numeracy; officially sponsored teaching methods had been implemented; and curriculum time allocations had been specified. The colonisation of the primary curriculum was complete.

Conclusion

I have constructed the period under review as a three-phased policy development over twenty-five years. It is doubtful whether policy makers actually operate with such long-term plans or rationality, but in retrospect the three-step colonisation, whether rationally planned or not, is supported by the available evidence. It is too early to be entirely sure about the long-term outcomes, but two factors which will have contributed most powerfully to any substantive change are the combined power of Barber and Woodhead, and the decision to narrow the reform objectives for the curriculum. If they succeed in raising teacher expectations and pupils' attainment in literacy and numeracy permanently, the Barber charm offensive and the Woodhead abrasiveness offensive will be judged to have worked.

There remain four substantial uncertainties, however. First, although test reliability has been improved since the standardisation in 1996, test validity remains highly problematic; we do not know whether the improving test scores reflect improvement in the ability to do the tests or improvement in sustainable literacy and numeracy skills in real life. Matthew Arnold (1908, cited in Richards 1999: 98), writing about the effect of testing the Revised Code, was as sceptical then as we might be now: 'It is now found possible by ingenious preparation, to get the children through the Revised Code examination in reading, writing and ciphering, without their really knowing how to read, write or cipher.'

Moreover, the measures of improved standards are almost entirely controlled by the government and exclusively concentrated on the core subjects. There is no independent agency systematically evaluating the impact of the new curriculum as a whole. This is not to argue that the evidence is in fact being manipulated unfairly, but that the government needs to demonstrate that it is not happening. As Richards (1998) pointed out, the assertion in the 1997 White Paper that we have, 'sound, consistent national measures of pupil achievement' is debatable. Most of the measures depend on the reliability and validity of national testing and Ofsted inspection data, which remain contested. A more independent agency for the monitoring of standards over time is called for if confidence in apparent improvement is to be secured.

Second, the *extent* of curriculum colonisation is unresolved. Richards (1999) has argued that a 'neo-elementary' curriculum, with a core of English, mathematics, religious education and science (supported by ICT) squeezing out other subjects, may be the outcome of the Labour reforms. Although the QCA review (QCA/DfEE 1999) argued for a broader curriculum to be specified nationally, the QCA was marginalised in the post-1996 developments. An equally convincing trajectory – a third way, so to speak – was that the neo-elementary core would become the limit of state control, with autonomy for primary schools in the rest of the curriculum. On this assumption, even if the time allocations of the literacy and numeracy hours remained in force, the state-prescribed core would account for roughly fourteen hours, freeing up the equivalent of about two days a week for school-based decisions. Such a development would, at a stroke, have been in line with neo-liberal ideology (e.g. Letwin 1988; Tooley 1998), with the 1997 White Paper's slogan 'intervention in inverse proportion to success', and with Barber's and Woodhead's priorities; it would also have handed back a restricted but significant amount of discretion to practitioners. As happens in real colonies, curriculum colonisation would have brought some freedoms as well as dependency. In the event, the revised curriculum for 2000 (QCA 2000) aligned the English and mathematics curriculum with the literacy and numeracy strategies, but brought back into statutory force all the non-core foundation subjects (with choice only from among prescribed elements) and religious education, and added a non-statutory expectation for a curriculum strand in personal social and health education. On the face of it, under the social authoritarianism that characterises the New Labour policies towards social and moral matters in general, the new curriculum is more strongly colonised than ever.

Third, since 1997, policy for raising standards has focused powerfully on pedagogical change: on training primary teachers to alter their teaching methods towards more whole class interaction. At the level of the individual classroom such a change may significantly affect the pupils, but the international studies of school effectiveness show, at the national level, relatively small contributions from teaching methods to variance in pupil outcome. Reynolds and Farrell's (1996) review puts the school contribution between 8 and 14 per cent. Within the school variable, the teaching method has been found to contribute little or nothing (Creemers 1994: 196). We are operating with an inexact science, and should not dismiss any potential basis for raising standards; but on the basis of the evidence available, the almost exclusive focus on teaching methods, however commonsensical, may not deliver the extent of change required nationally. Most interestingly, the follow-up study to the ORACLE project by Galton *et al.* (1999), showed that although there had been increases in amounts of whole class teaching in 1996 compared to 1976, there had been associated increases in 'easy riding' (i.e. slowing down of work rate) by pupils, reminding us that curriculum reform always has unintended consequences.

Finally, the performance culture has yet to prove it will maintain itself. Under the

1998 Green Paper's proposals, some one in seven heads and a substantial, but unquantified, minority of class teachers will either fail or choose not to cross the performance thresholds, and will thus be unresponsive to the rewards and recognitions offered by the performance culture. This unambitious and badly rewarded minority will not last for ever, but for the next twenty years or so may prove a substantial drag upon the government's project to modernise the profession as a means to implementing a performance curriculum. It is not necessary to care about the poor career prospects of these teachers to see that, disaffected or time-serving, they may pose a serious threat to the maintenance of improved standards.

Acknowledgements

I am grateful to my colleagues at Warwick University, Professor Chris Husbands, Martin Merson and Dr Wendy Robinson, for comments on an earlier draft of this chapter.

References

Acker, S. (1990) 'Teachers' culture in an English primary school: continuity and change', *British Journal of the Sociology of Education*, 11(3): 257–73.

Alexander, R.J. (1984) *Primary Teaching*, London: Cassell.

——(1997) *Policy and Practice in Primary Education*, London: Routledge.

Alexander, R., Rose, J. and Woodhead, C. (1992) *Curriculum Organisation and Classroom Practice in Primary Schools*, DES, London: HMSO.

Baker, K. (1993) *Turbulent Times*, London: Faber and Faber.

Barber, M. (1996) 'How to do the impossible: a guide for politicians with a passion for education', inaugural lecture, Institute of Education, University of London, 11 December.

Bennett, N. (1976) *Teaching Styles and Pupil Progress*, London: Open Books.

Bennett, N. and Desforges, C. (1984) *The Quality of Pupil Learning Experiences*, New York: Lawrence Erlbaum Associates.

Bichard, M. (1999) 'Modernising the policy process', http://ntweb1/GenBef Speeches/Michael%20Bichard/pmp/ahtm (25 January 1999).

Black, P. (1993) 'The shifting scenery of the National Curriculum', in C. Chitty and B. Simon (eds) *Education Answers Back*, London: Lawrence & Wishart.

Brooks, G. (1998) 'Trends in standards of literacy in the UK, 1948–1996', *Topic*, Slough: NFER.

Brown, M. (1996) 'FIMS and SIMS: the first two IEA International Mathematics Surveys', *Assessment in Education* 3(2): 193–212.

Campbell, R.J. (1985) *Developing the Primary School Curriculum*, London: Cassell.

——(1989) 'HMI and aspects of public policy for the primary school curriculum', in A. Hargreaves and D. Reynolds (eds) *Education Policies: Controversies and Critiques*, London: Falmer.

——(1993) 'The National Curriculum in primary schools: a dream at conception, a nightmare at delivery', in B. Simon and C. Chitty (eds) *Education Answers Back*, London: Lawrence & Wishart.

——(1996) 'Standards of literacy and numeracy in English primary schools: a real or imaginary crisis?' presidential address to the Education Section of the British Association for the Advancement of Science, University of Birmingham.

——(1998) 'Broader thinking about the primary curriculum,' in S. Dainton (ed.) *Take Care, Mr Blunkett*, London: Association of Teachers and Lecturers.

Campbell, R.J and Neill, S.R.St J. (1994a) *Curriculum Reform at Key Stage 1: Teacher Commitment and Policy Failure*, London: Longman.

——(1994b) *Primary Teachers at Work*, London: Routledge.

Carr, D. (1994) 'Wise men and clever tricks', *Cambridge Journal of Education*, 24(1): 89–112.

Creemers, B.P.M. (1994) 'Effective instruction: an empirical basis for a theory of educational effectiveness', in D. Reynolds, B.P.M. Creemers, P.S. Nesselrodt, E.C. Schaffer, S. Stringfield and C. Teddlie (eds) *Advances in School Effectiveness Research and Practice*, Oxford: Pergamon.

Dadds, M. (1992) 'Monty Python and the three wise men', *Cambridge Journal of Education*, 22(2): 129–41.

Dearing, R. (1993) *The National Curriculum and its Assessment: Final Report*, London: HMSO.

DES (1978) *Primary Education in England: A Survey by HMI*, London: HMSO.

——(1981) *The School Curriculum*, London: HMSO.

——(1985a) *The School Curriculum 5–16*, London: HMSO.

——(1985b) *Better Schools*, London: HMSO.

——(1993) *The Implementation of the National Curriculum in Primary Schools*, London: HMSO.

DfEE (1998) *Teachers: Meeting the Challenge of Change*, London: Stationery Office.

Education (1993) Article on time allocations, untitled, unattributed, p. 3.

Evetts, J. (1990) *Women in Primary Teaching*, London: Methuen.

Foxman, D. (1998) 'Monitoring trends in numeracy in the UK, 1953–1995', *Topic*, Slough: NFER.

Galton, M. and Simon, B. (1980) *Inside the Primary Classroom*, London: Routledge.

Galton, M. Simon, B. and Croll, P. (1980) *Progress and Performance in the Primary Classroom*, London: Routledge.

Galton, M., Hargreaves, L., Comber, C. and Wall, D., with Pell, A. (1999) *Inside the Primary Classroom, 20 Years On*, London: Routledge.

Graham D., with Tytler, D. (1993) *A Lesson for Us All*, London: Routledge.

House of Commons (1986) *Third Report of the Education Science and Arts Committee, Achievement in Primary School*, London: HMSO.

Labour Party (1996) *New Labour, New Life for Britain*, London: Labour Party.

Letwin, O. (1988) *A Core Curriculum*, London: Centre for Policy Studies.

Meyer, J.W., Kamens, D.H. and Benavot, A. (1992) *School Knowledge for the Masses: World Models and National Primary Curricular Categories in the Twentieth Century*, London: Falmer.

NCC (1993) *The National Curriculum at Key Stages 1 and 2: Advice to the Secretary of State for Education*, York: NCC.

Nias, J. (1989) *Primary Teachers Talking*, London: Routledge.

Ofsted (1993) *Curriculum Organisation and Classroom Practice in Primary Schools: A Follow-Up Report*, London: HMSO.

——(1996) *Annual Report of HMCI*, London: HMSO.

——(1999a) *Primary Education, 1994–98: A Review of Primary Schools in England*, London: Stationery Office.

——(1999b) *Annual Report of HMCI*, London: Stationery Office.

Pollard, A., Broadfoot, P., Croll, P., Osborn, M. and Abbott, D. (1994) *Changing English Primary Schools? The Impact of the Education Reform Act at Key Stage One*, London: Cassell.

QCA (2000) *The National Curriculum 2000*, London: QCA.

QCA/DfEE (1999) *The Review of the National Curriculum in England: The Consultation Materials*, London: QCA.

Reynolds, D. and Farrell, S. (1996) *A Review of International Surveys of Educational Achievement Involving England*, Ofsted, London: HMSO.

Ribbins, P. and Sherratt, N. (1997) *Radical Educational Policies and Conservative Secretaries of State*, London: Cassell.

Richards, C. (1998) 'The primary school curriculum: changes, challenges, questions', in C. Richards and P. Taylor (eds) *How Shall We School Our Children?* London: Falmer.

——(1999) *Primary Education – at a Hinge of History?* London: Falmer.

Steedman, C. (undated) *Impeccable Governesses, Rational Dames and Moral Mothers*, mimeo, Coventry: History Department, University of Warwick.

Tomlinson, J. (1993) *The Control of Education*, London: Cassell.

Tooley, J. (1998) 'Towards a state-free curriculum', in S. Dainton (ed.) *Take Care, Mr Blunkett*, London: Association of Teachers and Lecturers.

Travers, K.J. and Westbury, I. (1989) *The IEA Study of Mathematics. I: Analysis of Mathematics Curricula*, Oxford: Pergamon.

Webb, R. and Vulliamy, G. (1996) *Roles and Responsibilities in the Primary School*, London: Falmer.

White, J. (1982) 'The primary teacher as servant of the state', in C. Richards (ed.) *New Directions in Primary Education*, Lewes: Falmer.

Woodhead, C. (1998) *Blood on the Tracks: Lessons from the History of Education Reform*, annual lecture, 24 January 1998, London: Ofsted.

4 Affirming and contesting the comprehensive ideal

From common schooling to selection?

Geoffrey Walford

Introduction

In 1996 a series of lectures was held at the University of Oxford, subsequently published under the title *Affirming the Comprehensive Ideal* (Pring and Walford 1997). At that time, following seventeen years of Conservative government, many were strongly concerned about the politically charged attack that was being made upon the school system attended by 85 per cent of secondary school students. The ideals of that system, its considerable achievements and the daily success of many teachers were being ignored and negated. In a period just before a general election was expected, the series of lectures affirmed the moral and educational ideals which inspired the creation of a system of comprehensive schooling, and showed how those ideals might be reflected in the organisation and practice of schools and colleges in the future.

That anticipated 1997 general election brought a Labour government to power, but rather than the comprehensive system thereby being strengthened, Labour has introduced a series of measures which have deep continuities with previous Conservative policy. This chapter reviews the reasons for the need for comprehensive schooling, outlines Conservative attacks on that system, and demonstrates that Labour policy since their assumption of power has ignored many of the arguments for supporting comprehensive schooling.

The development of comprehensive schooling

As Brian Simon (1997: 14) has illustrated, there was quite widespread support for a comprehensive system from well before the Second World War, even from such an unlikely source as the male grammar school teachers who were members of the Assistant Masters' Association. As long ago as 1925 they passed a resolution at their annual conference in favour of secondary education for all – in *one* type of school. In the mover's words,

> If secondary schools of various types were set up, it would mean that there would be in secondary schools of the present type (that is, grammar schools) a class which was bound to be looked upon as something socially superior to the children who would attend the new schools of the distinct types.
>
> (quoted in Rubinstein and Simon 1973: 15)

But their voice was not heard. Following the war a tripartite or bipartite system was generally introduced, and progress towards comprehensive schooling only really began in 1956, when the beginnings of change occurred. From then until 1964–5 a speeding-up took place as Edward Boyle, then Secretary of State, removed some of the brakes on comprehensive education put in place by Conservative governments of the late 1950s. Following the general election of 1964, the Labour government published Circular 10/65, which formally declared that government's opposition to selection at 11 plus and requested all local education authorities to reorganise their secondary schools on comprehensive lines. The Circular was withdrawn in 1970 when the Conservatives returned to power, but the policy was effectively reinstated in 1974 on the return of Labour. However, throughout the entire period – no matter who was in power – the proportion of children attending comprehensive schools rapidly increased. In 1971 only about 40 per cent of children in British local education authority maintained secondary schools were in comprehensives; by 1981 this had risen to about 90 per cent.

As with most major social changes, this movement towards comprehensive education was the result of pressures from an uneasy alliance of groups and individuals with a range of ideologies, interests and visions for the future (Ball 1984; Benn and Simon 1972). By the mid 1950s there were many obvious problems with the tripartite (or more usually bipartite) system that was introduced after the war. For example, it became clear that there was a considerable social class bias between the intakes to the three types of school in the tripartite system (Floud *et al.* 1956; Douglas 1964). The grammar schools were dominated by middle-class children, while the secondary modern schools were largely the preserve of the working class. The problem was largely seen to be the IQ tests that were generally used to select children, and arguments centred on the fairness of these tests for children from different backgrounds, on the extent to which the tests were able to discriminate between children according to their abilities or their academic potential, and on the examinations having to be taken at an age when children were still developing at different rates (Yates and Pidgeon 1957). It was also found that the reliability of the tests was low and that children could be coached into obtaining higher scores in these examinations, even though they were supposed to measure some 'innate' abilities (Ford 1969). Even accepting a narrow definition of efficiency of selection based on what the IQ tests could measure, it was estimated that about 10 per cent of children were wrongly selected each year – half of these being wrongly selected for grammar schools and half wrongly going to secondary modern schools (Vernon 1957). By 1970, IQ tests were largely discredited as a means of selection, but most of the problems associated with them also occur in other ways of selecting.

But 'accurate' selection was only part of the problem. In the late 1960s a variety of sociological studies of grammar and secondary modern schools also began to raise questions about the desirability of selection at 11 independently of the degree to which selection could be accurately achieved. The classic case studies of grammar and secondary modern schools by Lacey (1970) and Hargreaves (1967) showed the detrimental effects of selection and differentiation between and within schools. Those children at the bottom of a grammar school tended to think of themselves as failures and developed anti-school attitudes. Other studies highlighted the cultural conflict experienced by a working-class child in a grammar school. Where working-class children did manage to enter grammar schools the cultural expectations were often in stark contrast to their own (Jackson and Marsden 1962; Dale and Griffith 1965).

A further important factor that led to comprehensive schools was an increased demand for a 'grammar school type' education. This was partly due to rising expectations on the part of parents, but demographic trends also had their effect. The post-war 'bulge' entered secondary education at a time when only a few new grammar schools had been created. As the percentage of children being selected varied markedly between local education authorities, in many areas middle-class parents were finding that their children were not being admitted to the grammar schools which they had themselves attended (Ford 1969). Instead, their children were being forced to attend secondary moderns which they perceived (often correctly) as funded at a lower level, having poorer-paid and poorer-qualified teachers, and able to enter children for only a limited range of public examinations. This individual concern about sons and daughters was largely transmuted to a call for greater equality of educational opportunity for all and greater national efficiency. It was believed that both of these would be provided through comprehensive education.

But comprehensive schools also developed because there were many who believed that educating all local children in a single school, where they would have equal physical facilities and equal access to high-quality teachers, would raise the aspirations of all children and teachers, bring about greater equity within the schools and lead to greater opportunities outside in the world of work. It was hoped that mixing children from different social class backgrounds in the same school would lead to a lowering of barriers between classes and a reduction in class antagonism and class differences. This reason for comprehensive schools is far stronger now than it has ever been. But such schools challenge the dominant principle on which the British system of schooling has been historically based – selection of children for unequal provision. Throughout British history, social class and gender have been the major determinants of the quality of schooling that children received. While there has been some decrease in gender inequalities, we now live in a multicultural society that is increasingly harshly divided by class and ethnicity. Social mixing gives at least some possibility for mutual understanding and greater equity.

I have summarised elsewhere the long and acrimonious debate about the relative effectiveness of the selective and comprehensive systems (Walford 1997). The most reasonable conclusion to be drawn from a variety of early studies is that any differences between the overall examination effectiveness of the two systems were small, but once comprehensives had become established they appeared to slightly reduce social class differences in attainment. A more recent study, but still using old data (Kerckhoff *et al.* 1996), agrees that the average output of selective and comprehensive systems is much the same, but found variations at school level suggesting that able children did better at grammar schools while less able children did better in comprehensives. However, as Crook *et al.* (1999: 48–9) argue in their thorough survey of the literature, even if one accepts a system-level tendency it cannot then be assumed that the 'superior' achievements of the academically able arise from the selective nature of the grammar schools rather than, for instance, the more favourable resourcing and teacher retention rates associated with these schools.

More significantly, all of the studies found that there were far larger differences between the examination successes of different schools of the same type than between the average examination results of different systems, even after such factors as social class had been taken into account (Gray 1990).

Yet, as Benn (1997: 123) argues, the myth still persists that better results flow from educating an academic elite separately, whether in their 'own' school or by streaming in comprehensive schools. Benn's own research (Benn and Chitty 1996: 286–7) compared schools where a majority of subjects were set against schools with a minority of subjects set, and found no difference in academic results.

Conservative attacks on the comprehensive ideal

However, in spite of the evidence generally in favour of comprehensives, during the early 1980s there were several attempts by Conservative-controlled local education authorities to try to reintroduce selection by academic ability. All these direct attempts failed. In Solihull and Richmond-upon-Thames, for example, local parents campaigned against the proposed changes and won their demands for the retention of existing comprehensive schools (Walford and Jones 1986).

As the all-out frontal attack on comprehensives did not work, a more gradual approach was adopted. Following the election of Margaret Thatcher's first government in 1979, a series of separate yet interlinked policies were introduced to support and encourage the selection of particular children for unequally funded schools. First came the Assisted Places Scheme of 1980, where poor but 'academically able' children were to be 'plucked like embers from the ashes' of the state system to enter private schools of high academic reputation. In practice, those families sufficiently knowledgeable about the procedures and able to negotiate the choice and selection processes inherent in the scheme were rewarded with more costly staffing and facilities than in the state sector (Edwards *et al.* 1989). The second support for selection occurred in 1986, when central government announced that it intended to establish a network of twenty City Technology Colleges (CTCs). These were intended to provide free technology-enhanced education to selected children within particular inner-city areas. Selection of specific children for inequitable provision was a central feature of the plan. In this case, selection was not to be on academic criteria but on 'deservingness'. In a study by Walford and Miller (1991) of the first CTC, it was shown that it was selecting those very parents who have the most interest in their children's education and those children who are most keen and enthusiastic. Heads and teachers in nearby local authority schools argued that the CTC was selecting children who, while they might not be particularly academically able, had special skills and interests in sport, art, drama or other activities. These children were seen as invigorating the atmosphere of any school, providing models for other children, and being the most rewarding for teachers to teach.

The 1988 Education Reform Act introduced further anti-comprehensive ideas. At first comprehensive grant-maintained schools were not officially allowed to select children by ability, but many demanded a high degree of commitment from parents and children, a separate application, an 'informative' interview and sometimes a test. They found that, if the barriers to entry were set high enough, self-selection can operate as an effective way of ensuring that 'deserving' families are selected. Giving grant-maintained schools the right to impose their own admissions procedures inevitably led to a form of selection where the children of parents who lacked the knowledge, interest or skills necessary to apply had no chance of being admitted.

There were several aspects of the 1993 Education Act that re-emphasised the government's attack on comprehensive education. The most important change was that all secondary schools were given the right to 'specialise' in one or more curriculum areas and select on the basis of particular aptitudes or abilities in music, drama, sport, art, technology or foreign languages. What is crucial is that it was deemed that the introduction of a 'specialism' did not necessitate an official 'change of character' as long as only up to 10 per cent of the intake were selected according to criteria related to the specialism. Further, greater specialisation was evident in the Technology Colleges launched in late 1993 as a far cheaper alternative to the CTC programme. Rather than establish entirely new independent schools, this new non-statutory plan enabled existing schools to seek a much smaller amount of sponsorship and become eligible for enhanced central government funding. Initially, the element of autonomy that the CTCs exhibited was reflected in the scheme's restriction to voluntary-aided and grant-maintained schools, but the scheme was soon extended to include all local education authority schools. The schools were expected to already have a strong and planned commitment to technology, science and mathematics and to be able to find sponsorship from industry in return for some seats on the school's governing body. The scheme was later developed into a Specialist Schools Programme with the announcement in 1994 of Language Colleges, and further extended to include Sports and Arts Colleges in June 1996. The results of such a raft of changes were not unexpected. The research by Gewirtz *et al.* (1995) indicates that, where curriculum specialisms were being introduced by schools, they were acting as selection mechanisms for high academic ability and middle-class children. In particular, the development of specialisms such as dance or music indirectly discriminated against working-class children and allowed schools a greater chance to select 'appropriate' children. They show that, in practice, rather than schools becoming more diverse, the pressures of competition between schools have led to schools becoming more similar in what they offer, but within a hierarchy of perceived ability to offer advantage. They conclude that local hierarchies of schools were developing where resources flowed from those children with greatest need to those with the least need.

A recent series of papers from Gorard and Fitz (Gorard 1999; Gorard and Fitz 1998a, 1998b) has partly challenged this general picture developed from qualitative research. In their several papers they draw year by year comparisons using statistical data, available from government sources, of the social composition of schools. Using indicators such as the percentage of children in each school who have the right to free school meals (which is a commonly used indicator of poverty), they argue that in most cases social segregation is actually decreasing, rather than increasing as the qualitative studies have found. They find reduced segregation in 84 out of 122 English LEAs. In their recent studies they have also used alternative indicators of deprivation such as the percentage of children with statemented special educational needs, with English as a second language or who are ethnically non-white. In all of these cases, their calculations lead them to conclude that, overall, increased marketisation and selection has not led to increased segregation. While they do find some cases where segregation appears to have increased, the balance of the evidence points in the opposite direction.

There has been considerable debate about these findings, but the main difficulty is that all the indicators used are indicators of deprivation. Only about 20 per cent of children are eligible for free school meals, and the percentage of children with state-mented special education needs, with English as a second language or who are ethnically non-white, is smaller. These are measures of social disadvantage, not social advantage, and are used as bipolar either/or indicators. Taking 'ethnically non-white' as a single category, for example, conceals the known differences in academic perfor-mance of children from different 'non-white' ethnic groups. These indicators thus do not give information on the whole distribution of social polarisation, but only on how the quite severely disadvantaged have coped with marketisation and selection compared with the rest. It is certainly not unimportant that this group may not have fared as badly as expected, but such data give no information at all about how the most advantaged or even the average students have fared. The qualitative and quantitative research is not necessarily in disagreement. Additionally, while the usual social indica-tors of social class, income, wealth, ethnicity and gender are important, the detrimental effects of selection do not depend on disadvantage being linked to these variables. The process of being chosen for a school has now become highly compli-cated with local knowledge, interest in education, and degree of motivation of parents and children being vital indicators of successful acceptance of a child in a leading school. Children and families where there is a low level of interest in education simply do not give this process sufficient attention.

The Conservative government's attack on comprehensive education was most clearly laid out in its last educational White Paper, *Self-Government for Schools* (DfEE 1996), which made several more proposals that challenged comprehensive schools. The Paper proposed that all grant-maintained schools should be able to select up to 50 per cent of their pupils by general ability, or by ability or aptitude in particular subjects, without needing central approval. LEA Specialist Technology and Language Colleges were to be allowed to select up to 30 per cent of their pupils according to abilities or aptitudes in their specialist subject, and all LEA schools were to be given the right to select up to 20 per cent of their intakes. Finally, and at last openly, the White Paper explicitly stated that the Conservative government wished to encourage the establishment of new grammar schools. It wished to encourage promoters of new sponsored grant-maintained schools to establish new grant-maintained grammar schools, and would encourage existing schools to become selective. In the period before the general election five new grammar schools were started through the sponsored grant-maintained schools programme (Walford 2000).

According to the estimate of Fitz and his colleagues (1997), the resulting diversity of status, funding and accountability meant that, while the Conservative government had only managed to increase the percentage of 'officially selective' schools by 1 per cent (Benn and Chitty 1996), by 1996 only 40 per cent of secondary schools were LEA-maintained and fully comprehensive. There were a growing number of schools which controlled their own admissions, and selection by ability, aptitude and a variety of other more covert mechanisms was increasing.

Labour attacks on the comprehensive ideal

The Education Bill that resulted from the 1996 White Paper was published on 30 October 1996, but large parts of the Bill were abandoned when the general election was called in early 1997. The resulting 1997 Education Act contained none of the controversial changes indicated above. However, in July of the same year the new Labour government published its own White Paper *Excellence in Schools* (DfEE 1997), which had a whole chapter devoted to 'Modernising the comprehensive principle'. This 'modernised' principle included firm backing for setting within schools and for a greater diversity of schools. The Paper stated that 'We are deeply committed to equal opportunities for all pupils', but emphasised that 'This does not mean a single model of schooling' (p. 40). The use of the concepts 'diversity' and 'specialisation' indicated distinct continuities with the previous government's policies (Edwards *et al.* 1999).

On the other hand, the government quickly legislated for the manifesto commitment to end the Assisted Places Scheme, thus ending this particular form of academic selection. However, the resulting 1998 School Standards and Framework Act had mixed implications for the comprehensive ideal. It replaced the system of county, voluntary and grant-maintained schools with a new system of community, voluntary and foundation schools which are funded using a common funding formula. This change meant that grant-maintained schools no longer had access to additional capital and current funding, and they now have local education authority representatives on their governing bodies.

The government's position on academic selection is more ambiguous. It has stated that it believes selection by academic ability is unfair and divisive, and that it is acting to prevent its increase. However, it is clearly not prepared to act positively to decrease such selection (Webster and Parsons 1999). In a letter to Margaret Tulloch, Executive Secretary of the Campaign for State Education, Stephen Byers, Minister of State for Education, explains the government's position on partial selection in the following way:

> And yes, it is true that we are allowing existing partial selection to continue ...
> We do, of course, recognise that partial selection clearly has created uncertainty and confusion for parents in some areas. But we also have to accept the possibility that there may be areas where partial selection by ability is not causing problems and there is no groundswell of opinion from parents or schools against it. In these circumstances it would be both heavy-handed and

unnecessary for us to put an end to it simply on dogmatic grounds – we want to take the dogma out of education.

(letter, 16 July 1998)

It would appear that the government believes it would be 'dogmatic' to act to reduce the effects of something that it openly recognises as divisive and unfair! Thus the 1998 Act contains several sections which deal with selection. While there is a general prohibition on selection by ability in all maintained schools, several major exceptions are established. The first permitted form of selection by academic ability reflects this desire to 'take the dogma out of education', for the Act allows partial selection arrangements based on ability or aptitude to continue if they were in place in 1997–8. But there must be no increase in the proportion of selective admission or any significant change in the method of selection. Where a school has been recognised as having a specialism in a particular subject, selection by aptitude for this subject may continue but must not exceed 10 per cent of the intake. The next exception actually enhances the comprehensive ideal, for selection is allowed where the purpose is to secure 'pupil banding' such that an appropriate range of abilities is achieved in each school. This is still done in several Inner London education authorities.

The final exception is, of course, grammar schools. On full selection by academic ability, the Act provided a complicated procedure whereby prospective and existing parents are able to vote to change the existing 164 state-maintained grammar schools into comprehensive schools. The details of the system that eventually followed through Regulations are seen by many as being designed to make it as difficult as possible for any change to occur. In particular, before any ballot can be held, parents have to obtain signatures supporting such a ballot from 20 per cent of those entitled to vote. In mainly selective areas a wide range of parents and prospective parents are entitled to vote, but where there are only a few isolated grammar schools only parents of children in feeder primary schools will have a vote. In this case, 'feeder' is defined as a school from which five or more children have progressed to the grammar school in the past three years. Private preparatory school users may thus have a disproportionate influence, while parents living near to the school may not have a vote at all. The Act thus leaves the reorganisation of the most divisive element of the state-maintained sector to the wishes of particular groups of parents who currently (or are about to) use the schools. The extent of this divisiveness for the most disadvantaged can be assessed from figures given to a written parliamentary question on 11 May 1999. The figures give the percentage of children known to be eligible for free school meals in grammar schools compared with those in maintained secondary schools for each of thirty-two local education authorities with grammar schools. The average ratio indicates that the proportion of children with free school meals in grammar schools is about a fifth of the national average. It is far lower in every local education authority, with Birmingham showing 5.1 to 34.3, Kent 3.4 to 12.9 and Buckinghamshire 1.6 to 7.0 (*Education Parliamentary Monitor* 1999).

Yet the Labour government has not only allowed existing full and partial selection by academic ability to continue, but has also encouraged an extension of the specialist schools programme where so-called 'comprehensive' schools can provide a 'specialism' and select up to 10 per cent of intake on the basis of 'aptitude' in that particular specialism. The Secretary of State has tried hard to argue that selection by aptitude for a specialism does not imply selection by ability or any ethnic or social class related criteria, but critics are unconvinced (Edwards 1998).

In contrast, one further aspect of the Act might have a positive effect on the comprehensive principle, for it established the office of adjudicator to make judgements on the fairness of aspects of school organisation and admissions. The decisions of the adjudicator will be crucial on the issue of partial selection, and early indications are that some schools with partial selection will be required to reduce the proportion selected. In the area around Watford, for example, five former grant-maintained schools have been forced to reduce their partial selection from 50 per cent to 35 per cent (Hackett 1999) to make it easier for local children to find a place. A small change, but at least in the right direction.

Various other policies of the Labour government can be seen as indirectly weakening the comprehensive principle. One such policy is the increased level of ideological support given to the private sector. Within the first few months the new Labour government had established an advisory group to focus on the development of partnership between the state and independent sectors. In the autumn 1997 edition of the *Independent Schools Information Service Magazine*, David Blunkett, Secretary of State for Education and Employment, wrote:

> Constructive collaboration and partnership is the way forward in education. We know that there is much that we can learn from the private sector and much that the private sector can share. We want to put aside the divisions of the past and build a new partnership which recognises that private schools can make a real contribution to the communities in which they are situated
>
> (Blunkett 1997: 10)

In November 1997 Stephen Byers, Minister for School Standards, echoed these views in a highly significant speech at the Girls' Schools Association annual conference. He announced an end to 'educational apartheid' between the state-maintained and private sectors and proposed a new partnership between them. He set out three 'golden rules' for Labour's new attitude towards private schools. First, high standards in independent schools will not be compromised, Second, change will be voluntary. Third, there will be no imposition from above. Further, he announced that £500,000 was to be made available for a partnership scheme between independent and state-maintained schools. This was later raised to £600,000 due to the large number of good applications, with about half of the funding coming from the Sutton Trust – a charitable trust. Small grants of up to £25,000 were made available for innovative schemes that made links between schools in the two sectors and contributed to raising standards. What is significant about this scheme is not the relatively small amounts of funding made available, but the major change in policy that it represents and the ideological support it gives to the private sector. The unspoken assumption behind the scheme is that private schools are 'better' than state-maintained schools, and that they should share some of their expertise and facilities with local state-maintained schools. While it is certainly correct that many of the major schools do have far better facilities for sport, science, music and so on, it is not clear that the teachers in such schools are necessarily 'better' or that they are ideally suited to 'help' children from comprehensive schools who often come from rather different social class backgrounds than the children they usually teach. In early 1999 the scheme was extended for a further two years.

As part of this new relationship with the private sector, the government also made it clear that it does not intend to remove charitable status from private schools. This had been seen as a significant threat in the 1992 general election, as it would have led to increases in school fees. While abolition of charitable status was not a part of Labour's 1997 programme, the clear abandonment of the policy only came in 1998.

A further major part of the 1988 legislation has a more mixed potential effect on the comprehensive ideal. Education Action Zones are designed to develop programmes that help raise educational standards in deprived inner cities or rural areas. Typically, a Zone comprises:

> between 15 and 25 primary, secondary and special schools, working in partnership with local parents, Early Years Providers, businesses, the LEA, community organisations, TEC(s), careers service, colleges, other statutory agencies (such as health authorities, the youth service and the police) and other. The strategic direction of the zone will be set by an Action Forum.
>
> (DfEE 1999: 5)

The basic idea behind the Zones is that schooling in certain deprived areas could be improved by targeting greater financial and human resources and by involving a wide variety of local people and organisations in a new partnership. The details of the policy have changed slightly since their original announcement in the 1997 White Paper (DfEE 1997), but each Zone receives up to £1 million extra funding a year for five years, of which the government provides £750,000. The additional £250,000 has to be found from sponsors who are able to contribute in cash or in kind. Here is one of the problems, for this need for sponsorship is linked to the way in which Zones are selected. Rather than identify target areas of deprivation where Action Zones are thought to be necessary, the government has left it to local initiative to develop proposals for Zones and to submit bids for funding.

Moreover, the Zones have been given various exemptions from the legal requirements under which all other state-maintained schools operate. First, they do not have to teach the National Curriculum, which Hatcher (1998) and Chitty (1998) both believe could lead to a limited and more directly work-related curriculum for some children in disadvantaged areas. Second, teachers do not need to be paid on the national agreed salary scale. The intention here is that teachers in the Zones will be paid more, but there are concerns that this could be another step towards local pay bargaining. Third, the Zones may put private consultants in management positions within schools, and they need not be trained teachers. All of these aspects are potential threats to the comprehensive ideal, but the idea of positive discrimination in school provision is one which accords well with increasing equity between groups.

Conclusion

The comprehensive ideal affirms that children's education should not be disadvantaged by their backgrounds, and that the state should provide free, high-quality education for all in comprehensive schools. With the exception of positive discrimination, selection of specific children for differentially funded and supported schools clearly violates this principle and encourages a move back to a discredited system. In contrast with what might be expected from a Labour government, many of their policies appear to be designed to generate greater fragmentation into different types of school, greater selection according to a range of different criteria and greater inequity in what schools offer. Market forces (under the guise of choice and diversity) reflect and promote a different set of values; growing inequalities between schools militate against social equity. Much of the present government's educational policy will increase injustice and inequity. It will lead to a system of unequally funded schools which will provide very different educational experiences for children of different abilities, social classes and ethnic groups. It will fail to raise educational standards for all.

I agree that the comprehensive ideal needs to be developed to take account of the very different social and economic circumstances of the new millennium. The future will demand that the need to develop a range of personal and social abilities is taken far more seriously. The different forms of intelligence will need to be nurtured; the new opportunities for organising learning which technology makes possible will need to be exploited. Most of all, however, there will be a need to ensure that every child has access to the highest possible quality schooling and that provision does not depend on privilege and social background. The demands and opportunities of the new millennium will require modification to the form of comprehensive schools that thrived in the 1970s, but the ideals on which they were based are very much worth re-examining and reaffirming. An acceptance of the inequities of selection is a retrogressive step.

Note

This chapter draws upon a previous joint publication (Walford and Pring 1997).

References

Ball, S.J. (1984) (ed.) *Comprehensive Schooling: A Reader*, Lewes: Falmer.
Benn, C. (1997) 'Effective comprehensive education', in R. Pring and G. Walford (eds) *Affirming the Comprehensive Ideal*, London: Falmer.
Benn, C. and Chitty, C. (1996) *Thirty Years On*, London: David Fulton.
Benn, C. and Simon, B. (1972) *Half Way There*, 2nd edition, Harmondsworth: Penguin.
Blunkett, D. (1997) 'Let's work together', *ISIS Magazine*, 18: 9–10.
Chitty, C. (1998) 'Education Action Zones: testbeds for privatisation?', *Forum*, 40(3): 79–81.
Crook, D., Power, S. and Whitty, G. (1999) *The Grammar School Question: A Review of Research on Comprehensive and Selective Education*, London: Institute of Education, University of London.

Dale, R.R. and Griffith, S. (1965) *Down Stream. Failure in the Grammar School*, London: Routledge & Kegan Paul.

DfEE (1996) *Self-Government for Schools*, London: DfEE.

——(1997) *Excellence in Schools*, London: DfEE.

——(1999) *Excellence in Cities*, London: DfEE.

Douglas, J.W.D. (1964) *The Home and the School*, London: MacGibbon & Kee.

Education Parliamentary Monitor (1999) 'Free school meals', *Education Parliamentary Monitor*, 3(9): 43–4.

Edwards, T. (1998) *Specialisation without selection?*, Research and Information on State Education Trust, Briefing Paper 1, London: RISE.

Edwards, T., Fitz, J. and Whitty, G. (1989) *The State and Private Education: An Evaluation of the Assisted Places Scheme*, Lewes: Falmer.

Edwards, T., Whitty, G. and Power, S. (1999) 'Moving back from comprehensive secondary education?' in Jack Demaine (ed.) *Education Policy and Contemporary Politics*, London: Macmillan.

Fitz, J., Halpin, D. and Power, S. (1997) 'Between a rock and a hard place: diversity, institutional identity and grant-maintained schools', *Oxford Review of Education*, 23(1): 17–30.

Floud, J.E., Halsey, A.H. and Martin, F.M. (1956) *Social Class and Educational Opportunity*, London: Heinemann.

Ford, J. (1969) *Social Class and the Comprehensive School*, London: Routledge & Kegan Paul.

Gewirtz, S., Ball, S.J. and Bowe, R. (1995) *Markets, Choice and Equity in Education*, Buckingham: Open University Press.

Gorard, S. (1999) ' "Well, that about wraps it up for school choice research": a state of the art review', *School Leadership and Management*, 19(1): 25–47.

Gorard, S. and Fitz, J. (1998a) 'Under starter's orders: the established market, the Cardiff study and the Smithfield project', *International Studies in Sociology of Education*, 8(3): 299–314.

——(1998b) 'The more things change ... the missing impact of marketisation', *British Journal of Sociology of Education*, 19(3): 365–76.

Gray, J. (1990) 'Has comprehensive education succeeded? Changes within schools and their effects in Great Britain', in A. Leschinsky and K.U. Mayer (eds) *The Comprehensive School Experiment Revisited: Evidence from Western Europe*, Frankfurt am Main: Verlag Peter Lang.

Hackett, G. (1999) 'Parents win battle to restrict selection', *Times Educational Supplement*, 13 August: 5.

Hargreaves, D. (1967) *Social Relations in a Secondary School*, London: Routledge & Kegan Paul.

Hatcher, R. (1998) 'Profiting from schools: Business and Education Action Zones', *Education and Social Justice*, 1(1): 9–16.

Jackson, B. and Marsden, D. (1962) *Education and the Working Class*, London: Routledge.

Kerckhoff, A.C., Fogelman, K., Crook, D. and Reeder, D. (1996) *Going Comprehensive in England and Wales*, London: Woburn.

Lacey, C. (1970) *Hightown Grammar*, Manchester: Manchester University Press.

Pring, R. and Walford, G. (1997) (eds) *Affirming the Comprehensive Ideal* , London: Falmer.

Rubinstein, D. and Simon, B. (1973) *The Evolution of the Comprehensive School, 1926–72*, 2nd edition, London: Routledge & Kegan Paul.

Simon, B. (1997) 'A seismic change: process and interpretation', in R. Pring and G. Walford (eds) *Affirming the Comprehensive Ideal*, London: Falmer.

Vernon, P.E. (1957) *Secondary School Selection*, London: Methuen.

Walford, G. (1997) 'Privatization and selection', in R. Pring and G. Walford (eds) *Affirming the Comprehensive Ideal*, London: Falmer.

——(2000) 'A policy adventure: sponsored grant-maintained schools', *Educational Studies*, 26(2): 247–62.

Walford, G. and Jones, S. (1986) 'The Solihull adventure. An attempt to reintroduce selective education', *Journal of Education Policy*, 1(3): 239–53.

Walford, G. and Miller, H. (1991) *City Technology College*, Buckingham: Open University Press.

Walford, G. and Pring, R. (1997) 'Introduction', in R. Pring and G. Walford (eds) *Affirming the Comprehensive Ideal*, London: Falmer.

Webster, D. and Parsons, K. (1999) 'British Labour Party policy on educational selection 1996–8: a sociological analysis', *Journal of Education Policy*, 14(5): 547–59.

Yates, A. and Pidgeon, D.A. (1957) *Admission to Grammar Schools*, London: NFER.

5 Further education

A suitable case for treatment?

Martin Jephcote and Prue Huddleston

Introduction

Unlike the growth of mass schooling, further education has taken a highly individualistic path, its expansion depending much on the patronage of industry, business and commerce and the ability to attract greater student numbers. Yet despite its resilience and resourcefulness in the market, post-16 provision has, over the past thirty years, been patchy, operating against a national backdrop of under-funding, low participation and policy neglect (Gleeson 1996: 87)

The further education (FE) colleges of England and Wales are unique in Europe. Some colleges have their roots in the Mechanics Institutes of the mid-nineteenth century; others were built with 'whisky money', duty levied in the late nineteenth century on beer and spirit and passed to local councils to be used for 'suitable' purposes, including the provision of 'technical instruction'. Other colleges were built more recently, as part of the general expansion of FE within the 1960s. Some colleges later became polytechnics and 'drifted' towards higher education. But whatever the origins, in 1993, as a result of the 1992 Further and Higher Education Act, all FE colleges became autonomous corporations, outside the control of their local education authorities; for the first time the FE sector had its own funding body, the Further Education Funding Council (FEFC), and was to become subject to a new funding regime. In addition it was to become further exposed to the education and training market.

Today, further education is big business. According to the FEFC's annual report (FEFC 1999), it currently allocates £3.2 billion per year to provide for the education and training of some 4 million students at 800 institutions throughout England. These are substantial figures, and yet the FE sector is one of the 'best-kept secrets' of the education landscape. Often referred to as the 'Cinderella' of education or as the 'no-man's land' which is neither schooling nor higher education (HE), the public perception of its purpose and range of provision is hazy, to say the least. It is tempting to suggest that, until recently, this myopia extended to government ministers and civil servants. This is surprising, since most people have an FE institution within a short distance of their homes, although few ministers or civil servants have been students there.

To be more specific, the term 'further education' covers not just the activities of the colleges, of which there are 437 (FEFC 1999), but also some of the work undertaken in HE and in external institutions (independent or local authority adult education centres). The colleges themselves may be further categorised as:

- general further education colleges;
- sixth form colleges;
- tertiary colleges;
- art, design and performing arts colleges;
- agriculture or horticulture colleges;
- specialist designated institutions.

Colleges vary greatly in their size, composition, student populations and range of provision. Ainley and Bailey (1997: 8) have suggested that 'there is no such thing as a typical college'. The smallest of these institutions may have fewer than 500 students, while the largest may have over 20,000. The student population is diverse, as is the provision. This may include everything from basic skills to undergraduate and professional courses, including a range of leisure and recreational activities. There are more students, both full- and part-time, within the FE sector than there are studying in HE. Most of these students are adults, although there are now small groups of pre-16 students coming into colleges as part of school link and access programmes. Today, FE colleges are the main providers of vocational education and training as well as providing a substantial number of A-level programmes.

The historical background

Historically it was the 1960s which saw a rapid expansion in FE and a shift in provision to full-time programmes, particularly general education courses for those young people who had been unsuccessful at school or who preferred the more adult environment of a college. The prosperity of the 1960s caused a concomitant need for an expansion in the provision of training in a range of skills. A wide range of vocational courses existed, many of them well respected as traditional entry routes to particular employment sectors, but these could not provide the economy and industry with what was needed in terms of skills and training. Colleges responded to the needs of the local labour market as best they could, but by the late 1970s that labour market was beginning to change irrevocably.

> Deepening recession, rising unemployment and the demographic bulge in school-leavers forced the education and training of the 16–19 age group upon the attention of politicians and the local and central education authorities. Discussion centred upon the range of courses available at 16 plus – a range that could be categorised as academic (A level), vocational (traditional technical qualifications) and training or work experience for the unemployed.
>
> (Ainley and Bailey 1997: 5)

This, then, was the context for Callaghan's Ruskin College speech in 1976; the stress in the speech on the need for education to provide industry and the economy in general with what it needed had a particular resonance as far as the FE sector was concerned. As Esland (1996: 47) has commented: 'In the international struggle for economic supremacy, the education and training systems were to be responsible for equipping the new model army of entrepreneurs and "captains of industry" with the skills of economic success.'

As the other chapters in this volume demonstrate, in the wake of the speech came a range of initiatives within both the compulsory and the post-compulsory phases of education which were intended to realign the outputs of the education and training system more closely with the needs of industry. Throughout our period, this has been the imperative for reform of the FE sector and, as we shall see, in the early twenty-first century the need for 'modernisation' has given this even greater impetus.

Rising youth unemployment and later adult unemployment in the 1970s and early 1980s not only created political panic but also brought new students into colleges. These students were enrolled on the plethora of schemes and initiatives designed to address, among other things, skills shortages, lack of work readiness, deficiencies in the adolescent population, basic skills and, perhaps written somewhere in the sub-text, deviant tendencies. The range of initiatives introduced during the course of the 1980s bears witness to the growing concerns about unemployment, the UK's lack of competitiveness, poor achievement and what has been described as an 'anti-industrial culture'. Examples include: 'A New Training Initiative' launched in 1981, a key element of which was the Youth Training Scheme (YTS), initiated in 1983 as a one-year scheme but extended to a two-year scheme in 1986; 'The Education and Training of Young People' in 1985; and, perhaps most famously of all, the Technical and Vocational Education Initiative (TVEI) introduced into pilot schools and colleges in 1983. All of these initiatives were direct attempts to respond to the reality of rising youth unemployment while at the same time aiming to make the FE curriculum more vocationally relevant, and thereby to prepare young people for the demands of the workplace. One important consequence of such government intervention was to make the FE sector more accountable to central government since it now had to bid, in competition with the increasing numbers of private training providers, to deliver vocational training. Faced with recession and closure, local businesses could no longer provide the steady flow of students to colleges. Colleges had to diversify and to seek new markets.

In 1992, the Further and Higher Education Act introduced radical changes to the governance of institutions. As a result of the Act, FE colleges were removed from the control of the LEAs and 'incorporated' as independent institutions, run only by their own governing bodies (which were required to have a substantial representation of employers). More fundamentally, the funding of FE was made the responsibility of Funding Councils in England and Wales, which were given the statutory responsibility to ensure sufficiency of provision for those under 19 and adequacy for those who were older. Funding became dependent on the numbers of students recruited to recognised programmes. Fuelled by the neo-liberal belief that competition would increase efficiency, a competitive 'quasi-market' was established, within which students became 'consumers' for whose 'custom' the post-16 institutions had to compete. These changes obviously had profound effects on the organisation of FE institutions, generating major new competitive pressures on colleges. With the removal of LEA control, colleges were forced to compete, not only with other colleges but also with school sixth forms. Internally, it contributed towards the 'intensification' of work for staff in colleges, who were required to undertake new forms of work specified in new contracts.

Running parallel to this were the changes being introduced into the curriculum, first at pre-16 and then, perhaps even more comprehensively, within the post-compulsory phase. The sweeping reforms introduced, among other things, a national qualification framework intended to cover all qualifications: vocational, academic and occupational. Since the FE sector was the main provider of most of these qualifications, the impact of the reforms was enormous. More recently still, FE has been the focus of a new set of demands placed upon it by central government – those of *inclusive learning, widening participation* and *lifelong learning*. The Tomlinson Committee's Report (FEFC 1996) and the Kennedy Report (1997) urged the sector to reach out to those groups at risk of exclusion, not just from education and training but from society more generally, and to contribute fully to the government's strategy for *lifelong learning*.

If during the 1960s, 1970s and early 1980s, the FE sector was left mainly unhindered by central government, today, particularly since incorporation, things have changed dramatically. As Merrill (2000: 45) puts it,

> Further education is still adjusting, redefining and shaping its boundaries, purpose and philosophy in the aftermath of the 1992 Further and Higher Education Act; it remains a varied and contested space ... Colleges continue to have many functions, catering for a heterogeneous student population ... [they] are characterised by a mixed economy offering vocational, academic, higher, adult and basic education.

This, then, is a brief overview of some of the main changes that have been experienced by the FE sector in the last twenty-five years. Central to those changes has been the increasing insistence by government that the FE sector take a key role in economic restructuring. It has been asked to provide a 'safe haven' for growing numbers of young people affected by unemployment, and hopefully to provide the forms of education and training needed for a rapidly changing workplace. It is now also being required to respond to the need to enhance social inclusion and lifelong learning. The obvious unanswered question is whether any institution could successfully discharge such diverse roles. In the remainder of this chapter we address this question by looking in more detail at some of these policies we have outlined – both the policy rhetoric and the reality. We conclude by briefly considering how such policies have been developed under New Labour.

FE policy and economic restructuring: the policy debate

As many of the chapters in this volume remind us, a major focus for all aspects of educational policy over the last twenty-five years has been the intractability of poor economic performance despite various initiatives designed to change the structure of education and training. Indeed, it is the case that many of the problems facing education and training and economic performance at the time of Callaghan's Ruskin College speech remain unsolved.

The view that education and training should be seen as an investment in human capital and as a means to economic growth and wealth creation was founded on the widespread belief that the prolonged relative decline of the UK economy was the result of poor education and training, and that the road to economic recovery was to be found by improving the quality of provision (see Esland 1996, above). From the late 1980s through to the early 1990s, numerous commentators drew attention to the deficits of the system. For example, Finegold and Soskice (1988) asserted that the UK had the worst-educated work force and poorest record of vocational training among industrial and economic competitors, and was caught in a 'low-skills equilibrium'. Corrigan *et al.* (1991) linked low levels of skill and training to low levels of productivity, and Daly *et al.* (1985) suggested that low levels of investment in capital left UK workers with less efficient machinery with which to produce, which, according to Jarvis and Prais (1988), was compounded by the failure to train new labour within the workplace. Poor economic performance was linked, therefore, to a supposedly inappropriate system of vocational education and training, and solutions to these problems were sought by making international comparisons.

Attempts were made to identify features of the education systems of those countries which outperformed the UK economically. The National Commission on Education (1993) drew on the work of Green and Steadman (1993) to show a 'substantial gap in performance' of 16- to 18-year-olds compared to Germany, France and Japan, and pinpointed inadequate vocational education and training as an explanation of the fact that UK manufacturing productivity rates were 20 per cent lower than in France and Germany. Furthermore, Cooke and Morgan (1991) identified Germany as having better vocational training: that is, the provision of technical skills and knowledge, and the promotion of generic skills such as the ability to work in teams, social skills and problem-solving abilities.

We should, of course, remind ourselves of the possible dangers of driving vocational education and training policy solely on the belief that there is a straightforward link between poor economic performance and perceived inadequacies of the system (Jephcote 1996); it is important to consider wider social issues and policies and the need to improve the overall quality of life, rather than simply measurable increases in overall wealth and the standard of living. Moreover, as the European Commission (European Commission 1994a, 1994b) have noted, other things being equal, countries such as Germany and Japan, which have the highest levels of general education and training, are least affected by problems of competitiveness and employment. As the Commission asserts, social and economic policy go 'hand-in-hand'. We would suggest that transferring attention within the policy debate from the 'economic problem', and the attempt to make it an 'educational problem', fulfilled a number of purposes. For example, it served to absolve government from the responsibility of previous economic ills; it also helped to legitimise changes to education and training (Finn 1985). Arguing in a similar vein, Merson (1995) asserts that the 'Great Debate' of 1976–7, premised on a view that education currently did not transmit the knowledge, understanding, skills and attitudes needed for economic and industrial success, was used as an explanation for the massive rise in youth unemployment. As such, it excluded other explanations such as increased overseas competition in manufacturing, low levels of investment in education and training, or poor industrial relations. However, despite these evident shortcomings, it was the view which dominated policy and provided justification for government intervention.

Therefore, from the 1980s on, post-16 education and training was increasingly regarded by politicians as a key means of responding to the demands of economic restructuring – both in a positive sense of developing the skills, knowledge understandings and attitudes necessary for a globally competitive economy, and as a palliative to the problems of youth unemployment.

In relation to unemployment, intervention began in earnest in 1983 with the launching of the Youth Training Scheme (YTS). YTS was officially intended to provide a high-quality programme of vocational preparation for its participants; it was portrayed as a means of resolving Britain's long-standing failures in creating a high-skill labour force. Participants were provided with twelve months' training which combined experience in the workplace with off-the-job training (by an FE college or private training provider). This was raised to two years in 1986. In line with other initiatives to increase central control over the curriculum, YTS was initially managed by a central government agency, the Manpower Services Commission (and its successors, the Training Commission and Training Agency). However, in 1990, responsibility was devolved to the newly created Training and Enterprise Councils (LECs in Scotland) and the programme was renamed Youth Training (YT).

A rather different intervention aimed at 'vocationalising' the 14–19 school and college curriculum began in 1983 with the introduction of the TVEI; through the initiative, local education authorities were effectively by-passed and funding was made available directly to support institutions willing to engage in curricular and pedagogical reform. There was, for example, an attempt to shift styles of teaching and learning from the dominant didactic methods, associated with academic subjects as preparation for universities and the professions, to learner-centred, problem-solving and participatory approaches thought to be a better preparation for the 'world of work'. The TVEI was indicative of how central government had lost confidence in the willingness or ability of schools, local authorities or the Department of Education and Science (DES) to deliver a vocational curriculum. Too many young people, it was felt, left school with low qualifications, low levels of literacy and numeracy and negative attitudes towards industry, and 'effectively immunised against further education or training' (Raggatt and Unwin 1991: xiii).

Investment in human capital, the primacy of economic goals and the need for an appropriate system of post-16 education and training continued as recurring themes throughout the 1980s and 1990s. Policy continued to be built around an appeal to the ideology of populism, so that the needs of industry were made a primary goal of education (Apple 1989). By 1990, the Employment Department had all but taken over the agenda-setting for post-16 education and training. For example, in 1990, the government launched what it called 'the Skills Decade'. The then Secretary of State for Employment stated that: 'Britain is faced with an unprecedented challenge to its international competitiveness. Our future economic growth and well being depend on our ability to overcome it' (Employment Department 1990).

Individuals were to take responsibility for their own development and to be willing and able to adapt rapidly to change. Providers of education and training were to offer high-quality and flexible provision which was to be based on a partnership between business and educational institutions.

From rhetoric to reality

To what extent, though, have these policies been successful, in practice, over the last twenty-five years? Recent research reported in the *Times Educational Supplement* (12 February 1999) conducted by the Organisation for Economic Co-operation and Development (OECD) reveals that, in the UK, unemployment rates have worsened despite the proliferation of youth employment programmes. They have failed to provide young people with the long-term flexible skills needed to manage the shift from manufacturing to service industries. Why is this the case? We would suggest that part of the answer at least lies in the mismatch between policy rhetoric, and the ensuing debates, and the realities of everyday college life. Perhaps herein lies a key problem, in that the focus of interest and debate may have shifted too far towards visions of a future and away from the reality of the educational experience of individuals. There are a number of factors that need to be identified here to explain this.

At the most general level, it is first necessary to recognise that, unlike schools, post-16 education is not mandatory; it is by definition 'post compulsory' and there is no prescribed curriculum. Whereas we do not necessarily advocate compulsion or prescription, at least in pre-16 education these features more easily facilitate an analysis of and a mechanism for controlling the purposes of schooling. Not only is it more difficult to present an analysis of the purposes of FE, but even where agreement can be reached it is more difficult to devise the means to bring any such purposes about.

Post-16 education might be regarded as a means to shape society in ways which either maintain the status quo or seek to change it 'for the better'. Thus, it would have a role in passing on or challenging the values and culture of a society. This would be achieved primarily through the selection of knowledge and the ways in which it is made available to students through, for example, the organisation of learning and teaching. Any attempts, however, to reach a common purpose through common provision or through notions of 'entitlement' are likely to be thwarted because of the voluntary nature of participation as well as the diverse routes which individuals are able to follow.

A second issue concerns the question as to whether the courses and qualifications offered through FE have, in fact, been appropriate to the task of economic restructuring. As we have already noted, the aspiration of YTS was that, in response to youth unemployment, it would provide high-quality training, similar to that developed within Germany. As with most state initiatives, the reality of implementation diverged very substantially from the officially articulated intentions (Lee *et al.* 1990). While the aim was to provide a uniformly high level of training provision, what actually emerged was a strongly differentiated system, with wide differences between types of provision. A minority of young people who enrolled on the scheme successfully used it as a basis of entry to high-quality occupations; the majority, however, found themselves little better off in terms of securing employment at the end of their course than they were at the beginning.

It seems that those countries that have been better able to deal with rising youth unemployment (e.g. Germany) are those which, rather than developing specialist courses for the unemployed, have maintained apprenticeship schemes and had a tradition of partnership between government, employers and trade unions. Moreover, against the expansion of part-time and temporary work which masks real levels of unemployment, we would suggest that there needs to be an improved and appropriate system of college- and work-based training. Recent initiatives such as Modern Apprenticeships, introduced in 1995, appeared to offer some hope in this regard, particularly of the ways in which colleges might work in partnership with local employers to develop high-quality vocational education and training programmes which effectively link, in a coherent way, off-the-job and on-the-job training (Huddleston 1999). However, despite the avowed policy intention that Modern Apprenticeships should provide a broader-based vocational education, including generic competences such as key skills, it appears that employers are unwilling to pay for anything beyond narrowly defined occupational skills.

Similarly, questions have to be asked about policy with respect to increased participation rates and qualifications. For example, Howson, reporting on the Government Youth Cohort Study, reveals a popular misconception when he states: 'Despite all its shortcomings, education seems to be working' (*Times Educational Supplement*, 29 January 1999). He was applauding the fact that the number of 18-year-olds with no academic qualifications fell from 13 per cent in 1987 to 5 per cent in 1996. Over the same time, the numbers gaining two or more A/AS levels more than doubled, from 14 per cent to 30 per cent. At first sight this would appear to be a major achievement for students, teachers, schools and colleges; looked at differently, however, it might reveal a major shortcoming. Why is it that we encourage so many young people to remain in full-time education, and why do we applaud the increase? Perhaps it is not the numbers involved in post-16 education and training which is the most telling factor; a more important consideration might be 'fitness for purpose'. As Renton reported in the *Sunday Times* (1 August 1999) there is a lack of vocational training, particularly at the craft level, with only one third of 19- to 21-year-olds in possession of a vocational qualification, compared with two thirds in Germany, the Netherlands and Sweden.

Whether Britain is faced with a skills gap or a skills shortage is a moot point. The fact is that there is a shortage of skilled craftsmen and -women and a lack of people appropriately skilled in information communication technologies. Hitherto, many have argued, there has been too much of a focus on academic and well-motivated students and their progression into higher education. Post-16 education continues to be highly stratified, with what counts as useful and worthwhile knowledge controlled through its content, form and rewards and, moreover, distributed through the ways in which access is controlled or regulated through existing social and economic advantage and disadvantage.

The introduction in 1993 to post-16 education of General National Vocational Qualifications (GNVQs) enabled government to tighten further its grip over assessment and examinations as a means to control curriculum content and, in turn, approaches to teaching and learning. However, as was demonstrated by the Dearing review (1996), there has been a continued reluctance to introduce radical change to the post-16 curriculum by abandoning the 'gold standard' of A levels. The rigour of A levels and the separation of academic and vocational routes remained throughout the 1980s and 1990s, it would seem, for fear of offending opposition from within the Conservative party (Halsall 1996). However, we would suggest that the ongoing refusal to consider seriously a unified system, in preference to the multi-track approach, virtually makes impossible the integration of the vocational and academic, even if this were desired. Moreover, it renders impossible the task of creating a coherent system of post-16 education built on sound educational principles rather than political and ideological dogma. The hegemony of the current economic discourse, perhaps no more than a happy coincidence of common interests, works to construct demands on education, so that satisfying economic requirements is seen as a way to fulfil other needs. Once this connection is questioned in turn, it allows for alternative combinations, which open up questions about the type of society we wish to live in and questions about the nature of education (Avis 1996), with an interest in knowledge, citizenship and democracy. Few ask such questions.

As well as questions about the appropriateness of qualifications, we would also suggest that, to date, not enough has been asked about what it is like to be a student or a teacher in FE. Increased staying-on rates often mask poor attendance, late arrival at classes and a less than enthusiastic attitude to learning on the part of some students. From September 2000 the introduction of Advanced Subsidiary levels will mean that students will take a broader programme of study, normally five subjects in the first year of their post-16 studies. Those in the policy arena have voiced concerns about student recruitment and retention, clearly influenced by the Audit Commission's report on student retention. A major study undertaken by the Further Education Development Agency (FEDA 1999) has highlighted the potential causes of student 'drop-out' and identified its multi-causality. Research currently being undertaken on recruitment and retention in five Midlands colleges by one of the authors of this chapter has identified the often troubled lives which students in college frequently experience. These are lives which have to juggle the competing demands of part-time employment – often up to thirty hours a week – of assignment writing and submission to deadlines, of re-engaging with the educational process which for many had previously been de-motivating and negative. To begin to recognise these problems produces a rather different conception of 'participation'.

It might be, as Ranson (1994) suggested, that the established pattern of disadvantage and underachievement is not because of any lack of capacity on the part of the disadvantaged. It is more to do with the conditions that have eroded the motivation to learn or to take seriously an education which provides little meaning or purpose to people's lives and which continues to lead to unemployment or low-paid work. The context for this disaffection is a period of widespread economic and political transformation, whereas the fundamental structure of society remains unchanged. The introduction of Individual Learning Accounts, first piloted in March 1999, whereby individuals will be given the means to 'buy' state-provided training of their choice up to specified value, will, according to recent research reported in the *TES* (12 May 2000), do little to help those with few or no qualifications, who tend to be from poorer social backgrounds. The disadvantaged and disaffected will remain disadvantaged and disaffected. We contend that FE cannot be a palliative for economic and social problems and, moreover, its contribution will be limited without economic, social and educational policies which complement each other. It is a symbiotic relationship so that, as Kennedy (1997: 15) asserts, 'learning is central to economic success and social cohesion'. However, a learning society depends upon creating the conditions which value and support learning and a society which values the contribution of individuals (Ranson 1994).

A further reason for the continued difficulties faced by FE concerns the changes in the governance of the sector, especially the move to incorporation. Incorporation effectively turned each college into an independent business. Yet despite having to deal with the realities of the 'market', many would question whether removing them from LEA control has in reality left them better able to respond to local needs. What is clear is that the changes to the governance of FE have created an atmosphere of competition, though the picture is complex (Jephcote and Salisbury 1996). Some colleges have been forced to compete with each other and with schools to increase student numbers in an attempt to maintain or increase funding; in other cases, there have been examples of collaboration. Recent mergers in the sector suggest that there may now be some rationalisation of provision. However, recent legislation has announced the opportunity for 11–16 schools to apply to reinstate or open new sixth forms – hence reinforcing competition.

The marketisation of FE and changing patterns of governance, together with the advent of new managerialism and greater public accountability, have all worked to undermine efforts to improve quality of provision and bring about economic recovery. There continues, for example, to be a lack of articulation between the market for qualifications and the market for skilled labour (Jephcote and Salisbury 2000). On the one hand, there is a market for qualifications, in which colleges are forced to respond to the demands of students seeking qualifications of their choice, as regulated by a funding mechanism which gives emphasis to high levels of participation, retention and assessment outcomes. On the other hand, there is the labour market, made up of employers with demands for labour with particular competencies. Typically, individual employers work in their own best interests rather than for those of the economy as a whole. Firms tend, therefore, to under-invest in training, relying instead on a ready-made pool of skilled labour, which if not forthcoming from training programmes will be 'poached' from other firms.

We would suggest that there is a need for strategic intervention in a regional vocational education and training system based upon an explicit model of what is expected to be achieved, rather than depending on the supposedly self-evident benefits of increased training (Jephcote and Salisbury 2000). The link between the labour market and the training and qualifications market should, therefore, be looked at in terms of the specific characteristics of a region. As Hodgson and

Spours (1999) point out, there are a number of hopeful signs contained in a recent Green Paper *The Learning Age* (DfEE 1998), which emphasises a strategic approach to the development of lifelong learning, the importance of regional planning and the link between education and the labour market. However, as they go on to suggest, the proposals look like a 'collection of interesting and potentially useful initiatives, rather than a coherent strategy' (Hodgson and Spours 1999: 40). Similarly, the White Paper *Learning to Succeed* (DfEE 1996) emphasised voluntarism, market forces and institutional competition (Marples 2000). It remains to be seen whether or not the move to devolved government and the reformed regional structure of the Local Learning and Skills Councils, to be introduced in 2001, will provide anything more than additional competing actors in an already complex policy arena.

New Labour, new deal?

As in other areas of educational policy, the coming to power of New Labour in 1997 has been associated with both continuity and change. For example, the 1998 Green Paper *The Learning Age: A Renaissance for a New Britain* (DfEE 1998) returns to the theme of learning as 'the key to a strong economy ... the key to prosperity ... Investment in human capital will be the foundation of success in the knowledge-based global economy.' The link between lifelong learning and the economy is obvious and taken for granted, so that, as Bagnall (2000) asserts, the focus is on instrumental, useful and performative knowledge, especially those skills which make people employable and increase earning potential. New Skills qualifications are likely to do little to change the status quo and are, according to Marples (2000: 135), 'symptomatic of a timid and backward-looking approach in so far as there is a piling on of yet more qualifications, within a divided and incoherent system, at the expense of addressing the issues of wholesale reform'.

At the same time, however, there is some recognition, at least at the level of rhetoric, of the need to combine economic policies with other priorities, including a greater commitment to equality by developing strategies for widening participation and increasing social inclusion. For example, the introduction of the Local Learning and Skills Councils in April 2001, it is claimed, will herald significant changes to the post-compulsory education and training landscape. A distinctive 16–19 phase of education will be created, and a new adult curriculum framework. Policy priorities are signposted as focusing upon:

- raising standards through the alleged depth, breadth and rigour offered by the new curriculum, operating from September 2000;
- widening participation, particularly for those at risk of exclusion;
- improvements to the quality of colleges' premises;
- where appropriate, the development of new institutions;
- supporting increased demand by adults through the provision of basic skills;
- engaging employers, in particular small and medium-sized enterprises (SMEs) in training and development;
- introducing qualification standards for FE staff;

- encouraging a commitment to lifelong learning.

How much this is new wine in old bottles remains to be seen. However, on some parts of the agenda the colleges have already made a promising start.

During the past five years, colleges have opened their doors to increasing numbers of pre-16 students. These 'new kids on the block' are often attending link courses designed to provide an introduction to vocational programmes which may prove more motivating than the compulsory, academically oriented National Curriculum. In 1998, under Section 363 of the Education Act, schools were able to 'disapply' pupils from part of the National Curriculum provided that an alternative, appropriate programme of study could be arranged. Colleges have, therefore, been increasing their provision for 14- to 16-year-olds, including access programmes, vocational taster courses and extended work experience linked to specific vocational routes, as well as basic skills provision.

The government's recent 'New Start' initiative, announced in 1997, was specifically designed to re-engage and re-motivate those young people at risk of exclusion from school. Colleges were seen as key partners in the initiative and were called upon to provide, in partnership with schools, the Youth Service, the Careers Service and in some cases employers, a vocationally oriented programme in an attempt to re-engage the young person with education and training.

The programme evaluation is positive and supports the view that FE is well placed to offer a 'New Start' to those for whom schooling has been a negative experience. Similarly, research conducted by one of the authors in a number of West Midlands colleges has identified the extent to which college has provided an opportunity for young people on the margins of education, and to some extent of society in general, to re-engage and re-orientate themselves in terms of their future destinations. Students have spoken positively about the college experience, in particular the support provided by tutors. The author has been struck by the amount of time spent by tutors in ensuring that students attend and that their personal and academic concerns are dealt with in a sensitive and wholly supportive manner. Every student in the interview sample reported that they preferred being in college to being at school. At least three quarters of the sample were considering continuing in further education at the end of their one-year course. All these students had entered college with low GCSE grades and often lower self-esteem.

FEDA (1999) has identified a yet further role for colleges within local communities: that of fostering local economic regeneration. It is suggested that colleges may act as service providers, stakeholders or strategic partners. Performance on the last of these appears uneven, with some colleges finding it difficult to engage with partners at the regional and sub-regional level. Others, however, are doing well and developing exciting outreach programmes to engage the wider community in learning.

One such project in the West Midlands has involved a partnership between the local college, the TEC, the local authority and private business in the development of a major distribution park, with the college providing training and development courses on site for employees. Another links a college with its local school in providing basic skills courses for parents of pupils. In this way the college is performing one of its traditional roles as community provider, but within a different context. As Merrill (2000: 49) suggests:

> The colleges' role in strategic partnerships and regeneration projects illustrates the FE sector's most entrenched characteristics both pre- and post-incorporation. The sector's strength lies in its diversity and comprehensiveness; its weakness lies in its very ubiquity as a jack of all trades.

Conclusion

For most of the period 1976–2001, FE policy, though not always FE practice, was driven by the explicit aspiration of linking post-compulsory education and training to the needs of the economy. Perhaps more than any other sector of education, FE directly felt the winds of change that followed James Callaghan's intervention and, as this chapter has sought to show, it was not always a comfortable time.

The future for FE is still not fully resolved. In the past twenty-five years it has undergone a dramatic and turbulent process of change involving new forms of organisation and management, new funding regimes, the imposition of new qualifications and curricula reform, changed terms and conditions of service for staff, and a plethora of initiatives and schemes for young and adult unemployed. In short, the FE sector has arguably been subjected to more rapid change than any other part of the education system. It now appears well positioned to respond to the new agenda of *widening participation* and *social inclusion* and to work locally to foster the development of learning communities.

References

Ainley, P. and Bailey, B. (1997) *The Business of Learning. Staff and Student Experiences of Further Education in the 1990s*, London: Cassell.

Apple, M.W. (1989) 'Critical introduction: ideology and the State in educational policy', in R. Dale (ed.) *Modern Educational Thought*, Milton Keynes: Open University Press.

Avis, J. (1996) 'The myth of the post-Fordist society', in J. Avis, M. Bloomer, G. Esland, D. Gleeson and P. Hodkinson (eds) *Knowledge and Nationhood*, London: Cassell.

Bagnall, R.G. (2000) 'Lifelong learning and the limitations of economic determinism', *International Journal of Lifelong Education*, 19(1): 20–35.

Cooke, P. and Morgan, K. (1991) *Industry, Training and Technology Transfer*, Cardiff: Regional Industrial Research.

Corrigan, P., Hayes, M. and Joyce, P. (1991) *The Cultural Development of Labour*, Basingstoke: Macmillan.

Daly, A., Hitchens, D.M.W.N. and Wagner, K. (1985) 'Productivity, machinery and skills', *National Institute Economic Review*, 111: 48–61.

Dearing, R. (1996) *Review of 16–19 Qualifications: Summary Report*, London: School Curriculum and Assessment Authority.

DfEE (1996) *Learning to Succeed*, London: DfEE.

——(1998) *The Learning Age: A Renaissance for a New Britain*, London: DfEE.

Employment Department (1990) *1990s: The Skills Decade. Strategic Guidance on Training and Enterprise*, Sheffield: Employment Department Group.

Esland, G. (1996) ' Education, training and nation-state capitalism: Britain's failing strategy', in J. Avis, M. Bloomer, G. Esland, D. Gleeson and P. Hodkinson (eds) *Knowledge and Nationhood: Education, Politics and Work*, London: Cassell.

European Commission (1994a) *European Social Policy: A Way Forward*, White Paper Com. (94) 333, Luxembourg: European Commission.

——(1994b) *Growth, Competitiveness, Employment: The Challenges and Ways Forward into the 21st Century*, Luxembourg: European Commission.

FEDA (1999) *Furthering Local Economies*, London: FEDA.

Finegold, D. and Soskice, D. (1988) 'The failure of British training: analysis and prescription', *Oxford Review of Economic Policy*, 4(3): 21–53.

Finn, D. (1985) 'The MSC and the Youth Training Scheme: a permanent bridge to work?' in R. Dale (ed.) *Education, Training and Employment*, Oxford: Pergamon.

Further Education Funding Council (1996) *Inclusive Learning*, Coventry: FEFC.

——(1999) *Annual Report 1998–99. Delivering the New Agenda*, Coventry: FEFC.

Gleeson, D. (1996) 'Post-compulsory education in a post-industrial and post-modern age' in J. Avis, M. Bloomer, G. Esland, D. Gleeson and P. Hodkinson (eds) *Knowledge and Nationhood: Education, Politics and Work*, London: Cassell.

Green, A. and Steadman, H. (1993) *Educational Provision, Education Achievement and the Needs of Industry: A Review*, London: National Institute of Economic and Social Research.

Halsall, R. (1996) 'Core skills: the continuing debate', in R. Halsall and M. Cockett (eds) *Education and Training 14–19: Chaos or Coherence?* London: David Fulton.

Hodgson, A. and Spours, K. (1999) *New Labour's Educational Agenda: Issues and Policies for Education and Training from 14+*, London: Kogan Page.

Huddleston, P. (1999) 'Modern apprentices in college: so what's new?', in P. Ainley and H. Rainbird (eds) *Apprenticeship: Towards a New Paradigm of Learning*, London: Macmillan.

Jarvis, V. and Prais, S.J. (1988) *Two Nations of Shopkeepers: Training for Retailing in France and Britain*, London: National Institute of Economic and Social Research.

Jephcote, M. (1996) 'Vocational education and training: problems and policy', in S. Hodkinson and M. Jephcote (eds) *Teaching Economics and Business*, London: Heinemann.

Jephcote, M. and Salisbury, J. (1996) 'Principals' responses to incorporation: a window on their culture', *Journal of Further and Higher Education*, 20(2): 33–48.

——(2000) 'From policy to practice in further education: patterns of governance in Wales', in R. Daugherty, R. Phillips and G. Rees (eds) *Education Policy-Making in Wales: Explorations in Devolved Governance*, Cardiff: University of Wales Press.

Kennedy, H. (1997) *Learning Works: Widening Participation in Further Education*, Coventry: FEFC.

Lee, D., Marsden, D., Rickman, P. and Duncombe, J. (1990) *Scheming for Youth: A Study of YTS in the Enterprise Culture*, Buckingham: Open University Press.

Marples, R. (2000) '14–19 lifelong learning' in J. Docking (ed.) *New Labour's Policies for Schools: Raising the Standard?* London: Kogan Page.

Merrill, B. (2000) *The FE College and its Communities*, London: FEDA.

Merson, M. (1995) 'Political explanations for economic decline in Britain and their relationship to policies for education and training', *Journal of Education Policy*, 10(3): 303–15.

National Commission on Education (1993) *Learning to Succeed*, London: Heinemann.

Raggat, P. and Unwin, L. (1991) (eds) *Change and Intervention: Vocational Education and Training*, London: Falmer.

Ranson, S. (1994) *Towards the Learning Society*, London: Cassell.

6 Creating a mass system of higher education

Participation, the economy and citizenship

Gareth Rees and Dean Stroud

Introduction

During the latter decades of the twentieth century, the place of higher education in British society has been transformed. Until the 1960s, the universities and other higher education institutions (HEIs) impinged relatively little on the lives of most people. The expansion of higher education since then – and especially during the later 1980s and early 1990s – has enormously widened its range of influence. Although at any one time it remains only a minority of people who participate in higher education directly, this minority is much larger than hitherto and is drawn from a wider cross-section of society. Moreover, probably the bulk of the population now have relatives and friends who are higher education students. Today, Britain much more closely approximates the USA's experience of higher education as a 'normal' phenomenon than it did even twenty years ago, although the effects of this on wider social relations are, as yet, only imperfectly understood.

Unsurprisingly, this social transformation has entailed a fundamental restructuring of the organisation of higher education itself. Perhaps most crucially, the basis upon which universities are funded has been radically altered. The financial implications of higher education expansion have been 'managed' by successive governments through a substantial reduction in the public funding of each student, necessitating HEIs to reshape their internal organisation and practices. To be a university student – or, indeed, member of staff – today implies a very different working environment from previously. The impacts of the substitution of student grants by loans and the more recent introduction of fees for undergraduates are further transforming the student experience of higher education. Equally, HEIs are currently much more dependent for their revenue on their 'entrepreneurial' capacity to recruit students and to raise money from research grants and contracts and from endowments. As in many other areas of the public sphere, higher education has been significantly 'marketised', especially since the mid 1980s.

These changes, in turn, have required the reformulation of the relationships between central government and the higher education sector. Higher education expansion and the consequent changes in the funding regime have necessitated the intensification of central government control over the universities and other HEIs. It is true that higher education funding continues to be implemented 'at arm's length', through the Higher Education Funding Councils (HEFCs). However, the latter are much more circumscribed in their real powers than their predecessor bodies (and the Universities Grants Committee (UGC) in particular). Moreover, the overall expansion of higher education has – to some extent at least – been imposed by central government upon a less than enthusiastic sector, especially in the traditional universities.

The principal rationale here has been the contribution of an enlarged higher education sector towards fulfilling the ambitions of successive governments to bring about a long-term improvement in the competitiveness and growth of the British economy. In this regard, the changes which have taken place in higher education echo the reforms in schools and elsewhere in the educational system, during the period since James Callaghan ushered in the 'Great Debate' with his speech at Ruskin College in Oxford in 1976. However, the connections between the economy and *higher* education are much more direct. They are reflected in the debates around the subjects which students should be funded to study, the nature of graduate employment and the consequent contributions which students should make to the costs of universities through fees. One of the great paradoxes here is that, despite their significance to these policy debates, the relationships between higher education, graduate employment and economic competitiveness are still only partly understood.

By any criteria, therefore, the restructuring of higher education has been profound. Moreover, this restructuring reflects fundamental changes in the role which higher education plays within British society, especially with respect to shifts in employment and economic life more generally. Given this, it is perhaps surprising that higher education remains only a very partially analysed element within Britain's overall educational system. More specifically, a number of studies are available which focus on changes in higher education as an administrative system (for example, Becher and Kogan 1992; Kogan and Hanney 2000; Salter and Tapper 1994; Shattock 1994). However, far less attention has been paid to higher education's shifting role as a set of social processes, within which the relationships between universities and the wider society are crucial (although see, for example, Halsey 1992; Scott 1995). In what follows, we attempt to redress this balance somewhat by examining some of the inter-relationships between these two dimensions of British higher education.

From an elite to a mass system of higher education

In his seminal analysis, Trow (1973) distinguishes between elite, mass and universal systems of higher education. Elite systems he defines as those which enrol up to 15 per cent of the age group; mass systems as those enrolling between 15 per cent and 40 per cent; and universal systems as those which enrol more than 40 per cent. In these terms, therefore, Britain now has what is clearly a mass system and, in fact, is rapidly approaching a universal one. However, the transition from an elite system is very recent and its effects have undoubtedly yet to be felt fully. The Age Participation Index (API) for 18- and 19-year-olds had risen from around 6 per cent at the beginning of the 1960s to just over 12 per cent some twenty years later (Halsey 1992: 95).[1] However, by the end of the 1990s, the API had risen spectacularly to almost 35 per cent, passing the crucial 15 per cent divide between elite and mass systems in the mid 1980s. Moreover, David Blunkett, at the time of writing the Secretary of State for Education and Employment, has recommended that participation should be increased to 40 per cent, and this has been echoed in Tony Blair's recent call for a further expansion of the higher education system to include 50 per cent of young people under 30 years old (albeit spread across institutions of both further and higher education).

Much the same sort of story can be told in terms of the numbers of students in British higher education. At the beginning of the 1960s, the total number of students was a little more than 300,000; and this more than doubled to over 800,000 during the following twenty years (Halsey 1992: 101). However, by 1998–9, this figure had jumped to almost 1.8 million. Even more dramatic was the meteoric growth in the numbers of first-year students entering the higher education system for the first time. These grew from some 200,000 at the beginning of the 1980s to almost 650,000 by 1998, with most of this growth occurring during the 1990s. This gives a clear indication of the dynamic of the sector, as well as emphasising the rapidity of the changes in recruitment which have been absorbed by the HEIs.

It should be emphasised, of course, that this spectacular growth in numbers has not been experienced evenly across the sector. Among students, about a third of the higher education population is accounted for by part-timers; and growth among part-time postgraduates was especially marked up until the mid 1990s and has recently begun to rise again. At the institutional level, growth rates in the universities were much lower than the then polytechnics during the 1980s (having been similar during the 1970s). Moreover, only recently have the older, civic universities embraced substantial expansion, while the new universities established during the 1960s, as well as Oxford, Cambridge and the colleges of the University of London, have expanded only slowly. For substantial parts of the British higher education system, therefore, 'massification' has been happening elsewhere; and this goes some way towards explaining why the impacts of the transition to a mass system have been somewhat muted (Scott 1995: 23).

This pattern of substantial growth in British higher education is attributable to a range of factors. At the most basic level, the expansion that we have documented would have been impossible in the absence of a demand for places in higher education from candidates with appropriate levels of entry qualifications. The Robbins Report (1963) envisaged that the proportion of 18-year-olds who should proceed to higher education should rise to 17 per cent by 1980, presumably giving some indication of what was then conceived as the 'pool' of available talent. This figure has, as we have seen, been substantially exceeded, and critics have argued that 'standards' have inevitably been eroded (for example, Phillips 1996). However, as Halsey (1993) has demonstrated (albeit for a period relatively early in the expansion), this has not been accompanied by any significant fall in the performance of those entering with A levels, although the number of students entering higher education using 'non-traditional' routes has increased. And certainly the Secretary of State for Education who instituted the period of most substantial growth, Kenneth Clarke, believed that there was 'enough innate intellectual material to take one third of its population to higher education standards' (MacGregor 1991: 3).

This latter point emphasises the part played by policy-makers in fostering the growth of higher education. Certainly, the measured growth and relative stability of the higher education system during the period after the Robbins Report (1963) was rudely shattered very shortly after the election to government of the Conservatives in 1979. Initially, the emphasis was on the restriction of public expenditure on higher education (as so much else). It was believed that entry to higher education would fall in any case, as a result of falling numbers of 18- and 19-year-olds in the population. Overseas students were charged full-cost fees after 1980, and in 1981 severe cuts in higher education expenditure were announced, reducing the recurrent grant to universities by some 15 per cent over three years. At least partly in consequence, the numbers of students attending universities actually fell between 1982 and 1985.

However, this strategy was dramatically superseded by the mid 1980s, as a succession of Conservative Secretaries of State initiated the most remarkable expansion of student numbers of the modern era, far in excess of anything which had gone before. The initial impetus here was provided by Kenneth Baker, whose White Paper of 1987, *Higher Education: Meeting the Challenge* (DES 1987), most clearly marked the break with previous policy. He initiated a period of major expansion through the mid 1980s, although the larger part of this was concentrated in the then polytechnics and other public sector institutions, which were better able to cope with the stringent financial constraints that operated. Through the early years of the 1990s, another Secretary of State, Kenneth Clarke, renewed the upward trend in numbers with an even more substantial increase in student numbers, very rapidly raising the API to almost 30 per cent and the total of students to almost 1.5 million (Higgins 1991). Moreover, it would appear that it was primarily the Treasury's concerns over the public expenditure implications of the government's obligation to fund undergraduate students' fees which induced Clarke's successor, John Patten, to call a halt to growth in 1993 (Bargh *et al.* 1996).

In fact, student numbers continued to grow during the latter part of the 1990s, albeit at a much slower rate. This pattern was scarcely disturbed by the election of the New Labour administration in 1997, although, as we have seen earlier, the present government has made clear its aspirations to bring about further very substantial increases in the size of British higher education. However, for these aspirations to become a reality, the seemingly intractable problem of how to finance a mass system of higher education needs to be resolved.

Financing a mass system of higher education

The appointment of the Dearing Committee of Inquiry into Higher Education in 1996, before the general election, in effect acknowledged that the implications of the transformation of British higher education to a mass system had not been fully worked out. While the expansion could be justified in terms of both contributing to the needs of a knowledge-based economy and widening access to what was increasingly identified as 'lifelong learning', the crucial question of how the transformed system could be funded remained to be answered (see, for example, the DfEE's 1997 submission of evidence to the Dearing Inquiry).

The fundamental issue here is that the 'massification' of higher education was certainly not matched by a corresponding growth in funding. More specifically, public funding for each student fell by around a third during the 1990s alone, with the rate of decline only bottoming out right at the end of the decade. In effect, Conservative governments throughout the 1980s and 1990s treated higher education as an inefficient nationalised industry, whose 'productivity' could be significantly improved by cuts in public funding, and bringing it closer to the rigours of the private sector (cf. Trow 1994). At the system level, this is reflected, for example, in the replacement of the UGC and its public sector parallel, the National Advisory Body for Public Sector Higher Education (NAB), by the Universities Funding Council (UFC) and the Polytechnic and Colleges Funding Council (PCFC), through the 1988 Education Reform Act. This required the latter two bodies to have significant involvement of industrialists and other representatives of the private sector, attuning the higher education sector more closely to the 'needs of the economy'. At the institutional level, the cuts in public funding have obliged the universities and other HEIs to absorb annual 'efficiency gains', and these have been translated into quite radical changes in their practices and internal organisation. Certainly, for example, the Jarrett Report's identification of inefficiencies, complacency and outmoded administrative structures, necessitating a shift towards more 'businesslike' institutional management, should be interpreted in this context (Committee of Vice Chancellors and Principals (CVCP) 1985). Equally, the dramatic rise in student to staff ratios to approaching 20:1 across the sector as a whole betokens fundamental changes in patterns of teaching and learning in British higher education, which have transformed the student experience, at least in those institutions which have embraced 'massification' most thoroughly (Ainley 1994).

A further critical element in the strategy of shifting British higher education towards the practices of the private sector was the attempt to introduce competitive market relations into the sector. In particular, Kenneth Baker, during his period as Secretary of State in the mid 1980s, moved to institute a system of funding in which HEIs would be rewarded on a per capita basis (differentiated between arts, science and medicine) for the number of students recruited. In the same way as schools and colleges, therefore, HEIs would be forced to compete for students and would also have clear incentives to expand at a lower cost (Baker 1993). In reality, however, a full-blown consumer market for higher education was not introduced. Rather, the balance between funding through block grant payments and that through student fees was shifted significantly in the direction of the latter. 'Money followed the student' to a much greater extent than hitherto. However, central government ultimately proved reluctant to relinquish control over higher education to the vagaries of the market.

As in many other policy areas, this tension between marketisation and central control was resolved through the organisational mechanism of the quango: HEIs were accorded the semblance of autonomy within a market, but the government retained effective control, albeit 'at arm's length' (Marginson 1997). Hence, the 1992 Further and Higher Education Act provided for the establishment of the HEFCs essentially to implement central government strategy with respect to the funding of the newly unified higher education sector. Moreover, the extent of continued central government control was graphically illustrated in 1993, when, in the face of Treasury pressure to curb overall expenditure on the rapidly expanding higher education sector, the freedom of the universities to recruit students was 'capped' to their Maximum Aggregate Student Number (Bargh *et al.* 1996). Nevertheless, despite this reassertion of directly *dirigiste* tendencies, a competitive ethos became part of the sector's routine.[2]

Concerns about the spiralling costs to the Treasury of the development of a mass higher education system had already been reflected in changes to the system of student maintenance grants, which had been introduced following the recommendations of the Anderson Report (1960) and had underpinned the expansion of the 1960s and 1970s. Initially, maintenance grants were frozen at their 1990 value, and student loans were introduced to fill the shortfall which would be created by inflation. However, by 1993, it was decided actually to cut maintenance grants by 10 per cent for each of the following three years, with the amount available for loans being correspondingly increased. Loans were to be repaid in instalments, once the borrower was earning close to the national average wage. By 1999, the New Labour government had opted to phase maintenance grants out altogether and had linked loan repayment to the taxation system. What remains much more controversial, however, is the introduction of tuition fees for undergraduate students. Here again, the crucial determining factor was the overall funding crisis brought about by the transition to a mass higher education system. Certainly, by 1997–8, it was projected that the whole sector would fall into financial deficit. Accordingly, the 1998 Teaching and Higher Education Act introduced standard tuition fees of £1,000 per year, although contrary to the recommendations of the Dearing Report (1997) this was on a means-tested basis.

As Hesketh (1999) has observed, it is remarkable how quickly student loans have moved from an ambivalent reception to becoming a normal part of student (and parental) life. What the then Parliamentary Under-Secretary of State for Education, Alan Howarth, described at the time as a more market-orientated system of financing students has become a routinised feature of British higher education. Similarly, while the experience of tuition fees is much shorter, it is striking that what was once generally regarded as a guaranteed vote-loser in middle-class Britain has actually been introduced with a relative absence of controversy. Nevertheless, the magnitude of the change brought about by these initiatives on student financing should not be underestimated. Certainly, from the 1960s onwards it had been widely accepted that the state had an obligation to provide access to higher education for all those 'who can benefit', as the Robbins Report (1963) put it. The substitution of loans for maintenance grants effectively removed a major element of state subsidy which had underpinned the provision of this access. Critics could, of course, argue that this subsidy was in reality hugely regressive, given the predominance of individuals from middle-class backgrounds in entry to full-time university programmes (e.g. Watson and Taylor 1998: 83–94). Nevertheless, legitimate concerns could equally be raised over the impacts which the introduction of loans would have on applications by people from social backgrounds which are disadvantaged in terms of entry to higher education. Similarly, the charging of tuition fees could be justified on the grounds that the individuals who would benefit from improved employment and higher salaries after graduating should bear some of the costs (25 per cent, according to the Dearing Report (1997) calculation) of their degrees (Purcell and Pitcher 1998). Here too, however, it is not clear how far fees payments are deterring 'non-traditional' applicants (despite the means-tested elements), especially where career prospects for graduates are highly differentiated according to social background and the type of HEI attended (Brown and Scase 1994). As Halsey (1992: 103) has commented, 'the movement from grants to loans [and to tuition fees] ... and the logic of education as a positional good might well produce greater class inequality in British higher education in the future'.

Students in a mass higher education system

The transformation of British higher education into a mass system is, therefore, beset with paradoxes. The enormous expansion has clearly brought about a sea change in the total opportunities for university-level education that are available. However, the funding regime which operates has in all probability reduced the overall quality of that university-level education, especially in those institutions which have expanded the most. Moreover, changes in the financing of students in higher education *may* have had the effect of restricting the benefits of expanded opportunities to particular sections of the population.

Some aspects of the changing social composition of the student population, however, are clear. Hence, the long-standing disadvantages experienced by women in entry to higher education have been very substantially redressed. Thirty years ago, women comprised only about a third of the total student population; and by the mid 1980s, this had grown to a little over 40 per cent. It was the great expansion in higher education which followed that created the conditions in which women grew to more than 50 per cent of the total (e.g. Dearing Report 1997). Moreover, in many respects women are distributed much more evenly through the university system than previously. For example, they are no longer enrolling predominantly at the former public sector HEIs; and women are not now concentrated into part-time programmes of study (Dearing Report 1997).

However, the situation in higher education is certainly not one of equality between men and women. Women remain concentrated into particular subject areas, especially the arts, humanities, social sciences and business studies; and are correspondingly under-represented in others, such as engineering, the non-biological natural sciences, and mathematics and computing (Dearing Report 1997). Although these patterns reflect choices made earlier in their educational careers, women's relationships to the graduate labour market are clearly affected by their distribution between subjects within higher education. It is also important to note that women are more likely than men to have entered higher education by an 'alternative route', such as an access programme. Indeed, the growth in significance of such 'alternative entry' to undergraduate study (conventional A-level entrants now account for less than 75 per cent of the total) is substantially accounted for by women's increased participation. This also means that they are likely to be older than men; the almost doubling of the proportion of 'mature-age' students on full-time undergraduate degrees that occurred through the expansion of the 1980s and

1990s is again largely attributable to women.[3] While these developments may be welcomed on grounds of widening participation, it remains the case that HEIs have not always been effective in providing appropriate conditions for mature-age female students to study effectively (Edwards 1993). Certainly, rates of drop-out among female and part-time students are higher than for other groups (Morrison 1996). It is also clear that women are substantially under-represented at higher levels of study, with only 35 per cent of research students being women (Dearing Report 1997). In other words, the principal obstacle to women's educational progress has shifted upwards in the system.

Entry to higher education by people from ethnic minorities has also been growing substantially. By the mid 1980s, ethnic minorities accounted for 11 per cent of the total intake to full-time first degrees.[4] This figure had risen to 13 per cent by the end of the great expansion through the 1980s and 1990s, an increase of almost a fifth (Dearing Report 1997). Moreover, the Dearing Report (1997) also records that by 1994, 8.2 per cent of the 18- to 20-year-olds in higher education were from ethnic minorities, compared with 5.2 per cent in the population as a whole. In simple terms, therefore, ethnic minorities overall are now substantially over-represented in higher education, compared with the general population.

There are, however, significant differences between ethnic groups. Hence, for example, it is striking that Afro-Caribbean students are significantly under-represented on technical programmes of study, but more than proportionately represented in arts and humanities ones; but the reverse is true of students from Chinese ethnic backgrounds (Rasekoala 1997). More generally, Afro-Caribbean men and Bangladeshi women remain under-represented to a significant degree in higher education (Dearing Report 1997). Moreover, it has been argued that Afro-Caribbean and Pakistani students were more likely to be located in public sector HEIs and continue to be concentrated in the new universities created in 1992, especially in regions with high concentrations of ethnic minority population, such as London and the Midlands. On the other hand, students from Chinese and some Asian ethnic backgrounds are more likely to be found in the pre-1992 universities (Madood and Shiner 1994; Madood 1993). These complex patterns of differential participation are, of course, the product of a complex set of determinants, including socio-economic background, previous educational attainment and cultural mores, as well as a residue of racial discrimination in admissions procedures (Madood 1993).

Even more complex questions are posed in respect of changes in the social class composition of students in higher education. At the most basic level, data are partial and are simply unavailable for students over 21 years old. However, the Dearing Report (1997) again provides the most systematic recent analysis and concludes that the proportion of young people entering full-time undergraduate degrees from broadly working-class backgrounds rose substantially during the later 1980s and early 1990s, from 23 per cent to 28 per cent, an increase of over a fifth.[5] A more precise picture is provided by an examination of the APIs for 18- and 19-year-olds from different social class backgrounds, as the social class composition of the general population is taken into account. Hence, the API for those whose backgrounds are classified as SEG IIIm rose from 11 per cent at the beginning of the 1990s to 18 per cent by 1995–6; that for SEG IV increased from 12 per cent to 17 per cent; and that for SEG V doubled from 6 per cent to 12 per cent (Dearing Report 1997). What this indicates, therefore, is that young people from skilled manual family backgrounds benefited particularly from the 'massification' of the higher education system; but that those from semi- and unskilled manual backgrounds also made significant progress.

However, while these changes clearly indicate some widening of access to higher education to those from working-class families, their *relative* position remains hugely disadvantaged. Hence, at the end of the period of most substantial expansion, almost 50 per cent of young people from professional, managerial and skilled non-manual family backgrounds went into higher education; compared with only 15 per cent of those from working-class families. Similarly, the APIs of young people from working-class backgrounds (see above) contrasted very sharply with those from the other SEGs. The API for those whose background is classified as SEG I (professional occupations) was almost 80 per cent; that for SEG II backgrounds (managerial and administrative occupations) was 45 per cent; and even that for SEG IIIn (skilled non-manual) was approaching double – at 31 per cent – that of the skilled manual equivalent (Dearing Report 1997). The share of participation in higher education of young people from professional and managerial families far exceeded their representation in the economically active population, while the share of those from the other SEGs was significantly less than their representation in the general population, especially for semi- and unskilled manual backgrounds (Dearing Report 1997). In short, therefore, although rates of participation in higher education have been increasing for all social classes, sharp differentials between them have remained an engrained feature of the British educational system (Egerton and Halsey 1993; Smithers and Robinson 1996). Moreover, these differentials have clearly persisted through the transition to a mass system of higher education; it remains the case that it is those from broadly middle-class backgrounds who are the principal beneficiaries of the British university system.

That these social class inequalities should persist in this way is not wholly surprising. Higher education draws upon the products of other parts of the educational system, and the schools and colleges in particular. Here, the general tendency for clear differentials in educational attainment between social classes to persist in relative terms is well established (Halsey *et al.* 1980). Certainly, towards the end of the period of higher education expansion in the 1990s, there remained very marked differences between the proportions of young people from different social class backgrounds who gained the two A levels or equivalent usually necessary to enter a degree programme; 50 per cent of those from the highest socio-economic groups did so, compared with only 16 per cent from the lowest ones. In addition, the A-level grades obtained by students from the highest socio-economic groups were on average more than twice as good as those achieved by young people from the lowest groups (as measured by the mean A-level points score for those achieving two A levels) (Dearing Report 1997).[6] However, these differences in educational attainment tell only part of the story. Hence, of those young people who did attain the two A-levels standard, almost 80 per cent from the highest social class backgrounds went on to higher education, compared with only 47 per cent from the lowest ones (Dearing Report 1997).

This differential propensity to enter higher education among appropriately qual-ified young people from different social class backgrounds clearly reflects a complex set of factors. Historical patterns of participation may well induce generalised atti-tudes among some social groups that exclude entry to university ('university is not for me'). More specifically, however, there is some evidence to suggest that changes in student financing – the introduction of loans and tuition fees – may well be inhibiting applications to higher education from individuals from working-class families. Certainly, during the latter years of the 1990s, after the period of greatest expansion, the rise in the proportion of university entrants from working-class back-grounds has ceased. A *Guardian*/Universities and Colleges Admissions Service (UCAS) study in 1998 reported that one in eight sixth formers from working-class backgrounds said that they could not afford to go to higher education (cited in MacLeod 1998: i). UCAS has also reported a decline in applications from mature-age students, as well as a growth in applications to local universities and colleges, permitting students to live at home and minimise maintenance costs.

None of this, of course, is in any way conclusive; and it will require more system-atic analysis, over an extended period of time, to establish with any confidence the impacts of the removal of maintenance grants and the introduction of tuition fees. Moreover, this analysis will need to take account of the changes which are also taking place in the employment opportunities available to graduates. Judgements about the future career benefits of being a graduate may influence how students evaluate the immediate costs of becoming one; and there may be systematic differ-ences between students from contrasting backgrounds in these terms. At the moment, however, it can simply be noted that the limited progress towards widening the social class basis of access to higher education that was made through the great expansion of the higher education system during the later 1980s and early 1990s may be under threat.

Mass higher education and graduate careers

As we noted briefly earlier in the chapter, one of the principal justifications of the enormous expansion of higher education places during the 1980s and 1990s was the needs of the economy. It is highly instructive, for example, that by the 1990s, the crucial role of higher (and further) education in producing individuals with the knowledge and skills increasingly deemed necessary in the knowledge-based economy could be powerfully emphasised in the series of 'Competitiveness' White Papers on economic development strategy, initiated by the then President of the Board of Trade, Michael Heseltine (Department of Trade and Industry (DTI) 1994, 1995 and 1996). What this highlights is that higher education – and, indeed, education more widely – has come to be seen as a critical element in *economic* policy; and this is clearly an emphasis which has persisted after the election of the New Labour government in 1997. It is in these terms, therefore, that the attempts to prioritise recruitment into science and engineering through the 1980s and 1990s, on the grounds that they are more 'vocationally' relevant, are to be understood. The persistence of well-qualified applicants in opting for arts and humanities degrees at prestigious universities has simply shifted the scope of the debate towards inculcating employment-related skills in all degree programmes (e.g. Dearing Report 1997).

For individuals, too, gaining a degree has come to be routinely presented as a means of increasing access to more desirable employment opportunities and consequent financial benefits (Majumdar 1983). However, the effects of this enhanced employability are seen to be more than simply economic. Hence, to the extent that universities are able to recruit able individuals, irrespective of their social backgrounds, and equip them to enter the higher echelons of the occupational structure, then higher education may be viewed as contributing to the flux of social mobility in British society, and thereby combating social exclusion (e.g. DfEE 1997). In these terms, therefore, governments have come to define higher education as a vehicle for achieving both economic competitiveness and a measure of greater social equity. As the Dearing Report (1997: 21) puts it, the first aim of higher education is 'to inspire and enable individuals to develop their capabilities to the highest potential levels throughout life, so that they can grow intellectually, are well equipped for work, can contribute effectively to society and achieve personal fulfilment'.

As we have already shown, however, entry to higher education remains sufficiently skewed in terms of students' social class backgrounds to indicate that recruitment does not reflect ability alone. Moreover, it is increasingly clear that, as a consequence of 'massification', those who do become graduates are less likely than previously to enjoy access to higher-level occupations.

Of course, it remains the case that, on average, graduates are more likely to be in employment than others in the labour market. Unemployment rates among graduates – and even more clearly for postgraduates – are significantly lower than for the population at large (e.g. Connor 1997: 171). Even when compared with others who gained the necessary entry qualifications and could have gone to university but decided not to, graduates retain significant employment advantages. Again, they are more likely to be employed, at least after the age when careers have settled down; and they earn significantly more, especially in the later stages of their careers. In fact, the Dearing Report (1997) calculates that graduates reap an average private rate of return on their investment in getting a degree of some 11 to 14 per cent.

Nevertheless, there have been profound changes in the *sorts* of occupations to which having a degree characteristically provides access. For graduates from an elite system of higher education, there was a relatively well-worn pathway to employment in a professional or managerial occupation, characterised by stable career progression to the higher occupational levels. It is this 'traditional graduate career' which has been substantially undermined. In part, this reflects changes in the workplace. In both the public and private sectors, many organisations have adopted 'flatter' occupational hierarchies, demanding greater 'flexibility' and willingness to adapt to new circumstances from their employees. Competitive pressures have increased the insecurity of employment; even managers and professionals are much more likely than hitherto to switch jobs, both willingly and under duress (Brown and Scase 1994). However, not only are graduates having to locate themselves within this very rapidly changing structure of employment, they are also in competition with very much larger numbers of others who are – nominally at least – as well qualified as they are.

A number of consequences flow from this. First, many employers are adjusting to the intensification of competition for the more desirable jobs by differentiating between applicants on the grounds not simply of being a graduate or not, but rather of being a particular sort of graduate. Here, being able to demonstrate requisite skills and aptitudes is crucial. However, the cultural capital amassed by an individual through his or her social background, the kind of university attended, the degree course completed and so forth, is a critical factor too. To this extent, therefore, graduates from less prestigious institutions, 'non-traditional' entrants to higher education, those who have completed newly established or unconventional degree programmes, and so on, are systematically disadvantaged in the competition for employment (Brown 1995). Second, graduates are entering a much more diverse range of occupations than was previously the case. Those who are unable (or do not wish) to enter conventional 'graduate jobs' are increasingly taking up employment in occupations which would in the past have been filled by people with lower levels of qualifications. Many employers are using a degree as an access criterion for jobs, where A levels or vocational qualifications were used before. For many graduates, their degree is not gaining the kind of labour-market advantage hitherto enjoyed and which they themselves may continue to expect (Purcell and Pitcher 1998). In short, the transition to a mass system of higher education has not simply extended the employment benefits of an elite system to a wider range of the population, but rather has significantly altered the nature of those benefits.

Conclusion

Britain's transition to a mass system of higher education embodies a profound – if not generally much noticed – educational and social transformation. At one level, the expansion of university places implies a fundamental restructuring of the education system and a reconstitution of higher education's relationships with the economy and with the social structure more widely. The state has significantly extended the access of citizens to educational opportunities and, thereby, to employment and the potential of social mobility. At the same time, the resources of knowledge and skills required in the knowledge-based economy have been substantially strengthened.

However, as we have seen, there are important caveats to be noted too. Most importantly, the basis on which educational opportunities have been expanded is not wholly consistent with the notion of higher education as a 'right of citizenship' in Marshall's (1950) sense. Despite the important widening of the social basis of recruitment to higher education, it remains clear that access still does not reflect the Robbins (1963) ideal of admitting to a university education all those 'who can benefit'. Moreover, the recent changes in student financing clearly reflect a shift away from the 'citizenship rights/common identity' model which underpinned the system inaugurated by the Robbins (1963) and Anderson Reports (1960), to one of 'market/individual consumer' (Plant and Barry 1990). And in this context, the enhanced employment benefits which are the cornerstone of the latter are themselves at the least ambiguous, precisely because of the transition to a mass system of higher education.

As with the other parts of Britain's educational system, therefore, it is difficult to avoid the conclusion that higher education will necessarily continue to change in the future. Certainly, the restructuring during recent decades has effected the transition to a mass higher education system. However, the terms on which this has been done are such that further instability is ensured. If the general aims of social equity and economic efficiency are to be reconciled successfully, the character of Britain's higher education system will have to be renegotiated afresh.

Notes

1   The API is calculated as the number of under 21-year-old, home-domiciled students entering a course of full-time higher education for the first time, expressed as a percentage of the 18- to 19-year-old population of Great Britain. Unless stated otherwise, all figures are derived from those produced by the Higher Education Statistics Agency (HESA).

2   Although not discussed here, it should be noted that the shift away from block grants applied not only to teaching, but also to research activities. The allocation to the research councils of the research funds which were previously distributed directly to universities and the introduction of the Research Assessment Exercise implied the strengthening of competitive relationships between HEIs.

3   Over 21-year-olds account for around 50 per cent of full-time students as a whole, and the overwhelming majority of part-time students.

4   Madood and Shiner (1994) give a figure of 8.4 per cent of undergraduate admissions accounted for by ethnic minorities in 1992.

5   The social class classification which is used is the Registrar General's, where Socio-Economic Groups (SEGs) IIIm, IV and V correspond respectively to skilled manual, semi-skilled manual and unskilled manual occupations.

6   This is clearly related to the much greater likelihood of students from SEGs IIIm, IV and V being at a new university created in 1992. It also goes some way to explaining the gross under-representation of these students at Oxbridge and some other so-called 'elite' universities.

References

Ainley, P. (1994) *Degrees of Difference: Higher Education in the 1990s*, London: Lawrence & Wishart.

Anderson Report (1960) *Grants to Students: Report of the Committee Appointed by the Minister of Education and the Secretary of State for Scotland*, London: HMSO.

Baker, K. (1993) *The Turbulent Years: My Life in Politics*, London: Faber & Faber.

Bargh, C., Scott, P. and Smith, D. (1996) *Governing Universities: Changing the Culture?* Buckingham: Open University Press.

Becher, T. and Kogan, M. (1992) *Process and Structure in Higher Education*, London: Routledge.

Brown, P. (1995) 'Cultural capital and social exclusion: some observations on recent trends in education, employment and the labour market', *Work, Employment and Society*, 9(1): 29–51.

Brown, P. and Scase, R. (1994) *Higher Education and Corporate Realities: Class, Culture and the Decline of Graduate Careers*, London: UCL Press.

Committee of Vice Chancellors and Principals (1985) *Report of the Steering Committee for Efficiency Studies in Universities (The Jarrett Report)*, London: CVCP.

Connor, H. (1997) 'Graduate employment trends: key issues in the labour market of the late 1990s and beyond', in R. Burgess (ed.) *Beyond the First Degree: Graduate Education, Lifelong Learning and Careers*, Buckingham: Open University Press.

Dearing Report (1997) *Higher Education in the Learning Society: Report of the National Committee of Inquiry into Higher Education*, London: NCIHE.

DES (1987) *Higher Education: Meeting the Challenge*, London: HMSO.

DfEE (1997) *Evidence to Dearing: The Size and Structure of Higher Education*, London: DfEE.

DTI (1994) *Competitiveness: Helping Business to Win*, London: HMSO.

——(1995) *Competitiveness: Forging Ahead*, London: HMSO.

——(1996) *Competitiveness: Creating the Enterprise Centre of Europe*, London: HMSO.

Edwards, R. (1993) *Mature Women Students: Separating or Connecting Family and Education*, London: Taylor & Francis.

Egerton, M. and Halsey, A.H. (1993) 'Trends by socio-economic group and gender in access to higher education in Britain', *Oxford Review of Education*, 19(2): 183–96.

Halsey, A.H. (1992) *The Decline of Donnish Dominion: The British Academic Professions in the Twentieth Century*, Oxford: Oxford University Press.

——(1993) 'Trends in access and equity in higher education: Britain in international perspective', *Oxford Review of Education*, 19(2): 129–40.

Halsey, A.H., Heath, A. and Ridge, J. (1980) *Origins and Destinations: Family, Class and Education in Modern Britain*, Oxford: Oxford University Press.

Hesketh, A. (1999) 'Towards an economic sociology of the student financial experience of higher education', *Journal of Education Policy*, 14(4): 385–410.

Higgins, M. (1991) 'The student market', *Higher Education Quarterly*, 45(1): 14–24.

Kogan, M. and Hanney, S. (2000) *Reforming Higher Education*, London: Jessica Kingsley.

MacGregor, K. (1991) 'Quality controller puts faith in money lever', *Times Higher Educational Supplement*, 13 December: 6.

MacLeod, D. (1998) 'Outside looking in', *Guardian Higher Education*, 24 March.

Madood, T. (1993) 'The number of ethnic minority students in higher education: grounds for some optimism', *Oxford Review of Education*, 19(2): 167–82.

Madood, T. and Shiner, M. (1994) *Ethnic Minorities and Higher Education: Why are there Differential Rates of Entry?*, London: Policy Studies Institute.

Majumdar, T. (1983) *Investment in Education and Social Choice*, Cambridge: Cambridge University Press.

Marginson, S. (1997) *Markets in Education*, Sydney: Allen and Unwin.

Marshall, T.H. (1950) *Citizenship and Social Class*, Cambridge: Cambridge University Press.

Morrison, M. (1996) 'Part-time: whose time? Women's lives and adult learning in England', in R. Edwards, A. Hanson and P. Raggett (eds) *Boundaries of Adult Learning*, London: Routledge.

Phillips, M. (1996) *All Must Have Prizes*, London: Little, Brown.

Plant, R. and Barry, N. (1990) *Citizenship and Rights in Thatcher's Britain: Two Views*, London: Institute of Economic Affairs Health and Welfare Unit.

Purcell, K. and Pitcher, J. (1998) 'Diverse expectations and access to opportunities: is there a graduate labour market?', *Higher Education Quarterly*, 52(2): 179–203.

Rasekoala, E. (1997) 'The black hole in the science ranks', *Times Education Supplement*, 24 January: 7.

Robbins Report (1963) *Higher Education: Report of the Committee Appointed by the Prime Minister under the Chairmanship of Lord Robbins*, London: HMSO.

Salter, B. and Tapper, T. (1994) *The State and Higher Education*, London: Woburn Press.

Scott, P. (1995) *The Meanings of Mass Higher Education*, Buckingham: Open University Press.

Shattock, M. (1994) *The UGC and the Management of British Universities*, Buckingham: Open University Press.

Smithers, A. and Robinson, P. (1996) *Trends in Higher Education*, London: Council for Industry and Higher Education.

Trow, M. (1973) *Problems in the Transition from Elite to Mass Higher Education*, Berkeley: Carnegie Commission on Higher Education.

——(1994) *Managerialism and the Academic Profession: The Case of England*, Institute of Governmental Studies Working Paper no. 94–5, Berkeley: Graduate School of Public Policy, University of California, Berkeley.

Watson, D. and Taylor, R. (1998) *Lifelong Learning and the University: A Post-Dearing Agenda*, London: Falmer.

7 Educational devolution and nation building in Wales

A different 'Great Debate'?

Robert Phillips and Richard Daugherty

Introduction

In a book which deals predominantly with the analysis and description of the growth of central state control over many spheres of education, this chapter traces the development of the parallel move towards educational devolution in Wales (Daugherty *et al.* 2000). It is both ironic and remarkable to reflect that during the period between 1988 and 1997, a period characterised by increasing policy centralisation by successive Conservative governments, Wales was able to develop a distinctive educational and institutional framework that preceded political and legislative devolution in 1999. The subtitle of our chapter is borrowed from Jones (1992); like him, we want to show in this chapter how the legacies of Ruskin influenced Wales in different ways, so much so, in fact, that at the beginning of the twenty-first century, when referring to education, it is no longer possible to refer in the same breath to 'England and Wales'. Rather, contemporary and future educational discourse will have to embrace the notion of an 'England or Wales' scenario in relation to education policies. We trace the origins of these developments, in particular in relation to the school curriculum, and consider their consequences, which, of course, have implications for the future of the nation-state. For, as Jones (1994: 13) suggests, the Education Reform Act (1988) (ERA) 'revolutionised the role of the state in education, thereby inadvertently raising questions about the relationship between the Welsh nation and the British state in a new context'. The history of education in Wales between 1976 and 2001 therefore provides an opportunity to analyse the ways in which educational reform, cultural politics and political nationalism became closely inter-related.

The historical background, 1944–76: for Wales, see England?

This link between education, nationhood and politics, focusing for the most part upon the relationship between England and Wales, has in some ways been a feature of political life in Wales since the so-called 'Treason of the Blue Books' in 1847 (Jones 1997). The 1889 Welsh Intermediate Act and the establishment of the Central Welsh Board for Education had created a distinctive educational administrative structure in Wales, and the inter-war years saw a small number of significant reports and discussion documents which centred upon distinctively Welsh aspects of the curriculum (Jones 2000). Yet the desire for post-war regeneration and rebuilding meant that the Education Act of 1944 concentrated upon structures rather than distinctiveness; the Act institutionalised the 'England and Wales' approach to the education system which was also a feature of post-war social policy more generally. Thus the Central Welsh Board was abolished in 1947 and for the next forty years, it could be argued, Welsh education policy was, effectively, indistinguishable in most respects from that of England.

Of course, there were some glimpses of expressions of a separate educational identity. At the political/regional level, as Jones (1990) has shown, although some local education authorities in Wales wanted to move towards comprehensivisation, they were prevented from doing so by central administration in London and by the Welsh Department of the Ministry of Education. In relation to the curriculum, the Welsh Department of the Ministry of Education publication *Curriculum and Community in Wales* (1952) tentatively raised the issue of introducing some Welsh cultural elements into schools. This was followed in 1963 when the Gittins Report (the Welsh equivalent to the Plowden Report) called for distinctively Welsh aspects of culture and social life to be expressed in the curriculum. Also, during the post-war period, the establishment of Welsh-medium and bilingual schools was becoming an increasingly significant feature of the educational landscape of Wales.

At the national level in Wales, it seemed that the establishment of an Education Department at the Welsh Office in 1970 might signal significant Welsh educational developments. However, as Jones (1997) has demonstrated, the period was characterised instead by civil service obfuscation, compounded by a Whitehall suspicion of allowing too much autonomy for Wales. Thus, when in 1974 the Schools Council in Wales published a discussion paper on the need (echoing Gittins) to develop the Welsh curriculum, nothing was done. It seemed that as far as education policy was concerned, even by 1976, the infamous 'for Wales, see England' jibe was still relevant.

As Jones (1992) has suggested, the Ruskin speech effectively signalled a 'different' 'Great Debate' in Wales. He argues that many of the perceived educational 'ills' implied by Callaghan had less relevance in Wales, whose primary schools had not witnessed the move towards progressive and child-centred pedagogy that had been seen in England. He cites HMI evidence in Wales which showed, first, that reading was satisfactory in four fifths of primary schools, and second, that criticisms were made by HMI that *too much* attention was being paid to the 'basic skills' in primary schools in Wales.

On the other hand, some of the central themes of Callaghan's speech, particularly those relating to the relationship between education and the economy and the notion of parental/governmental accountability, had a particular significance in Wales, for two reasons. First, Wales in the 1970s was dominated by the large, public-funded-sector industries (coal and steel) which were about to feel the cold wind of international competition and monetarism. Second, theoretically at least, parents, schools and local authorities in Wales could justifiably argue that, in terms of local accountability, people in Wales exercised relatively little control and autonomy over education policy. Characteristically, therefore, the only specifically 'different' aspect of the 'Great Debate' in Wales following Ruskin was the separate attention given to the future of the Welsh language in schools (Williams 1992).

The wasted years? Schooling for failure in Wales, 1976–88

It could be argued that Morris and Griggs' (1988) thesis that the 1980s were a period of 'wasted years' applied more to Wales than to England. Contrary to the well-established myth and cliché of a successful educational system and a supportive education-loving society, all the contemporary evidence after 1976 seemed to confirm that schooling in Wales was characterised by inertia, inefficiency, low standards and educational under-achievement. Criticism focused on the apparent failure of comprehensive schools, which since Circular 10/65 had almost completely replaced grammar and secondary modern schools in Wales by the beginning of the 1980s. Particular attention was paid to the apparent failure of the new comprehensive schools to respond to the needs of pupils in the middle or at the lower end of the range of attainment. Research evidence showed the high percentage of school leavers in Wales who left school well qualified, but also the high proportion who left without any qualifications at all (Rees and Rees 1980).

Following a Welsh Office conference in 1978 and associated publications documenting the attainments of pupils in Wales, what Reynolds (1995: 5) has called 'further quasi-official recognition of the existence of distinctive Welsh educational problems' came in 1981, with the publication of a report from the Schools Council Committee for Wales which came to be known as the Loosmore Report. It not only blamed underperformance on the continuation of the grammar school tradition, but in addition made reference to the educational ethos in Wales more generally, including the shortcomings of the Welsh Joint Education Committee (established in 1949) which was responsible for examinations and assessment in Wales (Loosmore 1981).

The performance of secondary schools was given particular attention in the work of Reynolds and his colleagues, research that was to prove profoundly controversial in Wales. In an article in the *Times Educational Supplement* (*TES*) on 4 December 1981, Reynolds and Murgatroyd argued that pupils in Welsh schools were essentially 'schooled to fail'. In particular, 'something transformed able Welsh eleven year olds into disaffected, underperforming Welsh fifteen years olds' (Reynolds 1990: 253). The following reasons were suggested for this 'schooled to fail' thesis:

- an over-emphasis and concentration upon the needs of high-ability children;
- continuation of streaming by ability;
- minimal levels of curriculum development and an irrelevant curriculum;
- a lack of pedagogical innovation;
- poor management, with former grammar school headteachers unable to cope with the complex demands of the new comprehensive schools;
- a 'ring-fenced' appointments system that excluded innovative thinking from outside Wales;
- distancing between schools and parents.

Reynolds' central claim was that 'the comprehensives of Wales were simply like grammar schools in their ethos, organisation and ultimate education purposes' (Reynolds 1990: 254). The attribution of low levels of attainment to the inappropriate continuation of these features of a selective system of schooling was also reported as being in evidence in some comprehensive schools in England (Hargreaves 1982).

Reynolds' work drew a furious response from the educational community in Wales, expressed in the pages of the *Western Mail* and the *TES*, and the Schools Council in Wales carefully distanced itself from the research. At the same time, Lapham (1981) claimed that any perceived 'under-performance' was caused by profound social deprivation in Wales, combined with the fact that pupils were being turned off by an English-dominated curriculum and assessment system. If these factors were taken into account, pupils in Wales could be said to be performing better than their counterparts in England. More recently, this theme has been developed by Gorard (1998a, 1998b, 2000), who has also challenged the 'schooled to fail' thesis. He argues that if social and economic background factors are taken into consideration, the assumed low standards and under-achievement of Welsh schools cannot be sustained. Moreover, given the particularly acute economic dislocation and social deprivation in Wales in the last two decades of the twentieth century, educational performance and attainment in Wales has actually been higher than one would have expected (see also Delamont and Rees 1999).

Whether or not in reality pupils were actually being 'schooled to fail' in Wales, the controversy in the press had certainly created that impression among sections of the public. Given this, why were there not more widespread demands in the early 1980s for political and educational devolution? The answer lies in the wider political traditions and complex cultural climate of Wales. Sociologists, political scientists and historians have for some time recognised the sometimes uncomfortable relationship between the 'two cultures' within Wales, namely the collective/industrial tradition (based predominantly in highly populated English-speaking south Wales) and the rural/cultural tradition (mainly associated with Welsh-speaking west, mid and north Wales) (see Davies 1991; Fevre and Thompson 1999). Raymond Williams referred to these as the 'two truths' (1985) while Gwyn Williams (1985) described them as the 'two tongues'. The dominant collective tradition remained suspicious that separate institutional structures and frameworks would provide a focus for cultural (and eventually) political separation. This in part explains the crushing defeat of the proposal for political devolution in the 1979 referendum.

The 'schooled to fail' debate was, however, an important stage in the development of a broader debate about political responsibility for education in Wales. The connection had been made between social deprivation, under-achievement and, crucially, an educational infrastructure (including a curriculum) that was not meeting the needs of pupils in Wales. Gradually, the political and educational climate began to change. There was the realisation in political and educational circles, as well as among elements of the public at large, that distinctively Welsh 'problems' could be solved by Welsh 'solutions'. Reynolds himself had claimed that Welsh educational problems could be partly overcome by a more distinctive and 'relevant' curriculum, a reformed assessment structure and an expanded institutional framework in Wales to implement change. By the end of the 1980s, as we shall see below, these 'solutions' had been initiated.

Scholars of education policy and curriculum in the UK have concentrated most attention on developments in England in the late 1980s, particularly the announcement of the National Curriculum by Baker in 1987, the subsequent development of the National Curriculum, and its assessment and the implementation of other important aspects of the ERA (Ball 1990; Chitty 1989). Yet in 1987, nearly a century and a half on from the Blue Books, the Welsh Office published its proposals for a National Curriculum for Wales (Welsh Office 1987). As Jones (1994) makes clear, this was a milestone in the development of the school curriculum, giving as it did official recognition to the distinctive cultural and educational existence of Wales.

Published six months after the DES/Welsh Office paper (DES/Welsh Office 1987), setting out the main features of what would become the 1988 Education Reform Act, *The National Curriculum for Wales* both stated some general principles of a National Curriculum and explained how such a curriculum would be implemented, in particular through the establishment of a Curriculum Council for Wales (CCW). It also made clear that Welsh would be a 'core' National Curriculum subject in schools where pupils were receiving their education through the medium of Welsh, and a 'foundation' subject in all other state-funded schools in Wales. As the subject components of the National Curriculum were drafted and finalised in the years which followed, the early 1990s saw a transformation in the ways in which this aspect of education policy in Wales was conceived, negotiated and implemented (Phillips 1996a).

How are these developments to be explained? Some research has been done into the National Curriculum (Elfed-Owens 1996) but, as we have argued elsewhere, the precise circumstances surrounding this crucial embryonic phase of educational devolution are in need of further empirical and analytical research (see Phillips and Sanders 2000). At this point we can only offer speculative suggestions. First, one has to consider the political context. Labour-dominated Wales had, effectively, been politically disenfranchised since the election of 1979. Gradually, even Labour politicians began to see some of the advantages and merits of some form of devolution as a bulwark against Thatcherism. Second, Wales had suffered particularly severely during the early 1980s: structural unemployment, compounded by the defeat of the miners in 1984, meant that the 'collective tradition' referred to earlier had been effectively destroyed. New solutions to old problems were now needed, not only in education (see above) but also in a range of policy spheres. Third, the ideological context of the ERA provided unexpected opportunities for those in Wales who favoured further devolution of education policy (James 1998). Racist New Right ideology distrusted ('black') multiculturalism and anti-racism more generally but was able to tolerate the notion of distinctively ('white') Welsh language and culture (Phillips 1996b). Fourth, a sympathetic Welsh Office Minister of State, Wyn Roberts (a Welsh speaker himself), probably convinced Baker and others of the need to grant expression to Welsh claims to distinctive elements of the curriculum, not only as an end in itself but also to counteract Welsh nationalism as represented by some 'direct action' groups. Finally, according to Jones (1992: 101), a culturally aware, 'ambitious bureaucracy' had developed in Wales during the 1980s, including officials at the Welsh Office and HMI in Wales, and therefore a range of factors combined to mean that 'there was potential for greater control of education in Wales from within Wales than ever before'.

Whatever the precise origins of the policies, aspects of the educational scene in Wales were to be changed quite radically over the next decade and in ways that were more transformative than the originators of the ERA could ever have anticipated.

Re-imagining the nation? Culture, curriculum and community, 1988–95

The duality of the curricular policy-making framework now established under the ERA meant that there were, by 1992, five National Curriculum subjects for which the statutory orders in Wales were wholly or partially distinct from the orders being implemented in England. One subject (Welsh) would be taught only in Wales, a second (history) had substantially different curriculum content within a common England and Wales framework, while three further subjects (geography, art, music) contained within them elements which were distinctive to Wales. The significance of these subjects for cultural transmission is clear. Using Anderson's analogy (1983) they provided ways in which the concept of nationhood and nation could be 'imagined' differently. For the rest of the century, Welsh education reform would be irrevocably linked to issues of nation building and cultural restoration (Phillips 1996b; Williams and Jones 1994).

The 'history of history' in Wales, for example, as in England during this period (Phillips 1998), provides an interesting insight not only into the changing cultural dynamics of nationhood but also the policy process itself (Phillips 1999). Prior to the establishment of the National Curriculum, Jeremy (1989: 1) described the history taught in schools in Wales for most of the twentieth century as 'mostly a jumble of Acts of Parliament, of kings and battles in English history, leavened in the latter decades by forays in social and local history'. The problem for nation builders, using Jeremy's phrase, was 'to establish that Wales had a history at all'. The National Curriculum History Committee for Wales' Final Report (Welsh Office 1990: 12) offered a robust assertion of the need to teach Welsh history because 'the history of Wales is the history of a distinct people and nation'. Like its English history counterpart (DES 1990), however, this was a carefully crafted, wily political document. Fearful perhaps of the accusation that a separate Welsh history curriculum provided a blueprint for quasi-nationalism, the document placed emphasis upon the fact that it was appealing to a 'range of historical inheritances' in Wales and to 'different interpretations' of the Welsh past (echoes of the 'two tongues'). Crucially, it argued that Welsh history should not be taught in isolation, for this would 'distort' the history of Wales. Rather, pupils would need to 'understand the separate identity of Wales, the close relationship between Wales and England, and the place of Wales within the history of the British Isles as a whole' (Welsh Office 1990: 13). Welsh history was on the march.

Perhaps the most remarkable feature of this period was the spate of cross-curricular and whole-school curricular documentation produced by the CCW, giving substantial credence to the thesis that institutional factors are vital for the construction of nationhood (Robbins 1998). In 1991 the CCW set out its vision for the whole curriculum in Wales, emphasising that 'the curriculum in Wales must aim to develop pupils' understanding of the distinctiveness and varied nature of the Welsh experience' (CCW 1991a: 3). Significantly, both the tone and substance of the documentation distinguished it from England, which was experiencing particularly contested and heated debates over cross-curricular themes (Graham 1993; Maw 1994). Two of the cross-curricular elements identified by the CCW – *Community Understanding* (CCW 1991b) and *Curriculum Cymreig* (CCW 1993) – were particularly significant as they could be said to represent the 'two truths' in Welsh cultural, social and political life outlined above. Both were given wider articulation in further texts produced by the CCW. A more detailed analysis of these discourses provides an important insight into the dynamics of Welsh educational reform, cultural life and national 're-imagining'.

As one of us has argued elsewhere, the *Community Understanding* document was, by any standards, a remarkable document (Phillips 2000). Initiated at the high tide of conservatism, when central governments and their New Right allies were profoundly suspicious of anything remotely cross-curricular or political, it was an extraordinary radical text, a symbolic statement and a representation, perhaps, of the CCW's newly found independence. It offered a complex, multi-faceted definition of the term 'community'. Communities, it was argued, consisted of varied, plural groups that 'raised issues of diversity, inequality and prejudice' (CCW 1991b: 6) The curriculum, it said, should provide a means by which these stereotypes, inequalities and prejudices could be combated. Pupils should also be provided with means of exploring what it meant to be a citizen at various levels (for example, the dual implications of being a citizen of Wales and the world), and Welsh children should be made aware of human rights. The document stated that the curriculum should not only be a vehicle for making pupils aware of the democratic processes available to them, but in a particularly frank statement (which reflected the reality of Welsh social and economic life at the end of the twentieth century) it argued that 'pupils should know how and why wealth and resources are distributed unevenly between individuals, groups, nations and continents' (p. 9).

Whereas *Community Understanding* provided a universalistic vision of identity and citizenship in Wales, *Curriculum Cymreig* (CCW 1993) was 'an unashamed attempt to promote the distinctive culture and heritage of Wales' (Phillips 1996c: 43; see also Phillips 1996b). The document stressed that although the Welsh language was seen as the primary form of expression of Welshness, Welsh identity could also be cultivated through place and heritage, a sense of belonging, literature and art and religion. This also was a remarkable development, given that for most of the century schools in Wales had been actively encouraged to relegate cultural aspects of Welshness; here was official documentation that was encouraging schools to promote it.

Interestingly, the subsequent history of these two documents gives us an insight into which educational discourse held sway among key personnel centred at the CCW and the inspectorate in Wales. Thus, following the Dearing reforms, it was

Curriculum Cymreig, not *Community Understanding*, that became a cross-curricular 'common requirement'. By September 1995, when the reformed Dearing curricular reforms were implemented, nation building had become statutory within the school curriculum in Wales.

In other areas of curriculum and assessment policy, however, the agenda set in England would overwhelm attempts in Wales to give expression to distinctive policy perspectives. The growing influence of the New Right on education policy in England after 1991 brought the English National Curriculum (common to Wales and England) once again to the forefront of the policy debate. The CCW advised the Welsh Office that time was needed for lessons to be learned from the experience of implementing National Curriculum English, a process which had only begun in September 1990. However, its counterpart in England, the National Curriculum Council (NCC), advocated an early review and a joint NCC/CCW review was begun in 1992. Teachers, CCW officers and HMI (Wales) sought to defend the 1990 English order, especially in relation to its stance on Standard English and the listing of required texts, from proposals emanating from the NCC which, led by Chief Executive Chris Woodhead, was responsive to the New Right ideas of lobby groups such as the Centre for Policy Studies. This 'battle for the English curriculum' (Cox 1995) may have been coloured by the fact that, as Cox himself makes clear, when the Right took over crucial positions of power in NCC they forgot to do the same for the CCW. But the Welsh Office, against the advice of CCW, was ultimately unwilling to countenance a separate NC English curriculum for Wales.

National Curriculum assessment is another aspect of policy where there is no evidence in the early 1990s of a distinctively Welsh perspective on policy formulation, implementation and practice, except in relation to the assessment of Welsh as a subject (Daugherty 2000a). An institutional framework capable of formulating assessment policy in Wales has been in place only since 1994, when CCW was transformed into ACAC (Curriculum and Assessment Authority for Wales) as it took on responsibility for assessment policy. There have been some instances where ACAC, and its successor ACCAC (Qualifications, Curriculum and Assessment Authority for Wales), has sought to distance itself from the assessment policies adopted in England, but few signs to date of substantive indigenous policy development within Wales (Daugherty 2000b).

Beyond the area of curriculum and assessment policy there are other examples of the supervisory and accountability elements of the state being less confrontational and more willing to accommodate a professional perspective in Wales than was the case in England. Changes to the schools inspectorate offer one such example. Ever since the nineteenth century, HMI in Wales had gained something of a reputation for independence. The 1992 Education (Schools) Act, while creating Ofsted in England, saw the establishment of the Welsh equivalent, OHMCI. As Thomas and Egan (2000) have demonstrated, OHMCI in Wales sought to build a more purposeful relationship with teaching professionals than the perceived confrontational approach of their counterparts in England. Thus, the Framework for Inspection Handbook in Wales contained significant variations on the Ofsted mode of inspection.

The year 1992 also saw the Further and Higher Education Act establish separate funding councils for Wales, which not only had important implications for the future direction of further and higher education policy in Wales (Jephcote and Salisbury 2000; Rees and Istance 1997) but provided a blueprint for the type of secondary supervisory responsibilities relating to education that would be afforded after 1999 to the National Assembly. Finally, whereas this period saw the direct impact of 'choice' in England, few schools in Wales opted out of local authority control and became grant maintained, and no City Technology Colleges were established. By ignoring the local options available from some of the provisions of the ERA, Wales had been able partially to cushion itself from the impact of the free market storm in education.

The BEST future? Institutional reform and devolution, 1995–2001

The contemporary history of education in Wales shows, however, that Wales, like England, was affected by the vital connection made by Callaghan between the apparent fall in standards in education and the demise of the economy. As was indicated in the introduction to this book, the major impetus behind many of the Tory educational reforms of the 1980s was the diagnosis, initiated publicly by Callaghan, that the education system did not provide adequately for the complex needs of the economy, a theme taken up by the modernising project of New Labour after the election in 1997.

In Wales, as we have seen, the relationship between low standards, failing schools and economic failure and social dislocation was particularly resonant during the period 1976–88. After 1995, this theme was resurrected by a series of policy documents produced by the Welsh Office. These 'general diagnoses of educational ills' took particular forms. Here, the argument was that in order to revitalise the economy after the traumatic decline of the staple industries, signal improvements were required in the skills and competencies of the Welsh labour force (Daugherty *et al.* 2000). The first of these documents contained a foreword by the Secretary of State John Redwood, arguing that 'the prosperity of Wales depends upon our people having the skills to match the best in the world. All in education, training and enterprise should help us carry this plan into effect' (Welsh Office 1995a: 4). The 'plan', therefore, involved encouraging pupils to 'do better at school' by 'tackling low expectations', 'setting clear standards' and 'targets for improvement', the 'effectiveness' of which would be 'examined' by school inspections. Moreover, 'successful' or 'popular' schools would be encouraged to expand, a policy presented as another distinctively 'Welsh' initiative. The major thrust of the document was to 'link employers and education'.

In the same year, a further document repeated why these goals were necessary, using images and points of reference that echoed Callaghan:

> The Government's commitment to education is profound. Very high levels of public money are being invested. But good schools and the best education come from making excellent use not only of money, but of talented and dedicated people.

Above all they come from teachers having the highest possible expectations of every pupil, and setting the highest possible standards. What might have been good enough yesterday, won't be good enough for tomorrow. Every school – whatever its achievements – needs to consider how to improve its performance, and to work out ways of bettering it as we move into the new millennium.

(Welsh Office 1995b: intro)

The concept of the role of the education system as having a determinate relationship with the economy also found expression in policies on lifelong learning (Welsh Office 1998). The Minister for Lifelong Learning in the Labour government, Peter Hain, asserted its importance in terms which could equally have been used by one of his Conservative predecessors:

Rapid change in technology and labour markets means everyone will increasingly have to re-train, re-educate and re-skill to achieve a rewarding career and a decent standard of living. The whirlwind of global economic forces means Wales needs a flexible, multi-skilled workforce. This can only be secured by having a place in a framework for lifelong learning.

(Welsh Office 1998: iii)

Conclusion

This chapter has focused on educational policy, and particularly curriculum policy, at the Wales level of policy formulation and implementation. The growing sense in the 1980s of an education system falling well short of its cherished ideals was resurfacing in the late 1990s, with a refocusing of the government's agenda on schools and other educational institutions being expected to meet targets framed in terms of the needs of economy. As we have argued elsewhere, once again the dominant discourse emphasised the economic necessity of educational reform (Daugherty *et al.* 2000). However, the intervening period from 1987 to 1994 had seen the emergence of a culturally driven agenda for the school curriculum. The way that agenda found expression in curriculum policy at the national Wales level, facilitated by a supportive curriculum agency, took on a character quite distinct from the contemporaneous debate in England. The idea of a school curriculum in Wales which was at least partially distinct from the curriculum in England, an idea discussed at intervals throughout the twentieth century, was at last taking shape as the legislative and institutional framework of the ERA made it possible.

Changes at the local level since the 1970s, in particular the emergence of a Welsh-medium school sector (Baker 1990), reinforced the development of a distinctive curriculum for Wales. By 1997 over 14 per cent of pupils at primary and secondary schools in Wales were reported to be being educated mainly through the medium of Welsh (Reynolds *et al.* 1998). This was not an example of centrally directed change but a parent-led phenomenon, starting in 1939 when seven pupils attended the first *ysgol gymraeg* in Aberystwyth. As parental demand increased, local education authorities across Wales, in English-speaking as well as Welsh-speaking areas, responded by establishing new Welsh-medium or bilingual schools.

In other respects, however, there were few signs of distinctively Welsh education policies developing during the 1990s. It is difficult to detect any significant differences between the policy discourse of the Welsh Office and that of its senior partner in policy-making, the DES/DfE/DfEE. Competition between educational institutions, the 'market' in educational services and nationally determined performance standards and accountability procedures dominated policy in Wales as in England. Opponents of such policies resorted to resistance at the local level, for example in the local campaigns to oppose schools opting for grant-maintained status.

The Welsh Office continued in its long-established customary role of implementing policies initiated in England, modifying some of the details but seldom embarking on its own processes of policy formulation and development. In an era of increasing centralisation in London of decisions about the education systems of Wales and England, those aspects of the system in Wales which have taken on a distinctive character during the last quarter of the twentieth century have emerged in two contrasting ways. On the one hand, the growth of Welsh-medium schooling is a product of decisions at the local level making use of the powers still resting with local education authorities. On the other, we have seen the UK government in London, largely inadvertently it would seem, creating through the ERA the framework for a distinctively Welsh curriculum.

The implications for education policy of the election, in May 1999, of a National Assembly for Wales have to be understood against this background. Of the main political parties contesting that election only Plaid Cymru, 'the Party of Wales', showed evidence in its manifesto of a disposition to develop and implement a distinctive education policy for Wales. If the National Assembly, together with its associated organisations and agencies, is to do more than replicate the experience of the last quarter of the twentieth century, its task will be to establish within Wales a process of policy formulation and implementation which is distinct from the process which is continuing to shape policy development in England.

References

Anderson, B. (1983) *Imagined Communities*, London: Verso.

Baker, C. (1990) 'The growth of bilingual education in Wales', in W.G. Evans (ed.) *Perspectives on a Century of Secondary Education in Wales*, Aberystwyth: Centre for Educational Studies.

Ball, S. (1990) *Politics and Policy Making in Education: Explorations in Policy Sociology*, London: Routledge.

CCW (1991a) *The Whole Curriculum 5–16 in Wales*, Cardiff: CCW.

——(1991b) *Advisory Paper 11 – Community Understanding: A Framework for the Development of a Cross-Curricular Theme in Wales*, Cardiff: CCW.

——(1993) *Advisory Paper 18 – Developing a Curriculum Cymreig*, Cardiff: CCW.

Chitty, C. (1989) *Towards a New Education System: The Victory of the New Right?*, London: Falmer.

Cox, B. (1995) *Cox on the Battle for the English Curriculum*, London: Hodder & Stoughton.

Daugherty, R. (2000a) 'National Curriculum assessment policies in Wales', in R. Daugherty, R. Phillips and G. Rees (eds) *Education Policy Making in Wales: Explorations in Devolved Governance*, Cardiff: University of Wales Press.

——(2000b) 'Assessing the National Curriculum in Wales: administrative devolution or indigenous policy development?' *The Welsh Journal of Education*, 9 (2): 4–17.

Daugherty, R., Phillips, R. and Rees, G. (eds) (2000) *Education Policy Making in Wales: Explorations in Devolved Governance*, Cardiff: University of Wales Press.

Davies, B. (1991) 'Welsh voices – more than just talk?' in G.E. Jones (ed.) *Education, Culture and Society*, Cardiff: University of Wales Press.

Delamont, S. and Rees, G. (1999) 'Education in Wales', in D. Dunkerley and A. Thompson (eds) *Wales Today*, Cardiff: University of Wales Press.

DES (1990) *National Curriculum History Working Group: Final Report*, London: HMSO.

DES/Welsh Office (1987) *The National Curriculum 5–16: A Consultation Document*, London: DES/Welsh Office.

Elfed-Owens, P. (1996) 'The implementation of the National Curriculum in Wales', unpublished Ph.D. thesis, Institute of Education, University of London.

Fevre, R. and Thompson, A. (1999) *Nation, Identity and Social Theory: Perspectives from Wales*, Cardiff: University of Wales Press.

Gorard, S. (1998a) ' "Schooled to fail?" Revisiting the Welsh school effect', *Journal of Education Policy*, 13(1): 115–24.

——(1998b) 'Four errors … and a conspiracy? The effectiveness of schools in Wales', *Oxford Review of Education*, 24(4): 459–72.

——(2000) 'A re-examination of the effectiveness of schools in Wales', in R. Daugherty, R. Phillips and G. Rees (eds) *Education Policy Making in Wales: Explorations in Devolved Governance*, Cardiff: University of Wales Press.

Graham, D., with Tytler, D. (1993) *A Lesson for Us All: The Making of the National Curriculum*, London: Routledge.

Hargreaves, D. (1982) *The Challenge for the Comprehensive School*, London: Routledge & Kegan Paul.

James, B. (1998) 'The origins, growth and development of a distinctive curriculum in Wales in the late twentieth century', unpublished master's thesis, University of Wales Swansea.

Jephcote, M. and Salisbury, J. (2000) 'From policy to practice in further education: patterns of governance in Wales', in R. Daugherty, R. Phillips and G. Rees (eds) *Education Policy Making in Wales: Explorations in Devolved Governance*, Cardiff: University of Wales Press.

Jeremy, P. (1989) 'History in the secondary schools of Wales: a centenary review', *Welsh Journal of Education*, 1(1): 11–17.

Jones, G.E. (1990) *Which Nation's Schools? Direction and Devolution in Welsh Education in the Twentieth Century*, Cardiff: University of Wales Press.

——(1992) 'Education in Wales: a different "Great Debate?" ' in M. Williams, R. Daugherty and F. Banks (eds) *Continuing the Education Debate*, London: Cassell.

——(1994) 'Which nation's curriculum? The case of Wales', *Curriculum Journal*, 5(1): 5–16.

——(1997) *The Education of a Nation*, Cardiff: University of Wales Press.

——(2000) 'The historical context', in R. Daugherty, R. Phillips and G. Rees (eds) *Education Policy Making in Wales: Explorations in Devolved Governance*, Cardiff: University of Wales Press.

Lapham, C. (1981) 'The Loosmore Report: an appraisal', *The Welsh Secondary Schools Review*, 68(2): 40–42.

Loosmore, F. (1981) *Curriculum and Assessment in Wales: An Exploratory Study*, Cardiff: Schools Council Committee for Wales.

Maw, J. (1994) 'The National Curriculum Council and the whole curriculum: reconstruction of a discourse?' *Curriculum Studies*, 1(1): 55–74.

Morris, M. and Griggs, C. (eds) (1988) *Education – The Wasted Years? 1973–1986*, London: Falmer.

Phillips, R. (1996a) 'Education policy making in Wales: a research agenda', *Welsh Journal of Education*, 5(2): 26–42.

——(1996b) 'History teaching, cultural restorationism and national identity in England and Wales', *Curriculum Studies*, 4(3): 385–99.

——(1996c) 'Informed citizens: who am I and why are we here? Some Welsh reflections on culture, curriculum and society', speech given to the SCAA International Invitation Conference on Culture, Curriculum and Society; also published in *Multicultural Teaching*, 14(3): 41–4.

——(1998) *History Teaching, Nationhood and the State: A Study in Educational Politics*, London: Cassell.

——(1999) 'History teaching, nationhood and politics in England and Wales in the late twentieth century: a historical comparison', *History of Education*, 28(3): 351–63.

——(2000) 'Culture, curriculum and community in Wales: citizenship education for the new democracy?' in R. Gardner (ed.) *Citizenship, Identity and Education*, London: Cassell.

Phillips, R. and Sanders, S. (2000) 'Contemporary education policy in Wales: theory, discourse and research', in R. Daugherty, R. Phillips and G. Rees (eds) *Education Policy Making in Wales: Explorations in Devolved Governance*, Cardiff: University of Wales Press.

Rees, G. and Istance, D. (1997) 'Higher education in Wales: the re-emergence of a national system?' *Higher Education Quarterly*, 51(1): 49–67.

Rees, G. and Rees, T. (1980) 'Educational inequality in Wales: some problems and paradoxes', in G. Rees and T. Rees (eds) *Poverty and Social Inequality in Wales*, London: Croom Helm.

Reynolds, D. (1990) 'The great Welsh education debate', *History of Education*, 19(3): 181–90.

——(1995) 'Creating an educational system for Wales', *The Welsh Journal of Education*, 4(5): 4–21.

Reynolds, D., Bellin, W. and ab Ieuan, R. (1998) *A Competitive Edge: Why Welsh-Medium Schools Perform Better*, Cardiff: Institute for Welsh Affairs.

Robbins, K. (1998) *Great Britain: Institutions, Identities and the Idea of Britishness*, London: Addison, Wesley Longman.

Thomas, G. and Egan, D. (2000) 'Policies on school inspection in Wales', in R. Daugherty, R. Phillips and G. Rees (eds) *Education Policy Making in Wales: Explorations in Devolved Governance*, Cardiff: University of Wales Press.

Welsh Office (1987) *The National Curriculum in Wales*, Cardiff: Welsh Office.

——(1990) *National Curriculum History Committee for Wales: Final Report*, Cardiff: Welsh Office.

——(1995a) *People and Prosperity: An Agenda for Action in Wales*, Cardiff: Welsh Office.

——(1995b) *A Bright Future: Getting the Best for Every Pupil at School in Wales*, Cardiff: Welsh Office.

——(1998) *Learning is for Everyone: The BEST for Lifelong Learning*, Cardiff: Welsh Office.

Williams, G. (1985) *When was Wales? The History, People and Culture of an Ancient Country*, London: Penguin.

Williams, M. (1992) 'Ruskin in context', in M. Williams, R. Daugherty and F. Banks (eds) *Continuing the Education Debate*, London: Cassell.

Williams, M. and Jones, B. (1994) 'Tensions between cultural restoration and nation building in the nationalised Welsh school curriculum', paper given at the European Curriculum Researchers' Network Conference, Enschede, Netherlands, August/September.

Williams, R. (1985) 'Community', *London Review of Books*, 21 January.

Part III

Professionalism, accountability and standards

8 The reinvention of teacher professionalism

Gary McCulloch

Introduction

Over the twenty-five years since James Callaghan's Ruskin College speech of October 1976, a major struggle has developed over teacher professionalism in England and Wales. Callaghan's intervention served to encourage a concerted challenge to inherited ideals and understandings of teacher professionalism that were based on teacher control and autonomy in the curriculum domain: the so-called 'secret garden' of the school curriculum. Callaghan emphasised the importance of ensuring that the education system was accountable to parents and the public in general, in the interests of improving educational standards (Morgan 1997: 503). Many of those involved in the self-styled 'Great Debate' that followed took this as an opportunity to undermine the vested interests of schools, teachers and their unions. For example, Kenneth Baker, Secretary of State for Education and Science in the late 1980s and primarily responsible for the Education Reform Act of 1988, insisted that 'producer capture', in which 'the interests of the producer prevail over the interests of the consumer', was one of the key problems facing the education system that needed to be tackled (Baker 1993: 168). This underlying trend fostered protracted and often heated conflict as to the character of teacher professionalism.

During this time, earlier ideals remained influential and resonant in helping to determine both the terms of debate and the direction and parameters of reform. The general undermining of these received ideals of teacher professionalism nonetheless created conditions for the emergence of a range of new approaches. In some cases, responses to the rapidly changing context of the 1990s suggested a pragmatic adjustment in the balance between teachers' rights and responsibilities in the classroom and public accountability. Meanwhile, more radical perspectives that became associated with the modernising project of New Labour prompted a wholesale recasting of the ideal of teacher professionalism, culminating in late 1998 in the self-styled 'new professionalism' of the Green Paper *Teachers: Meeting the Challenge Of Change* (DfEE 1998).

The death of teacher professionalism?

In 1976, the prevailing image of teacher professionalism in England and Wales revolved around an ideal of teachers individually and collectively possessing a high degree of autonomy and control in the curriculum domain. Within this sphere, it was widely assumed that their role included the freedom to decide not only how to teach but also what to teach, and that they had a primary responsibility for curriculum development and innovation. This prerogative was not subject to the fickle demands of parents and the community, and still less to the interests of the state or of political parties. Rather, it was to be carefully preserved as the province of teachers' experience, judgement and expertise, which would ensure the gradual evolution of content and methods in line with social and cultural change. This highly idealised set of assumptions came under systematic and concerted assault in the years that followed, and was decisively undermined as a result.

This general outlook was far from new, having been maintained already for more than thirty years. Lawn suggests that it dated from the mid 1920s, with the ending and restriction of regulations that had governed the curriculum and teacher training (Lawn 1987). The Education Act of 1944 had given responsibilities in this area to local education authorities (LEAs), but in practice the rights of schools and teachers were strongly emphasised. The Ministry of Education endorsed this approach, avoiding any direct intervention in the curriculum field until the early 1960s. Religious education was specifically provided for under Section 25(2) of the 1944 Act, but no other subject was prescribed by statute or regulation. Section 23 of the Act made the LEAs responsible for the control of secular instruction for the schools in their area (see also McCulloch 2000, and McCulloch *et al.* 2000, especially Chapter 3).

Sir David Eccles, as Minister of Education, in March 1960 described the school curriculum as a 'secret garden' into which it would be reasonable to venture more frequently, although he insisted at the same time that 'Parliament would never attempt to dictate the curriculum' (*Hansard* 1960). The principle of non-intervention was repeatedly endorsed by Ministry officials in private discussions. As the Ministry emphasised in September 1963:

> In England and Wales it has long been public policy to uphold the responsibility of the schools for their own work. This is the cardinal principle of national policy in relation to the schools' curriculum and examinations ... To the maximum possible extent, each school should therefore be free to adopt a curriculum and teaching method based on its own needs and evolved by its own staff.
>
> (Ministry of Education 1963)

A 'Curriculum Study Group' was established within the Ministry in 1962, but this innovation was rapidly abandoned in 1964 in favour of an arrangement involving representatives of the different partners involved, especially teachers, through the new Schools Council for the Curriculum and Examinations (Dean 1997). This 'professional autonomy' of teachers in the curriculum domain was widely acknowledged as a distinctive feature of an English tradition that was unlike that of other cultures and nations: indeed, as

the characteristic English contribution – to concentrate attention on the teacher, his role as a professional who must be directly implicated in the business of curriculum renewal; not as a mere purveyor of other people's bright ideas, but as an innovator himself.

(Schools Council 1968: 10; see also Helsby and McCulloch 1996)

This basic ideal or 'tradition' of teacher professionalism had been cultivated to accommodate the aspirations of partnership between teachers, LEAs and the Ministry that were emphasised in the 1950s and 1960s. However, in practice it was undermined by a wide range of competing pressures that became increasingly evident during the 1960s and 1970s. First, it was always questionable whether the reality of teacher autonomy matched the ideal, particularly because of the growing influence of examinations at all levels of the education system during the 1950s and 1960s. These tended to establish a uniformity of expectations and standards, reflected in the requirements of universities, colleges and employers, that constrained teacher-led innovation and belied the idea of each school being responsible for its own curriculum.

A related problem was the inertia of the system, despite the support offered by the Schools Council. It was unclear who was ultimately responsible for reform, how to promote change on a national basis, and even how to extend or encourage good practices identified by particular schools and teachers. The Schools Council itself acknowledged that such 'inertia' was a growing difficulty at a time of an 'increasing pace of advances in knowledge and social change' (Schools Council 1973: 16). Inertia, it affirmed, was 'largely a property of teaching materials, teachers' education and experience and, in some cases, external examinations', and yet no one agency was able to take an effective lead in all areas (ibid.). Teachers themselves were often acutely conscious of the limitations of their own role (Taylor 1970). Increasing demands on teachers' time also made it very difficult for them to respond to changing needs. According to one examining board representative in the late 1970s, seeking to account for the disappointing level of response to Schools Council projects:

> many teachers are now close to complete exhaustion and simply cannot take on any more work. And if they try, because of the fact that their basic work involves so much giving of themselves, they will simply be less effective. The law of diminishing returns begins to operate. A jaded teacher is probably little better than having no teacher at all, since so much work really depends on the leadership, enthusiasm, drive and energy of the teacher. It is a truism that teaching has become very much harder than in the secure, unchanging world of Mr Chips.
>
> (Goodall 1979)

In these circumstances, teachers' supposed rights in the curriculum field appeared little more than an illusion that effectively hindered reform.

The established tradition of teacher professionalism was therefore highly vulnerable to the criticisms that James Callaghan as prime minister levelled at the education service in 1976. Callaghan's principal target was the closed world of the 'educational Establishment', taken very broadly to include LEAs, teacher unions and schools that appeared unaccountable to public interests and impervious to change. Episodes such as the William Tyndale affair of 1975–6, in which the teachers at a London primary school insisted on maintaining a progressive, child-centred approach to the curriculum against the wishes of parents, tended to bring the cherished 'secret garden' of teachers into public disrepute (see also Dale 1989). As the historian Brian Simon has noted, this raised important concerns about the nature of teachers' professionalism: 'To whom *were* the teachers responsible – or accountable? … Teachers' [traditional] control of the curriculum – their autonomy – was now very sharply called into question' (Simon 1991: 446). No less significant, increasing economic difficulties, unemployment and industrial conflicts during the 1970s led to new doubts about the ability of the education system to generate economic productivity and competitiveness. Many critics complained that the school curriculum itself was not designed to promote practical skills or economic growth, nor to arrest Britain's long-term relative economic decline, and argued that it required a radical overhaul (for example, Barnett 1979). Yet if the state were to take the lead in promoting curriculum reform towards these ends, this would amount to a direct challenge to the assumptions around teacher professionalism that had been so potent over the past generation.

Teachers' unions and the increasingly embattled Schools Council became uncomfortably aware that the principle of teacher professionalism was in danger as a result of increasing government 'interference' in educational issues, especially after the election of a Conservative government under Margaret Thatcher in May 1979. Representatives of the National Union of Teachers insisted that teachers were best able to provide a local service for children and parents and that the 'national interest', which 'depended on the political climate', should not intrude on this (Schools Council 1979). The NUT therefore took the view that 'the Government should stop publishing documents of a prescriptive nature, which were incompatible with a local service' (ibid.). The Department of Education and Science (DES) remained sympathetic to the established role of teachers. However, the Manpower Services Commission (MSC), set up under the Employment and Training Act of 1973 and responsible to the Department of Employment rather than to the DES, was increasingly assertive about the need to intervene to promote employable skills and an adaptable work force. Against a background of high unemployment and industrial crisis in September 1981, Geoffrey Holland warned of a pressing need for schools to prepare young people for the workplace: 'There was no time, he said, for pilot schemes and experiments; something big and bold had to be done quickly' (Schools Council 1981).

Over the following year, two measures in particular responded to the call for 'something big and bold', and confirmed the worst fears of educational interest groups. First, in June 1982 the new Secretary of State for Education and Science, Sir Keith Joseph, decided to disband the Schools Council, replacing it with two separate nominated bodies which would be responsible for the curriculum and examinations. This decision was symbolic in that it abandoned a major agency that had been closely associated with the established principle of teacher profession-alism, in favour of a mechanism that would make it easier for the Secretary of State to control examinations and the curriculum. Members of the Schools Council's professional committee asserted that Joseph was 'intent on controlling examinations as a means of directing the curriculum', and pointed out that 'the present government was elected on a programme which promised more democracy, greater personal liberty and enhanced local autonomy' and that this centralising tendency in educational matters was the reverse of this and 'must be resisted' (Schools Council 1982). Second, in November 1982 the prime minister herself announced a new pilot programme of technical education for 14- to 18-year-olds, the Technical and Vocational Education Initiative (TVEI), which would be controlled by the MSC rather than the DES, 'where possible' in conjunction with LEAs. This initiative was again strongly condemned by teachers' interest groups because of its disregard for consultation and the 'professional prerogative' of teachers (McCulloch 1987).

The government's growing concern to regulate the school curriculum as a whole also gave rise to deep forebodings. In April 1983 the general secretary of the NUT, Fred Jarvis, declared that politicians were already well on the way to controlling what was taught in schools as a result of the government's initiatives, complaining that this was a 'dangerous development' that 'contradicted the British tradition, which was to leave the curriculum to the teachers' (*The Times* 1983). Sir Keith Joseph was cautious in his approach to this issue, and denied any intention of 'seeking to impose a centrally controlled curriculum, and to suppress the freedom to define the details of what is taught which had traditionally resided at local level' (Joseph 1984: 147). Kenneth Baker, who succeeded Joseph in 1986, did not share such caution, and began to plan for a new National Curriculum. This was influenced in part by a teachers' strike over pay and conditions in 1985–6 that had served to intensify government hostility to teachers' claims to professional status. The more general emphasis in Baker's education policies upon parental choice and the greater accountability of schools also suggested a hidden agenda, in which the National Curriculum would effectively undermine the position of teachers even in their most established domain.

Baker sought to allay such suspicions. Indeed, he declared in the House of Commons debate on his Education Reform Bill in December 1987 that 'We want to build upon the professionalism of the teacher in the classroom – the professionalism of the many fine and dedicated teachers throughout our education system' (*Hansard* 1987). Moreover, he insisted, 'We do not intend to lay down how lessons should be taught, how timetables should be organised, or which textbooks should be used' (ibid.). On this view, the National Curriculum would provide a loose framework for teachers' work, to maintain and even enhance their autonomy in curriculum development. Nevertheless, in spite of such assurances, the Education Reform Act of 1988, which introduced the National Curriculum, was widely regarded by its many critics as marking the demise of the long-held principle of teacher professionalism. As such, it marked the culmination of a decade of government intervention that had decisively undermined teachers' rights in this sphere deemed paramount over the preceding generation.

Professional discretion and public accountability

The wider context of teachers' work in the years following the Education Reform Act of 1988 was one of increasing demands created by new procedures designed to produce greater accountability. The growth of bureaucratic 'red tape' around testing and the curriculum increased teachers' workload and circumscribed their scope for individual judgement (see, for example, *Independent* 1994). At the same time, teachers were subjected to renewed pressure through the replacement of Her Majesty's Inspectorate (HMI) with the new Office for Standards in Education (Ofsted). This agency, under Chris Woodhead as chief inspector of schools, was widely blamed for lowering teachers' morale, especially through its tougher approach to school inspection and Woodhead's regular castigation of failing teachers. League tables of examination results, widely publicised to document differences between schools and changes from year to year, again enhanced the transparency of the system by which teachers were to be judged. New policies that affected teachers' work were regularly introduced with little notice or consultation. The physical conditions of schools – teachers' place of work – were often poor and little new funding was made available to improve them. Salaries were low in relation to other recognised professions. Teachers were often openly denigrated and blamed for low academic achievement as well as more generally for the social problems of the nation as a whole, often leading to stress and demoralisation (Helsby 1999).

These problems were vividly illustrated in the public accounts of teachers who, as it was put, 'retired, hurt, from a career that had changed beyond recognition' (*Independent* 1995). One, for example, went into teaching in 1986 and became a head of mathematics and science, but fell victim to the stresses produced by the National Curriculum and retired early, aged 45, in 1995 (ibid.). Another used the pages of the teachers' regular public forum, the *Times Educational Supplement* (*TES*), in 1998 to complain bitterly about the changes that had taken place over the twenty-two years since 1976 when he had first become a teacher:

> I've been appraised, inspected, observed, interviewed, chewed-up and spat out by all manner of experts telling me what to do ... I see people who are exhausted, who are insulted daily by the children in their care, and who know that they are not valued by anyone very much. I've tried, really tried, because I felt that teaching was a mission to help others but at the end of the day – teaching is just a bloody awful job.
>
> (*TES* 1998a)

On their own estimation, teachers appeared to have been systematically deskilled and deprofessionalised, a view that was reflected in persistently low teacher supply and recruitment throughout the 1990s as well as in early retirements.

Many observers responded to this rapidly changing situation by emphasising the loss of 'professional autonomy' that the 1988 Act and its associated reforms had engendered. Peter Gilroy, a critic of changing provision in teacher education, insisted that 'the professional autonomy of the teacher cannot long survive a situation where they have little or no control over the content of a curriculum which they are obliged by law to implement and test' (Gilroy 1991: 5). Denis Lawton, an experienced and shrewd analyst of curriculum change, noted the 'undermining of teacher professionalism' that had taken place since 1979 (Lawton 1996). For some critics, such as Martin Lawn, the notion of teacher professionalism could be consigned to history, the product of a specific phase of education in twentieth-century England that had now been lost for ever (Lawn 1996). The 'professional memories' (Ben-Peretz 1995) of teachers themselves also tended to highlight the supposed freedom enjoyed in earlier years, forgetting the complexities and constraints and often the problems to which it had given rise. In some cases, this established the basis for a critique of current policies, contrasting the failures and disappointments of contemporary changes with an idealised version of the past (McCulloch *et al.* 2000).

Nevertheless, in the decade that followed the 1988 Act, it was possible to discern a reformulation of teacher professionalism that involved finding a new accommodation or balance between the proper sphere of teachers' autonomy and discretion, on the one hand, and their accountability to the public, on the other. In many ways, this was a strategic response to the Conservatives' reforms. The earlier tradition of teacher autonomy was taken as a key reference point, with the aim of establishing a role for teachers as active interpreters rather than simply as passive implementers of the National Curriculum.

The Conservative government had usually conceded that although in its view teachers' freedom had gone too far and needed to be redressed, there should still be a proper role for teachers as 'professionals'. The White Paper *Better Schools*, published in 1985 when Sir Keith Joseph was Secretary of State for Education, attempted a detailed account of the 'professional work' of the teacher. This was taken to include the provision of information, the management of learning experiences, deciding how pupils should be grouped, the choice of teaching approaches and methods, and the choice of books, teaching materials and equipment. Overall, it concluded, 'These things may be seen as the means through which the curriculum is delivered: taken together, and combined with the attitudes and capabilities of the teacher, they also exercise a powerful influence on the teacher' (DES 1985: 41). In retrospect, this also reflected a distinction between what to teach and how to teach it, in that teachers' professional discretion was viewed as being principally in the area of pedagogy rather than in the choice of curriculum content.

This key distinction was strongly emphasised later in the decade in the policy documents that signalled the introduction of the National Curriculum. The consultation document on the National Curriculum published in July 1987, for example, noted that 'legislation should leave full scope for professional judgement and for schools to organise *how the curriculum is delivered* in the way best suited to the ages, circumstances, needs and abilities of the children in each classroom' (DES 1987: 11, emphasis added). Two years later, in explaining how the National Curriculum should be translated from policy into practice, the DES stated that the 'organisation of teaching and learning' should remain 'a professional matter for the head teacher and his or her staff' (DES 1989: par. 4.3). Moreover, it added,

What is specified will allow teachers considerable freedom in the way in which they teach, examples and materials used, selection of content and context, use of textbooks, etc. The legislation does not allow particular textbooks or teaching methods to be prescribed as part of a programme of study.

(ibid.: para. 4.15)

As has been seen, many critics were highly sceptical of such statements, but for others they offered at least some basis for constructing a new version of teacher professionalism in the changed milieu of the 1988 Act.

Some further grounds for optimism of this kind were also offered by the unexpected consequences of the TVEI in the 1980s. Initially regarded, with good reason, as a hostile incursion on the part of the state into the curriculum domain, it actually afforded many teachers unprecedented opportunities for innovation and experiment. Janet Harland noted in relation to the TVEI what she called the 'central paradox' of

the simultaneous emergence of two apparently or potentially conflicting features: on one hand, strong central control of a kind which has permitted the detailed intervention of a central government agency down to the level of the classroom; and on the other a teacher response which is, in many of the pilot schemes, creative and innovative, and often indeed experimental and down-right risky.

(Harland 1987: 39)

Harland described the teachers who were leading the TVEI 'crusade' as 'released prisoners', although she recognised at the same time that these were a very specific group of teachers, mainly drawn from practical, applied and technical areas of the curriculum, who had previously 'in many schools led rather isolated and low-status professional lives' (ibid.: 47). This experience suggested that teachers could interpret state policy in different ways, often leading it into unanticipated directions, with the implication that perhaps even the National Curriculum might be susceptible to similar treatment on the part of teachers (see also Helsby and McCulloch 1996).

The early years of the National Curriculum provided at least some support for this kind of approach to teacher professionalism. In primary schools, although many teachers experienced a loss of autonomy and an erosion of their professional judgement, there was also a tendency to incorporate the National Curriculum into their existing modes of working, and thus to interpret and mediate it in ways that suited their own preferred ends. One study of primary teachers concluded that:

the exercise of coercive power has challenged some teachers to explore their professional repertoire in order to find ways in which they can mediate the new requirements or incorporate them into their existing practices. They have thus sought to ensure that these new practices support, rather than undermine, their longstanding professional commitments.

(Pollard *et al.* 1994: 237–8)

Another researcher, Peter Woods, encountered a range of responses among primary school teachers, from active resistance to the constraints imposed by the National Curriculum, through appropriation of its provisions to their own concerns, to retreat and retirement (Woods 1994, 1997). Among secondary school teachers, too, there was evidence that the 'implementation' of the National Curriculum was by no means mechanistic. According to Ball and Bowe (1992), in some cases 'teachers' priorities, experience and professional expertise were set over and against the structure, content and progression of subject knowledge presented in the National Curriculum documents', leading to 'a lot of accommodation and minimal change' (p. 105). Other research also suggested that although the National Curriculum severely undermined the received tradition of teacher professionalism, its impact on secondary school teachers was not uniform (Helsby 1995, 2000). Teachers' scope for discretion in the domain of the curriculum appeared to vary in different subjects, from school to school, and according to experience (Helsby and McCulloch 1997).

The potential that existed for redefining teacher professionalism by shifting the boundaries between teachers' responsibilities and accountability in the area of the curriculum was vividly reflected in the Dearing Review of the National Curriculum and its assessment. This followed a phase in which the new demands of the National Curriculum produced widespread protests among teachers, reaching a climax in 1993 over a teachers' action to boycott tests for 7- and 14-year-olds. Much of this agitation again revolved around notions of teacher professionalism, and the Dearing Review may be read as an initiative designed to reinterpret this tradition in a new way that would be more acceptable for teachers. The Dearing Review restated an explicit link between teacher professionalism and the school curriculum by recognising that reducing the amount of prescriptive material in the National Curriculum would 'give more scope for professional judgement' (Dearing 1993: 17). In doing so, it made a key distinction between 'the essential matters, skills and processes which every school must by law teach' and 'the optional material which can be taught according to the professional judgement of teachers' (ibid.: 21–2). It concluded that while more should be left to the 'professional judgement' of teachers, this should be matched by an acceptance on the part of teachers that schools were ultimately accountable to parents and society.

Dearing's intervention, while not universally welcomed, provided a means by which to reassert ideals of teacher professionalism that involved at least a measure of autonomy, discretion and judgement in the curriculum field. The *TES* was in no doubt, for example, that this review of the National Curriculum effectively handed 'professional responsibility' back to the teachers, and would allow them 'to start thinking again about curriculum philosophy, and to introduce their own ideas within the framework' (*TES* 1994). Michael Barber, a former NUT official and now a professor of education (later to become a senior adviser on education for the Labour government elected in 1997), perceived in the Dearing Review what he described as an 'unwritten contract'. On the one side, teachers would need to accept that they were accountable for the public money that they received and the quality of education that they delivered, and this would require a national system of assessment and testing. On the other side, he asserted, 'teachers will get more freedom to exercise their professional judgement, particularly over what is taught in schools' (Barber 1994). This in turn, he argued, could establish a 'new partnership' based on a balance between 'professional discretion' and 'public accountability' (Barber 1993).

Thus, in spite of the constraints of the National Curriculum and the exigencies of the Conservative educational reforms of the 1990s which fundamentally affected the nature of teachers' work, there remained some scope for actively reinterpreting the received ideal of teacher professionalism and reasserting a measure of 'professional judgement'. Debates around exactly how to redraw the balance between what Barber termed professional discretion and public accountability continued throughout the 1990s, and were again reflected in the further review of the National Curriculum that took place in 1999–2000. Nicholas Tate, chief executive of the Qualifications and Curriculum Authority (QCA), argued, for example, that the National Curriculum did not undermine the professionalism of teachers, but instead gave them an important opportunity to enhance it. Tate pointed out that in France the existence of a national curriculum was taken for granted, but that it also allowed for reform of the school curriculum to be based on social, cultural and political aims. The lesson of this for the English education system, he suggested, was that while teachers in England should have some autonomy, this should go together with a 'more explicit vision' for the curriculum as a whole than had so far been attained (Tate 1998). Additional restrictions on teachers' discretion, such as the introduction of literacy and numeracy hours in primary schools, continued to fuel scepticism about the practical limits of teacher professionalism at a time of persistent intervention in the classroom by central government. Nevertheless, by the turn of the century such arguments began to be largely overshadowed by a new and quite separate policy agenda that was set in train by Tony Blair's Labour government after 1997.

'Modernising' teacher professionalism

If the Dearing Review had represented a reformist account of teacher professionalism, there was also scope for a fundamental reappraisal that openly challenged the earlier tradition. This was what Tony Blair's Labour government set out to achieve after 1997. Just as it aspired to 'modernise' other established features of the education system such as comprehensive schools (DfEE 1997), so it attempted to reinvent and re-position the ideal of teacher professionalism. No longer related principally to the curriculum domain or based in notions of autonomy and discretion, teacher professionalism was redefined in terms of improving the status, conditions and financial rewards of the most successful teachers in a more competitive environment.

This recasting of teacher professionalism was not wholly new. The pursuit of 'professional' status and recognition, or professionalisation, had been important to teachers' groups throughout the century (Tropp 1957). *Better Schools* (DES 1985) had attempted, tentatively and not altogether coherently, to broaden the idea of professionalism by including taking part in the corporate development of the school, showing teamwork with other teachers, and involving themselves with parents and the community. According to *Better Schools*, 'This professionalism requires not only appropriate training and experience but also the professional attitude which gives priority to the interests of those served and is constantly concerned to increase effectiveness through professional development' (DES 1985: 44). In 1996, Anthea Millett, chief executive of the Teacher Training Agency (TTA), argued strongly that the curriculum did not lie at the heart of teacher professionalism since 'it is and always has been pedagogy which occupies that key position' (Millett 1996: 1). Chris Woodhead, while conceding that teacher professionalism in England and Wales had traditionally been identified with controlling the school curriculum, also insisted that it should instead be focused on classroom practice or pedagogy in order to move towards a more 'outcome-based' model of professionalism, 'to devolve as much as possible, and then hold people accountable' (*TES* 1998b). However, it fell to the new Labour government to interpret and develop such ideas in a more concerted way.

In March 1998, the new Secretary of State for Education and Employment, David Blunkett, was able to declare that 'professionalism is back at the very heart of teaching', as an integral part of the government's priority to raise standards and expectations for all pupils (Blunkett 1998). The prime minister underlined his government's commitment to teachers' professionalism in a speech to the National Association of Head Teachers (NAHT) annual conference in Cardiff in June 1999:

> The Government's objective is simple but highly ambitious. It is to restore teaching to its rightful place as one of Britain's foremost professions ... recognising the need for a step-change in the reputation, rewards and image of teaching, raising it to the status of other professions such as medicine and law, which are natural choices for our most able graduates.
>
> (Blair 1999)

However, this would be a 'modernised' professionalism, very different from that of the past. It would make teachers responsible for improving standards for pupils, including those in socially disadvantaged areas. It would provide successful teachers with greater status and the most successful with higher salaries than they had received in the past. But it would bring penalties for those teachers and school principals who were unable or unwilling to rise to the challenge of raising standards as judged by examination results.

A consultative Green Paper was published in December 1998 to support these developments. This major policy document, entitled *Teachers: Meeting the Challenge of Change*, set out a case for 'modernising the teaching profession', and related this to an agenda of specific reforms. The first chapter, 'The imperative of modernisation', underlined the need for schools to respond to major social and technological changes. This would entail in part the provision of new resources in the form of modern facilities for pupils and improved working conditions for teachers: 'The shabby staffroom and the battered electric kettle – which endured for so long because teachers always choose to put their pupils first – can become things of the past' (DfEE 1998: 13). At the same time, it would demand 'changes in the classroom', which would have 'profound implications' for teachers as individuals and for the profession as a whole:

> At the heart of what teachers do will remain the good, well-taught lesson – which has proved its effectiveness. But many new possibilities are emerging. Throughout this century, teachers have had to choose between prioritising the needs of large groups or following up the diverse needs of individuals. Now for the first time they can realistically do both.
>
> (ibid.: 12–13)

This in turn, according to the Green Paper, would mean teachers embracing a 'new professionalism'. Nevertheless, it specifically ruled out a return to older notions of professionalism of the 'secret garden' type: 'The time has long gone when isolated, unaccountable professionals made curriculum and pedagogical decisions alone, without reference to the outside world' (ibid.: 14). Instead, teachers would need to promote high expectations, to expect accountability, to take responsibility for improving their skills and subject knowledge, to seek to base decisions on evidence of what works in schools, to work in partnership with other staff in schools, to welcome the contribution of parents, business and others outside a school, to anticipate change, and to promote innovation (ibid.: 14). They would require greater incentives for excellent performance, which again would challenge inherited ideals: 'The tradition in teaching is to treat all teachers as if their performance was similar, even though in every staffroom teachers themselves know this is not true' (ibid.: 15). They would also need more systematic opportunities for their professional development. Most fundamentally of all, these aspirations would involve introducing a new staffing framework for schools that the Green Paper insisted would reward teachers for high performance and offer incentives for success.

This approach to teacher professionalism was accompanied by well-targeted initiatives to improve the public image and status of teachers that contrasted vividly with the vilification of a decade before. These included the creation of a General Teaching Council, the establishment of a National College for School Leadership, and the award of knighthoods to successful headteachers. Such innovations marked the beginnings of a campaign to relaunch teacher professionalism for the fresh challenges of a new century. Ironically, they also prompted the Conservative Party, now in opposition, to rediscover the virtues of older principles of teacher autonomy, which the Conservative governments of the 1980s had effectively overridden. According to David Willetts, the education spokesperson of the Conservative Party in 1998, the imposition of what he called a 'command and control model' in which 'instructions flow down from the Department of Education and Employment to local authorities and schools as if they were junior outposts of a colonial administration' was 'no way to raise educational standards and enhance the professionalism of teachers' (Willetts 1998). With the zeal of a convert, Willetts insisted that higher standards and enhanced professionalism would be more likely if schools and teachers had greater freedom and autonomy rather than less. This was an argument that gained ground among a range of critics of the Labour government's relentless policy interventions in this field. James Porter, for example, complained that 'in the past twenty-five years, the country has moved from having the most independent and professionally based system in the world to one of the most controlled and centralised' (Porter 1999; Burgess 1998; Price 1999).

Conclusion

The relationship between teachers and the state continued to be central in helping to shape ideas about teacher professionalism, just as it had been throughout the twentieth century. The benign indifference of the Ministry of Education in the 1950s had created conditions in which ideals of teacher autonomy could flourish, whatever the problems of interpreting them in practice. The active intervention of the state on a regular basis from 1976 led to a more circumscribed and closely policed approach, under the regime of the National Curriculum and enforced by Ofsted. In a comparatively short time span, within the professional lifetime of many teachers working in state schools, the expectations of teacher professionalism had changed so far as to be virtually unrecognisable, and in many respects in a hostile and threatening way.

Nevertheless, far from witnessing the demise of teacher professionalism, the twenty-five years that followed Callaghan's Ruskin speech saw a vigorous debate over its character and implications. Callaghan had stressed the need for accountability and standards. This reorientation proved decisive in undermining and dismantling the ideal of teacher professionalism that had held sway over the previous generation. The myths and memories attached to this older professionalism proved to have considerable residual power, even growing in their talismanic significance when set against contemporary innovations. They were sufficient indeed to continue to shape the thinking of teachers, and often to constrain and limit the ambitions of new policy initiatives including the National Curriculum. Meanwhile, into the gap left by the progressive decline of this older professionalism there poured new ideas and precepts, often incoherent and inconsistent, some reformist and pragmatic, others more radical in nature, which jostled with each other and against older ideals in the process of reinventing teacher professionalism.

Acknowledgement

I should like to acknowledge the Economic and Social Research Council for its support for the research project 'Teachers' professional culture and the secondary school curriculum' (R000234738) on which some of the research for this chapter is based, and my colleagues in this project, Gill Helsby, Peter Knight, Murray Saunders and Terry Warburton.

References

Baker, K. (1993) *The Turbulent Years*, London: Faber & Faber.
Ball, S. and Bowe, R. (1992) 'Subject departments and the "implementation" of National Curriculum policy: an overview of the issues', *Journal of Curriculum Studies*, 24(2): 97–115.
Barber, M. (ed.) (1993) *Sense, Nonsense and the National Curriculum*, London: Falmer.
——(1994) 'Union's testing boycott threatens drive to raise standards', *Sunday Times*, 22 May.
Barnett, C. (1979) 'Technology, education and industrial and economic strength', *Journal of Royal Society of Arts*, 5271: 117–30.
Ben-Peretz, M. (1995) *Learning from Experience: Memory and the Teacher's Account of Teaching*, Albany: SUNY Press.

Blair, T. (1999) 'Quality is key to progress', *TES*, 4 June.

Blunkett, D. (1998) 'Professionalism is back at the very heart of teaching', *Guardian*, 7 April.

Burgess, T. (1998) 'Doubt of the benefit', *TES*, 11 December.

Dale, R. (1989) *The State and Education Policy*, Milton Keynes: Open University Press.

Dean, D.W. (1997) 'The rise and demise of the Curriculum Study Group, 1962–64', *Contemporary British History*, 11(1): 31–8.

Dearing, R. (1993) *The National Curriculum and its Assessment: Final Report*, London: SCAA.

DES (1985) *Better Schools*, London: HMSO.

——(1987) *The National Curriculum 5–16: A Consultation Document*, London: HMSO.

——(1989) *The National Curriculum: From Policy to Practice*, London: HMSO.

DfEE (1997) *Excellence in Schools*, London: Stationery Office.

——(1998) *Teachers: Meeting the Challenge of Change*, London: Stationery Office.

Gilroy, P. (1991) 'The loss of professional autonomy: the relevance of Olga Matyash's paper to the brave new world of British education', *Journal of Education for Teaching*, 17(11): 1–5.

Goodall, G.T. (1979) 'Schools Council projects for the future', paper delivered at 3rd Meeting of Schools Council Convocation, 4 July, Schools Council Papers, Public Record Office, EJ 13/6.

Hansard (1960) House of Commons debate on the Crowther Report, 21 March, vol. 620, cols. 51–2.

——(1987) House of Commons debate on the Education Reform Bill, 1 December, vol. 123, Parliamentary Debates 1987–88, col. 774.

Harland, J. (1987) 'The TVEI experience: issues of control, response and the professional role of teachers', in D. Gleeson (ed.) *TVEI and Secondary Education: A Critical Appraisal*, Milton Keynes: Open University Press.

Helsby, G. (1995) 'Teachers' construction of professionalism in England in the 1990s', *Journal of Education for Teaching*, 21(3): 317–32.

——(1999) *Changing Teachers' Work: The 'Reform' of Secondary Schooling*, Buckingham: Open University Press.

——(2000) 'Multiple truths and contested realities: the changing faces of teacher professionalism in England', in C. Day, A. Fernandez, T. Hauge and J. Moller (eds) *The Life and Work of Teachers: International Perspectives in Changing Times*, London: Falmer.

Helsby, G. and McCulloch, G. (1996) 'Teacher professionalism and curriculum control', in I. Goodson and A. Hargreaves (eds) *Teachers' Professional Lives*, London: Falmer.

——(eds.) (1997) *Teachers and the National Curriculum*, London: Cassell.

Independent (1994) 'How red tape tied the hands of teachers', 12 May.

——(1995) 'Who'd be a state school teacher? Retired, hurt, from a career that had changed beyond recognition', 28 December.

Joseph, K. (1984) 'Postscript', *Oxford Review of Education*, 10(2): 147–8.

Lawn, M. (1987) 'The spur and the bridle: changing the mode of curriculum control', *Journal of Curriculum Studies*, 19(3): 227–36.

——(1996) *Modern Times? Work, Professionalism and Citizenship in Teaching*, London: Falmer.

Lawton, D. (1996) *Beyond the National Curriculum: Teacher Professionalism and Empowerment*, London: Hodder & Stoughton.

McCulloch, G. (1987) 'History and policy: the politics of the TVEI', in D. Gleeson (ed.) *TVEI and Secondary Education: A Critical Appraisal*, Milton Keynes: Open University Press.

——(2000) 'The politics of the secret garden: teachers and the school curriculum in England and Wales', in C. Day, A. Fernandez, T. Hauge and J. Moller (eds) *The Life and Work of Teachers: International Perspectives in Changing Times*, London: Falmer.

McCulloch, G., Helsby, G. and Knight, P. (2000) *The Politics of Professionalism: Teachers and the Curriculum*, London: Continuum.

Millett, A. (1996) 'Pedagogy – the last corner of the secret garden', the 3rd Annual Education Lecture, TTA/King's College London, July.

Ministry of Education (1963) 'Memorandum to the Working Party on Curriculum and Examinations, "The outlines of the problem"', September, Ministry of Education Papers, Public Record Office, ED 147/814.

Morgan, K. (1997) *Callaghan: A Life*, Oxford: Oxford University Press.

Pollard, A., Broadfoot, P., Croll, P., Osborn, M. and Abbott, D. (1994) *Changing English Primary Schools? The Impact of the Education Reform Act at Key Stage One*, London: Cassell.

Porter, J. (1999) 'Mission for special agents in schools', *TES*, 17 September.

Price, C. (1999) 'We need less slap and more tickle', *TES*, 8 January.

Schools Council (1968) *Curriculum Innovation in Practice: A Report by J. Stuart Maclure of the 3rd International Curriculum Conference, 1967*, London: Schools Council.

——(1973) *Pattern and Variation in Curriculum Development Projects*, London: Macmillan.

——(1979) 'Report of 4th Meeting of Schools Council Convocation', 11 December, Schools Council Papers, Public Record Office, EJ 13/7.

——(1981) 'Report of 10th meeting of Schools Council Convocation', 21–3 September, Schools Council Papers, Public Record Office, EJ 13/13.

——(1982) 'Minutes of the Professional Committee, 17th Meeting', 15 June, Schools Council Papers, Public Record Office, EJ 13/15.

Simon, B. (1991) *Education and the Social Order, 1940–1990*, London: Lawrence & Wishart.

Tate, N. (1998) 'Core Anglais', *TES*, 13 February.

Taylor, P. (1970) *How Teachers Plan Their Courses: Studies in Curriculum Planning*, London: NFER.

The Times (1983) 'Politicians well on way to controlling school curriculum, union is told', 5 April.

Times Educational Supplement (1994) 'Back with the teachers' (editorial), 11 November.

——(1998a) 'Dear Mr Blunkett' (Platform opinion), 6 November.

——(1998b) 'Pedagogue with a pugilistic streak', 13 February.

Tropp, A. (1957) *The School Teachers: The Growth of the Teaching Profession in England and Wales from 1800 to the Present Day*, London: Heinemann.

Willetts, D. (1998) 'Blunkett's colonial rule', *TES*, 13 November.

Woods, P. (1994) 'Adaptation and self-determination in English primary schools', *Oxford Review of Education*, 20(4): 387–410.

——(1997) 'Creative teaching in the primary National Curriculum', in G. Helsby and G. McCulloch (eds) *Teachers and the National Curriculum*, London: Cassell.

9 Reforming teacher education, re-forming teachers

Accountability, professionalism and competence

John Furlong

Introduction

Despite his protestations to the contrary, in his Ruskin speech James Callaghan was highly critical of the teaching profession. How could it be otherwise? At a time when teachers' claim to be a profession primarily rested on the fact that they had considerable autonomy in deciding what they taught their pupils, how they taught them and how they assessed them (Grace 1987), any critique as fundamental as that made by Callaghan was inevitably a criticism of the teaching profession itself. What Callaghan wished for, perhaps naively, was a world where teachers were different, where they were willing to work with others in society whom he believed had a legitimate interest in the education of the nation's children. In short, what he implied was a new professionalism among teachers, one based on the recognition of the legitimacy of accountability rather than the practice of autonomy.

Changing the behaviour, values and commitments of a professional group such as teachers is of course a long-term project; it is also likely to involve conflict. As many of the other chapters in this volume document, almost all of the changes introduced into the education service over the last twenty-five years have not been the result of voluntary reform by the teaching profession itself, as Callaghan might have hoped. In order to change the curriculum, to change assessment procedures, to introduce new measures of performance, successive governments have considered it necessary explicitly to challenge the autonomy of the teaching profession, and as McCulloch so clearly documents in his chapter, these challenges have had major implications for the nature of teacher professionalism itself.

But at the same time as this 'top down' approach to reform, there has also been a recognition on the part of successive governments that if the change process was to be a success in the longer term, then it was essential to win the hearts and minds of teachers themselves, especially new teachers entering the profession. As a result, throughout the last twenty-five years, initial teacher education has become an increasingly important area of educational policy development. It may be a false assumption, but nevertheless it has been assumed that one way of changing the nature of teacher professionalism is to change the structure and content of initial teacher education and training (ITET). As a result, the period has seen initial education and training move from being a relative backwater in terms of educational policy to a position of key strategic significance.

In this chapter I want to argue that over the last twenty-five years there have been two different sorts of changes which have influenced the structure and content of initial teacher education and training in England and Wales. The first, directly following on from Callaghan's Ruskin speech, has been the growing insistence on increased accountability within the system. As we will see below, in the mid 1970s initial teacher education and training was managed and led almost entirely autonomously by those in higher education. A key aim underlying many of the changes introduced since then has therefore been to wrest power from higher education and re-establish a national, publicly accountable system.

The second source of change has been varying and sometimes competing definitions about what the outcomes of initial education and training should be; in other words, the forms of professionalism that should be engendered in the next generation of teachers. In what follows, I identify five different phases of policy development, four of which were based on different visions of teacher professionalism. At the opening of the period the assumption was that the professional teacher should be educated as a 'scholar' where academic knowledge was to the fore; later, the aim was to make them an 'expert', proficient in practical as well as theoretical knowledge; then the aim was to make them merely a 'competent practitioner'. Today the current Labour government is promoting a different view yet again – what it calls the 'new professionalism'. Visions of professionalism implicit in initial education and training policies have therefore changed considerably over the last twenty-five years; what has not changed, however, has been the determination of successive governments to re-establish accountability within the system so that it is they, rather than those in higher education, who can take the lead in defining what professionalism should be.

In analysing the changes that have taken place, I will be drawing to a significant degree on two ESRC-funded research projects known as the MOTE studies.[1] These two projects examined the changing face of initial teacher education and training in England and Wales throughout the 1990s, and many of the ideas set out in this chapter are developed more fully in the book reviewing that research (Furlong *et al.* 2000). I will also be drawing on the well-known theoretical framework developed by Ball and his colleagues (Bowe and Ball 1992) which highlights the possible distinctions between a number of different 'contexts' within the policy process. The 'context of influence', in which public policy debate occurs, may in reality, they argue, be quite distinct from the 'context of text production' where specific policy texts emerge; and both of these may be different from what happens in the 'context of practice'. As Ball and his colleagues would predict, in the field of initial teacher education, the last twenty-five years have demonstrated again and again that there can be important differences, disjunctions as well as continuities, between each of these different 'moments' in the policy process; achieving change in practice has not always been as easy as politicians would have liked. Indeed, one might argue that it was precisely because those involved in public policy debate (in the context of influence) so frequently found that their intentions had not been fully realised that there have been constant calls for further and more stringent reforms.

Table 9.1 provides a schematic overview of the major phases of policy development in the last twenty-five years; in each case it identifies a key policy theme for the period and summarises changes in each of the main policy contexts identified by Bowe and Ball (1992).

Pre 1976: the professional teacher as 'scholar'

In the early and mid 1970s, when our period opens, debate within the context of influence on the form and content of initial teacher education, was still to a considerable extent shaped by the social democratic ideals and policies of the post-war

Table 9.1 Change in initial teacher education and training in England and Wales, 1976–2001

	The context of influence	**The context of text production**
	Key policy debates	*Key policy 'texts'*
Pre 1976 Key theme: the professional teacher as 'scholar'	The search for 'degree worthiness'	University regulations define 'degree worthiness'; teacher educators are autonomous experts
1976–84 Key theme: fragmentation and autonomy	Little centrally directed policy debate; among teacher educators, growing dissatisfaction with academic model	Few national policy texts; teacher educators remain autonomous experts
1984–92 Key theme: the professional teacher as 'expert'	Emerging New Right critique; ITET criticised as too academic and unresponsive to changing world of schools – marketisation, National Curriculum; challenge of teacher shortages	Circulars 3/84 and 24/89. Establishment of CATE to 'manage' HE; Articled and Licensed Teacher schemes introduced
1992–7 Key theme: the professional teacher as competent practitioner	Mounting neo-conservative critique argues for more focus on subject teaching and end to 'trendy left-wing ideology'; continued concern over 'low quality' and variability in the system	TTA bureaucrats take control; utilise Ofsted inspection framework linked to 'quality' ratings as mechanism of controlling the system
1997– Key theme: the new professionalism?	Government-led demand for modern labour force – flexible, with collective rather than individual values, responsive to changing national policy priorities	Strengthening of control through publication of 'league tables'; some institutions close. New documents on content – 'Standards' and National Curriculum; Green Paper 1998

settlement (Wilkin 1996). In the field of higher education, social democratic ideals found their expression in the Robbins Report of 1963 which argued that 'The good society desires equality of opportunity for its citizens to become not merely good producers but also good men and women'. Higher education qualifications 'should be available for all those who are qualified by ability and attainment to pursue them and who wish to do so' (Robbins 1963: para. 31). It should therefore aim to develop learners as a 'rationally autonomous' individuals; if it was to achieve that aim, then higher education had to be centrally concerned with learning which was both fundamental and general, for only in this way could autonomy be promoted and the learner freed from the constraints of the 'present and the particular' (Bailey 1984).

The context of practice

Influence on

(i) Pathways	(ii) Content	(iii) Links to school
B.Ed. as conventional academic degree established	Academically led	Academic courses largely insulated from practice
HE-provided courses continue but some limited experimentation with 'school-based' models	General trend to 'relevance' but great diversity of content	Still largely insulated from practice but some experimentation; CNAA gave some lead to 'professional relevance'
Conventional courses develop new strategies for 'integration'; new routes developed for new populations; new models (Articled and Licensed Teacher schemes) emphasising school experience	Relevant degree subjects defined; time in school defined; hours on English and maths defined; content broadly defined	Recent and relevant experience for tutors established; increasing time in school; curriculum much more school-focused but left to HE to define how that was interpreted; Emergence of 'reflective practice' as key concept for linking theory and practice
HE-provided courses develop 'partnerships' of different sorts, mainly still HE-led; new routes (SCITT and OU) developed to challenge control of HE	Competences introduced but combined with 'reflection' by HE; inspection framework increases pressure on content; pedagogy as key area of autonomy for HE	Student time in schools increased; funding to schools, financially destabilises HE; 'mentoring' and competences emerge as key aspects of school practice; inspection framework progressively imposed on schools too
Conventional courses continue to be strictly 'policed' through Ofsted	More elaborate 'standards' and National Curriculum in English, maths, science and ICT introduced	Schools must contribute to training in relation to 'standards' and National Curriculum

This social democratic ideal had a strong influence on the Robbins Committee's conception of teacher education. The Committee's vision of a professional teacher was of someone who was 'rationally autonomous' – how else could they develop rationally autonomous children? Teachers therefore needed a strong personal education based on 'fundamental and general knowledge', and this form of education had to take priority over practical training. Teacher training colleges were to be rapidly expanded to respond to the growing demand for teachers, and courses were to be made 'degree worthy'; university regulations, which defined what degree worthiness was, became the key policy texts that teacher educators of the day had to observe. The main vehicles for ensuring the 'degree worthiness' of the newly born B.Ed. degree were subject studies and 'education' – reinterpreted as the study of the four 'ologies' – sociology, history, psychology and philosophy. In line with the social democratic ideal, the academic study of the disciplines was justified as part of the liberal education of the well-rounded teacher, 'the scholar who happened to want to be a teacher' (Bell 1981: 13), and courses became increasingly theoretical and insulated from the world of school.

In retrospect, it is now clear that the Robbins conception of the professional teacher and professional education was untenable. There were significant unresolved epistemological difficulties concerning the relationship between 'theory' and 'practice', and the majority of lecturers and students remained sceptical about the value of an overly academic approach to professional preparation. Once the 'degree worthiness' of the new B.Ed. had been accepted, the Robbins' conception of a liberally educated professional started to be challenged, and the search for a professionally oriented degree gained momentum. But despite its obvious weaknesses, the academic approach to teacher education was to remain an important dimension of the policy debate for the rest of the century – if nothing else, it served as a highly significant shibboleth for those intent on reform in the periods that followed.

From 1976 to 1984: fragmentation and autonomy

In contrast to the early 1970s, the middle and later 1970s, as Wilkin (1996) suggests, were a period of ideological confusion. In education in general, including teacher education, there was no well-developed context of influence inside or outside the government, no coherent presentation of principles and priorities and few national policy texts. The decade opened promisingly enough with the new Conservative government establishing a series of 'expert' committees to tackle the major problems of the day. The James Committee, established to examine teacher education, was the first of these. Its proposals were radical, with its vision of 'three cycles' of linked education and training (personal, initial training and in-service) and statutory rights for teachers to have one term's study leave every seven years. However, the report of 1972 was not followed up in any significant way by the governments of the mid 1970s; it remained one voice among many. In the event, during the 1970s central government's involvement in teacher education policy was largely limited to managing provision in line with changes in demography; the result was a severe reduction in student numbers and the closure of many colleges of education in the wake of the unfortunately named 1972 White Paper, *Education: A Framework for Expansion.*

The ideological vacuum that developed around educational policy allowed the professionals themselves – teacher educators, the Council for National Academic Awards (CNAA), philosophers of education, the teaching unions and Her Majesty's Inspectorate (HMI) – to take a lead in shaping the practice of teacher education. The result, at the level of practice, was increasing fragmentation. As Wilkin (1996: 121) comments, 'Throughout the 1970s there was considerable variation in courses of initial training on almost every dimension; the weighting of theory and practice, integration of the elements, time spent in school, relationships with teachers and so on.' On the one hand, there were the fiercely autonomous 'old' universities where, with some important exceptions, a strong emphasis on theory continued to hold sway (Patrick *et al.* 1981). By contrast, among CNAA-validated institutions, there was a slow trend towards a curriculum in which the disciplines of education became less prominent, where the status of professionally oriented courses (curriculum studies; language and education) rose and students spent more time in school. Overall, Wilkin suggests that the professionals involved in leading the debate and practice of teacher education were slowly changing their vision of professionalism from an emphasis on the need for personal intellectual development to one of professional expertise. However, even in CNAA-validated courses, the system was still managed and run by those in higher education. Although the language of 'partnership' with schools started to emerge in some institutions, the practice of partnership was largely illusory and most courses remained distant from schools. As a result, many students and practising teachers remained critical of what they felt still to be an over-academic approach to professional education.

When the Thatcher government came to power in 1979, it inherited a system of initial teacher education that had in recent years rapidly expanded and then contracted as projections of teacher supply had changed. The need to maintain a flexible system of supply therefore remained a high priority for successive Conservative Secretaries of State. In the context of practice, the system of the late 1970s had a number of distinctive features about it. First, despite some general trends, it was highly diverse. There were three different types of institutional providers – universities, polytechnics and colleges – each with their own histories, commitments and professional associations; course content and structure varied widely, too. Second, despite the slow trend towards professional relevance, courses remained distant from schools, and as a result student and teacher criticism of the system remained strong. Third, as a professional group, teacher educators were divided among themselves. Even within the same institution, they were often heterogeneous, having been recruited at different historical periods. Some were highly academic in their commitments; others, particularly those recruited before the development of the B.Ed., were much more professionally oriented. Finally, what those lecturers as a group did have in common was that they were used to being largely autonomous in the management of what they considered to be their own system.

From 1984 to 1992: the professional teacher as 'expert'

Interestingly, the incoming Conservative government of 1979 was at first slow to develop any significant policies in initial teacher education. In fact, it was not until its second term of office, when a neo-liberal critique of teacher education started to come to the fore in the public policy debate, that it made any significant moves.

Central to the neo-liberal position is the claim that market forces are both an efficient and a fair means for allocating resources, in that they are more responsive to the felt needs of individuals, helping them become self-reliant and independent of the state (Gamble 1983, 1988). In the field of initial teacher education, there was an assertion among neo-liberals that initial training was unnecessary, even harmful – the product of 'producer capture' by the educational establishment. As O'Hear (1988: 6), one of the leading neo-liberal critics of the time, wrote:

> A large and vested interest has arisen in the form of a teacher training establishment, which runs, directs and assesses the courses of teacher training. In assessing the value of this training, we shall thereby indirectly consider whose interests it really serves.

The implication of such critiques was that teacher training courses actually diminish the effectiveness of teachers. From a neo-liberal point of view, if the quality of training itself was to be improved, then government needed to insist that it was opened up as much as possible to the 'market' of schools so that practical work took precedence over higher-education based training. Market realities were the best 'educator'. Ideally, there would be a free market in training itself, where schools would be allowed to recruit whomsoever they wanted – trained or untrained. If this was the case then it was assumed that head teachers would favour straightforward graduates over those who had 'suffered' from professional training.

While radical critiques of this sort were articulated with increasing force in the early 1980s, actual policy texts of the time were only partially influenced by them. Specific intervention first began in 1984 with the issuing of DES Circular 3/84 (DES 1984). It was this circular that established the Council for the Accreditation of Teacher Education (CATE), which was charged with the responsibility of overseeing initial teacher education in England and Wales on behalf of the Secretary of State.

In retrospect, the substantive changes introduced by Circular 3/84 do not seem particularly radical, though they do indicate some influence of neo-liberal thinking – in particular the idea that opening up teacher education to the 'realities of the market' would in itself improve quality. As a result, college and university lecturers responsible for 'pedagogy' had to return periodically to schools to undertake 'recent and relevant' school experience; teachers had to be involved in the process of interviewing students; the time that students had to spend in schools during their training was defined for the first time. Such proposals now seem relatively modest, but constitutionally the circular was revolutionary (Wilkin 1992, 1996) in that it established a new framework for accountability. As a result of the circular, the Secretary of State was given the right to have a say in the detailed content and structure of initial teacher education in this country, thereby marking the end of higher education's (and even the old universities') autonomy. In establishing the mechanism of increased accountability and central control, the circular was therefore of fundamental and lasting significance.

In 1989, a second and more radical circular (Circular 24/89) (DES 1989) was issued. The new circular took a number of steps to strengthen accountability and central control of training courses and further challenge the autonomy of higher education institutions. The circular revised and extended the powers of CATE and added a new layer of bureaucracy to the accreditation system – local CATE committees were set up to oversee all teacher training courses. In addition, the amount of time students had to spend in school was increased, and experienced teachers from their schools had to be involved in course planning and evaluation, student selection and the assessment of practical work. Teachers also had to be invited to contribute to appropriate lectures, seminars and other activities.

In relation to the content of training, the circular broke new ground by defining a range of topics that had to be addressed within courses. Importantly, parts of this emerging curriculum for initial teacher education, notably those concerned with information technology, were expressed in terms of 'outputs' or 'exit criteria' – 'statements of what students should be able to show they know, understand and can do by the end of their training' (para. 16). In the next round of reforms, these were to be further developed into 'competences'.

Two further interventions at this time that were also intended to challenge existing notions of professionalism were the introduction of the Articled and Licensed Teacher schemes. The Articled Teacher scheme, which ran from 1989 to 1994, was an entirely new form of school-based PGCE. Students, who had to be graduates, spent two years rather than one year in training, with 80 per cent of their time in school. The Licensed Teacher scheme was a far more radical departure from conventional training routes. Whereas the Articled Teacher scheme was a PGCE with a systematic and structured training programme organised through higher education, the Licensed Teacher scheme allowed mature entrants with a minimum of two years of higher education to be recruited directly to positions in schools and provided with any necessary training by their employers 'on the job'.

Taken together, government policy texts in the 1980s therefore had two interrelated purposes. First, they aimed to re-establish a national system of accountability in initial teacher education, challenging the right of those in higher education to define the nature of teacher professionalism underpinning initial teacher education. In addition, they aimed progressively to introduce a more practically focused professionalism, by opening up training courses to the realities of the 'market' of school. Yet, despite the challenges to its autonomy, higher education was still seen as making a very important contribution to professional education. Its contribution was now defined by government: it had to be practically oriented, focusing sharply on the realities of school life. Nevertheless, there was little doubt that those in higher education had an important contribution to make.

In reality, therefore, despite the aspirations of the neo-liberals, the vision of professionalism promoted by the majority of the policy texts of the time was not so different from that put forward by the James Report a decade earlier, which wanted a form of teacher education that was 'unashamedly specialised and functional' (James 1972). The aim of teacher education courses in the 1980s was to produce an 'expert teacher': someone who had access to the specialised, research-based and 'theoretical' knowledge that was sharply practically focused, and someone who was also highly practically competent. And as the MOTE studies demonstrated (Furlong *et al.* 2000), this was the form of teacher education that was established in the context of practice throughout England and Wales in the late 1980s and early 1990s. The contribution of higher education to initial education and training remained strong, but it had moved sharply away from the academic concerns of the earlier period. Courses were no longer dominated by 'disciplines of education'; instead, the idea of the 'reflective practitioner' became increasingly fashionable. By developing work in higher education that was increasingly practical in its focus, universities and colleges were able to avoid ceding significant power to schools. Schoolteachers did become more involved than in the past, but few were asked, or wanted, to take real responsibility. During the 1980s, therefore, the practice of initial education and training certainly changed, but the end of the decade, like the beginning, saw those in higher education firmly in charge.

From 1992 to 1997: the professional teacher as competent practitioner

By the early 1990s, therefore, initial teacher education was much more profession-ally and practically focused than in the past. However, such changes did nothing to stem the tide of criticism within the powerful context of influence that surrounded the Conservative government of the day. Neo-conservative critics became particu-larly influential (Hillgate 1989). Lawlor (1990: 21), for example, wrote:

> Contrary to the intentions of the 1980's reforms, general theory continues to dominate at the expense of individual practice; and students are not encour-aged to approach classroom teaching with an open mind or to develop individually as teachers. Instead, they are expected to bring to the classroom, and to apply to their teaching, the generalised educational theories which they have been taught.

Although in practice they have much in common, neo-conservative ideas are rather different from neo-liberal ones, for they emphasise traditional authority and national identity. From the neo-conservative perspective, the central aim of educa-tion is the preservation of a refined cultural heritage; in the words of the Hillgate Group (1989: 1), education 'depends on ... the preservation of knowledge, skills, culture and moral values and their transmission to the young'. The primary task for initial teacher education, from this perspective, is therefore to develop professionals who are themselves experts in their own subject area. Such preparation should take precedence over training in pedagogy; indeed, according to Lawlor (1990), the chief weakness of initial training at the time was that it was dominated by a concern to prepare students in how to teach rather than what to teach.

So much for debates in the context of influence: how did they influence policy texts and practice? In the autumn of 1991, a new Secretary of State for Education was appointed – Kenneth Clarke – and shortly after his appointment he issued a major new set of proposals for the reform of initial teacher education in England and Wales (Clarke 1992). These proposals were radical in many ways, most particularly in their suggestion that secondary students should spend 80 per cent of their time in school. After a period of consultation, however, this particular suggestion was modified to 66 per cent. But despite this concession, the new criteria for secondary (DfE 1992) and primary courses (DfE 1993) involved a major restructuring of the organisation and the curriculum of initial teacher education. Moreover, the fact that those in higher education were now required to pay schools up to 25 per cent of their fee income to support students' work in schools had a major effect in destabilising many schools and departments of education.

Clarke's appointment as Secretary of State marked the beginning of a very different and much more confrontational period of reform in the demand for increased accountability; much of the confrontation was with those in higher education. Over the next three years, new policies came thick and fast, each of them seeming more radical than the last. The year 1994 saw the establishment of the Teacher Training Agency (TTA) and the abolition of CATE; the transfer of funding for teacher education from the Higher Education Funding Council for England (HEFCE) to the TTA; and the development of a new Ofsted inspection framework for teacher education. Other policy changes introduced at the same time included the ending of the Articled Teacher scheme, and the establishment of School Centred Initial Teacher Training (SCITT) schemes and the Open University distance learning scheme.

The post 1992 policies had a number of aims, but two stand out as of particular significance. First, there was a much more concerted attempt than hitherto to establish a more practically based form of professionalism; that meant further curtailing the power of those in higher education in initial teacher education and increasing the role of schools. Almost equally important, however, was the concern to use a newly devised competency framework in order to increase direct control of the curriculum and the assessment process, whoever was responsible for delivering them. The secondary regulations, Circular 9/92 (DfE 1992), required higher education institutions, schools and students to 'focus on the competences of teaching throughout the whole period of initial training'. A similar phrase was used in Circular 14/93 on primary training issued the following year (DfE 1993). Although it was indicated that the statements of competence were not intended to provide a complete syllabus for initial teacher education, they were intended to define the issues on which courses would be accredited by the government. In other words, individual courses were free to devise syllabi that went beyond the competences listed, but that fact would not be of relevance in the application for accreditation. In order to ensure conformity to the new competency framework, the remit of HMI (later to become Ofsted) in teacher education was extended to include the inspection of schools where students were based for their training.

In 1993, the challenge to the role of higher education was taken a stage further with the launching of the 'school-centred' teacher training initiative (SCITT), which allowed schools to 'opt out' of links with higher education provision entirely and receive direct government funding to run their own postgraduate training schemes. Within SCITT schemes, small groups of schools work together as consortia, buying in higher education expertise and/or accreditation if and when they see fit. Even if they do choose to involve higher education, it is the school or consortium, rather than the higher education institution, that initially receives the funding for such courses.

The early 1990s were therefore a period of considerable influence for neo-conservative thinkers in relation to initial teacher education. Their stated aim was the suppression of 'lengthy, doctrinaire and demoralising' training courses (Lawlor 1990) and the creation of a 'neutral' system, in which teachers, rather than teacher educators, prepared students on a list of pre-defined competences. Their hope was that by these means they would see the rise of a different generation of teachers, whose professional values were untainted by views of the teacher education establishment. As has been indicated above, much of the thrust behind the key policy texts of the day (the 1992 and 1993 circulars and the creation of the SCITT scheme) seemed to be in accord with these aspirations. However, the passing of the 1994 Education Act and establishment of the TTA meant that the next five years were to see some significant changes in this policy agenda.

In 1994, the TTA took over most of the functions of CATE, as well as the funding of all initial teacher education in England (though not Wales, Scotland and Northern Ireland) whoever provided it. Indeed, one rationale used by the government for the setting up of the TTA was the need to find a way to fund SCITT schemes permanently. It was because such schemes, which were central to the government's vision of the future of teacher education, were outside existing funding arrangements that a new agency had to be invented. In a sense, then, the agency was explicitly established as part of the government's ongoing attempt to increase accountability by challenging the autonomy of higher education. It was fundamentally based on the assumption that higher education did not have a necessary and distinctive contribution to make to initial teacher education; that was why a new national body was needed.

The initial remit letter for the TTA from the Secretary of State was broad, and by 1995 the TTA was assuming responsibility for an ever-widening range of activities (Mahony and Hextall 1996). In relation to initial teacher education, two requirements in the remit letter were particularly important. The first, giving sustenance to 'New Right' ideas, was the formal requirement for the TTA to promote SCITT. The second concerned the requirement to develop a strategy for linking funding to quality. It was this formal requirement that became the main strategy used by the TTA to gain progressively more control over the system as a whole. In its aspiration to develop greater control of the system, inspections and inspection frameworks used by Ofsted, which was charged with working with the TTA on this issue, became increasingly important tools. Between 1993 and 1995, nearly all teacher education courses were inspected by Ofsted and 'quality' ratings applied. The TTA then developed mechanisms which linked Ofsted 'quality ratings' directly to funding. Not surprisingly, this new mechanism did much to encourage rapid conformity to the 1992 and 1993 circulars.

This, then, was the changing policy context in the second period of Conservative reform – one of dramatically increased central control. In the early 1990s, SCITT schemes were being established and courses provided by higher education were in the process of implementing the 1992 and 1993 circulars. Later in the decade, courses were having to come to terms with the workings of the TTA – with new accreditation arrangements, with new funding arrangements and with progressively more specific inspection regimes. The aim of all these interventions was first to increase accountability within the system, and second to establish a narrower and more practically oriented form of professionalism. Those in higher education and in schools were intended to have less and less autonomy in how to interpret their responsibilities. The second MOTE study (Furlong *et al.* 2000) found that, in the context of practice, this aspiration was largely achieved. Despite the hope on the part of those in higher education that they would be able to maintain the vision of the 'reflective practitioner' by collaborating with teachers in schools, thereby ensuring that students were offered more than 'merely' practical training, in reality this proved hard to achieve. Students now spent a significant part of their time in schools away from the influence of those in higher education; reduced funding and increasing pressures from Ofsted meant that what was offered to students inevitably became a narrower, largely practical form of training. The character of the training they received was to a significant degree influenced by the two or three schools they happened to be attached to during their training. Those in higher education found that they had to spend an increasing amount of their time managing what was now a highly devolved system rather than working directly with 'their' students.

From 1997: towards a new professionalism?

If the aspiration of successive Conservative governments in the early and mid 1990s was to increase public accountability and to challenge the nature of teacher professionalism embedded within initial teacher education, then it is hard to avoid the conclusion that, during that period, they did indeed make considerable progress towards achieving these goals. As the MOTE project demonstrated (Furlong *et al.* 2000), the cumulative effect of many policies introduced – the invention of new routes into teaching that specifically excluded higher education, the definition of competences, the prescription of how partnerships were to be formed, the undermining of the financial stability of schools of education in universities and colleges – all of these factors served progressively to curtail the influence of those in higher education on the professional development of new teachers. What students in the mid 1990s increasingly received was a form of preparation that was in its own way highly professional: it was demanding, relevant and practical, and closely mirrored current work in schools. However, because of its overwhelmingly practical focus, it was a view of professionalism and professional education that was very different from that argued for by teacher educators themselves (Furlong *et al.* 1988; Furlong 1996; Hirst 1996; Smith 1996).

The aim of this final section is to bring this review up to date by examining policy in the late 1990s. As we will see, the late 1990s represented a period of important transition in teacher education policy; there was continuity, but there was real change, too. The continuity was in the continued attempts, by an increasingly assertive Ofsted and TTA, to develop ever tighter forms of control – to insist even more than before that initial teacher education conform to the patterns of provision defined centrally. And in order to achieve this aim, new and more effective 'technologies of control' were developed. What was different was the aspiration on the part of government for the first time to define a content to the new professionalism Once control had been taken, it was no longer necessary for those in power to accept that 'the market' should determine the content of professionalism; that students should learn what it is to be a teacher of English or science or mathematics simply through enculturation in current practice in schools. Instead, through the development of a new National Curriculum for initial teacher education, there has been an asserted attempt to use initial teacher education to define the nature of teaching in those subjects – to set out the content of professional knowledge and even to define the pedagogy that trainee teachers must use. As we will see, the New Labour government of 1997 was quick to recognise the importance of maintaining tight control through the discipline of the market and then the potential for using that control to achieve its own policy aspirations. Central to maintaining that tight control has been the role played by Ofsted

Throughout the 1990s, Ofsted pursued its highly controversial inspection strategy in relation to schools; many considered it hostile and invasive. To begin with, its work in initial teacher education was less confrontational, perhaps reflecting the more tentative role HMI had had in the past in relation to higher education institutions and particularly to the older universities. However, with the appointment of Chris Woodhead as Chief Inspector in 1994, things began to change.

The move to more quantitative forms of measurement in inspection initiated by Ofsted necessitated the development of a publicly available inspection framework. For the first time, HMI began to work with explicit and publicly available criteria, and the inspection framework documents quickly became key policy texts for course leaders to interrogate; they constituted the criteria on which they were to be publicly judged. In its first format (Ofsted 1993), the inspection framework was broadly based. Its aim, as in earlier inspections, was to provide a holistic assessment of the quality of a particular training course. However, a revised framework issued in 1996 (Ofsted/TTA 1996) and then later refined in 1998 (Ofsted/TTA 1998) was much more tightly focused and detailed. By the late 1990s, therefore, the inspection process of initial teacher education had become as controversial and perhaps even more politicised than inspection in schools. It had also become a major undertaking. Over the next two and a half years, the Ofsted teacher education and training team inspected some 80, mostly postgraduate, primary courses and over 500 secondary subject specialisms, and in 1998 a further cycle commenced. Given that each inspection was conducted over the course of a year, for many institutions Ofsted inspections became a continuous affair.

Generally, the response to the inspection process from teacher educators was negative (Sutherland 1997) – they were seen as heavy-handed and invasive. Nevertheless, as a means of increasing accountability with conformity to the spirit and the letter of government regulations, the inspections were highly effective. The fact that a revised circular (DfEE 1997) was reflected immediately in a revised inspection framework meant that conformity to the new regulations was extremely rapid. And despite the voluntary nature of their involvement, there was also increasing pressure on schools to provide more effective and consistent forms of training. Higher education simply could not afford to take the risk of under-performing schools.

By the end of the 1990s, therefore, government, through the work of the TTA and Ofsted, had developed a system of initial teacher education that was highly responsive to policy changes. In the course of just fifteen years, the system had been moved from one of diversity and autonomy to a 'command economy' with unanimity and central control. What the government, and particularly the TTA, had wanted was a common system with common standards and procedures, no matter where or by whom the training was provided; this was how the TTA defined quality. By the end of the 1990s, this had largely been achieved.

It is important to recognise that, in relation to the development of that 'command economy', the aspirations of the Conservative and Labour governments of the late 1990s were identical. However, there is a sense in which once that aspiration was achieved, a different policy agenda became possible. That was the aim of intervening in the content of training itself.

Until 1996, the content of training had been only broadly prescribed. During the middle 1990s in particular, the most important influence on the content of training was 'the market' to which students were increasingly exposed, i.e. practice in schools. Because of their substantially increased time in schools and because of the growing role for school-based mentors, what students inevitably came to learn was significantly influenced by current practice in the limited numbers of schools to which they were attached. It was, potentially at least, a very localised market.

In sharp contrast, policies in the late 1990s increasingly sought to exploit the new control of the system to begin specifying the content of professional education in much more detail. Two strategies were involved: first, the transformation of competences into more elaborate 'standards'; and second, the development of a National Curriculum for initial teacher education in English, mathematics, science and information and communication technology (ICT).

The TTA first produced its 'standards' for initial teacher education in early 1997, and after a period of consultation (which covered the 1997 general election) they were then incorporated into a revised government circular – Circular 10/97 – which was published in June of that year (DfEE 1997). It was the first policy document in this field by the New Labour government, but despite this the document changed very little from its initial drafts a year earlier. As well as the much more detailed definition of content for courses, there was a reassertion of the need for subject specialist teachers at the upper primary phase, and the regulations for SCITT schemes remained unchanged.

The second and more explicit strategy for establishing greater control of the content of initial teacher education courses was the development of a National Curriculum in four subject areas – English, mathematics, science and ICT for both primary and secondary school teachers. Again, the idea of a National Curriculum for initial teacher education was first put forward on the advice of the TTA by the Conservative government in 1996, though it was not formally put in place until 1997, after the general election.

For the TTA, the National Curriculum has been seen as representing an important marker of the type of intervention they hoped to establish at all levels of professional development. As Anthea Millett (Millett 1997), then chief executive of the TTA, wrote in her covering letter introducing the new curriculum:

> The benefits of the standards and curricula extend far beyond initial teacher training. I have no doubt that the new standards for the award of QTS will come to be seen as a landmark for serving teachers in making clear the expectations of them in this most demanding yet rewarding of professions.

And the Labour minister responsible for initial teacher education, Estelle Morris, explicitly recognised the link between such initiatives and the government's wider agenda within education. As she wrote in a letter to the TTA only six weeks after the election (Morris 1997): 'Raising the standards we expect of new teachers in this way is clearly essential to delivering the government's commitment to raising pupil performance across the education system and in particular, to delivering the major new literacy and numeracy targets.'

Conclusion: the teachers of the future?

In conclusion, we might ask where this leaves teacher professionalism at the beginning of the new century. Certainly, the vision of the TTA is of a form of professionalism where the voice of the individual teacher is almost wholly silenced. As Anthea Millett wrote in 1999,

> I believe that teachers need to be: better regarded; better qualified to enter initial training; better trained initially; better inducted; better developed, after entering teaching; better deployed; better assisted; better led; better managed, appraised and rewarded; and better represented.
>
> (Millett 1999)

Yet after eighteen months in office, the New Labour government set out in a new Green Paper (DfEE 1998) what might possibly be seen as a rather different vision of the future of the profession. The Green Paper was an up-beat, future-oriented document with talk of creating a 'world-class education service for all our children'. 'Pupils will need education for a world of rapid change in which both flexible attitudes and enduring values have a part to play' (DfEE 1998; para. 1). Schools, it argued, will need to be outward-looking, constantly striving to change to meet the challenges of the future. In addition, most controversially of all, employment practices will need to change, with greater flexibility and a need for all teachers to keep their skills and subject knowledge up to date. All this, the Green Paper argued, demands:

> a new professionalism among teachers. The time has long gone when isolated, unaccountable professionals made curriculum and pedagogical decisions alone, without reference to the outside world.

Teachers in a modern teaching profession need:

- to have high expectations of themselves and of all pupils;
- to accept accountability;
- to take personal and collective responsibility for improving their skills and subject knowledge;
- to seek to base decisions on evidence of what works in schools in this country and internationally;
- to work in partnership with other staff in schools;
- to welcome the contribution that parents, business and others outside a school can make to its success; and
- to anticipate change and promote innovation.

(DfEE 1998: para. 13)

The 'new professionalism' of the Green Paper could therefore be different from 'competent practitioner' of the earlier period. High levels of practical competence remain essential, but now the nature of that competence is being defined in new ways. The contradiction at the heart of current policies is that the vision of the new professionalism set out here would demand a rather different form of initial education and training from that currently in place. As I have argued elsewhere (Furlong 1996, 2000), if the new generation of teachers are to seek to base decisions on evidence of what works in schools in this country and internationally, if they are to take responsibility constantly to improve their skills and subject knowledge, if they are to anticipate change and promote innovation, if they are to promote enduring values among their pupils, then they need more than practical training on a predefined list of competences. The irony is that in the past it is precisely these dimensions of 'extended professionalism' (Hoyle 1974) which those in higher education in the past sought to develop. At the time of writing, the 'standards' framework for initial teacher education and training (DfEE 1997) is under review. It will be interesting to see whether this key text, once it is published, in reality moves away from a narrow competency framework and recognises the contribution that higher education can make to the development of these broader attributes that the government claims to be central to their vision for the teachers of the future.

Notes

1   The two MOTE (Modes of Teacher Education) studies were: 'Modes of teacher education: towards a basis for comparison' (ESRC project no. R000232810) and 'Changing modes of professionalism? A case study of teacher education in transition' (ESRC project no. R000234185). The generic title of MOTE was used informally for both projects.

References

Bailey, C. (1984) *Beyond the Present and the Particular: A Theory of Liberal Education*, London: Routledge.

Bell, A. (1981) 'Structure, knowledge and relationships in teacher education', *British Journal of Sociology of Education*, 2(1): 3–23.

Bowe, R. and Ball, S., with Gold, A. (1992) *Reforming Education and Changing Schools: Case Studies in Policy Sociology*, London: Routledge.

Clarke, K. (1992) Speech for North of England education conference, 4 January.

DES (1984) *Initial Teacher Training: Approval of Courses*, Circular 3/84, London: DES.

——(1989) *Initial Teacher Training: Approval of Courses*, Circular 24/89, London: DES.

DfE (1992) *Initial Teacher Training (Secondary Phase)*, Circular 9/92, London: DfE.

——(1993) *The Initial Training of Primary School Teachers: New Criteria for Courses*, Circular 14/93, London: DfE.

DfEE (1997) *Teaching: High Status, High Standards*, Circular 10/97, London: DfEE.

——(1998) *Teachers: Meeting the Challenge of Change*, London: DfEE.

Furlong, J. (1996) 'Do student teachers need higher education?' in J. Furlong and R. Smith (eds) *The Role of Higher Education in Initial Teacher Training*, London: Kogan Page.

——(2000) *Higher Education and the New Professionalism for Teachers: Realising the Potential of Partnership*, London: SCOP/CVCP.

Furlong, J., Hirst, P., Pocklington, K. and Miles, S. (1988) *Initial Teacher Education and the Role of the School*, Buckingham: Open University Press.

Furlong, J., Barton, L., Miles, S., Whiting, C. and Whitty, G. (2000) *Teacher Education in Transition: Re-Forming Teacher Professionalism?*, Buckingham: Open University Press.

Gamble, A. (1983) 'Thatcherism and Conservative politics', in S. Hall and M. Jacques (eds) *The Politics of Thatcherism*, London: Lawrence & Wishart.

——(1988) *The Free Economy and the Strong State*, London: Macmillan.

Grace, G. (1987) 'Teachers and the state in Britain: a changing relation', in M. Lawn and G. Grace (eds) *Teachers: The Culture and Politics of Work*, Lewes: Falmer.

Hillgate Group (1989) *Learning to Teach*, London: Claridge.

Hirst, P (1996) 'The demands of professional practice and preparation for teaching', in J. Furlong and R. Smith (eds) *The Role of Higher Education in Initial Teacher Training*, London: Kogan Page.

Hoyle. E. (1974). 'Professionality, professionalism and control in teaching', *London Education Review*, 3(2): 13–19.

James, Lord (1972) *Teacher Education and Training (James Report)*, London: HMSO.

Lawlor, S. (1990) *Teachers Mistaught: Training Theories or Education in Subjects?* London: Centre for Policy Studies.

Mahony, P. and Hextall I. (1996) 'Trailing the TTA, paper presented at the annual meeting of the British Educational Research Association, University of Lancaster, September.

Millett, A. (1997) *Letter to Providers*, 26 June, London: TTA.

——(1999) *The Implications for Teacher Training of the Government's Green Paper – 'Teachers: Meeting the Challenge of Change'*, London: TTA.

Morris, E. (1997) *Letter to TTA*, 26 June, London: DfEE.

Ofsted (1993) *Working Papers for the Inspection of Secondary Initial Teacher Training*, London: Ofsted.

Ofsted/TTA (1996) *Framework for the Assessment of Quality and Standards in Initial Teacher Training 1996/7*, London: Ofsted.

——(1998) *Framework for the Assessment of Quality and Standards in Initial Teacher Training*, London: Ofsted.

O'Hear, A. (1988) *Who Teaches the Teachers?* London: Social Affairs Unit.

Patrick, H. Bernbaum, G. and Reid, K. (1981) *The Structure and Process of Initial Teacher Education within Universities in England and Wales*, Leicester: Leicester School of Education.

Robbins, Lord (1963) *Higher Education (Robbins Report)*, London: HMSO.

Smith, R. (1996) 'Something for the grown-ups', in J. Furlong and R. Smith (eds) *The Role of Higher Education in Initial Teacher Training*, London: Kogan Page.

Sutherland, Sir S. (1997) *Teacher Education and Training: A Study. Report 10 of the National Committee of Inquiry into Higher Education*, London: HMSO.

Wilkin, M. (1992) 'The challenge of diversity', *Cambridge Journal of Education*, 22(3): 307–31.

——(1996) *Initial Teacher Training: The Dialogue of Ideology and Culture*, London: Falmer.

10 Empowerment or performativity?

Assessment policy in the late twentieth century

Patricia Broadfoot

Introduction

When New Labour came to power in the UK in 1997, many in education believed that the worst excesses of a dirigiste, divisive and punitive system would be replaced with policies that revived the notion of partnership between professionals and central government, which had been the hallmark of previous Labour administrations. Yet, despite the undoubted commitment to education that the current government has made and its explicit concern with supporting the more disadvantaged sections of society, there has been little change in the underpinning policy strategies which are being adopted to achieve these goals. The mantra of themes that have characterised English/Welsh educational policy over the last twenty-five years – marketisation and choice, the centralisation of power, new forms of institutional management, inspection, accountability, standards and effectiveness – are, if anything, more central to government education policy than before, as the introduction to this book makes clear. They remain the defining policy themes of our present time. Indeed, as Maclure (1998) has argued, their pursuit by a government which much more readily attracts the commitment and loyalty of educational professionals is potentially even more dangerous, since the sense of common cause may dull the opposition to what are in some cases misguided policies, as I shall argue later in this chapter.

These policy themes provide the supporting skeleton for the analyses of the different limbs and organs of educational provision that make up this book. There is one theme that underpins all these various developments to a greater or lesser extent, a theme that may come to be seen in historical perspective as the defining principle of education policy in the late twentieth century. This theme, I suggest, is assessment, as I hope to make clear in this chapter. In what follows I first delineate briefly some of the key assessment policy developments in education which have taken place during the last twenty-five years; these are located in terms of the powerful assumptions that have dominated the thinking that informed them. I shall seek to account for this domination in terms of both broad trends in the international zeitgeist and specific features of the English/Welsh educational tradition, which together have served to reinforce the growing power of a very particular assessment discourse – that of 'performativity', to use Lyotard's (1984) now familiar term. Rooted in a rationalistic assumption that it is possible – and, indeed, desirable

– to 'measure' performance, whether this be of the individual pupil or of the institution as a whole, the concept of 'performativity' arguably represents one of the clearest expressions of modernist thinking. The quest to understand the source and significance of the current domination of 'performativity' in this particular context necessarily involves a consideration of the unique cultural and institutional traditions of English/Welsh education and society, as well as of the more general changes currently impacting on society, and of the nature and state of the modernist project itself.

Key themes and assumptions in recent assessment policy

Two decades ago, educational visitors from other countries who visited England and Wales found it almost impossible to credit that there was no national curriculum – indeed, very little central direction of any kind to constrain the activities of either local education authorities (LEAs) or schools. They marvelled at how free individual teachers appeared to be in their own classrooms to decide what to teach, how and when. If they stayed a little longer, they would gradually realise the essential role played by assessment procedures in controlling an otherwise almost anarchic system (Broadfoot 1983). Such an experience would not have prepared them, however, for a similar visit today, when they would find an education system that is arguably not only as tightly controlled and centrally directed as any in the world – at least in principle – but also a system that might appear to them to be infected by 'a kind of madness' (Alberge 1999), by the rampant growth of a forest of assessment procedures which threatens to throttle the whole education system within a dense canopy of externally imposed performance indicators. Coming from a different educational tradition, they would perhaps once again be bemused by an obsessive neurosis that manifests itself in an almost pathological belief in the value of assessment, for there is no other country in the world that subjects its schoolchildren to more external testing or spends more money on it (Whetton 1999).

Thus, at present, pupils begin to be subject to the process of formal assessment with 'baseline assessment' on entry to primary school. Thereafter they are subject to a continuous and ineluctable process of testing and target-setting throughout their primary and secondary schooling, until the pupil retires exhausted from the fray with the tangible reward of a certificate, degree or diploma. Coupled with this, the steadily spreading tentacles of institutional assessment, based on standardised performance indicators, value-added calculations and benchmarking, increasingly determine both the funding of institutions and the pay of individuals. The now ubiquitous presence of the Office for Standards in Education (Ofsted), which both defines the parameters of quality and judges how far individual institutions have met them, provides powerful reinforcement for these requirements. Published league tables of results provide consumers with a public index of apparent quality, which becomes the currency of an increasingly divisive educational market. Add to this the pervasive climate of 'quality assurance' which is manifest in a whole culture of target-setting, performance indicators, development plans, departmental reviews and annual reports, and the sheer scale of this trend becomes clear.

Assessment is a dangerously ambiguous concept; essentially, it is a 'technical craft' but it is also a social technology (Madaus 2000) and, in that sense, it is not the techniques themselves that need to be a focus for concern but how they are used (Haney *et al.* 1993). Like all technologies, the utilisation of assessment in practice has social implications and needs to be understood as such. Thus, the attempt to trace the essential themes which have informed recent assessment policy must necessarily centre not on the particular techniques employed but on the assumptions which underpin these applications. For example, the driving force for the currently pervasive preoccupation with monitoring and evaluation in this country appears to be a concern for, on the one hand, maximum dependability of assessment information and, on the other, value for money. Behind many of the current assessment initiatives, notably the reporting of results in comparative 'league tables', is also the assumption that competition between both individuals and institutions is a valuable spur to improvement. Both these ways of using assessment information make the implicit assumption that it is possible to 'measure' quality by applying criteria to the available evidence, and that it is both appropriate and desirable to express the resultant judgement in a 'categoric' form (Pollard *et al.* 1994).

These 'categories' may take the form of grades or marks, ranks or percentages. However, they all share the underlying rationale that it is meaningful to compare some aspect of quality on a common scale: to locate various aspects of institutional or individual performance, such as a school's value for money, on a common, objectified scale. In short, that it is both possible and desirable to identify objectified *standards* and to use these to judge some aspect of performance (see Cresswell 1998). In England and Wales, at least, the current combination of pervasive external assessment together with the creation of an educational market based on a currency of indicators, ranks and grades comprises elements which create a contemporary categoric discourse of competition and control – a new hegemony of 'performance'.

This approach to assessment is essentially punitive. It is increasingly being used by policy-makers in the belief that it is one of the most effective ways of ensuring results. For example, Haney *et al.* (1993: 265) argue in relation to the United States that assessments are 'not simply sources of information but are instruments of reform in themselves'. Hence, we find ourselves in a situation where a number of powerful assumptions are so dominant in current policy thinking that their validity is unquestioned. These include the following:

- that decisions concerning curriculum (inputs), pedagogy (process) and assessment (outcomes) should be centralised;
- that there are standards of 'quality' that can be objectively measured;
- that it is necessary and desirable to assess institutional quality according to externally defined 'performance indicators';
- that the punitive use of league tables and other publicly shaming devices will help to drive up educational performance.
- that assessment is a 'neutral' measuring instrument which only requires further technical developments to make it more effective.

Beneath the penumbra of performativity, however, other assessment policy developments have also struggled to grow. Most notable of these have been various initiatives which cast assessment in the very different role of supporting learning. Initially associated particularly with the Records of Achievement (RoA) initiative, this has now been translated into a cluster of more broadly based policies which include action planning, the use of portfolios, and self-assessment. Here the term 'assessment' is linked to notions of empowerment through its utilisation in processes of self-reflection. Indeed, professional counsellors use the term 'restorative' assessment to refer to the process by which individuals can be helped to overcome the damage of previous painful episodes in their lives through a guided process of self-reflection and positive reinforcement. There is now a substantial body of research which documents the powerful positive effects that can be achieved through the appropriate use of formative feedback and, particularly, self-assessment (Sadler 1987; Black and Wiliam 1998).

In between these very different extremes, there have been other assessment policy initiatives that can loosely be grouped under the broad heading of 'certification', including the attestation of competency and selection – the more familiar territory of assessment purposes.

These three broad themes constitute the connecting narratives in the history of assessment policy in England and Wales during the last twenty-five years. At times, their essential incompatibility has been almost completely hidden. At other times, the stark choice between the different epistemologies on which they are based has been an explicit feature of policy debates. The next section traces some of these historical developments in terms of these three broad policy strands of 'empowerment', 'performativity' and 'certification' initiatives.

Empowerment: the Records of Achievement (RoA) initiative

In 1984, the Department of Education and Science in England and the Welsh Office published a document entitled: *Records of Achievement: A Statement of Policy* (DES/WO 1984). It committed the government to supporting a national pilot of RoA development and implementation in secondary schools in nine different areas around the country. The overall aim was to generate enough practical experience to form a basis for the formulation of national policy guidelines by the end of the decade. It was anticipated that by this time all young people leaving school would be provided with an RoA.

By the beginning of the 1990s, the initiative had evolved into procedures and products which were typically associated with generic approaches to teaching, learning and assessment. A national evaluation of RoA schemes (Broadfoot *et al.* 1991: 8) identified the following three definitions of RoAs which, in some combination, informed the work of staff in schools and LEAs:

- a range of documents developed for the purposes of recording and reporting pupils' achievements (both summative and formative);
- specific processes and activities which have been developed to enable the recording of achievement, such as teacher–pupil discussions, target-setting and review, pupil self-assessment, the preparation of statements, and so on;

- a set of principles which can be applied to all teaching and learning, such as 'pupil involvement and ownership', 'widening notions of achievement in all learning contexts', 'positive portrayal', 'description rather than grades', 'grounding assessment in evidence' and so on.

Arguably, the definitive stage in this process of policy development was the publication in 1989 of the DES/WO National Guidelines for RoA (DES/WO 1989), which endorsed the aims for RoA which had been set out in the 1984 policy statement. These national policy guidelines explicitly drew attention to the formative role of recording achievement in enhancing and guiding student learning as well as to the summative role of the RoA in celebrating every student's achievements at school in a comprehensive way. For the first time, mention was made in this document of the role that RoAs could play in reporting students' achievements in relation to what were later to be known as 'key skills' – 'communication, working with others, organizing work, information handling, personal qualities' (para. 3.40) – and their achievements in the newly introduced National Curriculum.

The rationale for the RoA initiative was as much about improving student motivation and learning as it was about reporting achievements. Its origins lay in a conscious reaction to the perceived shortcomings of conventional modes of assessment, particularly the latter's emphasis on recognising only a narrow range of achievements, and the tendency, in the UK at least, to exclude significant numbers of students from the opportunity to gain formal accreditation for their achievements. A key informing principle of RoA has been the aspiration to record the full range of a student's skills, qualities and achievements by using a wide variety of evidence and a more descriptive approach to reporting. This kind of approach necessarily involves a number of people in the assessment process who have had the opportunity to observe a student's achievements. By definition, it challenged the dominance of conventional written tests and their necessarily limited scope.

The tension of pursuing greater validity in assessment while at the same time ensuring a sufficient measure of reliability for summative purposes has been central to RoA development, as it has been to many other recent assessment policy initiatives, such as General National Vocational Qualifications (GNVQ) (Stobart 1999) and National Assessment (Butterfield 1995). Related to this, and perhaps even more important, has been the tension between the capacity of the formative processes associated with recording achievement, such as reviewing progress and target-setting to empower both students and teachers, and the reality of a system in which the dominance of very different assessment priorities largely inhibits the fulfilment of this potential. The core rationale of this policy development was to break the mould of conventional assessment and associated teaching and learning practices in order to raise student motivation and achievement. Thus, RoAs provide a good example of what the realisation of the challenge to create a 'learning society' is likely to mean in practice. The RoA development played a crucial part in helping to formulate what can now be understood as an alternative 'emancipatory' assessment discourse: a different vocabulary and language, a different set of concepts for thinking about the content and delivery of education and, crucially, the role that assessment ought to play in this. The key assumptions of such an 'emancipatory' discourse are that:

- both motivation and achievement can be enhanced by giving students a measure of responsibility for, and control over, their own learning;
- learning can be enhanced if students understand clearly what they are trying to achieve, and are provided with personal and substantive feedback in trying to reach their target;
- assessment which celebrates achievement on an ipsative or criterion-referenced basis rather than drawing attention to failure through the use of grades and marks – particularly on a norm-referenced basis – builds students' confidence and ultimately enhances their performance;
- the use of student self-assessment is valuable in training students to be more effective learners by being able to monitor their own learning;
- collecting, sorting and annotating evidence to demonstrate achievement in the form of a portfolio of work is a valuable aid to developing the skills of reviewing and target-setting, as well as for communicating standards in a relatively unambiguous and accessible way.

The development of RoA arguably reflected a number of different influences which combined at that time to bring about change. Employers expressed enthusiasm for more comprehensive documentation; teachers wanted to have something to meet the needs of a non-traditional school population; the government was aware of the impact of technology and of the need to encourage the development of new skills. Thus, the RoA movement arguably acted as a catalyst for the development of a range of radically new educational insights and practices which are increasingly now being recognised as the foundation for achieving the educational goals of the twenty-first century – active, strategic and effective involvement in learning for everyone throughout their life.

But if the RoA initiative played a crucial part in the formulation of an 'emancipatory' assessment discourse, it has arguably been signally unsuccessful in establishing this discourse in such a way as to challenge established assessment thinking. As Hodgson (1997: 225) argues, commentators in the mid 1990s were broadly in agreement that the 'NRA has had limited success as an instrument of national policy'. A government report (DfEE 1997) emphasised the variation in quality of RoA processes in schools. This was explicitly acknowledged in the influential 1996 *Review of Qualifications for 16–19 Year Olds* (Dearing 1996). Chaired by Sir Ron Dearing, it asserted that the ubiquitous National Record of Achievement maroon folder had had relatively little impact in terms of its potential role of supporting and encouraging learning.

The RoA was relaunched as 'Progress File', accompanied by extensive supporting guidance for educational institutions and learners of all kinds. It uses the latest technologies and has been designed with the government's strategies to encourage lifelong learning explicitly in mind. Rather than speculating on the likely success of 'Progress File', which is beyond the historical scope of this chapter, I want to consider briefly why the National Record of Achievement, despite having an established national role, appears not to have fulfilled its intended goals. Although there are several possible explanations for this, among which, as with any initiative, the difficulties of managing change were undoubtedly significant, the main reason lies in the growing preoccupation with 'performativity'.

'Performativity': the impact of the 1988 Education Reform Act

In England and Wales, the passing of the 1988 Education Reform Act provided for the introduction of a National Curriculum and a national assessment system to cover the ten years of compulsory schooling. The rationale for this legislation was the desire to ensure the provision of a broad and balanced but subject-based curriculum, the effective delivery of which was to be 'policed' by the regular public testing of all pupils. Although the design of the assessment part of the framework was initially innovatory, involving as it did a criterion-referenced approach, subsequent policy developments were such as to provide for a steady increase in its 'categoric' assessment emphasis.

The expressed aim of the Education Reform Act 1988, a policy initiative almost unprecedented in its ambition and scope, was quite simply to raise standards. This was to be achieved by raising expectations about pupil achievement and through the imposition of a broad and balanced National Curriculum for all pupils to provide continuity and coherence in their learning experience. The introduction of the National Curriculum was complemented by provision for a standard and comprehensive assessment system. This national system was designed not only to measure the performance of pupils at the end of four Key Stages (Years 1–2, 3–6, 7–10 and 11–12), but also to make it possible for market forces to operate by providing a currency of information which would fuel competition between schools.

The original aim of the national assessment system was that it should provide formative and diagnostic information to guide teachers in the classroom, as well as summative information for students, teachers and parents about the level of attainment of a given child at a given stage. Thus, the government's Task Group on Assessment and Testing (TGAT) envisaged an elaborate, criterion-referenced structure of attainment targets. Pupils' achievement was to be recorded and reported at the end of Key Stages 1, 2 and 3 by means of a combination of teacher assessment and results from externally provided standard assessment tasks. At the end of Key Stage 4, external assessment was to be in the form of the newly introduced GCSE examination. Significantly, such a comprehensive national assessment system could, and subsequently did, provide attainment data with which to compare not only individual students, but also the results of their schools, of LEAs and indeed of the nation as a whole in comparative league tables. Slowly, the formative purpose of assessment waned in significance, and its role as a summative measure of performance became dominant.

One of the major reasons for this change was the advent of explicit competition between schools. Central to the rationale of the 1988 Act was the creation of an educational market in which the availability of assessment information about students and about institutions in the form of inspection reports played a key role. In a situation in which an individual school's results in relation to national assessments at the age of 11 and 14 (Key Stages 2 and 3), as well as those of GCSE at 16 and A Level at 18, were explicitly intended to provide much of the hard currency for parents to use to inform their choice of school, it became virtually impossible for schools to avoid focusing their efforts on the immediate goal of 'getting the scores up'.

More recent policy initiatives which require schools to achieve specific target levels of pupil achievements in these terms at each of the Key Stages have served further to reinforce this trend. Increasing emphasis has been put on the traditional roles of assessment within the governmental policy machine, with growing interest in the publication of test and exam scores in the form of 'league tables' of school results and other 'indicators': significantly extended and strengthened school inspections; a reaction against coursework in external examinations; and, more recently, the requirement for schools to engage in target-setting and benchmarking to establish their 'value-added' component. The most recent of these initiatives at the time of writing is the requirement for all schools to achieve at least 20 per cent of their pupils gaining an A–C grade at GCSE, or face being closed down.

In short, the clear policy emphasis of the last ten years or so in the UK has been on assessment as a measurement device, the results of which are used to goad students, teachers and institutions as a whole to try harder. It is not surprising that, faced with these pressures, schools have typically succumbed to them.

Behind all these policies is the explicit assumption that it is *test results* of one kind or another that are the best indicator of educational quality. This increasingly powerful and explicit assessment discourse is essentially 'categoric', in that its central purpose is to categorise individuals and/or institutions in relation to each other on an externally defined scale of performance. Thus the pervasive power of this particular assessment discourse is well illustrated by the subtle redefinition of the 'emancipatory discourse' associated with RoA initiatives into the 'categoric' discourse of 'recording achievement'. In a 1990 government circular, the many primary and secondary schools which had already put in place procedures for recording and reporting achievement to support the production of RoAs, were invited to refocus them as a means for supporting the reporting of academic achievements under the National Curriculum to parents. The purpose, scope and form of reporting was to be external to the pupil, on nationally designated targets. Rather than the empowerment of learners, the informing rationale of such reporting was the need for accountability to parents and their need, rather than the student's, for information:

> The Government sees Records of Achievement as integrally linked with the National Curriculum. The underlying principles of recognising positive achievement in all pupils are common to both. Recording of achievement schemes have often served to bring together schools' policies and practices on assessment, recording and reporting into a coherent whole. The Secretary of State applauds such developments, which are very much in the spirit of the National Curriculum. For the future, he sees Records of Achievement as a means by which achievement across the National Curriculum and beyond can be most effectively reported to a range of audiences.
>
> (DES/WO 1990: section 30)

This was a clear example of performativity taking priority over empowerment in assessment. In addition, performativity has been paralleled by an exponential growth in externally accredited qualifications in recent years, and it is to this that I now want to turn.

Certification: qualifications reform

The long struggle to introduce a common system of examination at 16 plus was finally resolved in 1988, when the GCE O Level and Certificate of Secondary Education (CSE) were replaced by the introduction of the General Certificate of Secondary Education (GCSE). This new examination had its roots in the protracted search for a public examination that would be appropriate to certificate the achievements of the entire age cohort at the end of compulsory schooling (age 16). It followed the creation of the Certificate of Secondary Education (CSE) examination in 1965, which was designed to provide an alternative certification goal for the increasing numbers of 16-year-olds in school for whom the O-level examination, designed to test only the top 30 per cent of the year group, was unsuitable. This new qualification for 'the middle 40 per cent' introduced a number of significant innovations in public examination practices. In particular, it gave an important role to teachers in both developing examination syllabuses and conducting school-based assessment. It was operated by a large number of local examination boards. The net effect was to give teachers considerable control over the content and conduct of the examination.

However, it proved increasingly difficult to run two national examinations for the same age group, especially given the explicitly lower status of CSE. Thus in 1971 the Schools Council – the body at that time in charge of examination policy – initiated the first of what were to be many initiatives to introduce a common system of examinations at 16 plus. In 1978, the Waddell Committee recommended a single system based on the integration of existing GCE and CSE grades. Notable in their proposals was the recommendation that the new examinations be run by three or four regional consortia of combined GCE and CSE examination boards, and the introduction of national criteria to define subject titles and coverage. These latter proposals were highly significant in heralding the growing trend towards greater central control of the education system through assessment arrangements which, I have argued, has been one of the defining characteristics of education policy in the latter part of the twentieth century.

So controversial was the proposal to introduce such a new system that it was not finally achieved until 1980. The examination was launched in 1984, and the first candidates examined, finally, in 1988. Initially, this new system of examinations was characterised by many of the innovatory, even 'emancipatory' assessment procedures that had been pioneered within the CSE examination, especially the strong emphasis on teacher-assessed coursework. However, the tensions between the different objectives for the examination rapidly became apparent. The 1978 White Paper had made explicit the expectation that 'that there will be a need for stronger central co-ordination of the new examining system' (DES 1978: 26). The subsequent demise of the teacher-dominated Schools Council in 1983 and its replacement by a powerful National Examinations Council gives weight to Nuttall's (1979) speculation that the government's real motive for introducing a common system of examining at 16 plus was not to secure its undoubted pedagogic, educational and administrative advantages, but to obtain much firmer control of the activities of the exam boards, and hence of the curriculum.

Nuttall's speculation was to prove correct. Unlike the GCE examinations, for which the DES had laid down only a framework, the GCSE was tightly controlled from the centre. In most subjects there was a detailed and restrictive framework, setting out a common core for each subject, detailed assessment objectives and methods, specified weighting in the marking schemes, and compulsory assessment by teachers of coursework. So the new common system of examinations at 16+ was not just a unification of the old GCE and CSE. Rather, it reflected the new priorities in public examinations which were set out by the Secretary of State in a much-publicised speech in Sheffield at the North of England Conference in January 1984. This speech heralded a new emphasis on criterion-referencing in examinations in order to communicate what candidates could actually do. It also heralded what was to become the increasingly explicit agenda of the decades which followed: the need to raise standards within the education system as a whole through innovations in assessment and examinations.

From this time, public examinations increasingly became the focus for efforts to reform the education system in order to raise standards. It was not that examinations had been unimportant before. On the contrary, as I have suggested, they have always had a pivotal role to play in the often almost anarchic arrangements for educational provision in England (and Wales). As HMI wrote in 1979:

> public examinations were a major preoccupation of the schools inspected ... too many teachers and pupils were concerned with the pursuit of examination success to the relative neglect of other considerations ... The style and quality of pupils' work in the fourth and fifth years are dominated by the requirements – as most teachers perceive them – of public examinations.
>
> (DES 1979: 246)

Although this judgement provides telling evidence of the potential power of assessment arrangements as a policy tool within English/Welsh education, it also highlights the significant changes that were to take place during the 1980s – not least the shift that has subsequently taken place in the role of school inspections, another element of the assessment edifice. If HMI were deploring schools' obsession with examinations in 1980, their contemporary successors – Ofsted – have more or less willingly embraced the discourse of marks and grades, examinations and testing, as a key element in promoting standards in schools.

Nuttall (1984) predicted, almost before it was operative, that the GCSE would become divisive, with its 'tiered' papers for different levels of 'ability'; bureaucratic, because of the need to conform to national criteria and accreditation of syllabuses; retrogressive, because it led to the curriculum becoming more 'monolithic, more subject-based and more traditional in its specification' (p. 470); and obsolescent, because of its increasing irrelevance to the changing structure of education and training and the needs of the labour market. If Nuttall was correct in his description then, how much more is it true now of a qualification in which the percentage of achievement of an A–C grade in GCSE is regarded as a key performance indicator of school quality? As such, it has served to redefine the old O-level standard once again as a 'pass', in defiance of the formal GCSE grading scheme. Also, the possibility for coursework has been substantially reduced and the individual subject syllabuses must be approved centrally by the Qualifications and Curriculum Authority (QCA).

Another significant strand of examination reform since the 1960s has been the search for an appropriate form of certification of students' achievement post-16. As the numbers staying on at school have steadily increased, so the problem of finding an alternative qualification to the academic A-level examination, designed to accredit only the top 20 to 30 per cent of the age group, has become increasingly pressing. Initial ideas in the early 1970s included 'Qualifying' and 'Further' examinations and, later, 'N' and 'F' levels, both approaches based on a modular sixth-form course of major and minor subjects. These initiatives succumbed to the combined pressure of the universities and the GCE examination boards, who resisted what they saw as the prospect of academic standards, and indeed their own influence over them, being eroded.

In 1976, the Schools Council tried again, this time recommending the establishment of the Certificate of Extended Education (CEE) – a new, one-year, five-subject course – followed, in 1977, by proposals for an Intermediate or 'I' level, equivalent to about half an A-level course. Although the latter idea was eventually to be incorporated within the Advanced Supplementary (AS) examination finally launched in 1984, it was the Certificate of Pre-Vocational Education (CPVE) which arguably broke the deadlock on providing a real alternative for the non-traditional sixth-former. To be run by a consortium of further education, GCE and CSE examining boards as well as local authority associations, the CPVE was intended to provide a means of linking the great variety of courses on offer in schools and colleges. Rapidly becoming the preserve of the further education examining boards, the Business and Technical Education Council and the City and Guilds examining boards, the CPVE pioneered many new examining approaches. It was a unitary qualification with a strong element of profile assessment in relation to specified targets and work experience. Perhaps even more significant was the emphasis on collaborative pedagogies and negotiated curricula, in which students were regarded much more as responsible, active learners than would typically be the case in more conventional courses. Many of these approaches were incorporated in the next initiative in relation to this agenda, GNVQ – which, unlike its predecessors, has so far stood the test of time.

In May 1991, the British government published *Education and Training in the 21st Century*. This document stressed the need for parity of esteem between academic and vocational routes and initiated the GNVQ, which would be the vehicle for more general qualifications linking vocational and academic courses and in which the recording of 'core skills' would be a central feature. This so-called 'third route to excellence' (GNVQ) was launched on a pilot basis in Autumn 1992 with Level 3 GNVQs ('advanced') intended to be on a par with two A levels, and GNVQ Level 2 ('interme-

diate') equal to four GCSEs. Subsequently, Part 1 GNVQs w
pre-GCSE standard. Each course is inclusive of a core of cor
some optional elements, like the CPVE which preceded it durin

When it was first launched, GNVQ represented a radic
approaches to curriculum, pedagogy and assessment in t'
qualification. The emphasis was on a detailed specification ᴏₗ
criteria' students needed to be able to meet, notably in terms oₗ
included investigation and evaluation. Students and teachers were left to deciᴜ
themselves what and how to study to meet these goals. As with RoAs, the emphasis
was on empowering students, many of whom had not been particularly successful
on more conventional courses, with the skills and confidence to take responsibility
for their own learning.

But despite the clear indication from the rapid growth in the number of students
taking GNVQs that this approach was attractive to them, other evidence documented significant problems of reliability in the assessment procedures being used.
The result, as Stobart (1999: 10) describes, is that:

> In less than ten years, GNVQ has moved from a qualification based on a
> pass/fail criterion-referenced model to one which will use the same five grade
> scale as GCE, have examiner-marked tests which are graded and use externally
> set and marked key skills assignments.

Once more, the power of the policy assumptions underpinning the emphasis on
'performativity' has triumphed over the less familiar discourse of 'empowerment'.
There are many more examples that could be cited to illustrate the contemporary
triumph of this particular policy trajectory. The requirement in a range of professional settings, such as teacher training and nursing, for accreditation to be based on
assessment against standardised and explicit criteria of competence which have
been centrally derived and imposed, is one such. The uneasy co-existence of such
'performative' approaches side by side with more 'emancipatory' practices, such as
the production of reflective journals and portfolios, provides another, perhaps even
more pointed example of the tensions between these two assessment traditions. It is
not surprising that a range of studies suggests that the resultant outcome for the
individual in terms of liberation or control is far from predictable (Taylor 1998;
Lawson and Harrison 1999).

Assessment policy in the late twentieth century: a critique

The assumptions that inform current assessment policy in this country, especially
the intense emphasis on performativity, have proved remarkably resistant to criticism. They are rooted in the earliest history of publicly provided education in
England and Wales and the need to find a means of controlling and legitimating
the form of its provision in the context of deeply entrenched social divisions (Archer
1979; Broadfoot 1996).

Despite sustained, and at times impassioned, debates about either the technical

ions of testing or its harmful impact on both pupils and the curriculum over
y years, such concerns have been but glancing blows. There does not appear to
ve been, as yet, any effective challenge to this hegemony. Indeed, the apparently
inexorable advance of 'performative' assessment into every aspect of educational
activity looks set to continue. As Berlak (2000: 2) argues, referring to both the US
and the UK:

> Although there is an increasing body of sceptical and critical professional and
> public opinion, there are no signs that the rush of governments to impose more
> testing and ranking of students, educational institutions and teachers is dimin-
> ishing. Indeed the inclination of elected officials is toward more public
> accountability, which in the US and the UK translates to greater use of mass
> administered, high stakes testing and rankings.

A fundamentally modernist creation, educational assessment in its traditional guise
can be seen as the archetypal representation of the Enlightenment project to discipline
an irrational social world in order that rationality and efficiency could prevail. The
engine that drove its rapid development was the aspiration that merit and competence
should define access to power and privilege; that investment in education could be
tailored to identified potential; that value for money could be convincingly demonstrated. All these were worthy aspirations, and they remain the dominant agenda of
examinations and test agencies around the world, even today continuing what is often
an heroic struggle to provide equitable and defensible accreditation and selection
mechanisms; to hold back the tide of corruption and nepotism that threatens to engulf
the whole enterprise (Greaney and Kellaghan 1998).

But if the explanation for the remarkable persistence of assessment could be
located solely in the search for equity and efficiency, it is doubtful that it would have
been as resistant to criticism as it has proved to be. For, since the earliest days of
public examinations and intelligence tests in the nineteenth century, there has been
a growing body of evidence that testifies to the serious shortcomings of these assessment devices in achieving their intended ends. There is now copious evidence to
attest to the fact that standards of 'quality' cannot be objectively measured (Satterly
1994; Filer 2000) and that assessment is not, and can never be, a 'neutral'
measuring device (Broadfoot 1996).

Those who have responsibility for designing and administering tests are well
aware of their unavoidable limitations, which are rooted in the fact that, in all its
stages, the assessment process is a social one; that no matter how technically sophisticated the techniques employed, it is human beings who design the test, human
beings who take it and human beings who use the results (Goldstein and Cresswell
1996; Carlton 1999). Whether the context is a primary school classroom (Torrance
and Pryor 1998) or a university course (James 2000), there are a significant number
of studies that make it clear how powerfully an individual's performance is likely to
be influenced by a host of personal and social factors, such as their understanding
of what is required, their motivation to perform, their confidence in a successful
outcome, their gender, their culture, their home background and even their physical
state (Filer 2000).

By the same token, the measurement of institutional quality is an equally social phenomenon. The ability of an institution to present itself effectively, 'to tell a good story' for Ofsted, for the university 'Research Assessment Exercise' (RAE) or for Teaching Quality Assessment (TQA), is now widely accepted as an important contribution to the subsequent grading. Not only the production of institutional assessments but also the way in which they are used cannot be regarded as objective. League tables, for example, are constructed in different ways according to the perceived interests at hand. Maw (1998, 1999) has shown how Ofsted reports are constructed to convey particular messages and do important ideological work.

There is equally little evidence to support the other assumptions listed: that it is desirable to assess institutional quality in relation to externally defined 'performance indicators', that the punitive use of league tables and other publicly shaming devices will help to drive up standards. Aldrich (1998), for example, describes the rapid disillusion with the 'Payment by Results' system for elementary schools that set in when it was recognised that the very substantial cost of the system – over £1 million – had done little to enhance standards of basic literacy and numeracy, and a great deal to limit the vision of education down to narrow coaching in test-taking skills rather than being a liberating force. Likewise, in the USA Madaus (2000) has documented the development of a technology of testing which expediency rapidly elevated to a position of influence that could only have been politically inspired, since it has signally failed either to achieve higher standards or to change teachers'' practice (see Firestone *et al.* 2000).

Similarly, there is little evidence to support the belief that 'standards' have risen as a result of the recent intense emphasis on assessment in this country. The fact that scores on intelligence tests and public examinations have risen steadily over the years can have many possible explanations (Neisser 1996). To the extent that they are the results of effort put into 'getting the scores up' or 'teaching the test', they may indeed have been achieved at the price of more genuine but less measurable learning. International comparisons suggest that, with regard to academic achievement, both the USA and the UK do about as well or as badly as they did in the 1980s (Berlak 2000).

But if there appears to be little evidence to sustain the positive benefits of the underpinning policy assumptions of performativity, there is other evidence that points to some significant negative effects. In both the USA and the UK, for example, educational inequalities are widening (Kozol 1992; Wilby 1997). As Edwards (1998: 144) makes clear, the 'hierarchies of income, power and advantage in Britain, as elsewhere, are matters of fact not of opinion, however often they are denied'. Given this, how can the commitment to performativity during this period be explained?

'Living in a time-warp': explaining assessment policy

Foucault, (1977) suggests that the advent of the examination was associated with a qualitatively new form of control, in which the relatively anonymous individual of traditional society becomes subject to 'hierarchical observation' and 'normalising judgement'. As Hoskin (1979: 137) argues:

> Written performance and written records ... make it possible to generate a 'history' of each student and also to classify students en masse into categories ... This new form of power locates each of us in a place in society. Because it is a technique of knowledge, we overlook the fact that it is simultaneously a technique of power.

But, as Madaus (2000: 7) points out, 'it is the coupling of the device and its outcomes with important rewards or sanctions which give those who control the testing technology real power over the action of others'. Crucial to this latter point is Madaus' argument that technologies are not neutral but, he argues, citing Winner (1986: 19), they can be 'judged not only for their contributions to efficiency and productivity and their positive and negative environmental side effects, but also for the ways they can embody specific forms of power and authority'. Or, as Power (1997: 213) describes it, referring specifically to auditing, it

> is not a neutral process. It imposes its own values on the activities that it regulates, and this means that the process can have unintended and indeed dysfunctional consequences – the efficiency and effectiveness of the organisation is not so much verified as constructed around the audit process.

The advent of formal educational assessment was thus associated with the moment when the sciences of man became possible. The subsequent powerful development of the discipline of psychology in particular became the foundation for psychometrics, and hence the discourse that is now the source of the worldwide domination of educational assessment. As such, as Foucault suggested, it is an instrument of power. However, the significance of this power is not that it is exercised by a particular group to the detriment of another. Nor, in his terms, can it be conceived as emanating from any particular point such as 'the state'. Hill (1981: 7) articulates this as follows:

> Political power, from this perspective, is not the possession of a social class, but a proliferating, anonymous force which cannot be attributed to the ideological self-expression of a unified economic group ... disseminated through many and varied discourses and institutions, power possesses no single determining centre and cannot be identified with a monolithic state apparatus which it largely outstrips ... his [Foucault's] work invites a radical rethinking of such notions as the neutrality of scientific truth.

As Popkewitz (1996: 47) suggests, 'While the production is never totally coercive, the production of knowledge positions and produces power through the regulatory principles applied as "reason" and "truth".'

With regard to education policy, therefore, the situation we find ourselves in today is, in these terms, the result of a language whose very familiarity has the power to constrain the way problems are defined and to render alternatives almost literally inconceivable. We are in a 'catch-22' situation, since:

Our errors are so entrenched in our tradition that it is not possible for us entirely to escape from them. For example, if you wish to criticize the Western idea of reason your criticisms will take no force unless they take the form of rational arguments … which therefore will have the effect of confirming it rather than undermining it. So you cannot win. You fight the enemy only with the weapons of his choice, and by your use of them you acknowledge that he has won because you have conceded his right to define the rules.

(Cupitt 1987: 6)

The assumptions that appear to underpin current UK government assessment policy, which I identified at the beginning of this chapter, are now revealed as the products of a particular assessment discourse which is rooted in modernist notions of science, as these were translated during the nineteenth century into the powerful development of psychometrics. However, in itself this does not explain the particular configuration of education policy emphases at the present time, either in England in particular or internationally. This requires, rather, the unravelling of a range of different factors, in this case, as Callaghan's Ruskin College speech so clearly demonstrated, a politically motivated desire to exercise hitherto covert central government powers, as well as the enactment of fundamentally new powers of control in response to apparent public concern over standards, the threat of international economic competition and an increasing preoccupation with managerialism.

Moreover, as the scale of assessment activity within our education system increases, so different groups within the education system seek to accommodate to the new requirements being placed on them through a variety of mediations based on their own values and understandings, with regard to the goals of education and how these may best be achieved. Gradually, this changes the discourse through which the ideology and practice of education is expressed. We have seen a good example of this in English primary schools during the last decade, as teachers' initial intense hostility to national testing has gradually evolved into a resigned acceptance, or even the complete professional integration of testing and associated practices of target-setting as part of their professional language (Osborn *et al.* 2000). To the extent that this is so, the domination of the discourse of 'performativity' is daily reinforced. This is evidenced by a *Times Educational Supplement* (*TES*) report on 'The buzz words of 1998'. They report that the word 'standards' was mentioned 2,272 times – nearly twice as many mentions as the nearest competitor, which was 'reading'. 'Standards' was mentioned in almost a quarter of *TES* articles in that year. Other frequently mentioned terms were: 'achievement' (826 mentions), 'assessment' (782 mentions), 'choice' (709 mentions) and 'inspection' (627 mentions). As Davies and Edwards (1999: 262) so succinctly put it, 'Under New Labour "standards" has replaced "curriculum" as the discursive hub of educational policy-making.'

Conclusion

By contrast to the discourse described above, there is now a very considerable body of research evidence that documents how assessment can best promote learning

(Black and Wiliam 1998). It centres on the harnessing of individual ownership of learning, the engagement of both mind and emotions, on the pupil as 'sense maker' and the effective support of the teacher as 'cognitive guide' (Roelofs and Terwel 1999). A growing body of research literature underlines the crucial importance of the development of appropriate learning dispositions and attitudes, emotions and attributions, to subsequent lifelong success as a learner (Claxton 1999). The significance of 'emotional intelligence' (Goleman 1995) which incorporates personal and social as well as intellectual skills, is also increasingly being recognised.

As I have argued elsewhere, (Broadfoot 2000), the conventional technologies of testing cannot recognise the possession of these attributes. Nor do they typically encourage their development. On the contrary, there is considerable evidence that both conventionally successful and unsuccessful learners alike have been more or less damaged by their experiences of assessment:

> The combined effect of recent policy changes in assessment has been to reinforce traditionalist conceptions of teaching and learning which are associated with a greater instrumentalism on the part of pupils. From this it can be argued that rather than acquiring life-long learning skills and attitudes, the effect of recent reforms has been to make pupils more dependent on the teacher and less ready and able to engage in 'deep' learning.
>
> (Broadfoot and Pollard 2000: 23)

This chapter has sought to show that educational assessment needs to be seen as a social as much as a scientific activity, and hence one that is deeply imbued with the bias and subjectivity inherent in any human interaction. The question remains, however, how to demonstrate that 'the emperor has no clothes'; how to break out from the pervasive influence of the discourse that informs our contemporary culture, and hence, our educational thinking. Before the education system becomes even more fatally infected with the contagion of 'performativity' and its symptoms of pervasive judgement and comparison, there is a pressing need to articulate the evidence from research – indeed, even from common sense – of the limitations of educational assessment. There is an urgent need to demonstrate, from research evidence and from the personal experiences that almost every individual possesses, that assessment is a 'social process' which affects, intimately and often for ever, the quality of an individual's capacity to learn. By the same token, there is a pressing need for a more socio-cultural understanding of assessment as a 'social product', in which the values and traditions of particular cultures and the interests of specific groups within them combine to produce particular definitions of quality or merit, as well as different policy emphases.

It is both chilling and ironic to consider that, at the beginning of the twenty-first century, we have an assessment structure – endorsed by a New Labour government supposedly committed to undermining disadvantage and to promoting a more just society – that reinforces existing social divisions and causes a great deal of unnecessary pain for both individuals and institutions. It is an assessment system that is of doubtful validity as a representation of what individuals can do and that inhibits the effective learning of many. Above all, it is essentially ineffective in preparing individuals to meet the challenges of tomorrow. It underpins assumptions about curriculum and pedagogy that are rooted in an outmoded vision of what students need to be able to do, and it clouds our collective capacity to work towards an education that embraces processes and relationships as well as knowledge and skills.

References

Alberge, D. (1999) 'Author brings "stifling" school systems to book', *The Times*, 15 July.

Aldrich, R. (1998) 'Educational standards in historical perspective', British Academy Seminar on Educational Standards, 9 October.

Archer, M. (1979) *Social Origins of Educational Systems*, London: Sage.

Berlak, H. (2000) 'Cultural politics, the science of assessment and democratic renewal of public education', in A. Filer (ed.) *Assessment, Social Practice and Social Product*, London: Falmer.

Black, P. and Wiliam, D. (1998) 'Assessment and classroom learning', *Assessment in Education*, 5(1): 7–74.

Broadfoot, P. (1983) 'Assessment constraints on curriculum practice: a comparative study', in M. Hammersley and A. Hargreaves (eds) *Curriculum Practice: Some Sociological Case Studies*, Lewes: Falmer.

——(1996) *Education, Assessment and Society*, Buckingham: Open University Press.

——(2000) 'Culture, learning and comparison: Lawrence Stenhouse's views of education for empowerment', *British Education Research Journal* (in press).

Broadfoot P. and Pollard, A. (2000) 'The changing discourse of assessment policy: the case of English primary education' in A. Filer (ed.) *Assessment, Social Practice and Social Product*, London: Falmer.

Broadfoot, P., Grant, M., James, M., Nuttall, D. and Stierer, B. (1991) *Records of Achievement: Report of the Extension Work in Pilot Schemes*, London: HMSO.

Butterfield, S. (1995) *Educational Objectives and National Assessment*, Buckingham: Open University Press.

Carlton, S. (1999) 'Issues in equality of opportunity in testing', International Association for Educational Assessment Conference, Bled, Slovenia, 23–8 May.

Claxton, G. (1999) *Wise Up: The Challenges of Life-Long Learning*, Basingstoke: Picador.

Cresswell, M. (1998) 'The problem of standards', paper given to British Academy Seminar on Educational Standards, 9 October.

Cupitt, D. (1987) *The Long-Legged Fly*, London: SCM.

Davies, M. and Edwards, G. (1999) 'Will the curriculum caterpillar ever learn to fly?', *Cambridge Journal of Education*, 29(2): 265–77.

Dearing, R. (1996) *Review of 16–19 Qualifications: Summary Report*, London: School Curriculum and Assessment Authority.

DES (1978) *Secondary School Examinations: A Single System at 16+*, White Paper, London: HMSO.

——1979) *Aspects of Secondary Education in England: A Survey by HM Inspectors of Schools*, London: HMSO.

DES/Welsh Office (1984) *Records of Achievement: A Statement of Policy*, London: HMSO.

——(1989) *Records of Achievement: Report of the National Steering Committee*, London: HMSO.

——(1990) *Records of Achievement*, Circular 8/90, London: HMSO.

——(1991) *Education and Training for the 21st Century*, London: HMSO.

DfEE (1997) *Review, Recording Achievement and Action Planning in Schools*, London: DfEE.

Edwards, T. (1998). 'A daunting enterprise', *British Journal of Sociology of Education*, 19(1): 143–7.

Filer, A. (ed.) (2000) *Assessment, Social Practice and Social Product*, London: Falmer.

Firestone, W., Fitz, J. and Broadfoot, P. (2000) 'Power, learning and legitimation: assessment implementation across levels in the US and the UK', *American Educational Research Journal* (in press).

Foucault, M. (1977) *Discipline and Punish*, London: Allen Lane.

Goldstein, H. and Cresswell, M. (1996) 'The comparability of different subjects in public examinations: a theoretical and practical critique', *Oxford Review of Education*, 22(4): 435–43.

Goleman, D. (1995) *Emotional Intelligence: Why It Can Matter More than IQ*, London: Bloomsbury.

Greaney, V. and Kellaghan, T. (1998) 'Cheating in examinations', IAEA Conference, Barbados, 10–15 May.

Haney, W.M., Madaus, G.F. and Lyons, R. (1993) *The Fractured Marketplace for Standardized Testing*, Boston: Kluwer.

Hill, L. (1981) 'Shades of the prison house', *Times Higher Education Supplement*, 2 January.

Hodgson, E.A. (1997) 'The National Record of Achievement: another initiative or a useful tool for the future?', unpublished Ph.D. thesis, Institute of Education, University of London.

Hoskin, K. (1979) 'The examination, disciplinary powers and rational schooling', *History of Education*, 8(2): 135–46.

James, D. (2000) 'Making the graduate: perspectives on student experience of assessment in higher education', in A. Filer (ed.) *Assessment, Social Practice and Social Product*, London: Falmer.

Kozol, J. (1992) *Savage Inequalities: Children in America's Schools*, New York: HarperCollins.

Lawson, T. and Harrison, J. (1999) 'Individual action planning in initial teacher training: empowerment or discipline?' *British Journal of Sociology of Education*, 20(1): 89–105.

Lyotard, J. (1984) *The Post-Modern Condition*, Manchester: Manchester University Press.

Maclure, S. (1998) 'Through the revolution and out the other side', *Oxford Review of Education*, 24(1): 5–24.

Madaus, G. (2000) 'Testing technology: the need for oversight', in A. Filer (ed.) *Assessment, Social Practice and Social Product*, London: Falmer.

Maw, J. (1998) 'An inspector speaks: the annual report of Her Majesty's Chief Inspector of Schools', *The Curriculum Journal*, 9(2): 145–53.

——(1999) 'League-tables and the press – value added?' *The Curriculum Journal*, 10(1): 3–11.

Neisser, U. (1996) 'Intelligence: knowns and unknowns', *American Psychologist*, 51(2): 77–101.

Nuttall, D. (1979) 'A review of accountability in the era of examinations', in T. Becher and S. Maclure (eds) *The Politics of Curriculum Change*, London: Hutchinson.

——(1984) 'Doomsday or a new dawn? The prospects for a common system of examining at 16+', in P. Broadfoot (ed.) *Selection, Certification and Control*, London: Falmer.

Osborn, M., McNess, E. and Broadfoot, P., with Pollard, A. and Triggs, P. (2000) *Polity, Practice and Teacher Experience: Changing English Primary Education*, London: Cassell.

Pollard, A., Broadfoot, P., Croll, P., Osborn, M. and Abbott, D. (1994) *Changing English Primary Schools*, London: Cassell.

Popkewitz, T.K. (1996) 'Rethinking decentralization and state/civil society distinctions: the state as a problematic of governing', *Journal of Education Policy*, 11(1): 27–53.

Power, M. (1997) 'The audit society: rituals of verification', *Quality in Higher Education*, 1: 211–22.

Roelofs, E. and Terwel, J. (1999) 'Constructivism and authentic pedagogy; state of the art and recent developments in the Dutch national curriculum in secondary education,' *Journal of Curriculum Studies*, 31(2): 201–27.

Sadler, R. (1987) 'Specifying and promulgating achievement standards', *Oxford Review of Education*, 13(2): 191–209.

Satterly, D. (1994) 'External assessment', in W. Harlen (ed.) *Enhancing Quality in Assessment*, London: Paul Chapman.

Stobart, G. (1999) 'Merging academic and vocational qualifications in England: two steps forward and one step back?' International Association for Educational Assessment, Bled, Slovenia, 23–8 May.

Taylor, A. (1998) 'Employability skills: from corporate "wish list" to government policy', *Journal of Curriculum Studies*, 30(2): 143–64.

Torrance, H. and Pryor, J. (1998) *Investigating: Teaching, Learning and Assessment in the Classroom*, Buckingham: Open University Press.

Whetton, C. (1999) 'Attempting to find the true cost of assessment systems', International Association for Educational Assessment, Bled, Slovenia, 23–8 May.

Wilby, P. (1997) 'Stopping the clocks on inequality will not stem it', *Times Educational Supplement*, 28 November.

Winner, L. (1986) *The Whale and the Reactor: A Search for Limits in an Age of High Technology*, Chicago: University of Chicago Press.

11 Standards, achievement and educational performance

A cause for celebration?

Peter Tymms and Carol Fitz-Gibbon

Introduction

This chapter considers one of the most important and controversial issues relating to the period 1976–2001, namely the question of educational standards in primary and secondary schools in England and Wales. It begins by exploring the inter-relationship between educational reform and the drive for higher educational standards. Using a number of sources of data, it analyses standards in both primary and secondary schools during the period. The chapter not only attempts to make some tentative judgements about whether educational standards can be said to have risen or fallen during the period, but also raises issues about the ways in which performance is measured in England and Wales.

Politics, standards and the imperative of reform

As the other chapters in this volume amply demonstrate, the last twenty-five years have seen remarkable changes in education in England and Wales. The period has seen the introduction of a statutory curriculum, as well as fundamental changes to the ways in which schools are organised, managed and controlled. As Broadfoot has shown in her chapter, the last fifteen or so of those years have witnessed increasing attempts to monitor and control state schools through statutory assessments. The major reason for the statutory changes was a political supposition – initiated first by the authors of the Black Papers and continued by Callaghan at Ruskin in 1976 – that all was not well in schools and that, in particular, educational standards were low and falling.

It could be argued, therefore, that the essential driving force for many of the reforms during this period was putatively a drive for standards (Shorrocks-Taylor 1999). A fairly simple hypothesis guided the drive for reform: economic success would be enhanced by increasing the levels of skills and qualifications that are needed to compete in a changing world; secondary schools should deliver these skills and qualifications; pupils in primary schools would have to reach certain levels in the basics to benefit from secondary education. Therefore, priority had to be given to the basics in primary schools (Blunkett 1997).

Until just over a decade ago, the main external assessments were Advanced level (A level) examinations, designed originally to select pupils for university, and

Ordinary level (O level), to which the Certificate of Secondary Education (CSE) had been added for the less able pupils. However, the fact that there was a dual system for pupils at the age of 16 was increasingly seen as a problem, and from 1988 onwards the CSE and O-level examinations were replaced by a single system, the General Certificate of Secondary Education (GCSE) in 1988. Both A levels and GCSEs were 'high stakes' in the sense of controlling access to employment and further and higher education, yet as a means of monitoring standards in particular schools and in the nation as a whole they were of limited value. Moreover, although there were clear views about what constituted 'good' schools in particular areas, there were no league tables and LEAs did not monitor the results by school.

In 1987, the Conservative government therefore initiated the extension of formal assessment to all pupils of ages 7, 11, 14 and 16. In order to facilitate the change, Kenneth Baker, the then Secretary of State for Education, established the Task Group on Assessment and Testing (TGAT). Its task was to devise a series of statutory assessments that would operate at the ends of what have now become known as Key Stages 1, 2 and 3; the final Key Stage of compulsory education – Key Stage 4 (KS4) – coincides with the end of GCSE. The Education Reform Act of 1988, which introduced the National Curriculum, ensured that these new assessments were phased in and started to work their way through the system in parallel with the new curriculum. The assessments took a while to become stabilised, as the pure criterion referenced approach proved to be unworkable and as some of the pupil tasks similarly failed to live up to expectations. But these Key Stage tests have now become part of the established education scene in England and Wales. A further addition to statutory assessment is the 'baseline assessment' of pupils on entry to school, which was introduced in 1999.

As a result of these changes, there is now in place a system of national testing of children's achievement throughout the school system, and the results are starting to generate an extensive longitudinal database. These data can now be added to findings from a series of earlier surveys of educational attainment. The National Foundation for Educational Research (NFER), for example, conducted repeated surveys of reading, and some of this work goes back to 1948 (Brooks *et al.* 1995). The Assessment of Performance Unit (APU), which was created in 1976, also contributed to the monitoring of standards from 1977 until it was terminated in 1990, when the National Curriculum was introduced. And our own Curriculum Evaluation and Management (CEM) Centre has specialised in providing, directly to schools, measures of the relative progress of each student ('value added') along with a wide range of other indicators of the behavioural and attitudinal outcomes of schooling (www.cem.dur.ac.uk; Fitz-Gibbon 1996; Tymms 1999).

There is, therefore, very extensive data now available on children's educational achievement throughout their school careers. Given the importance attached by successive governments during this period to the nation's educational standards, it seems reasonable at this point to pose the question of how pupils' performance has changed. Following the very extensive programme of educational reform described throughout the rest of this volume, to what extent have educational standards risen?

As we will see, a first glance at the evidence does seem to confirm that standards have risen in recent years and, indeed, in some instances the rise has been truly impressive. So should such a rise be a cause for celebration? Given the new forms of assessment that have been introduced, can we be confident that standards are indeed rising? Assessing standards over time is never easy and, as we will demonstrate below, a more careful review of the monitoring procedures that have been established inexorably leads us to the conclusion that, despite the assessment reforms, it remains extremely difficult to measure changes in national standards with complete confidence. We therefore conclude our chapter with some suggestions for the future.

National Curriculum data in primary schools

Official data are available from 1995 onwards for the end of Key Stage 2 (KS2) assessments in mathematics, English and science. We shall concentrate on the percentage of pupils attaining a 'Level 4' or above. The data are summarised in Figure 11.1. This shows that in English the results have risen fairly steadily from 1995, when 48 per cent of children gained a Level 4 or above, up to 1999, when 70 per cent of children gained the same result. The rise seemed to be levelling off in 1998, but a sudden rise was observed the following year. The overall change is impressive and has largely been paralleled by the results of the two other core subjects – mathematics and science.

The science results started in 1995 with a surprisingly high 70 per cent of

Figure 11.1   End of primary, percentage achieving Level 4 and over

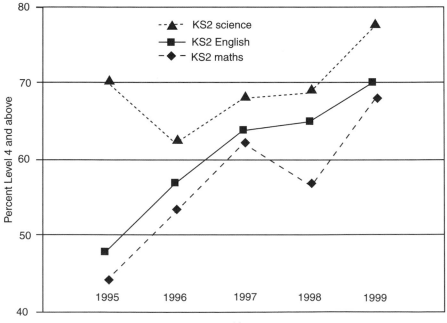

children gaining a Level 4 or above, but this dropped to 62 per cent the following year. The drop brought the severity of science grading more into line with English and mathematics. One can speculate that the Schools Curriculum and Assessment Authority (SCAA), the body responsible for overseeing the tests at the time, decided that science was somewhat out of line with the other two subjects, and an effort was made to pull the three into line with one another in 1996. Careful analysis of the data (Tymms 1996) showed that the three subjects were more or less aligned for more able pupils in 1995. In other words, there was little tendency for the more able pupils to get higher or lower grades in science, mathematics or English. But for the less able, higher levels were much easier to gain in science than in mathematics and English. Mathematics performance started at a very low level in 1995 (44 per cent), lower than either English or science, and this improved quite dramatically, up to 54 per cent in 1997, only to drop in 1998, possibly because a new mental arithmetic test had been introduced. Then, along with the two other subjects, it experienced a significant boost in 1999.

The data shown in Figure 11.1 raise many issues. Most of these will be discussed later in the chapter when comparative data from a variety of sources have been presented. However, a single point is emphasised here: there are difficulties associated with the use of percentages when reporting schools results and this is compounded when monitoring standards. The percentage of children who achieved a Level 4 or above tells us nothing about the children at the bottom end or top end of the distribution, and there has for some years been talk of a long 'tail' in reading (see, for example, Brooks 1998: 6). (The term 'tail' refers here to the group of individuals with low scores on a test, and comes from a consideration of distribution curves.)

How significant are these apparent achievements? In order to assess the magnitude of changes, various other sources of primary school data have to be brought together, which have been converted to a scale in which the mean is 100 and the standard deviation is 15. This allows the reading specialist to pass judgement using a familiar metric and also allows researchers to make assessments about the magnitude of the changes by comparing the changes with the results from carefully evaluated interventions (Cohen 1977). Table 11.1 sets out the metrics.

Figure 11.2 shows the results from a series of longitudinal studies for the reading scores of 11-year-olds. The chart includes data for the KS2 English assessment, which, of course, is not simply a test of reading, since it includes writing and spelling. The KS2 data are the same as those shown in Figure 11.1, but they have been converted to standardised scores by taking the 1995 results as being equivalent

Table 11.1 Changes from a score of 100

New reading score	Characterisation in well-controlled experiments
100	No change
103	Small change
106	Modest change
112	Large change

to 100. As expected, the KS2 results show a steady and impressive rise, amounting to a 9-point rise over four years. Table 11.1 suggests that this might be characterised as something between 'modest' and 'large', but that would be for well-controlled research-based interventions. For a national change, 9 must be regarded as very large indeed.

By far the most comprehensive data set relating to standards over time comes from the USA and gives a valuable backdrop against which the English data can be seen. It comes from the National Assessment of Education Progress (NAEP) which aims to monitor standards 'by administering materials and replicating procedures from assessment to assessment' (Campbell *et al.* 1996: 1). Over two decades there is little evidence of even modest changes in standards. The 1996 average reading scores are imperceptibly different from the scores on the same tests in 1975. Detailed investigations of the data do show some interesting changes for minority groups, but constancy is the dominant feature.

The research of Brooks *et al.* (1995: 1), using English data, demonstrates a similar finding: they comment that 'reading standards among 10/11- and 15/16-year-olds have changed little since 1945 apart from slight rises around 1950 and in the early 1980s'. The Assessment of Performance Unit (APU) surveys of reading in 1978, 1983 and 1988 confirm the picture. There appears to have been a slight rise

Figure 11.2   Reading trends

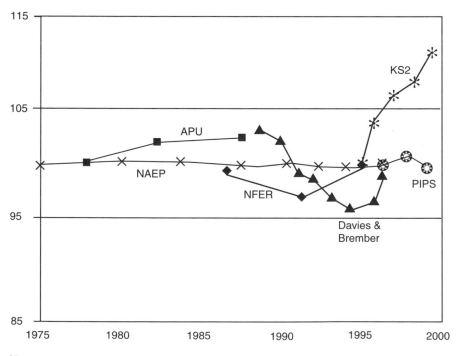

Note
The NAEP data presented here are an average of data for 9- and 13-year-olds.

in 1983, but again the impression is one of stability. An NFER study between 1987 and 1995 suggested stability with a slight dip in 1991.

The ongoing study by Davies and Brember (1997, 1998) involves testing all Year 6 pupils in the same six randomly chosen schools within one LEA, year on year, using the same test materials. Their data show a fall between the start of the study in 1989 and 1994, followed by a rise for the next two years. These data show the largest fluctuations of the surveys, perhaps because they used the smallest samples. Nevertheless, the data do not jump around erratically over the years. Detailed investigations prompted Davies and Brember (1997: 620) to comment that 'the considerable cost of implementing the National Curriculum and assessment arrangements has not appeared to result in either raising standards or producing an effective system for monitoring reading standards throughout England and Wales'.

The final set of independent data over three years is available from the Performance Indicators in Primary Schools (PIPS) project (Tymms 1999). The project includes a half-hour reading test, and data are available from the same 155 schools, collected at the same time of year, every year, for three years. The samples involved more than 7,000 pupils each year. The results are remarkably stable and cover a period when the Key Stage results were steadily rising.

Assessing the changes in primary schools

We have, then, a considerable amount of information. Some of this information is contradictory and the challenge is to make sense of it and to make a judgement about whether standards have increased over the period as a whole. In particular, we need to assess whether the changes that have been seen in the national assessment results at the end of primary school over the last four years represent real changes in pupils' achievements. It might be that the changes shown in Figure 11.1 should be taken at face value, but on the basis of the other data presented so far there are a number of reasons to suppose that they do not tell the whole story. In particular, there are three specifics that suggest other interpretations.

First, the 1996 drop in the percentage of pupils gaining a Level 4 or above in science could be perceived to be an attempt to bring the severity of science grading into line with mathematics and English. Second, the small drop in mathematics between 1997 and 1998 could perhaps also be explained by the introduction of a mental arithmetic test. Third, it seems reasonable to suppose that the schools were becoming used to the new testing system and beginning to coach their pupils to prepare them for the end-of-Key-Stage primary tests. This might be called 'teaching to the test'. If schools were working independently on the curriculum and were not looking at the tests, then the changes, if they can be accepted at face value, would represent a remarkable rise. If, on the other hand, the teachers were very concerned about the results and were teaching exam techniques, then what we might see is a capacity to pass tests rather than an indication of pupils being better at English, science or mathematics. This third point highlights the problems associated with the accountability/assessment system currently in existence in England and Wales.

The changes seen between 1995 and 1999 are so dramatic and so out of step with the other longitudinal data as to raise questions about their being true representations of changes in standards. The cynical view is that the Qualifications and Curriculum Authority (QCA, formerly SCAA) are quietly adjusting the cut-off marks in order to make sure that the government targets are met. We are not at all inclined to take that position; it does seem as though QCA attempt to do an honest job. We can say this with some confidence having worked with SCAA/QCA and also having read Rose *et al.* (1999).

The present English and Welsh systems of monitoring of standards over time are complicated and require that new tests be produced each year. If this were not done then some teachers would inevitably teach the items known to be on the test. In the kind of official accountability system being run for primary schools, it is not advisable to use the same tests year on year. When a new test is produced, every effort must be made to ensure equivalent standards are maintained.

How is this done? The English and Welsh approach is well documented (Quinlan and Scharaschkin 1999), with four procedures being used. First, the same anchor test is employed each year against which the results of the new test are checked. Second, a sample of pupils who are about to take, or have just taken, the real test from one year are given next year's test (the 'second pre-testing') so that equivalent scores can be estimated. Third, expert judgements are made of the scripts. Fourth, expert judgements are made of the questions by employing the Angoff procedure (Angoff 1971).

Judgements about the cut-off scores, which are used to define the levels, are apparently made using all four sets of information. A retrospective account of the way that the process worked in 1999 is given in Rose *et al.* (1999), which raises issues about how marks are assigned, particularly at the borderlines of different levels. Despite these concerns, we can expect the system to be quite good at ensuring comparable standards from one year to the next. Nevertheless, the consistency could never be more accurate than one mark (about 1 to 2 percentage points). On the evidence of the 1999 KS2 decision-making meeting, the variation from year to year might be as much as five marks (between 5 and 10 percentage points). This seems quite high, but it could be argued that an error rate of a few percentage points from year to year is not unreasonable.

However, in a system that always looks at the previous year to standardise the present year's data, there is a problem. There will be a drift in standards, as over several years differences will accumulate. The only guard against this drift is the anchor test, but this may eventually be thought to lose its relevance as curricula evolve and language changes. In any case, it seems that the anchor test is not used to check standards across the years, as one might expect. It is only used to check standards from one year to the next (Quinlan and Scharaschkin 1999: 10).

A random drift may be acceptable, but the real concern is that the drift is not random. There might be a tendency for borderline decisions to be influenced by targets – especially with the data on the consequences of their decisions being explicitly made available at decision-making meetings. There is also a mechanism in the present arrangements that might create a systematic movement towards lower standards (more pupils getting higher levels for the same performance). Rose *et al.* (1999) quite rightly note that the 'second pre-testing', the one on which the marks are based, is 'adrenaline-free' as the pupils know that the test is not the real thing and will not count for anything. This may result in pupils gaining lower marks on the pre-test than they would if the test were 'live'. The same lowering of standards will result from a pre-test taken earlier than the live test – pupils are younger, by the odd month, and less prepared. So when equivalents are created, standards will be lowered. This will apply not just to the statistical procedures employed but also to the script examinations. The effect does not have to be great for an important slipping in standards to be observed – it might simply be the odd mark every year.

Another way in which the standards procedure may not provide the nation with valid information on trends over time arises from the way the marking is carried out. The markers know that primary schools are under increasing pressure to gain Level 4s, and this might have some impact on the results. It seems unlikely that this would have a large effect, since markers might be expected to try to mark as accurately as they can, but it could result in a steady upward trend. Of more significance is the effect of the new proposal of returning scripts to schools. This is an innovative and positive step, which is to be welcomed. However, over the years markers are increasingly likely to find that their judgements are challenged. The challenges are unlikely to be for errors that result in higher marks, and this may mean that an additional mark here and there might be given where before it was not.

We have, then, four mechanisms by which standards at KS2 might have been lowered over the years:

- Decision-making about cut-off marks may be influenced by knowledge of the impact that they will have on published 'high stakes' targets.
- Pre-test results are equated to live results, and yet the pre-test is adrenaline-free and taken earlier than the live test.
- Markers may be looking more kindly on borderline cases as the stakes are raised.
- The return of scripts to schools may increasingly involve challenges and a reaction among markers to give pupils the benefit of the doubt.

If any of these mechanisms are in operation, then one should ask why it is that similar drifting has not been noticed at Key Stage 3 (KS3). The simple answer is that there has been a fairly steady, but slow, drift upwards in mathematics and English, although not in science. Further, the pressure at KS3 has not been as acute as at KS2, and all four mechanisms might not be expected to operate with such bite. Finally, the 'second pre-testing' may not have followed the same timing for the two key stages. It is worth noting at this point that the large gains in 1996 in English and mathematics (Figure 11.1) at KS2 were followed by a very slight drop and a very slight rise respectively by the same cohorts when they reached KS3 in 1999. The simple idea that better results in primary school will be followed by secondary gains has not been borne out.

The kind of monitoring structure that has been put in place nationally, then, driven as it is by accountability, cannot guard against drifting standards. The only way to be sure that consistency is maintained is to employ the same secret questions, administered under the same conditions, to equivalent samples of pupils, on almost the same date over many years. Changes in language and in the curriculum always have to be taken into consideration. But when the data displayed in Figure 11.1 are taken into account, one certainly would not expect the English language to have changed much over five years, and the kinds of reading skills needed for children to access the secondary curriculum have hardly changed. We can reflect at this point that to have had yearly independent representative samples of pupils assessed on the same test at the same time each year would have been invaluable.

Standards over time at ages 16 and 18

For external examinations taken at the ages of 16 and 18, we can apply similar approaches. Do the data sets that are available indicate a possible change in 'standards', and if so how might this have happened? The answers again require careful scrutiny of available data.

Two major features of the data are that enrolments in advanced courses have increased and grades have increased. In 1955 only 13 per cent continued directly into the sixth form or some type of post-16 provision, whereas twenty years later, in 1975, the figure had almost trebled to 38 per cent, and then in the next twenty years it almost doubled to 72 per cent. The proportions of students going into higher education showed similar growth in the same twenty-year periods, from 4 per cent to 14 per cent to 31 per cent in 1955, 1975 and 1995 respectively.

During these substantial increases in the proportions of students continuing in education, the failure rate declined. At A level the failure rate was about 30 per cent in almost all subjects until 1986. This rate was recommended by the then Secondary School Examinations Council, formed by the university-led examination boards. Not only were almost one in three candidates failed in most A-level subjects, but also a further 20 per cent were given an E grade. Thus a D grade was a grade in the top half of the distribution for many years at A level (Fitz-Gibbon 1985: 55; SCAA/Ofsted 1996).

Latin was exempt from the recommended 30 per cent failure rate because it was recognised that the entrants to A-level Latin were an exceptionally able group; to fail 30 per cent would be to set a very high standard indeed for A-level Latin. However, differences in the ranges of ability of candidates choosing other subjects were not taken into account. This resulted in unrecognised differences in difficulty between A-level subjects. For example, in 1988 students taking A-level mathematics were on average awarded a grade that was two grades lower than those obtained by similar students who had opted for A-level English (Fitz-Gibbon 1988). Lack of knowledge of this general national pattern led many headteachers to blame mathematics departments for having lower grades than the English department. Indeed, it was such a situation that led to the development of the A-level Information System (ALIS) in 1983 (see Fitz-Gibbon 1996: chapter 7).

Subsequent research for SCAA/QCA showed that the sciences, mathematics and foreign languages also attracted more able students, as did Latin, but since no adjustments were made to the failure rates, unlike Latin, they were all severely graded compared with most other subjects (Fitz-Gibbon and Vincent 1994). The research study for SCAA used four methods to compare the difficulties of various subjects: comparing the grades achieved by individual students taking the same 'hard' and 'easy' subjects; comparing grades awarded to large samples of students who had the same previous levels of achievement; comparing grades awarded to large samples of students who had the same previous levels on a measure of developed abilities; and using comparisons with the collection of grades each student obtained in all the subjects taken, using the method of 'relative ratings' (Kelly 1976).

It was quite clear from all four methods that A-level grades could not be considered equivalent to each other. Thus, a B grade in one subject might be obtained on average by students who in another subject would average a C grade. This was important, given the growing agenda for judging schools on the basis of examination data, and the situation helped to stimulate interest in the use of 'value added' (i.e. measures of relative progress). If examination results were heavily determined by the difficulty levels of the subjects taken and by the intake to the school, then these factors needed to be taken into account in judging schools.

The data in the Fitz-Gibbon and Vincent (1994) report mentioned above were based on schools that voluntarily participated in the A-level Information System, and it was possible that this voluntary sample was not nationally representative. However, Sir Ron Dearing had the DfEE check the findings using 100 per cent national samples, and the findings were broadly confirmed. For example:

> Replication of the Fitz-Gibbon and Vincent work shows that, broadly speaking, the general pattern of variation across subjects reported by these authors is confirmed by the national data ... in terms of the value-added from GCSE to 'A'-level, boys made greater progress than girls and ... the maximum value-added scores were obtained in the arts subjects. Again, these findings are confirmed by the national data.
>
> (Dearing 1996: 4–5)

The concept of subject 'difficulty' is intimately linked with 'standards'. More students achieving higher grades could be interpreted as the result of better teaching, more effort on the part of students, more use of private tutors, and other such factors that might have led to 'really' improved achievement. But, on the other hand, the grade inflation could be due to easier examinations or easier grading. The former explanation would denote improving standards, and the latter would denote falling standards. The reality might be a mixture of declining difficulties and improved learning.

Are we seeing grade inflation, where an A grade is now 'worth' less than previously? Or are we seeing many more students reaching the original high standards that put the UK in very highly ranked positions in international comparisons in the sciences (Smithers and Robinson 1991)? Have standards fallen or risen?

There is no doubt regarding the fact that more students have been achieving higher grades in recent years, and not only at A level. There have been similar grade changes at GCSE. Indeed, the introduction of an A* grade (higher than an A) in 1994 was clearly symptomatic. Table 11.2 shows the decreases in the percentage of students obtaining low grades and the increases in the percentage of students obtaining high grades between 1988 and 1995, using GCSE candidates of all ages in England, Wales and Northern Ireland. Additional data in the same report showed the percentage achieving five grades of C or better rose from 23 per cent in 1975 to 43 per cent in 1995 (SCAA 1996: figure 6).

The data are not in doubt. The difficulty that faces us lies in the interpretation: distinguishing between declining standards and improved actual achievements. One SCAA report stated that 'No attempt is made within the report to interpret the findings' (SCAA 1996: introduction). Another SCAA report, prepared jointly with Ofsted, investigated three subjects (English, mathematics and chemistry) at GCSE and A level. It noted that many changes had taken place over the years in syllabuses, content, question type, coursework and question structuring, making 'comparing standards over time a complex task' (SCAA/OFSTED 1996: 10). It suggested that Codes of Practice now ensure 'greater consistency of procedures' between examination boards, but conceded:

> It is possible that the emphasis given to awarders' judgement of the quality of candidates' work rather than to statistical data, coupled with a tendency to choose the lower of two scores when there is a decision to be made about setting the minimum mark for a grade, *may have allowed small, unintended but cumulative reductions in grade standards in successive years.*
>
> (ibid.: 15, emphasis added)

This frank admission regarding the process of standard setting lends further credence to the points made about drifting standards earlier in this chapter. The most valuable parts of the SCAA/Ofsted (1996) report are probably the qualitative descriptions of the changing content of the syllabuses. But, given a concern with standards, these are not the topic of interest here. As the report notes: 'Standards of attainment refer to the *demands* of syllabuses' (p. 1, emphasis added). The appropriate statistical treatment is therefore to examine results in the framework of 'demand', this being understood as how easy or difficult it was for students to attain certain grades. Using this statistical monitoring approach, the aim is to make fair comparisons, whether these be from subject to subject or (the focus of this chapter) of the same subject over time. How can like be compared with like so that the changing demands can be interpreted?

That either prior achievement or a good measure of general academic aptitude predicts about 50 per cent of subsequent variation in results is now widely known as

Table 11.2 Percentages of candidates awarded various grades: GCSE in 1995

Grade awarded	U	G	F	E	D	C	B	A[a]
For all candidates and subjects, 1995	1.7%	4.7%	9%	14%	18%	22%	18%	10%
Change in % from 1988 to 1995	−1.8	−2.1	−3.0	−2.0	0.1	2.2	5.5	5.0

Notes:
Based upon data in SCAA 1996
[a] A and A* grades combined

a result of decades of school effectiveness research (e.g. Madaus *et al.* 1979; Fitz-Gibbon 1985; Gray *et al.* 1986; Nuttall *et al.* 1989; Tymms 1993; Goldstein and Thomas 1996; Tymms 1999). This fact permits comparisons to be made between the grades awarded to candidates who are similar in terms of prior achievement/aptitude. This framework in which predictions can be made has been called the '50 per cent framework' (Fitz-Gibbon 1997) and it can be used now to illustrate how subjects differ in difficulty, how these differences probably arose, and how these differences in difficulty can be examined over time.

Examples of the use of the 50 per cent framework

A 'demanding' course is one in which it is difficult to obtain a high grade; i.e. one in which grading is severe. Thus a hallmark of severe grading is that the average grade achieved by average students is low, whereas in easier subjects the average grade for average students is higher. These differences can be represented graphically, as in Figure 11.3. There we see differences between three A-level subjects, using actual data from students in 1999.

Each sloping line shows, roughly, the average A-level grade obtained by students with the average GCSE score shown on the horizontal axis. The business studies line is to the left because it was a subject chosen largely by lower achieving students.

Figure 11.3   Illustrating subject difficulties (data from 1999): business studies was easier than physics

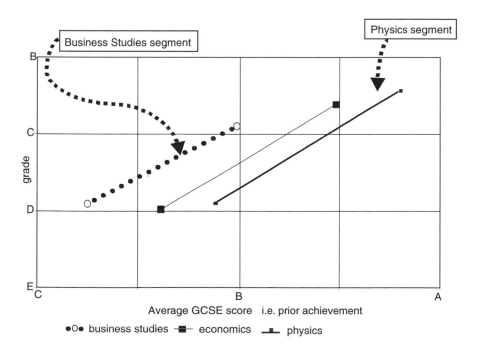

For business studies, the average A-level grade achieved was C for the hundreds of students who had had an average of B at age 16 (average GCSE score). In contrast, for students who had had an average of B at GCSE and took physics, we can read from the trend lines that they obtained, on average, only slightly above a D grade. Their most likely grade was thus a D. Economics was intermediate between the demanding subject, physics, and the easier subject, business studies.

If subject difficulties (or severity of grading) are not recognised, then schools will find that the lower grades in A level in mathematics, science and foreign language departments are blamed on poor teaching, whereas much, if not all, of the difference will be the result of severe grading. The 50 per cent framework and regression *segments* (rather than regression *lines*) provide the graphical representation that best captures both the range of the intake to a subject or syllabus and the difficulty or severity of grading. A regression segment is simply a trend line through the actual data. Instead of continuing the line across the whole graph, it is only as long as is appropriate to the intake.

There is a national problem with regard to monitoring standards over time using prior achievement measures (e.g. the average GCSE scores). These measures change their meaning each year. GCSE itself might be getting harder or easier. *In order to monitor standards we need a benchmark that does not alter.* We have such benchmarks, or baseline tests, in the Curriculum, Evaluation and Management (CEM) Centre. For A levels we have given the International Test of Developed Abilities (ITDA) since 1988. Data already published showed mathematics grades becoming easier to obtain from 1988 to 1994 (Fitz-Gibbon and Vincent 1997). In Figure 11.4, that trend is shown to be continuing recently, at least in applied mechanics. Students scoring 60 per cent, for example, on the ITDA scored on average between a C and a D in 1996, but in 1999 they scored on average almost a grade higher. Other data not illustrated here show less change in English, and varying amounts of change over time in other subjects, but for none of them is the trend towards the subject becoming more difficult from year to year.

Another reason for leaning towards a 'declining standards' interpretation at A level, rather than improved performance, is corroborating evidence from university lecturers. For those subjects in which university admissions officers expect actual mastery of basic content, such as mathematics or chemistry, lecturers often have views as to the extent to which students with high grades do or do not know as much as in previous years. This source of professional judgement may be unreliable but we would be inclined to believe otherwise, particularly in those cases where there is corroborating evidence. For example, the Royal Society of Chemistry published extensive records of the same test given across many years (Barber *et al.* 1994). Furthermore, opinion among mathematics lecturers is quite consistent, and theirs is a rather measurable subject.

Turning to GCSE results over several years, we also find many regression segments floating up the page (i.e. indicating easier grading) for some subjects when plotted against an unchanging baseline. This suggests that the GCSE examinations in some subjects were becoming easier. In no subjects do they appear to have been becoming more difficult. The suspicion of falling standards is aroused, though not proved.

Figure 11.4   Comparing difficulties of mathematics (applied mechanics) over four years: it was easier in 1999 than in 1996

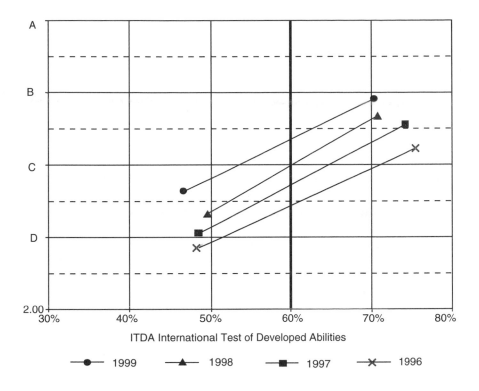

The changes at A level and at GCSE have not been uniform across all subjects. The difficulty or demand of English has changed very little, whereas there have been larger changes in mathematics and the physical sciences, subjects that were severely graded for many years. They are now more in line with other subjects. Could it be that, despite the upwardly floating regression segments, there has in fact been no change in standards, just a great leap forward in student achievement? Could it be that the target-setting agenda, the inspection system and the publishing of examination results in 'league tables' has led to much hard work, and some of the 'fall in standards' is actually higher achievement? Perhaps students are working harder. If they are, this is strange, because hundreds of thousands of independent reports from students, made on confidential questionnaires completed in more than nine hundred schools and colleges per year, sealed in plastic envelopes and sent to the CEM Centre, state that they are not. The amount of homework reported by A-level candidates has fallen in the very years when enrolments were increasing and grades were getting better. Although not important in primary schools, in secondary schools more homework *is* associated with higher achievement. It would therefore be surprising if there were real improvements in achievement when the amount of homework reported is declining.

Judgements about grade inflation

It seems clear in the external examinations at age 16 and 18 that there has been a less severe grading, particularly in mathematics and the sciences. This is not necessarily regrettable at all – indeed, an examination system that produced large numbers of failing grades after honest effort by teachers and students would be wrong; that used to be the case at A levels, and objections were raised at the time (Fitz-Gibbon 1985).

Furthermore, a policy of inclusion demands the opportunity to obtain qualifications that are suitable for a wide range of aptitudes. It should be noted that the inclusion of lower socio-economic status students does not of itself require much change in standards since, rather than the 50 per cent prediction from prior achievement/aptitude, socio-economic status (SES) measures predict only 9 per cent of the variation. The change in standards is driven by the increased staying on of less able students, only some of whom are from low SES backgrounds. Many from such backgrounds are very able.

There is another policy reason for reducing the difficulty of mathematics, science and foreign language subjects. These subjects are seen as contributing to our economic competitiveness: were they allowed to remain much more difficult than other subjects, this would drive schools towards steering students away from such subjects, as it might be feared that the lower grades could damage their standing in the School Performance Tables. However, the situation is more subtle, since high grades may be more reliably obtained in the more quantitative subjects.

The inflation cannot go on indefinitely. Already an extra grade has been added at the top end of GCSEs, an A*, better than an A. Where is it to end, and will every Secretary of State stake his or her future on ever-increasing grades, as the current one has done? Some non-verbal aptitudes of students have slowly increased by as much as an Effect Size of 1.0 in a thirty-year generation; although this effect is welcome it is not well understood. It cannot, however, account for recent rapid increases in grades, even though it might contribute some effects.

Reasonable conclusions for secondary education are that standards in external examinations towards the end of secondary schooling have been adjusted downwards to meet the needs of a larger cohort and a more inclusive system. This situation reinforces the need for detailed monitoring, syllabus by syllabus, if employers and admissions officers are to interpret the data accurately and if comparisons that are made between departments in schools and between schools are to be fair.

Conclusion

We believe that many of the changes that have been introduced into schools in England and Wales over the past twenty-five years have been beneficial. Local Management of Schools (LMS), for example, involving a greater degree of autonomy at individual school level, has in many ways been an empowering development for the teaching force, a change no one seems keen to reverse. Even the development of examinations for primary schools has been welcomed by some teachers and has led to an increased amount of data for measuring performance.

But, as we have tried to demonstrate in this chapter, a serious problem surrounds the monitoring of standards over time. There is good evidence to suggest that standards have not been maintained at A level – and yet the extent of the change is not known with accuracy. In primary schools there appears to have been a rise in numeracy and literacy, but it is difficult to know whether what we are seeing in the data is real or imaginary. The published results show a steady rapid rise, but the rise has been so great as to question aspects of its validity and accuracy. Further, the ways in which standards are maintained contain within them mechanisms whereby an upward drift can be expected even if standards remain steady.

Given that the period under investigation began with a call for higher standards, we find this a rather ironic state of affairs. A more accurate and reliable system of measurement is needed, as called for by a number of scholars. Davies and Brember (1997: 621) thus suggest 'a continuous policy of research is needed to try to unravel the effects of the National Curriculum and major policy changes on schools and on children's reading attainment'. The Assistant Chief Executive of SCAA responsible for testing wrote in 1996 that 'an independent benchmark could be useful in showing that standards have not slipped, *particularly if national performance improves over the years*' (Hawker 1996, emphasis added). Foxman *et al.* (1992: 4) wrote that a system to monitor standards effectively should 'include nationally representative samples of pupils tackling appropriate tasks repeated at regular intervals ... monitoring surveys and National Curriculum assessment could complement each other'.

We would suggest that a small group should be established with the explicit and sole task of tracking educational standards in England and Wales. This need not be an expensive exercise, but it needs to be – and to be seen to be – independent from government. The group will need a brief that defines its task in general terms but leaves the specifics to be worked out, since they need considerable thought and care. The terms would dictate the areas of interest (literacy, numeracy, etc.) and the ages to be studied. The dates for reports would be specified, as would the destinations for a number of the reports that would automatically be sent to a specified number of bodies, including non-governmental organisations.

England and Wales probably now have the most monitored educational systems in the world. We can rightly speak of the lessons that have been learned and of the progress that has been made. But a new structure is needed that can provide the nation with crucial high-quality data on standards over time.

Acknowledgements

We wish to thank all the staff at the CEM Centre for their dedicated work, and, in particular, Dr Paul Skinner of the ALIS (A-level Information System) project and Neil Defty of the YELSIS (Years of Late Secondary Information System) project who have accepted requests for data on top of their already demanding responsibilities.

References

Angoff, W. (1971) 'Scales norms and equivalent scores', in R. Thorndike (ed.) *Educational Measurement*, Washington DC: American Council on Education.

Barber, N., J. Brockington and D. Jones (1994) *Research in Assessment XI: A Skills Test Survey of Chemistry Degree Course Entrants*, London: Royal Society of Chemistry, Education Division.

Blunkett, D. (1997) Speech to the North of England Education Conference, 4 January, the Octagon Centre, Sheffield University.

Brooks, G. (1998) 'Trends in standards of literacy in the United Kingdom, 1948–1996', *Topic*, 19: 1–10.

Brooks, G., Foxman, D. and Gorman, T. (1995) *Standards in Literacy and Numeracy 1948–1994*, NCE Briefing, New Series 7.

Campbell, J.R, Voelkl, K.E. and Donahue, P.L. (1996) *Report in Brief: NAEP 1996 Trends in Academic Progress*, National Centre for Educational Statistics, http://nces.ed.gov/nationsreportcard/96report/97986.shtml.

Cohen, J. (1977) *Statistical Power Analysis for the Behavioral Sciences*, New York: Academic Press.

Davies, J. and Brember, I. (1997) 'Monitoring reading standards in Year 6: a seven year cross-sectional study', *British Educational Research Journal*, 23(5): 615–22.

——(1998) 'Reading and mathematics attainments and self-esteem in years 2 and 5: an eight-year cross-sectional study', paper presented at the ECER conference, Ljubljana, September.

Dearing, R. (1996) *Review of 16–19 Qualifications*, London: SCAA.

Fitz-Gibbon, C.T. (1985) 'A-level results in comprehensive schools: the Combse project, year 1', *Oxford Review of Education*, 11(1): 43–58 (Combse: Confidential, Measurement-based Self-Evaluation, the original name of the project later renamed ALIS, the A-level Information System).

——(1988) 'Recalculating the standard', *Times Educational Supplement*, 26 August: 15.

——(1996) *Monitoring Education: Indicators, Quality and Effectiveness*, London: Cassell.

——(1997) 'Listening to students and the 50 per cent framework', in A.D. Edwards, C.T. Fitz-Gibbon, F. Hardman, R. Haywood and N. Meagher (eds) *Separate but Equal? A Levels and GNVQs*, London: Routledge.

Fitz-Gibbon, C.T. and Vincent, L. (1994) *Candidates' Performance in Public Examinations in Mathematics and Science*, London: SCAA.

——(1997) 'Difficulties regarding subject difficulties', *Oxford Review of Education*, 23(3): 291–8.

Foxman, D., Gorman, T. and Brooks, G. (1992) *Standards in Literacy and Numeracy*, NCE Briefing 10.

Goldstein, H. and Thomas, S. (1996) 'Using examination results as indicators of school and college performance', *Journal of the Royal Statistical Society*, 159(1): 149–65.

Gray, J., Jesson, D. and Jones, B. (1986) 'The search for a fairer way of comparing schools' examination results', *Research Papers in Education*, 1(2): 91–122.

Hawker, D. (1996) *Can we really trust the tests?*, *Times Educational Supplement*, 16 February.

Kelly, A. (1976) 'A study of the comparability of external examinations in different subjects', *Research in Education*, 16: 50–63.

Madaus, G.F., Kellaghan, T., Rakow, E.A. and King, D.J. (1979) 'The sensitivity of measures of school effectiveness', *Harvard Educational Review*, 49(2): 207–30.

Nuttall, D.L., Goldstein, H., Prosser, R. and Rasbash, J. (1989) 'Differential school effectiveness international', *Journal of Educational Research*, 13: 769–76.

Quinlan, M. and Scharaschkin, A. (1999) 'National Curriculum testing: problems and practicalities', paper presented at BERA Annual Conference, University of Sussex, September.

Rose, J., Downes, P., Grant, M., O'Leary, J. and Wallace, J. (1999) *Weighing the Baby, the Report of the Independent Scrutiny Panel on the Key Stage 2 National Curriculum Tests in English and Mathematics*, DfEE: http://www.dfee.gov.uk/panel/report.htm.

SCAA (1996) *GCE Results Analysis: An Analysis of the 1995 GCE Results and Trends over Time*, London: SCAA.

SCAA/Ofsted (1996) *Standards in Public Examinations 1975 to 1995*, London: SCAA.

Shorrocks-Taylor, D. (1999) *National Testing: Past, Present and Future*, Leicester: British Psychological Society.

Smithers, A. and Robinson, P. (1991) *Beyond Compulsory Schooling: A Numerical Picture*, London: Council of Industry and Higher Education.

Tymms, P. (1993) 'Accountability – can it be fair?' *Oxford Review of Education*, 19(3): 291–9.

——(1996) *The Value Added National Project Second Primary Technical Report: An Analysis of the 1991 Key Stage 1 Data Linked to the 1995 KS2 Data Provided by Avon LEA* (Ref: COM/96/554), London: SCAA.

——(1999) *Baseline Assessment and Monitoring in Primary Schools: Achievements, Attitudes and Value-Added Indicators*, London: David Fulton.

Part IV

Issues of equality

12 Special needs education from Warnock to Salamanca

The triumph of liberalism?

Alan Dyson and Roger Slee

Introduction

In October 1997, the recently installed Labour government in Britain issued a Green Paper on special needs education which contained the following statement:

> We want to see more pupils with SEN included within mainstream primary and secondary schools. We support the United Nations Educational, Scientific and Cultural Organisation (UNESCO) Salamanca World Statement on Special Needs Education 1994. This calls on governments to adopt the principle of inclusive education, enrolling all children in regular schools, unless there are compelling reasons for doing otherwise. This implies a progressive extension of the capacity of mainstream schools to provide for children with a wide range of needs.
>
> (DFEE 1997: 44)

In many ways, this statement marks the culmination of a liberal and progressive tradition in special education policy in England and Wales. On the face of it, the government was adopting a policy of inclusion which would have been regarded as unacceptably radical only a few years before; indeed, at the time of this statement, only one LEA had formally declared in favour of inclusion and – according to Booth (1996) at any rate – few if any English/Welsh schools could, then or now, claim to be inclusive. Moreover, for the first time, a British government abandoned its traditional insularity and aligned its special needs education policy not simply with an international declaration, but with a world-wide movement – albeit, some might argue, more a movement in discourse than in practice.

This does indeed seem to be a triumph of liberalism, particularly, given that the most important policy legacy of the outgoing administration had been the introduction of a special needs Code of Practice (DfE 1994) which was seen in many quarters as a somewhat backward-looking and over-bureaucratic document (Bines and Loxley 1995; Dyson *et al.* 1997; Garner 1996; Lewis *et al.* 1996). However, our analysis of special education policy in England and Wales adopts a somewhat sceptical perspective on such apparent triumphs. In common with the American special education commentator, Tom Skrtic (1991), we start from the assumption that it is necessary to look 'behind' the rational and benevolent appearance of special education in order to understand critically the assumptions upon which it is founded, the interests which are at work to maintain it, and the often perverse impacts which it has upon its supposed beneficiaries. In so doing, of course, we call upon a tradition of critique which has been evident in England and Wales throughout the period with which we are concerned (see, for instance, Barton 1988; Barton and Tomlinson 1981, 1984; Booth 1981, 1983a, 1983b; Tomlinson 1982, 1985).

In particular, we wish to suggest that special education policy can be read as an attempt to deal with a fundamental problem which besets mass education systems in Western democracies. That problem is the problem of 'difference' (Artiles 1998; Franklin 1994; Norwich 2000; Richardson 1994). States develop education systems in order to achieve certain ends. However implicit, confused and contested those ends may be in detail, they presuppose that all – or very nearly all – of the country's children will be offered something that is recognisable as 'an education', with some degree of state control over the nature of that education, over the institutions in which it is offered and over the professionals who are responsible for its delivery. Within such a context, differences between learners become problematic insofar as they create difficulties for the state project of mass education. Hence, learners who resist schooling, who have a language other than the language(s) of instruction, who have disabilities and difficulties which make it hard for them to learn in 'common' schools, create problems which call not only for responses in practice, but for responses at the level of national policy.

It is our contention that, in England and Wales, those responses have drawn heavily upon a liberal, perhaps even progressive, tradition. By this we mean that they have been marked by a concern for the well-being of the disadvantaged or disabled individual and that they have been concerned with values of equity (in terms, for instance, of resource distribution, opportunities and outcomes) and participation (in shared curricular experiences, 'common' schools and social interaction). However, we suggest, those responses, precisely because of their liberal tendencies, have, in recent years, failed to challenge the structural features of the English/Welsh education systems which produce disadvantage and disability and have, moreover, been marked by deep ambiguity in terms of the very values which they appear to embody.

It is from this perspective that we wish to review the course of special education policy in England and Wales over the past two and a half decades and to explore how current New Labour policy can be understood.

The liberal tradition

Commentators on the recent history of special education in England and Wales, whatever their ideological stance, tend to agree in seeing the Warnock Report (DES 1978), and the 1981 Education Act which, in part at least, implemented its recommendations, as the principal watershed between post-war and contemporary special education policy (Barton and Landman 1993; Hegarty 1994; Stakes and Hornby 1997). Certainly, it is true that the 1981 Act established a legislative framework for special education that was significantly different from what had gone before and that remains substantially unaltered. However, it is important to remember that both the Act and the report on which it was based arose out of a long liberal tradition in English/Welsh special education.

The 1944 Act and after

The 1944 Education Act, for instance, is best remembered for establishing a system of separate schooling for children of different aptitudes and abilities, paralleled by a segregated special education system with different types of schools for children in each of eleven categories of 'handicap'. Although segregated schooling is now much criticised for its divisive and discriminatory effects, it is also possible to read the Act as an attempt to set up a more coherent and less stigmatising system of provision to replace a pre-war system that had become widely discredited (Stakes and Hornby 1997). It is important to remember that the 1944 Act placed a duty on LEAs to ascertain the needs of children for special education wherever they were placed, and anticipated that such treatment would be provided in many cases in regular schools.

The post-1944 period can also be read in similar liberal terms. The development of special classes (Tansley and Gulliford 1960) and of remedial teaching (Sampson 1975) in mainstream schools, for instance, were both means of extending the supposed benefits of special education to pupils in mainstream schools and, equally importantly, of doing so without the need to segregate those pupils entirely from their peers. In an important sense, therefore, the experiments with the 'integration' of pupils from special into mainstream schools, which gathered pace in the 1970s, were simply an extension of practices and values that had long been in place (Galloway and Goodwin 1979; Hegarty *et al.* 1981, 1982; Jones 1983).

Warnock and the 1981 Act

The Warnock Report likewise, therefore, was an embodiment of long-established trends. At the core of its approach to special education is the notion that 'the purpose of education for all children is the same; the goals are the same' (DES 1978: 1.4).

Starting from this humanistic basis, it sought to dismantle a system of categorisation which it saw as unnecessarily arbitrary and divisive, replacing it instead with a process of individual assessment which would identify each child's 'special educational needs' and lead to an individualised 'package' of provision to meet those needs. This in turn meant that the link between ascertainment, provision and placement could be broken. The post-war system of responding to children's difficulties by placing them in special schools for that 'category of handicap' was no longer necessary. Provision was to be as individualised as assessment and could, therefore, be made in whatever institution – including the mainstream school – was deemed most appropriate for that child. This certainly did not imply the abolition of special schools, nor even the unequivocal promotion of 'integration'. However, it did mean removing any legislative obstacles to integration. It also meant that, just as the preceding decades had seen an extension of special education practices to children in mainstream schools, so the new system meant an extension of the legislative framework governing assessment and provision to those same children. It was, therefore, no longer a matter for the whim of the headteacher or local authority to determine what provision a child with 'special educational needs' should receive. For the first time, some degree of *legally guaranteed* special provision was available other than in special schools.

If the years following the 1981 Act saw something of a hiatus in national policy initiatives regarding special education, the gap was more than filled at local authority and school level. These local initiatives were focused both on extending the scope of integration on the one hand and exploring the possibilities of the 'whole school approach' on the other. The Fish Report for the Inner London Education Authority (ILEA 1985) was typical, though more high profile and perhaps more ambitious than most, envisaging as it did the delegation of special education provision to 'clusters' of mainstream schools. However, these initiatives were soon overtaken by the major changes brought about by the 1988 Education Reform Act.

The 1988 Education Reform Act

It may seem perverse, given the critique to which the 1988 Act has subsequently been subjected, to view it as an embodiment of a long-standing liberal approach to special education. Nonetheless, this is precisely what we wish to suggest, at least in its provisions regarding the introduction of a National Curriculum. Arguably, the 1988 Act is liberal by default. Its interests are clearly to do with the 'reform' of mainstream schooling, and it is, perhaps, no coincidence that the consultation paper on the National Curriculum (DES 1987) which preceded the Act itself made virtually no mention of special needs education. The implication of this, however, was that, for the first time, a curriculum was introduced which constituted an entitlement for all – or very nearly all – pupils in English state schools. Moreover, the guidance issued by the National Curriculum Council (NCC) on the implementation of the new curriculum for children with special educational needs promoted a strongly inclusive view of the curriculum, emphasising the importance of 'access' and of 'differentiation' rather than segregation as a means of ensuring that access (NCC 1989a). Indeed, it is arguable that a brief – and, sadly, largely forgotten – circular issued as an interim document by NCC (1989b) came close to recommending the abandonment of the 'special educational needs' label entirely, in favour of a much more flexible notion of individual differences which made more sense in terms of access to a differentiated entitlement curriculum.

The 1993 Act and the Code of Practice

Following the 1988 Act, national policy attention in respect of special education turned away from curriculum matters towards underlying problems in the resourcing and management of special needs education. Two Audit Commission/HMI reports in the early 1990s (Audit Commission/ HMI 1992a, 1992b) pointed to a range of difficulties in the system: a lack of incentives for LEAs to move towards further integration, a lack of clarity regarding the relative responsibilities of schools and

LEAs for special needs provision, and a lack of accountability in both schools and LEAs for the efficient and effective use of special needs resources. The government's response was the special needs provisions of the 1993 Education Act and, in particular, the introduction of the special educational needs *Code of Practice* (DfE 1994).

As with the 1988 Act, it is sometimes difficult to disentangle from all the subsequent critique of the Code some of its fundamentally liberal elements. Essentially, the 1993 Act in general and the Code in particular had two main thrusts. One was to place pressure on LEAs to conduct the assessment and statementing procedures of the 1981 Act more efficiently and expeditiously. This meant, among other things, establishing an SEN tribunal to which parents could appeal if they were dissatisfied with LEA process or decisions. Since parents were seen in the Code as acting as proxies for their children, the new 'partnership' (Russell 1994) between LEAs and parents appeared to offer a higher degree of protection for children with special educational needs than had previously been the case.

The second thrust was to set out for schools in some detail the procedures they were to follow in assessing and responding to children's special needs. Not only was this the first time that schools had had access to such guidance at national level, but the procedures were organised in a series of 'stages', of which the first three were unequivocally based in mainstream schools; and the first one, equally unequivocally, located responsibility for special needs provision with the class teacher. In other words, the expectation which had been embodied in the 1944 Act that mainstream schools would make provision for pupils with special needs was, for the first time, formalised and operationalised in a way which promised some degree of consistency in schools across the country.

New Labour and the Green Paper

Returning now to the 1997 Green Paper (DfEE 1997a) and the subsequent Programme of Action (DfEE 1998), it should be evident even from this brief review that the policy initiatives introduced by the incoming New Labour government have roots that extend back at least half a century and that have relatively little to do with change of political control. The rhetoric of the Green Paper and Programme of Action may indeed sound new. However, many of their themes – integration (albeit rebadged as 'inclusion'), working with parents, improving provision in mainstream schools, improving the management of special needs provision at local level, and so on – would not have been unfamiliar at the time of Warnock or before.

Moreover, these are essentially liberal themes. They are, in other words, concerned with safeguarding individuals (children with special needs and their families) who are vulnerable insofar as they represent a minority interest in the mainstream education system. They are concerned with ensuring that parents have a voice in decision-making and that appropriate provision is made for their children effectively and expeditiously. Above all, they are concerned with extending the participation of children with special needs in mainstream schools and the mainstream curriculum. Indeed, for the first time such participation is, however tentatively, aligned with a wider concern for the rights of disabled people (Disability Rights Task Force 1999).

It is important not to overlook the contribution of these liberal concerns to shaping special needs education policy in England and Wales over recent decades. However, it is important also not to overlook the other principles that have been at work over the same period. It is to these that we now turn.

The illiberal context

Implicit in the liberal approach to special needs policy has been the assumption that the concern for individual needs, and for access and participation, would be sufficiently widespread and powerful within the education system to ensure that appropriate special needs provision would be sustainable without recourse to special school placement. Indeed, some within the special needs education 'community' have gone further than this, in suggesting that those concerns might be powerful enough to bring about a transformation of mainstream schools – that the 'ordinary school' might be made 'special' (Dessent 1987), that it would be possible to develop mainstream schools that were 'effective for all' (Ainscow 1991), or that special needs education was inextricably bound up with 'change' in the mainstream system (Dyson 1990). Our contention is that these hopes have, in practice, been disappointed.

It is possible to support this contention by looking at two policy 'moments' over the past quarter-century. The first is the period around and immediately after the Warnock Report when the restructuring of mainstream special needs provision that became known as the 'whole school approach' was undertaken. As we suggested above, much of the energy for this restructuring came from local level, though it was at the very least strongly foreshadowed by Warnock (Roaf 1989). The expectation was that it would be possible for special educators in mainstream schools to break out from their semi-segregated worlds of special classes and remedial groups towards developing 'remedial work across the curriculum' (Gulliford 1979) and a 'new role' which would see them offering in-class support and acting as consultant to their mainstream teacher colleagues on how best to teach pupils with special needs (Gains 1980; Gains and McNicholas 1979).

The persistence of attempts to implement and, indeed, extend the notion of the whole school approach long after the initial flush of enthusiasm had died down should not be underestimated (Clark *et al.* 1995; Dyson *et al.* 1994). Nonetheless, the hoped-for transformation of mainstream schools simply did not occur: support teaching was patchy, changes in curriculum and pedagogy were sporadic, the commitment of senior managers was ambiguous, and many mainstream teachers resisted the extended role of their special educator colleagues (Clark *et al.* 1997). Writing on the basis of a study undertaken at the time of this 'redefinition of remedial education', Bines (1986, 1988) concluded that the difficulties experienced by the whole school approach represented a contradiction between a potentially radical reconstruction of educational practice and values and the much more conservative practices and values embedded in mainstream schools. Although remaining optimistic about the eventual potential of the whole school approach, she comments particularly on the somewhat debilitating effect of its liberal basis:

To date, it [the whole school approach] has largely been regarded as a change in structure and methodology, following from a traditional view in special education which has largely ignored its social and political aspects in favour of a concentration on an humanitarian approach to individuals ... The development of the 'whole school approach' to special educational provision, whatever its limitations, does represent a welcome shift in ideology and practice. It will, however, require a critical awareness both of traditional legacies and current and future issues and constraints if its potential is indeed to be fulfilled.

(Bines 1988: 158)

In fact, at the time Bines was writing, this radical potential was, as we have seen, about to be given considerable impetus by the introduction of the National Curriculum. In some schools, it did indeed seem for a time that the heritage of the whole school approach, combined with the nationally guaranteed entitlement of very nearly all students to a common curriculum and the greater autonomy available to schools as a result of other provisions of the 1988 Act, would combine to produce a genuinely radical approach to 'special needs' education. Here and there, the separate structures which had grown up in and around schools began to be dismantled, and the language and ideology of 'special needs' education were abandoned in favour of more flexible and less discriminatory notions of 'individual difference', enacted through sophisticated practices of differentiation and support (Clark *et al.*1995; Dyson *et al.* 1994).

However, these apparently radical developments took place in the context of a 'reform' of mainstream education which saw it become significantly more inimical to the interests of marginalised students. Not only was the curriculum to which they were avowedly entitled somewhat rigid, over-prescriptive and exclusive in effect (Bines 1993; Swann 1992), but the introduction of competition between schools, supported in due course by the apparatus of inspection, 'league tables' and 'naming and shaming' eroded the willingness of some schools at least to embrace positively the diversity of their student body (Bines 1995; Booth 1996; Booth *et al.* 1997, 1998; Clark *et al.* 1999a, 1999b; Gold *et al.* 1993; Riddell and Brown 1994; Rouse and Florian 1997). What became apparent, therefore, as the 1988 Education Reform Act took full effect, was that the entitlement to a common curriculum, far from ushering in a radical reconstruction of special needs education, was bringing about a renewed wave of exclusions from school and referrals to special education – a situation which the incoming New Labour government in 1997 realised was running out of control, and which they felt demanded urgent corrective action (DfEE 1997a; SXU 1998).

Writing at a time when tight centralised control of education was on the horizon rather than a present reality, Jeffs (1988) summarised developments since the 1981 Act in the following way:

The fears of many following the 1981 Education Act have been fully realized in some instances. The 'illusion of progress' has produced in full measure 'confusion, inefficiency and demoralisation'. Labels have changed, empires have been renamed and tenuous consultative procedures held up as partnership. In such settings those teachers designated for training and given responsibility for the range of special educational needs within school have laboured long, but to little avail.

(Jeffs 1988: 75)

Jeffs was still able to believe in 1988 that the models of more liberal practice, evident here and there, might be spread more widely; that, as central government took ever tighter control of the education system, it would build on these liberal principles; and that just a little extra training of just the right kind would be enough to bring about the sort of radical transformation for which he hoped. It has to be said, however, that the experience of a further twelve years of 'reform' and, in particular, of what central control of education has actually meant, suggests that Jeffs was unjustifiably – if understandably – optimistic.

In a recent study of special needs provision in primary schools, Croll and Moses (2000) replicate a survey which they first undertook at the start of the period with which we are concerned (Croll and Moses 1985). What they report throws grave doubts over any assertion that this period has been one of the progressive realisation of liberal principles. They argue that the Warnock Report estimate of one in five children 'having' special educational needs is now a significant underestimate; the true figure is nearer one in four. They suggest that the reason for this growth is not so much any increase in the incidence of children's difficulties as 'changes in school and LEA procedures which resulted in more children being identified' (Croll and Moses 2000: 145). The 'incidence' of special needs continues, they report, to be associated strongly with social deprivation, with an over-representation of boys and of certain ethnic groups in particular 'categories' of need. In terms of practice, they identify a significant formalisation of roles and procedures over the period, but not necessarily any radical change in practice – withdrawal remains as popular as ever, inclusion is an issue of limited significance for schools, and 'extra provision' rather than change in pedagogical practice remains the preferred response to children's difficulties.

In other words, there is an important sense in which, in the twenty and more years since the Warnock Report, very little has changed in special needs education. Liberal principles have not, by and large, produced liberal practices. If anything, schools have become *more* resistant to children presenting difficulties and challenges than they were in the past. It is evident that teachers, schools and the wider education system have been responding to something other than the apparently liberal policies which have been pursued at both national and local level throughout this period. Indeed, it is difficult to resist the argument which Sally Tomlinson has been propounding throughout this time, that special needs education is to be understood not so much a manifestation of liberal and humanitarian impulses but rather as a product of vested social interests which seek to marginalise deviant children, but which use a smokescreen of liberal rhetoric to camouflage their true purposes (Tomlinson 1982, 1985, 1995).

Certainly, what is clear is that the liberal principles which appear to have informed special needs policy have not been powerful enough to transform the rather illiberal context within which they have had to be realised. Indeed, how could it be otherwise? As Bines (1988) pointed out, in the 1980s that very liberalism had led to a focus on individual 'need' and the accommodation of the majority system to minority differences – what Corbett (1996) identifies as an essentially 'charitable' discourse – without a critical social and political awareness which would allow it to address the fundamental issue not only of *how* the mainstream system excluded and marginalised children, but also of *why* it should seek so to do. Under the circumstances, the impact of liberal policies has been confined to the 'ghetto' of the special needs sub-system; endless contortions and reconstructions in that ghetto have achieved little beyond its immediate confines (Clark *et al.* 1997).

New Labour: can things only get better?

Gloomy as this analysis may be, there is one crucial factor which may give cause for hope: throughout this period, special needs policy has been in the hands of right-of-centre administrations. The Warnock Report was commissioned and received by a Conservative government; the 1981 Act was a piece of Conservative legislation; the major 'reforms' of 1988 were the product of neo-liberal ideology in full flow; and the SEN Code of Practice was the attempt of yet another Conservative administration to rein in a system careering out of control. Only in the last few years has a more leftward-leaning administration been in a position to make a significant impact on special needs education. Given that the 1997 SEN Green Paper (DfEE 1997a) with which we opened this chapter marked a significant shift in tone and language from what had gone before, it is worth asking whether some more fundamental change is under way which might bring about genuinely radical shifts in the structural marginalisation of children 'with special needs'.

The answer we wish to give is marked by ambivalence. There is no doubting the radical rhetoric of the government's commitment to inclusion, of its aligning of inclusion with wider issues in the civil and human rights of disabled people (Disability Rights Task Force 1999) and of its attempts to reunite a liberal agenda in special needs education with a more wide-ranging concern for the impacts of social and economic disadvantage as part of its 'social inclusion' agenda (Blunkett 1999a, 1999b). There is no doubting either that some real changes in patterns of provision are resulting from these new emphases. Not only are local education authorities looking with new seriousness at the issue of inclusion (Ainscow *et al.* 1999), but a revision of the Code of Practice is under way which promises to remove a significant proportion of children from the special needs apparatus, and a whole raft of measures are being directed towards children and young people in socially and economically disadvantaged areas (DfEE 1999a, 1999b, 1999c, 1999d).

Our ambivalence arises from a closer look at the ideological bases of these developments. First, the commitment to inclusion itself is highly qualified. Even in the 1997 Green Paper (DfEE 1997a), a version of inclusion is presented which in practice amounts to the perpetuation of the current twin-track system of special needs provision. Inclusion, it seems, is about 'enrolling all children in regular schools, *unless there are compelling reasons for doing otherwise*', where 'the needs of individual children are paramount', where 'specialist provision is seen as an integral part of overall provision', and in which 'inclusion is a process, not a fixed state'

(p. 44, our emphasis). By the time of the 1998 Programme of Action, even more qualifications have been entered:

> Promoting inclusion within mainstream schools, *where parents want it and appropriate support can be provided*, will remain a cornerstone of our strategy ... Our approach will be practical, not dogmatic, and will put the needs of individual children first ... For some children, a mainstream placement may not be right, or not right just yet. We therefore confirm that specialist provision – *often, but not always in special schools* – will continue to play a vital role.
>
> (DfEE 1998: 23, our emphasis)

Second, the commitment to inclusion is set in the context of a system-wide 'crusade for standards', realised through a 'combination of pressure and support' (DfEE 1997b: 24). In practice, the mechanisms for exerting pressure – target-setting, continued competition between schools, the extension of Ofsted inspections to LEAs, the 'naming and shaming' of failing schools and LEAs, competitive bidding, the encouragement of private sector take-overs of schools and services, the introduction of prescriptive literacy and numeracy 'hours' and so on – may have been somewhat stronger than the supports. In the circumstances, it seems highly likely that the sorts of resistances which were generated in the system following the 1988 Education Reform Act will be perpetuated or even heightened by this powerful central drive for standards. Indeed, it is already becoming apparent that the tensions between the two agendas are creating real dilemmas for schools and LEAs, and that there are real dangers that a somewhat weakly enforced inclusion agenda will simply be steam-rollered by the more forceful 'standards' agenda (Ainscow *et al.* 1999).

Third, and perhaps most significant, the context for the government's avowed commitment to inclusion is formed not merely by its even more powerfully enacted commitment to raising standards, but by a far-reaching analysis of the role of education in contemporary society. This analysis has most recently been articulated by the Secretary of State, David Blunkett, in his annual speech to the North of England Education Conference (Blunkett 2000). Education, Blunkett suggests, has four fundamental purposes: economic, social, liberating and problem-solving. In order to compete in the global economy, he argues, the country needs a supply of highly skilled, and hence highly educated, workers. Such highly educated citizens are, he continues, less likely to experience 'social exclusion' and more likely to be able to play a part in society as active citizens. Moreover, given the challenges which the 'global society' will have to face in the near future (he cites the 'environmental challenge' and the ethical dilemmas posed by advances in genetic sciences as examples), only highly educated citizens will have the knowledge and problem-solving skills necessary to make the difficult decisions that are likely to be necessary.

From this perspective, inclusion is at one and the same time part of a grand vision of the educational future and a somewhat minor side-issue. This is evident when Blunkett explain what he means by the 'drive for inclusion' (Blunkett 2000: 7–8). Significantly, inclusion as an issue about the nature, future and purpose of the special education system warrants only a brief mention. Here, as on other occasions

(Blunkett 1999a, 1999b), Blunkett focuses on disaffected pupils, pupils who are excluded from schools for disciplinary reasons, the education of children from ethnic minorities, out-of-hours support for children from less advantageous backgrounds, the extension of participation in higher education, equipping young people for the job market and the teaching of 'citizenship'. In other words, Blunkett's focus is primarily on *social* inclusion, and on inclusion in the SEN Green Paper sense only insofar as it contributes to this wider agenda.

The ambiguities in this view of inclusion are subtle, but nonetheless real. On the one hand, the alignment of inclusion with a wider social inclusion agenda and, beyond that, with a 'grand vision' of education is, in many ways, an apotheosis of the liberal view of special needs education. At last, the egalitarian and participatory values which have driven developments in special needs education for over twenty years have broken out of the ghetto and permeated the education system as a whole. On the other hand, inclusion becomes not an end in itself, but simply a contributory strategy to reducing disaffection, raising standards and training a high-skills work force. What happens, we need to ask, when the liberal values of inclusion conflict with these wider social and economic goals – when children and young people fail to become economically productive or fail to respond to the social inclusion strategies currently multiplying in the education system? What happens, more importantly, if their failures and resistances threaten to impair the capacity of the education system as a whole to deliver the government's grand vision?

Conclusion: the circle and the line – policy change in special needs education

At the start of the period we have reviewed, England and Wales had a system of special needs education which placed 1.8 per cent of children in special school, which categorised children by 'handicap', which gave medical personnel a central role in ascertainment procedures, which offered little or no formal protection of children with special needs in ordinary school, and which expected such children routinely to be taught in 'bottom' streams, special classes and withdrawal groups (DES 1978). At the end of the period, the proportion of children in special school has dropped to 1.2 per cent (DfEE 1999e); the system of categorisation has been replaced by a more responsive assessment of individual 'need'; the assessment process itself has become much more educationally oriented; there is elaborate guidance which offers protection to children in ordinary schools; and such children are now routinely expected to have access to a common curriculum delivered, in part at least, in ordinary classrooms alongside their peers.

If we add to these impressive developments the more recent governmental commitment to inclusion, it is difficult not to argue that change in special needs policy over this period has taken the form of a linear development in line with liberal, progressive principles. At the same time, there is also a depressing circularity about the changes that have taken place: special schools remain; special classes, withdrawal groups and 'bottom' sets are still with us; the legislative commitment to inclusion is, in practice, no greater than in the 1976 Education Act; above all, there is still a thriving special needs education 'industry' which finds enormous amounts of work for itself to do, but which shows little evidence of bringing about radical change in the mainstream system.

If we are to make sense of this situation, we need to understand the weakness of the liberal values which have underpinned at least some of the developments of the past twenty years – weakness in terms of the relative size of the special needs and mainstream systems, weakness in terms of the strength with which those values have been held and the forcefulness with which they have been advocated, and, above all, perhaps, the inherent weakness of an essentially individualised approach in addressing fundamental structural issues. It is arguable, at least, that the tendency of such approaches to deflect attention from these structural issues is precisely what explains the apparent paradox of their survival, in a period when education policy generally has moved markedly to the right.

There is, however, some cause for hope. Whatever these weaknesses, the interaction of linear and circular change is change nonetheless. Things are not as they were in 1978. In the process of change, new spaces have opened up, old ones have been reshaped. If there are problems, inequities and injustices in the English/Welsh education system that have not changed, then there are also possibilities to address these issues that were not available twenty years ago. The challenge, therefore, remains: will the system accept short-term 'fixes' of the policy problems generated by learner diversity; or will it respond more fully to the cultural politics of identity, difference and disadvantage?

References

Ainscow, M. (1991) 'Effective schools for all: an alternative approach to special needs in education', in M. Ainscow (ed.) *Effective Schools for All*, London: David Fulton.

Ainscow, M., Farrell, P., Tweddle, D. and Malki, G. (1999) *Effective Practice in Inclusion and in Special and Mainstream Schools Working Together*, London: DfEE.

Artiles, A.J. (1998) 'The dilemma of difference: enriching the disproportionality discourse with theory and context', *The Journal of Special Education*, 32(1): 32–6.

Audit Commission/HMI (1992a) *Getting the Act Together: Provision for Pupils with Special Educational Needs: A Management Handbook for Schools and Local Education Authorities*, London: HMSO.

——(1992b) *Getting in on the Act: Provision for Pupils with Special Educational Needs: The National Picture*, London: HMSO.

Barton, L. (ed.) (1988) *The Politics of Special Educational Needs*, London: Falmer.

Barton, L. and Landman, M. (1993) 'The politics of integration: observations on the Warnock Report', in R. Slee (ed.) *Is There a Desk with My Name on It? The Politics of Integration*, London: Falmer.

Barton, L. and Tomlinson, S. (eds) (1981) *Special Education: Policy, Practices and Social Issues*, London: Harper & Row.

——(eds) (1984) *Special Education and Social Interests*, London: Croom Helm.

Bines, H. (1986) *Redefining Remedial Education*, Beckenham: Croom Helm.

——(1988) 'Equality, community and individualism: the development and implementation of the "whole school approach" to special educational needs', in L. Barton (ed.) *The Politics of Special Educational Needs*, London: Falmer.

——(1993) 'Curriculum change: the case of special education', *British Journal of Sociology of Education*, 14(1): 75–90.

——(1995) 'Special educational needs in the market place', *Journal of Education Policy*, 10(2): 157–72.

Bines, H. and Loxley, A. (1995) 'Implementing the Code of Practice for special educational needs', *Oxford Review of Education*, 21(4): 381–94.

Blunkett, D. (1999a) *Excellence for the Many, Not Just the Few: Raising Standards and Extending Opportunities in our Schools. The CBI President's Reception Address by the Rt Hon. David Blunkett MP 19 July 1999*, London: DfEE.

——(1999b) *Social Exclusion and the Politics of Opportunity: A Mid-Term Progress Check. A Speech by the Rt Hon. David Blunkett MP*, London: DfEE.

——(2000) *Raising Aspirations for the 21st Century. Speech to the North of England Education Conference, Wigan, 6 January 2000*, London: DfEE.

Booth, T. (1981) 'Demystifying integration', in W. Swann (ed.) *The Practice of Special Education*, Oxford: Blackwell.

——(1983a) 'Integrating special education', in T. Booth and P. Potts (eds) *Integrating Special Education*, Oxford: Blackwell.

——(1983b) 'Integration and participation in comprehensive schools', *Forum*, 25(2): 40–2.

——(1996) 'A perspective on inclusion from England', *Cambridge Journal of Education*, 26(1): 87–99.

Booth, T., Ainscow, M. and Dyson, A. (1997) 'Understanding inclusion and exclusion in the English competitive education system', *International Journal of Inclusive Education*, 1(4): 337–54.

——(1998) 'England: inclusion and exclusion in a competitive system', in T. Booth and M. Ainscow (eds) *From Them to Us: An International Study of Inclusion in Education*, London: Routledge.

Clark, C., Dyson, A., Millward, A. and Skidmore, D. (1995) *Innovatory Practice in Mainstream Schools for Special Educational Needs*, London: HMSO.

——(1997) *New Directions in Special Needs: Innovations in Mainstream Schools*, London: Cassell.

Clark, C., Dyson, A., Millward, A. and Robson, S. (1999a) 'Inclusive education and schools as organizations', *International Journal of Inclusive Education*, 3(1): 37–51.

——(1999b) 'Theories of inclusion, theories of schools: deconstructing and reconstructing the "inclusive school"', *British Educational Research Journal*, 25(2): 157–77.

Corbett, J. (1996) *Bad-Mouthing: The Language of Special Needs*, London: Falmer.

Croll, P. and Moses, D. (1985) *One in Five – the Assessment and Incidence of Special Educational Needs*, London: Routledge & Kegan Paul.

——(2000) *Special Needs in the Primary School: One in Five?* London: Cassell.

DES (1978) *Special Educational Needs: Report of the Committee of Enquiry into the Education of Handicapped Children and Young People (The Warnock Report)*, London: HMSO.

——(1987) *The National Curriculum 5–16: A Consultation Document*, London: DES.

Dessent, T. (1987) *Making the Ordinary School Special*, London: Falmer.

DfE (1994) *Code of Practice on the Identification and Assessment of Special Educational Needs*, London: DfE.

DfEE (1997a) *Excellence for All Children: Meeting Special Educational Needs*, London: Stationery Office.

——(1997b) *Excellence in Schools*, London: Stationery Office.

——(1998) *Meeting Special Educational Needs: A Programme of Action*, London: DfEE.

——(1999a) *Excellence in Cities*, London: DfEE.

——(1999b) *Learning to Succeed: A New Framework for Post-16 Learning*, London: Stationery Office.

——(1999c) *Meet the Challenge: Education Action Zones*, London: DfEE.

——(1999d) *Sure Start: Making a Difference for Children and Families*, London: DfEE.

——(1999e) *Statistics of Education: Special Educational Needs in England: January 1999, DfEE Statistical Bulletin, Issue no. 12/99*, October, London: Stationery Office.

Disability Rights Task Force (1999) *From Exclusion to Inclusion: A Report of the Disability Rights Task Force on Civil Rights for Disabled People*, London: DfEE.

Dyson, A. (1990) 'Special educational needs and the concept of change', *Oxford Review of Education*, 16(1): 55–66.

Dyson, A., Millward, A. and Skidmore, D. (1994) 'Beyond the whole school approach: an emerging model of special needs practice and provision in mainstream secondary schools', *British Educational Research Journal*, 20(3): 301–17.

Dyson, A., Lin, M. and Millward, A. (1997). *The Role of Special Educational Needs Coordinators in Schools*, Newcastle: Special Needs Research Centre, University of Newcastle for DfEE.

Franklin, B.M. (1994) *From 'Backwardness' to 'At-Risk': Childhood Learning Difficulties and the Contradictions of School Reform*, Albany, NY: State University of New York Press.

Gains, C.W. (1980) 'Remedial education in the 1980s', *Remedial Education*, 15(1): 5–9.

Gains, C.W. and McNicholas, J.A. (eds) (1979) *Remedial Education: Guidelines for the Future*, London: Longman.

Galloway, D. and Goodwin, C. (1979) *Educating Slow-Learning and Maladjusted Children: Integration or Segregation*, London: Longman.

Garner, P. (1996) 'Go forth and coordinate! What special needs coordinators think about the Code of Practice', *School Organisation*, 6(2): 179–86.

Gold, A., Bowe, R. and Ball, S. (1993) 'Special educational needs in new context: micropolitics, money and "education for all"', in R. Slee (ed.) *Is There a Desk with My Name on It? The Politics of Integration*, London: Falmer.

Gulliford, R. (1979) 'Remedial work across the curriculum', in C. Gains and J.A. McNicholas (eds) *Remedial Education: Guidelines for the Future*, London: Longman.

Hegarty, S. (1994) 'England and Wales', in C.J.W. Meijer, S.J. Pijl and S. Hegarty (eds) *New Perspectives on Special Education: A Six-Country Study of Integration*, London: Routledge.

Hegarty, S. and Pocklington, K., with Lucas, D. (1981) *Educating Pupils with Special Needs in the Ordinary School*, Windsor: NFER–Nelson.

——(1982) *Integration in Action*, Windsor: NFER–Nelson.

Inner London Education Authority (ILEA) (1985) *Educational Opportunities for All? Report of the Committee Reviewing Provision to Meet Special Educational Needs (The Fish Report)*, London: ILEA.

Jeffs, A. (1988) 'The appearance and reality of change within special educational needs', in L. Barton (ed.) *The Politics of Special Educational Needs*, London: Falmer.

Jones, N. (1983) 'The management of integration: the Oxfordshire experience', in T. Booth and P. Potts (eds) *Integrating Special Education*, Oxford: Blackwell.

Lewis, A., Neill, S.R.S.J. and Campbell, R.J. (1996) *The Implementation of the Code of Practice in Primary and Secondary Schools: A National Survey of Perceptions of Special Educational Needs Co-ordinators*, Warwick: University of Warwick for the National Union of Teachers.

National Curriculum Council (NCC) (1989a) *Curriculum Guidance 2: A Curriculum for All*, York: National Curriculum Council.

——(1989b) *Circular no. 5: Implementing the National Curriculum – Participation by Pupils with Special Educational Needs*, York: National Curriculum Council.

Norwich, B. (2000) 'Inclusion in education: from concepts, values and critique to practice', in H. Daniels (ed.) *Special Education Re-Formed: Beyond Rhetoric?* London: Routledge.

Richardson, J.G. (1994) 'Common, delinquent, and special: on the formalization of common schooling in the American states', *American Educational Research Journal*, 31(4): 695–723.

Riddell, S. and Brown, S. (eds) (1994) *Special Educational Needs Policy in the 1990s: Warnock in the Market Place*, London: Routledge.

Roaf, C. (1989) 'Whole school policies: a question of rights?', in N. Jones and T. Southgate (eds) *The Management of Special Needs in Ordinary Schools*, London: Routledge.

Rouse, M. and Florian, L. (1997) 'Inclusive education in the market-place', *International Journal of Inclusive Education*, 1(4): 323–36.

Russell, P. (1994) 'The Code of Practice: new partnerships for children with special educational needs', *British Journal of Special Education*, 21(2): 48–52.

Sampson, O. (1975) *Remedial Education*, London: Routledge & Kegan Paul.

Skrtic, T.M. (1991) *Behind Special Education: A Critical Analysis of Professional Culture and School Organization*, Denver: Love.

Social Exclusion Unit (SXU) (1998) *Truancy and School Exclusion: Report by the Social Exclusion Unit*, London: Cabinet Office Social Exclusion Unit.

Stakes, R. and Hornby, G. (1997) *Change in Special Education: What Brings it About?* London: Cassell.

Swann, W. (1992) 'Hardening the hierarchies: the National Curriculum as a system of classification', in T. Booth, W. Swann, M. Masterton and P. Potts (eds) *Curricula for Diversity in Education*, London: Routledge.

Tansley, A.E. and Gulliford, R. (1960) *The Education of Slow Learning Children*, London: Routledge & Kegan Paul.

Tomlinson, S. (1982) *A Sociology of Special Education*, London: Routledge & Kegan Paul.

——(1985) 'The expansion of special education', *Oxford Review of Education*, 11(2): 157–65.

——(1995) 'The radical structuralist view of special education and disability: unpopular perspectives on their origins and development', in T.M. Skrtic (ed.) *Disability and Democracy: Reconstructing (Special) Education for Postmodernity*, New York: Teachers College Press.

13 Some success, could do better

Education and race 1976–2000

Sally Tomlinson

Introduction

In all post-industrial, post-colonial societies, racial and ethnic minorities[1] experience problems in negotiating a position that will guarantee them incorporation into the economy and into the civil society, with equal treatment, opportunities and respect. Education is the key institution which will assist this process. It is thus important to discuss whether the educational changes and reforms of the past twenty-five years have assisted or disadvantaged minorities in their search to achieve the educational credentials that provide employment opportunities and the chance of occupational and social mobility. Education is also a key institution in persuading the white majority that they now live in a diverse multicultural society which allows all its members to have multiple identities, that minority cultures can be accorded recognition and respect without threatening the national identity, and that post-imperial racist attitudes and beliefs are outdated and counter-productive.

From the early 1960s the children of migrants entering the UK from the Caribbean, the Asian sub-continent, East Asia, East and West Africa, Cyprus and other existing or former colonial countries[2] were greatly disadvantaged as they entered the education system. Minority parents rapidly became aware of the increased importance of education credentials in the modern world and the higher levels of qualifications demanded for any kind of employment. Whatever their social class position, minority parents have consistently demonstrated the high aspirations and expectations for their children associated with the middle classes, and despite a good deal of racism and xenophobia there has been considerable success in 'reversing the initial downward mobility produced by migration and racial discrimination in the early years of British settlement' (Madood 1998: 70). Some minority young people have begun to achieve educational success and a small 'black' and 'Asian' middle class is emerging. However the failure of the education system to deliver equal access and educational success to many minority children became and remains a source of considerable tension. Disadvantages experienced by minorities from the 1950s to the 1980s have been well documented (see Kirp 1979; Taylor 1981, 1985, 1988; Tomlinson 1983; Troyna 1987). New disadvantages stemming from market policies and from an absence of race-specific policy post-1988 became apparent in the 1990s. The introduction of a National Curriculum signalled an end to many of the multicultural curriculum initiatives developed during the 1970s and 1980s, and there was a silence over issues of race and ethnicity in education for much of the 1990s.

This chapter briefly examines the situation of racial and ethnic minorities in education pre-1988, then goes on to discuss the post-1988 effects of education markets which have created new disadvantages – notably the disadvantages associated with social class position, location in inner cities, inequitable funding, the 'failing schools' policy and the increase in the exclusion of minority students from mainstream education. Despite a rhetoric of social inclusion and a plethora of government policies to alleviate disadvantage, there are still structural barriers to race equality, many of them created by policies associated with an education market. The chapter particularly notes the improved educational achievements of minorities in the 1990s – improvements set in train well before the impact of market forces, the failure to think through a revised National Curriculum appropriate for a diverse society in the twenty-first century, and the implications for the whole society as minorities become more successful educationally. The chronology of events since 1976 demonstrates liberal efforts made to include minorities, particularly evident in some policies of the 1980s, hostile responses to racial diversity from some parents and teachers and white youth, including two notorious murders, and the contradictions in government policies over two decades.

Minorities in education from the 1960s

From the early 1960s through to the 1980s, the children of ethnic minority parents entered a school system in which overt selection was gradually disappearing and comprehensive education was becoming the norm. Where selection remained, minorities were less likely to be successful (Rex and Tomlinson 1979; Walford and Miller 1991). However, once selection at 11 was phased out in most LEAs, pupils mainly attended neighbourhood schools. Policies in the 1960s to 'spread the children' in order to prevent high concentrations of minority children in urban schools were soon abandoned, and central and local government were at least notionally committed to widening access to a broad secondary education for all social and racial groups.

Initial disadvantages faced by immigrant children were associated with the need for English language teaching, an inappropriate curriculum, selective systems which worked against minorities, lack of extra funding, teachers who, if not overtly racist, had no training or awareness of minority issues, and the use of special education placement to remove black children from the mainstream. The hostility of some white parents to their children being educated alongside racial and ethnic minority children has been an ongoing issue since the 1960s (Richards 1983; Lane 1987; Gewirtz *et al.* 1995). Local authorities with high numbers of immigrant minority children made policy on an ad hoc basis, but other than encouragement by HMI, there were no national policies to assist in the incorporation and successful education of minority children. Kirp (1979: 40) noted that educational policy was characterised by racial inexplicitness and by embedding issues concerned with race and ethnicity in 'some broad policy context such as educational disadvantage'. By 1978 it was official policy to subsume minority issues under disadvantage. A Home

Office report noted that a 'good deal of the disadvantage that minorities suffer is shared by less well-off members of the indigenous population, and their fundamental needs – jobs, housing. education, health, are essentially the same as those of the general population' (Home Office 1978: 1).

Conflating minority disadvantages with general disadvantage had some merit, especially when poverty and inequality began to affect larger numbers in the majority society, but minorities have continued to experience disadvantages considerably in excess of the indigenous population. An analysis of 1991 census data in London, for example, demonstrated housing overcrowding among Bangladeshi and Pakistani groups, rates of unemployment three times higher than whites for black Africans and Bangladeshis, less chance of qualified minority people obtaining jobs than whites, and higher rates of long-term illness among black children (Storkey 1991). A report on inequalities in health in 1998 recorded 'many indications of poorer health among ethnic minority groups in England' (Acheson 1998: 23). In Tower Hamlets during the 1980s, a situation arose in which a severe shortage of school places led to over 500 Bangladeshi children being known to the local authority as having no school place, a situation that would never have been tolerated in a white area (Tomlinson 1992).

During the 1970s the lack of national policy to deal with the incorporation and successful education of minorities became more obvious, and during an eight-year period from 1973 to 1981 reports produced by government-sponsored committees, parliamentary committees and the Commission for Racial Equality (CRE) made some 228 recommendations for improving the education of minority children (Tomlinson 1983: 21). The third Race Relations Act, passed in 1976, which set up the CRE, included measures to combat any racial discrimination in education. In a Green Paper published in 1977, the Labour government commented on the school curriculum, which continued to incorporate beliefs and stereotypes about minorities (DES 1977) and, responding to anxieties expressed by the Afro-Caribbean community, set up an inquiry into the educational performance of their children. Teachers, particularly those working in multi-racial schools, and minority parents were instrumental in beginning to change school practices (see, for example, Lynch 1983; Craft and Bardell 1984). Local authorities began to develop multicultural policies, and by 1981 some twenty-five LEAs had appointed multicultural advisers. The 1981 report of the Rampton Committee (DES 1981) suggested that West Indian children were disadvantaged by the education system, which incorporated 'intentional and unintentional racism', and stressed that teachers needed training to teach properly in a multi-ethnic society.

The 1980s

Despite a good deal of xenophobia and racism, indicated by hostility to multicultural education of any kind or to any special focus on the education of minorities, advances were made during the 1980s. Opposition to any moves to make the curriculum more appropriate for a multicultural society was expressed by the New Right. On a political level, opposition centred on the criticism that multicultural education was left-of-centre egalitarianism, political subversion and a threat to traditional British values, culture and heritage (Hillgate Group 1986; Pearce 1986; Scruton *et al.* 1985). Urban rioting in St Paul's in Bristol, in Brixton, Liverpool and other cities during the early 1980s, by both black and white young people, was condemned by the Conservative government as criminal, but was diagnosed by the liberal Law Lord Scarman as a response to poor education and employment prospects (Scarman 1982). Lord Scarman's report on the Brixton riots of 1981 took the view that much work was being done by local authorities, especially the Inner London Education Authority (ILEA), and by schools and teachers to adapt education to minority needs. His report recommended a major government initiative to ensure that young black people had equal chances in society. However, no such initiative was forthcoming, and the ILEA was abolished by the 1988 Education Act.

The final report of the Committee of Inquiry into the education of ethnic minority children, chaired by Lord Swann, was published in 1985, making seventy-one recommendations for improving education for *all* young people growing up in a multi-ethnic society (DES 1985). It was given cautious approval by Keith Joseph, then Education Secretary of State, although the *Sun* newspaper advised him to 'shove it in the Whitehall incinerator' and Pearce, a right-wing commentator, claimed that the report was 'a profoundly dangerous document aimed at reshaping British society' (Pearce 1986: 136). The parts of the Swann Report which particularly upset traditionalists were the comments that a 'fundamental reappraisal' of values and attitudes in education was needed (DES 1985: 324) and that a 'redefined concept of what it means to live in British society' as a plural society should be a major goal (p. 8).

Other high-profile cases of opposition to education taking account of the multicultural nature of the society included those of the Bradford headteacher Ray Honeyford whose views on multicultural education were at odds with his employing LEA (Honeyford 1988), parents in Dewsbury who in 1987 refused to send their children to a school with a majority of Asian children, and a parent in Cleveland who won the right to remove her daughter from a multi-racial school on the judgment that 'choice' legislation overrode race relations legislation (Tomlinson 1990). The murder of Ahmed Ullah, an Asian boy, in the playground of Burnage School in Manchester, also sparked opposition to multicultural and anti-racist education, as the school had attempted to produce and put into practice an anti-racist policy (MacDonald 1989). At government level, ministers consistently refused requests from the Muslim community to receive state funding for Islamic schools on a par with voluntary-aided Anglican, Catholic and Jewish schools, and in a speech to the 1987 Conservative Party Conference, Margaret Thatcher expressed populist and ministerial fears that multicultural and anti-racist education was linked to left-wing extremism and lowered standards (Hughill 1987).

Despite all this, the 1980s was a period of educational advance for minorities. It could fairly be claimed that the raised awareness of practitioners and teacher unions, some central and local policy, plus pressure from minority communities, and both national and international groups concerned with equity, were all factors leading to the improved treatment of minorities in education, their raised educational performance and some curriculum change. Formal requirements that teachers in training should be made aware that they would be teaching in a multi-ethnic society were made by the Council for the Accreditation of Teacher Education (CATE) set up in 1984, which led to the question 'Who trains the trainers?' This began to be addressed by courses pioneered by Maurice Craft at Nottingham University (Craft 1996) and in-service courses for teachers, run by local authorities with Grant-Related In-Service Training (GRIST) funding. The Swann Committee believed that a major way of ensuring curriculum issues could be addressed was through the 1984 Education (Grants and Awards) Act, which allowed government to pay education support grants (ESG) for innovation in education. Eventually some 120 ESG projects were supported, especially in 'white' areas of the country, running from 1985 to 1991. The projects did generate new ideas, produced new materials and raised awareness, although there was resistance in areas with few or no minorities to the idea that change was needed, referred to by some as the 'no problem here syndrome' (Gaine 1987; see also Tomlinson 1990).

Further positive moves included the adoption by over two-thirds of LEAs of some kind of a multicultural or anti-racist policy by 1988; increasing numbers of schools working on their own policies; HMI and local advisers offering help and advice; a number of Teachers' Centres and Multicultural Centres set up around the country acting as resource bases; and a requirement that the new GCSE examination boards have regard to linguistic and cultural diversity. Organisations such as the teacher-led National Anti-Racist Movement in Education, and the Early Years Trainers Anti-Racist Network focused attention on the major problem of racism and racist stereotyping that was manifest in education from nursery classes upwards.

After 1988: the education market

After 1988, however, the slow but steady progress towards the more equitable incorporation of minorities into the education system was considerably impeded. Overt policies for dealing with race and minority issues were almost completely removed from the educational agenda and race became an absent presence (Apple 1999: 12), not to be rediscovered until the end of the 1990s. The new framework for funding, administering and monitoring all aspects of education, and the competition between schools based on parental 'choice' of school (fuelled by the annual publication of raw scores of examination results) gradually introduced new ways of disadvantaging minorities. The intention of the education market was to change the balance of power from producers to consumers of education; choice and competition were to ensure that good schools prospered while weaker schools closed, and ostensibly free consumers were to embrace the laws of the market and the values of self-interest and personal and familial profit.

While a variety of school choice movements were in operation globally by the end of the 1980s and arguments were being advanced that there had been an international welcome for greater choice, school accountability and less local bureaucratic intervention (Chubb and Moe 1992), others were pointing out that geographical location, social class and the history of particular schools all combined to reduce choice for some groups and increase segregation by class and race (OECD 1994; Gewirtz *et al.* 1995; Benn and Chitty 1996). There was no 'level playing field' from which all schools started out fairly in the bid to attract students and associated funding. In the UK, the 1991 census showed clearly 'the concentration of minorities in the most urbanised parts of Britain' (Centre for Research in Ethnic Relations 1992), with 60 per cent of those of Afro-Caribbean and Indian origin living in Greater London and the West Midlands, Bangladeshis concentrated in East London, and some cities settled by specific migrant groups – East African Asians in Leicester, for example. In some areas of cities, minorities *were* the majority, and their younger age profile ensured that their school and college age profile remained high.

While there had been some gentrification of inner-city areas, with whites moving back into renovated housing, the areas minorities lived in had major indices of disadvantage. The urban schools most minority students moved into from the 1960s to the 1990s, although nominally comprehensive, were intended for the working class and never designed to prepare students for high-level academic work and higher education. Most were renamed secondary modern schools, and until the early 1960s were actually forbidden to enter students for public examinations (Simon 1991). In a survey of over 1,500 comprehensive schools and colleges carried out in 1994, distinct social class differences were apparent. Those with black and other minority groups had higher working-class and lower middle-class intakes than the survey average. Some 81 per cent of schools with Afro-Caribbean students had predominantly working-class intakes, as did 71 per cent of schools with Indian and 72 per cent of those with Irish students (Benn and Chitty 1996: 175). Research by Ball and his colleagues indicated that social class differences enabled privileged 'choosers' – largely white middle-class – to avoid schools with negative characteristics, one of these being high numbers of minority students (Gewirtz *et al.* 1995). Following their research cohort into post-school education, they found that white students avoided colleges of further education with 'high black' attendance, although some colleges were marketing themselves to attract black students (Ball *et al.* 1998)

The competitive market situation which emerged in the UK in the 1990s did encourage schools to orient themselves to attract the middle classes, and while this included the small emergent black and Asian middle class, whose choices mirrored those of the white middle class (Noden *et al.* 1998), class and location continued to disadvantage racial minorities, still predominantly part of the lower socio-economic groups and with all the well-documented disadvantages of these groups. Racial and ethnic segregation is exacerbated by choice policies, and in the UK it soon became apparent that choice was offering white parents a legitimate way of avoiding schools with high intakes of minority students. This had been foreseen during the passage of the 1988 Education Act by opposition peers in the House of Lords, who, in conjunction with the CRE, sought to amend the requirements on parental choice, arguing that this would lead to racial segregation by school. Lady Hooper, a Minister of State for Education, conceded this, but concluded in a television interview in November 1987 that 'racial segregation may be a price to be paid for giving some parents more opportunity to choose' (Tomlinson 1988).

Funding and failing in the 1990s

As a precondition for an education market, schools after 1988 were given control of their own budgets and LEAs were required to devolve most of the funding they received to schools. Research found that funding was 'disproportionately damaging to inner urban schools' (Guy and Mentor 1992: 165), and minority students were further disadvantaged as LEAs closed down multicultural education centres and local authority multicultural advisers lost their jobs. Money given under Section 11 of the 1966 Local Government Act for the special needs of ethnic minorities became discretionary, and LEAs had to bid for the grant.

The New Labour government, taking over in 1997, committed itself to 'fair funding' policies and set in train a number of initiatives designed to combat the disadvantage suffered by lower socio-economic groups, with the assumption – as in the 1970s – that measures to benefit all disadvantaged groups would benefit minorities. In 1997 a Social Exclusion Unit was set up in the Cabinet Office, opened by Prime Minister Blair with the assertion that he wished to see 'Britain rebuilt as a nation in which each citizen is valued and no one is excluded' (Blair 1997: 1). The Unit focused initially on school truancy and exclusions, particularly of Afro-Caribbean boys. A major policy initiative created Education Action Zones. These were to be in disadvantaged areas in which a mix of public and business money partnerships were intended to raise educational achievement. The first twenty-five of these operated from September 1998. A programme aimed at disadvantaged 0- to 3-year-olds, 'Sure Start', was also announced in 1998, and again the assumption was that minority children would benefit. The one policy directed specifically at ethnic minorities was the replacement of the Section 11 grant with an Ethnic Minority Achievement Grant (EMAG) to be distributed, after bids from LEAs, by the DfEE, and the use of the grant evaluated by research. In 1999 the grant became EMTAG with the inclusion of travellers' children, and the proposal to evaluate the grant was dropped.

However, the contradictions in government policies which characterised the 1990s continued to affect minorities disproportionately. While the New Labour government was preaching 'inclusiveness', it was continuing the market policies set in train by the previous government which had the effect of excluding working-class and minority pupils from 'desirable' schools and disproportionately from mainstream education. There was a targeting of schools described as 'failing' and a public pillorying of largely urban schools deemed to be offering an inadequate education. Under the 1992 Education (Schools) Act, when a school was deemed to be failing 'special measures' could be taken by the newly privatised inspectorate (Ofsted). Press coverage of failing schools was negative and derisory, with the accolade of 'the worst school in Britain' handed out to different schools every few months (Brace 1994). The first survey of ninety-two failing schools, with data provided by the DfEE, showed that over 70 per cent of the schools included disadvantaged children (DfEE 1995). The first, and only, supposedly 'failing' school to be closed after the appointment of an Education Association,[3] Hackney Downs in the London borough of Hackney, had 80 per cent of pupils from an ethnic minority background, half speaking English as a second language and 70 per cent qualifying for free school meals. A second school threatened with such treatment had similar proportions of minority and second-language speakers, including numbers of refugee children (Gardiner 1996). The responsibility for the schools' problems was chiefly assigned to teachers, governors, parents and pupils rather than to historical, structural, economic or political factors. Market reforms exacerbated the difficulties of schools attended by minorities by taking money, resources and the middle classes away, and the schools were then blamed for ensuing difficulties. The 'failing schools' policy proved a new way of scapegoating and disadvantaging minorities.

Minority students were also disadvantaged by policies of school selection, either overt or covert, particularly operated by the grant-maintained (now foundation) schools set up from 1998, and by streaming (tracking) and setting of pupils within schools. Research by Gillborn and Youdell (1999) found that black students were disproportionately placed on low-level GCSE examination tracks, making it impossible for them to achieve higher grades.

The market encouraged schools to get rid of students who disrupted the smooth running of the school or who interfered with the credentialling of other students. Since the 1960s, special education had provided one way in which minority (particularly Afro-Caribbean) students could be removed from the mainstream. Black students were four times over-represented in the stigmatised category of 'educationally sub-normal' in the 1970s (Tomlinson 1981), and in the 1980s and 1990s were over-represented in the category of 'emotionally and behaviourally disturbed'. Removal from mainstream to special education has always been a lengthy process, and in the 1990s straight exclusion from school became the major means for removing the troublesome. Again, black students were over-represented. In 1992, black Afro-Caribbean students constituted 2 per cent of the school population but 8 per cent of those excluded from school (DfEE 1992). Gillborn, after researching black exclusions, commented that 'exclusion operates in a racist manner, they deny a disproportionate number of black students access to mainstream education.' (Gillborn 1995: 36). The whole stereotype of the 'undesirable' student attending a failing school became, in the 1990s, implicitly linked to racial minorities.

Racism

Throughout the period surveyed in this chapter, racism in schools and society continued to create a major barrier to the fair and just incorporation of minority young people into the education system. Although the 1976 Race Relations Act made racial discrimination illegal, racist beliefs and attitudes, and racist behaviour continued to affect the lives and learning of minority children (CRE 1987; Tomlinson 1990). Racism was directed at 'visible minorities' by physical or verbal harassment and bullying. Cultural racism was directed against minority religions and cultural practices, and institutional racism – beliefs and practices embedded in organisations – was manifest in school organisation, curricula and teacher behaviour. Despite the raised awareness of teachers noted in the 1980s, high degrees of conflict between teachers and black students and stereotyping of Asian students (particularly Muslim girls) were evident into the 1990s (see Bhatti 1999; Gillborn and Youdell 1999). The Teacher Training Agency (TTA), created in 1994 after the abolition of CATE to oversee the recruitment and training of teachers, initially took little account of teacher training for a diverse society. The initiatives in both pre- and in-service training had disappeared from the agenda by the early

1990s, with politicians from the prime minister downwards deploring anti-racist initiatives.[4] The TTA was criticised by Sir Hermann Ousley, head of the CRE, in 1998 for its inertia over multiculturalism and anti-racism, and the national standards for qualified teacher status have never prioritised teacher preparation for a society still demonstrating much racism.

Ironically, Ofsted was more pro-active; Ofsted handbooks for nursery, primary, secondary and special schools required inspectors to take account of ethnicity and background and provision for pupils with English as a second language (Ofsted 1995). After having been criticised for failing to take equality issues seriously, Ofsted commissioned a review of the achievement of ethnic minority pupils (Gillborn and Gipps 1996) and undertook a further review in 1998 (Ofsted 1999).

While LEAs and schools during the 1980s continued to develop anti-racist policies, racial minorities continued to experience much violence and harassment. In 1986, 13-year-old Ahmed Ullah was murdered in the playground of Burnage School, Manchester, by a white fellow-pupil, and the media attempted to blame the school as it had formulated an anti-racist policy (MacDonald 1989). In 1993, the murder of 18-year-old college student Stephen Lawrence by five white youths became *the* focus in the 1990s for debate on racism in the police force and all other social institutions. An inquiry into the murder, set up in 1997, eventually reported in 1999, making four recommendations on education: that the National Curriculum be amended to help value cultural diversity and prevent racism; that LEAs and schools develop strategies to address racism, including reporting racist incidents; that Ofsted should monitor strategies; and that local government and other agencies should implement local and community initiatives to address racism (MacPherson Report 1998: 334–5). By the late 1990s, racism directed at refugees, asylum seekers and travellers had become an issue (Home Office 1996) and Ofsted had begun to take account of the experiences of these groups (Ofsted 1999).

Curriculum policies and practices

Moves to disentangle the school curriculum from the imperial past were evident from the early 1970s, and in 1977 a Labour Green Paper acknowledged that 'The curriculum appropriate for our Imperial past' needed changing (DES 1977). During the 1980s, a considerable literature emerged on a multicultural curriculum practice, and practitioners and the Inspectorate supported the notion that all pupils should learn to respect other religions and ways of life and understand the interdependence of individuals and nations. The Swann Committee pointed out that it was the school curriculum which was the vehicle for bringing about the 'fundamental re-orientation of attitudes which were needed in an ethnically diverse society' (DES 1985: 324). In the mid-1980s, in-service training courses covering 'teaching and the curriculum in a multi-ethnic society' were a notional priority for two years, and central government gave Educational Support Grants to some 120 projects concerned with curriculum change and development for an ethnically diverse society (Tomlinson 1990). During the passage of the 1988 Act, an amendment that Section 1.2 of the Act should assert that the National Curriculum would 'prepare pupils for the opportunities, responsibilities and experiences of adult life *in a multi-*

cultural, multiracial society' was defeated, but in 1988 Kenneth Baker, then Secretary of State for Education, instructed his new National Curriculum Council to 'take account of ethnic and cultural diversity, and the importance of the curriculum in promoting equal opportunity for all regardless of ethnic origin or gender' (DES 1988). However, by 1990, an editorial in the *Times Educational Supplement* (*TES*) noted that 'there seems to be an unformulated intent to starve multicultural education of resources and let it wither on the vine' (*TES* 23 October 1990). The intent was deliberate, not unformulated, as Duncan Graham, first chair of the NCC, made clear in his book (Graham 1993). A report of a multicultural Task Group set up in 1989 to consider ways in which the curriculum could broaden the horizons of *all* pupils and address the needs of minority – and bilingual – pupils was never published (Tomlinson 1993; Tomlinson and Craft 1995), and the political interference in the Working Groups appointed to decide curriculum content in each subject area has been well documented (Cox 1995; Phillips 1998). In particular, Margaret Thatcher attempted in 1990 to influence the history curriculum, and there was much conflict over the inclusion of 'world', as against 'British', literature in English.

In 1993 an overloaded National Curriculum was slimmed down by Sir Ron Dearing (Dearing 1993) with no reappraisal of its appropriateness for a diverse society, and a further reappraisal was undertaken in 1999 by the Qualifications and Curriculum Authority (QCA) in preparation for a re-launched National Curriculum in September 2000. Following the recommendations of a Citizenship Advisory Group (Crick 1998), citizenship education became a compulsory element, taking at least 5 per cent of curriculum time. Secretary of State David Blunkett, introducing the new National Curriculum proposals, asserted that personal and social education and citizenship education could make a contribution to 'combating racism, promoting equal opportunities, and teaching about fairness, justice, rights and responsibilities through an understanding of diversity' (DfEE 1999: 13). There was little guidance for schools as to how they should make this contribution, no suggestion of specific training for teachers, and no 'fundamental reappraisal' of the other subject areas. In addition, religion continued to be a source of some conflict. The National Curriculum of 1988 prioritised the Christian religion (Education Act 1988, sections 6–9) while 'taking account' of other religions, and eventually each local authority individually developed an 'agreed syllabus'. Faith communities around the country continued to demand state-funded separate schooling, particularly after the passing of the 1993 Education Act, which encouraged this. The Conservative government resisted demands from non-Christian faiths, but in 1998 New Labour agreed that a Seventh-Day Adventist school attended by black students and Muslim and Sikh schools could become voluntary aided, on a par with state-funded Anglican, Catholic and Jewish schools.

Achievement

The possession of education credentials increased in importance all over the world towards the end of the twentieth century. What Dore in 1976 had regarded as a 'Diploma Disease' of the developing world, had spread to developed countries (Dore 1976). Educational qualifications had become ever more crucial in selection and allocation for any kind of employment, and a higher education had become a necessity for professional, managerial and executive jobs. Thus, the educational performance of minority pupils assumed even greater importance for their parents, and a continued focus for tension and anxiety. During the 1990s there were widespread improvements in the performance of all young people in public examinations – GCSE, A levels and associated vocational qualifications. The improvement was shared by all minority groups, although patterns of achievement among different groups emerged more strongly. The two Ofsted-commissioned reports on school achievement (Gillborn and Gipps 1996; Ofsted 1999) indicated, as did other research, that the greatest improvement was among East African Asian, Indian and Chinese pupils, with Bangladeshi and Pakistani pupils doing less well, particularly in the early years, but closing the gap between themselves and others in the course of their education. Black Caribbean pupils performed well in primary schools but performance declined at secondary school, especially among boys. Girls from all minority groups attained more highly than boys throughout schooling. Traveller and refugee children were not well served by schools.

As with white pupils, social class was associated with achievement for all ethnic groups. Pupils from higher social class backgrounds performed better all through schooling and achieved more qualifications (Smith and Tomlinson 1989; Cheng 1995). Muslim pupils tended to achieve less well, but a large proportion came from lower socio-economic backgrounds and were more recent arrivals in the UK. Research from the 1970s to the 1990s demonstrated that ethnic minority young people showed greater persistence in continuing in education, usually in further education colleges, partly due to greater motivation to improve their qualifications and partly due to greater difficulty finding work (Cheng 1995). Afro-Caribbean and white students were more likely to take vocational courses and seek work after college. The fourth PSI study of ethnic minorities in Britain (Madood *et al.* 1997) found that Afro-Caribbean men in their early twenties were more highly qualified vocationally than any other group. Minority students were thus more likely to catch up on qualifications not obtained at school, and to be older than white students when entering higher education.

Some minorities' students aspire to, and are successful in reaching, higher education. University participation ratios for Indian and Pakistani young men and Indian, Pakistani and Afro-Caribbean young women exceed those for white men and women, and they are less likely to come from middle-class homes than white students. Ballard has noted that 'the capacity of visible minorities to overcome the British education system's well-known obstacle of class is truly remarkable' (Ballard 1999: 11). However, minority students are more likely to attend 'new' urban universities, be older on entry, and pursue part-time courses more (HEFCE 1996: 11).

Conclusion

A verdict on the way in which the education system has incorporated racial and ethnic minority young people over the past twenty-five years would probably be, then, 'some success, could do better!' Improvements in the education performance of minority groups were set in train well before the impact of market forces.

Schools, teachers and local authorities had become more responsive to the needs of minorities during the 1970s and 1980s, and despite hostility from the New Right there were political initiatives from both major parties to encourage this. One result of improved performance was that minorities began to enter higher education in large numbers and seek further education and vocational qualifications at college. Disadvantages associated with this are that students attend less prestigious universities and urban colleges and are older on entry and on attaining qualifications. A further disadvantage for minorities – not the subject of this chapter – is the 'ethnic penalty' minorities experience on entering the labour market, whereby whatever their level of qualification they find it harder to find work and promotion (Heath and McMahon 1997; see also the chapter in this volume by Robertson and Lauder). The Commission on the Future of Multi-Ethnic Britain, reporting in October 2000, made twenty-one recommendations for the improvement of the education service (Parekh Report 2000).

The education market in schools has certainly led to disadvantages for minority pupils. All parents have benefited from more information offered by schools and, initially, many minority parents supported the promise of more power for consumers. While there is some evidence of black and Asian middle-class parents taking advantage of choice policies and making similar choices to the white middle class, minority parents in many urban areas do not have access to historically well-resourced schools. Minority parents, in common with other parents, discovered that the rhetoric of choice did not match the reality whereby children were selected or rejected by schools. Education markets enhance the life choices of middle-class minorities, leading to the situation described by Wilson in the USA whereby 'talented and educated blacks ... continue to enjoy the advantages and privileges of their class status' (Wilson 1979: 153). In addition, educational success on the part of minority groups does not necessarily lead to congratulation from the white majority. The educational success of any minority group or individual is more likely to be resented by the increasing numbers in the majority population who are, or fear, becoming downwardly mobile. Education has become a competitive positional good, and from the point of view of the white majority the fewer competitors the better. At the same time, the concentration of minorities in urban areas and often 'failing schools' perpetuates the xenophobic reaction that the presence of minorities lowers standards. Despite the rediscovery of race in the later 1990s, with the New Labour government opening up more dialogue with minorities and attempting more inclusive policies, the retention of market policies and the increasing segregation in schools and colleges has created new and additional disadvantages. Minority young people bear market burdens that have set back their just and equitable incorporation into the education system. Ultimately, demography and aspiration may win over xenophobia and racism as larger numbers of educated and skilled young racial and ethnic minorities become absorbed into the labour market in the twenty-first century.

Notes

1　This chapter does not enter into the long-standing debate of definitions of race and ethnicity. It refers to groups defined as racial or ethnic on the basis of characteristics imputed to them by others (Rex 1986: chapter 1), and when quoting from policies or literature employs the language used in the text. The Commission on the Future of Multi-Ethnic Britain (Parekh Report 2000) have urged that a new vocabulary is needed to reflect a new understanding of British society.

2　Self-assignment to 'ethnic' groups in the 1991 census comprised 94.5 per cent white and 5.5 per cent ethnic minority, of which 1.6 per cent defined themselves as black African, Afro-Caribbean or black Other, 2.7 per cent as South Asian (Indian, Pakistani or Bangladeshi), and 1.2 per cent as Chinese or other Asian.

3　The 1993 Education Act made provision for the setting up, by the Secretary of State, of Educational Associations which would take over the governance of 'failing' schools and recommend either closure or grant-maintained status. The first and only Association to be appointed had its actions questioned in the High Court (O'Connor *et al.* 1999).

4　At the 1992 Conservative Party Conference, Prime Minister Major asserted that 'teachers should teach children how to read – not waste their time on the politics of race, class and gender'.

References

Acheson, Sir D. (1998) *Inequalities in Health Report*, London: HMSO.

Apple, M. (1999) 'The absent presence of race in educational reform', *Race Ethnicity and Education*, 2(1): 9–16.

Ball, S.J., Maguire, M. and Macrea, S. (1998) 'Race, space and the further education market place', *Race Ethnicity and Education*, 1(2): 171–90.

Ballard, R. (1999) *Paper for the Commission of the Future of Multi-Ethnic Britain*, London: Runnymede Trust.

Benn, C. and Chitty, C. (1996) *Thirty Years On*, London: David Fulton.

Bhatti, G. (1999) *Asian Children at Home and at School*, London: Routledge.

Blair, T. (1997) 'My vision for Britain', in G. Radice (ed.) *What Needs to Change: New Visions of Britain*, London: Labour Party.

Brace, A. (1994) 'Is this the worst school in Britain?' *Mail on Sunday*, 20 March.

Centre for Research in Ethnic Relations (1992) *Ethnic Minorities in Britain: Settlement Patterns*, Warwick: University of Warwick.

Cheng, Y. (1995) *Staying on in Full-Time Education after 16*, Youth Cohort Report no. 37, London: DfEE.

Chubb, J. and Moe, T. (1992) *Politics, Markets and American Schools*, Washington: Brookings Institute.

Commission for Racial Equality (1987) *Learning in Terror*, London: CRE.

Cox, B. (1995) *The Battle for the English Curriculum*, London: Hodder & Stoughton.

Craft, A. and Bardell, G. (1984) *Curriculum Opportunities in a Multicultural Society*, London: Harper.

Craft, M. (ed.) (1996) *Teacher Education in Plural Societies*, London: Falmer.

Crick, B. (1998) *Education for Citizenship and the Teaching of Democracy in Schools*, Report of the Advisory Group, London: DfEE.

Dearing, Sir R. (1993) *The National Curriculum and its Assessments*, London: SCAA.

DES (1977) *Education in Schools – A Consultative Document (Green Paper)*, London: DES.

——(1981) *West Indian Children in Our Schools (Rampton Report)*, London: HMSO.

——(1985) *Education for All: Report of the Committee of Inquiry on the Education of Children from Ethnic Minority Groups (Swann Report)*, London: HMSO.

——(1988) *Letter to Chair of NCC from the Rt Hon. Kenneth Baker*, London: DES.

DfEE (1992) *Exclusions from School*, London: DfEE.

——(1995) *The Improvement of Failing Schools: UK Policy and Practice – Ofsted/OECD seminar organised by the DfEE*, London: DfEE.

——(1999) *Excellence in Cities*, London: DfEE.

Dore, R. (1976) *The Diploma Disease*, London: Unwin Educational Books.

Gaine, C. (1987) *No Problem Here*, London: Hutchinson.

Gardiner, J. (1996) 'Hit squad's target wins reprieve in climbdown', *Times Educational Supplement*, 26 July.

Gewirtz, S., Ball, S.J. and Bowe, R. (1995) *Markets, Choice and Equity in Education*, Buckingham: Open University Press.

Gillborn, D. (1995) *Racism and Anti-Racism in Real Schools*, Buckingham: Open University Press.

Gillborn, D. and Gipps, C. (1996) *A Review of Recent Research on Achievement by Ethnic Minority Pupils*, London: Ofsted.

Gillborn, D. and Youdell, D. (1999) *Rationing Education*, Buckingham: Open University Press.

Graham, D. (1993) *A Lesson for Us All*, London: Routledge.

Guy, W. and Mentor, I. (1992) 'Local management: who benefits', in D. Gill, B. Mayor and M. Blair (eds) *Racism and Education: Structures and Strategies*, Buckingham: Open University Press.

Haque, Z. (1999) 'Exploring the validity and possible causes of the apparently poor performance of Bangladeshi pupils in British secondary school', unpublished Ph.D. thesis, School of Education, University of Cambridge.

Heath, A. and McMahon, D. (1997) 'Educational and occupational attainments: the impact of ethnic origin', in V. Karn (ed.) *Education, Employment and Housing among Ethnic Minorities in Britain*, London: HMSO.

HEFCE (1996) *Widening Access to Higher Education*, London: HEFCE.

Hillgate Group (1986) *Whose Schools? A Radical Manifesto*, London: Hillgate Group.

Home Office (1978) *Proposals for Replacing Section 11 of the Local Government Act. A Consultative Document*, London: Home Office.

——(1996) *Racial Attacks*, London: Home Office.

Honeyford, R. (1988) *Integration or Disintegration: Towards a Non-Racist Society*, London: Claridge.

Hughill, B. (1987) 'Dramatic steps that will carry Britain forward', *Times Educational Supplement*, 16 October.

Kirp, D. (1979) *Doing Good by Doing Little; Race and Schooling in Britain*, Berkeley: University of California Press.

Lane, Sir D. (1987) 'The Commission for Racial Equality – the first five years', *New Community*, 14(1–2): 12–16.

Lynch, J. (1983) *The Multicultural Curriculum*, London: Batsford.

MacDonald, I. (1989) *Murder in the Playground: The Burnage Report*, London: Longsight Press.

MacPherson Report (1998) *The Stephen Lawrence Inquiry: Report of an Inquiry by Sir William MacPherson*, Cm 4262–1 London: Home Office.

Modood, T. (1998) 'Ethnic diversity and racial disadvantage in employment', in T. Blackstone, B. Parekh and P. Sanders (eds) *Race Relations in Britain: A Developing Agenda*, London: Routledge.

Modood, T., Berthoud, R., Lakey, J., Nazroo, J., Smith, P., Virdee, S. and Beishon, S. (1997) *Ethnic Minorities in Britain (The Fourth PSI Survey)*, London: Policy Studies Institute.

Noden, P., West, A., David, M. and Edge, A. (1998) 'Choices and destinations at transfer to secondary schools in London', *Journal of Educational Policy*, 13: 221–36.

O'Connor, M., Hales, E., Davies, J. and Tomlinson, S. (1999) *Hackney Downs: The School that Dared to Fight*, London: Cassell.

OECD (1994) *School: A Matter of Choice*, Paris: OECD.

Ofsted (1995) *Handbooks for Inspection for Primary and Secondary Schools*, London: Ofsted.

——(1999) *Raising the Attainment of Ethnic Minority Pupils. School and LEA Responses*, London: Ofsted.

Parekh Report (2000) *The Future of Multi-Ethnic Britain*, London: Profile Books.

Pearce, S. (1986) 'Swann and the spirit of the age', in F. Palmer (ed.) *Anti-Racism: An Assault on Education and Value*, London: Sherwood Press.

Phillips, R. (1998) *History Teaching, Nationhood and the State: A Study in Educational Politics*, London: Cassell.

Rex, J. (1986) *Race and Ethnicity*, Milton Keynes: Open University Press.

Rex, J. and Tomlinson, S. (1979) *Colonial Immigrants in a British City: A Class Analysis*, London: Routledge.

Richards, K. (1983) 'A contribution to the multicultural education debate', *New Community*, 10(2): 222–5.

Scarman Report (1982) *The Brixton Disorders 10–12th April (1981)*, London: Penguin.

Scruton, R., with Ellis-Jones, A. and O'Keefe, D. (1985) *Education and Indoctrination*, London: Education Research Centre.

Simon, B. (1991) *Education and the Social Order 1940–1990*, London: Lawrence & Wishart.

Smith, D.J. and Tomlinson, S. (1989) *The School Effect*, London: Policy Studies Institute.

Storkey, M. (1991) *London's Ethnic Minorities: One City, Many Communities*, London: London Research Centre.

Taylor, M. (1981) *Caught Between*, Slough: NFER.

——(1985) *The Best of Both Worlds*, Slough: NFER.

——(1988) *Worlds Apart*, Slough: NFER.

Tomlinson, S. (1981) *Educational Subnormality: A Study in Decision Making*, London: Routledge.

——(1983) *Ethnic Minorities in British Schools: A Review of the Literature*, London: Heinemann.

——(1988) 'Education and training', *New Community*, 15: 103–9.

——(1990) *Multicultural Education in White Schools*, London: Batsford.

——(1992) 'Disadvantaging the disadvantaged: Bangladeshis and education in Tower Hamlets', *British Journal of Sociology of Education*, 13(2): 337–46.

——(1993) 'The Multicultural Task Group; the Group that never was', in A. King and M.J. Reiss (eds) *The Multicultural Dimension of the National Curriculum*, London: Falmer.

Tomlinson, S. and Craft, M. (eds.) (1995) *Ethnic Relations and Schooling: Policy and Practice in the 1990s*, London: Athlone Press.

Troyna, B. (1987) *Racial Inequality in Education*, London: Tavistock.

Walford, G. and Miller, H. (1991) *City Technology College*, Buckingham: Open University Press.

Wilson, W.J. (1979) *The Declining Significance of Race*, Chicago: University of Chicago Press.

14 Gender and education policy

Continuities, transformations and critical engagements

Madeleine Arnot, Miriam David and Gaby Weiner

Introduction

Transformation in the schooling of boys and girls was one of the most significant educational changes in the late twentieth century. Yet gender equality in education has rarely been on the UK government policy agenda. In this chapter, we explore the intended and unintended effects of government policies since the 1970s, by comparing the continuities and discontinuities between social democratic and New Right policies and by pinpointing the effects of central and local relations on gender. We emphasise the complex interplay between educational policy and the often neglected key part played by family policy and values. We also focus on the role of a major social movement of the late twentieth century – education feminism.

In our analysis of post-war education and social change in *Closing the Gender Gap* (Arnot *et al.* 1999), we argued that the end of the twentieth century saw the culmination of attempts to break the hold of Victorian family values over the education of schoolboys and schoolgirls. Until then, the culture and curriculum provision of state schools was designed to sustain a sexual division of labour which presumed a wage-earning male head of household and a female dependent housewife. The challenge to such values was not the immediate goal of either post-war social democratic or New Right governments under Margaret Thatcher and John Major. Nevertheless, economic and social policy changes detached female education from women's domestic lives and reshaped male and female pupils' aspirations and identities. The actions taken by the women's movement were critical to gender transformations. In the UK, the constellation of these official hegemonic and feminist counter-hegemonic projects were found largely at school level.

In this chapter, we briefly explore how the challenge to Victorian gender values was found in social democratic educational reforms between the 1960s and 1970s and how women's economic position and their education were transformed by the welfare state. We then consider the uneven social consequences of the socio-economic policies and educational restructuring promoted by the Thatcher and Major Conservative governments from 1979 to 1997 and their effects on gender. In our discussion of both political eras, we describe how feminists reshaped educational policies and their outcomes. We conclude by speculating briefly on how New Labour approaches to gender issues might create new agendas which promote gender equality.

Schools as agents of change: social justice in the 1970s and 1980s

The year 1975 was pivotal in the history of gender relations in the UK when the Labour government passed the Sex Discrimination Act. In Britain, as in most advanced industrial/capitalist societies, women's employment opportunities had already mushroomed as a result of the expansion of educational, welfare and other social services. Women had tasted economic independence as job opportunities became available, but they also experienced the contradictions between their roles in the public world of work and in the family. In the new economic climates of the 1960s and 1970s and the new awareness of 'civil rights', women began consciously to transform their private lives. Under pressure from women and also partly in response to changing labour market conditions and the liberalisation of divorce laws, contraception and abortion practices, the patterns of family formation and dissolution in the UK began to change (Coote *et al.* 1990).

These stirrings had led to the formation at the end of the 1960s of the Women's Liberation Movement (WLM) which demanded social changes for women. The state could, if it so chose, redefine the boundaries between the public and private, between family, work and government. In 1969, the WLM formulated four demands on the state, namely: equal pay for equal work; equal educational opportunity; free contraception and abortion on demand; 24-hour nurseries (Coote and Campbell 1982). Feminists consequently put considerable pressure on the Labour government of the time to consider gender equality as part of its policy agenda.

Evidence at the time pointed to high levels of sex discrimination in employment, social policy and education. The Labour government responded by passing the Equal Pay Act in 1970, to be implemented by 1975. However, its White Paper on Equal Opportunities was diluted by the incoming Conservatives. Once back in government, Labour passed the Sex Discrimination Act 1975 (SDA). Surprisingly, unlike other areas of social policy, education was included in the legislation (Rendel 1985). The Race Relations Act passed in 1976 focused on racial discrimination. The two regulatory bodies, the Equal Opportunities Commission (EOC) and the Commission for Racial Equality (CRE), were both designed to be pro-active in consultation on policy, conducting formal investigations into possible discrimination, responding to complaints under the law, and promoting greater opportunities through educational activities. Both pieces of legislation signified major shifts in the understanding and interpretation of equal opportunities from social class towards sex/gender, race and ethnicity.

The passage of anti-discriminatory legislation in the UK was claimed as a victory for equal opportunities campaigners. (Rendel 1985). This was the first time that the concept of *discrimination* was used and that schools were given responsibility for promoting gender equality. The courts and the law could be used to police discriminatory practice (albeit only if victims of discrimination or harassment could prove their case). The aim of the legislation, however, was to provide a gender-neutral educational framework. The legislation rendered illegal the practice of excluding pupils from school subjects or courses on the grounds of sex. Yet, while it removed some discriminatory practices, it allowed others to continue. Textbooks and their content were excluded; co-educational schools were covered by the legislation but single-sex schools remained able to offer sex-specific curricula. Thus, girls in one school could be (and were) treated less favourably than boys in another. It was also left to non-statutory guidelines to urge secondary schools to avoid less overt biases and forms of sex discrimination. Secondary schools were warned 'not to organise the earlier stages of the secondary curriculum in such a way that it prevents a choice of the full range of options at a later stage' (EOC 1975: para. 4.10).

Another aim was to ensure that both girls and boys had a wider range of subject choice at secondary schools than the previous narrow sex-divided curriculum. However, subject take-up remained sex-divided and optional throughout the 1970s and early 1980s, as students at 13 plus were allowed relatively free choice of between four and six subjects (in addition to the 'core' subjects of English, mathematics and PE) to carry to the end of compulsory schooling. While a wide range of subjects was theoretically available, Pratt *et al.* (1984) found that girls tended to choose arts, humanities, commercial and 'caring' subjects, and boys science, mathematics and craft subjects. This was despite calls from teachers and academics for a more sex-equitable secondary school curriculum structure (Byrne 1978). Thus the outcomes of student choice and performance continued to reflect Victorian family values on private/female and public/male dualisms.

Although the first set of EOC commissioners were criticised for leaving their 'feminist hats at home' (Meehan 1982: 15), in its first ten years of existence the EOC cajoled teachers and the educational establishment to consider gender issues as important. This was at a time when schools and teachers saw themselves as autonomous from government and as largely responsible for the form and content of education. The strategy of reform relied heavily upon consent rather than coercion. It drew upon rational and legal arguments about the benefits of change, particularly in relation to women's economic advancement and their contribution to the economy. Thus, policy-makers encouraged changes through awareness-raising and professional teacher development.

While characterised by what can only be described as lukewarm government action on gender equality, the two decades which followed nevertheless witnessed a plethora of feminist action in schools. Schools (and particularly the teaching profession) were seen as potential agents of social change, able to reduce if not eliminate gender inequalities in education, and also in the economy and family. The opportunities afforded by devolved curricular and organisational structures and teacher autonomy in the English/Welsh context were exploited by those wishing to shape the content and structure of school teaching. *Voluntarist bottom-up* approaches to change, which encouraged teachers to become pioneers of anti-sexist and 'girl-friendly' educational reform, were used to persuade pupils, classroom practitioners and educational policy-makers of the need for gender equality.

There was little discussion of the merits of comprehensive education for gender equality (Shaw 1980; Deem 1984; Dale 1969, 1971, 1974) even though most comprehensive schools were co-educational. Such schools began to have considerable significance for the development of educational feminism in the UK. Evidence collected by the HMI for the DES (1975) revealed that boys and girls were channelled into different subject areas and that, at secondary school, girls seemed to lose the educational advantages gained at primary school. Debates about the respective merits of single-sex and mixed-sex secondary schooling were taken up by education feminists. They called for the reform of co-educational state schooling as a major focus of feminist activity in education.

Similarly, the discourse of progressivism, which as a result of the Plowden Report (1966) had influenced primary education from the 1960s, was shown by feminists to be inimical to concerns about male and female educational inequalities. Progressivism drew upon a concept of liberatory pedagogy where educational development and learning were seen as distinctive to the individual child within normative assumptions about age-related achievement (Walkerdine 1981). A child's social background, sex and ethnicity were relegated to the personal; thus, little interest was expressed in countering what were perceived as 'natural' gender patterns. Grounded in such a discourse, girls' early success in reading and language skills was viewed as transgressive, abnormal and 'not real learning' (Walkerdine 1983).

The challenges mounted by feminists appealed to the large audience of female teachers who were vital to the success of the movement. The appeal was to teachers to become 'insider reformers' to improve girls' schooling and the discriminatory practices in teachers' employment. Few women had risen to the top of the education profession, where men dominated headships, the inspectorate, university education departments and administrative/policy-making positions. Moreover, women had received scant support from the male-led teacher union movement largely uninterested in the problems women faced as employees (Oram 1987).

Increased professional awareness was, therefore, a prime target of feminist teachers and of the growing number of feminist academics engaged in promoting gender equality. The existence of the anti-discrimination legislation was used to open up debates about inequalities in the schooling for girls, a theme which, despite its challenge to patriarchal relations, resonated with both the radical politics of the new social movements and the economic rationalism of the time. In the event, backed by the municipal socialism of a number of inner-city Labour-controlled LEAs, such political campaigning received some official recognition and small-scale funding through in-service budgets, the provision of specialist advisers, and the seeding of action research projects (Myers 2000). Although in some notable instances pressure was put on headteachers to deliver action plans on gender equality (and even compulsory attendance on in-service courses), for the most part teacher-led change aiming at gender equality relied upon voluntary efforts. Those using the SDA as a catalyst urged schools to implement the spirit of the legislation and take on self-assessment. A common strategy was to provide evidence that inequalities existed in schooling, thus to put on record 'the hard facts of inequality' (Yates 1985).

Despite the election of a Conservative government in 1979, feminist teachers continued their challenge to pupils' conventional sex roles, focusing specifically on girls' education and female career opportunities. Although the EOC published guidance booklets to encourage boys to take up home economics, on the whole the main thrust of this 'unofficial' reform movement was directed towards making schools more 'girl friendly' (Whyte *et al.* 1985) and reducing the level of sexism found among boys and teachers.

Paradoxically, by 1980, campaigns to widen female career opportunities and curricular choices received an added boost from the effects of stringent government cutbacks on teacher training and the teaching profession. Teacher training colleges, up to the l970s, had been used as 'the cheap solution' to meeting the requirements of higher education expansion recommended in the Robbins Report (Committee on Higher Education l963) and the demands of a rising number of newly qualified, female school leavers. However, the falling birth rate, the falling pound, the economic crisis and a changed government led to the closure or merger of a hundred teacher training colleges and the subsequent reduction in places from 43,700 in 1970 to 8,700 in 1980. Yet this was also a time when girls' A-level results had risen faster than boys. As a result, a substantial proportion of academically successful girls joined the university system in order to take up professions and vocations other than teaching (Crompton 1992). The new paths and careers they chose were thus less 'domestically' oriented (Hutchinson 1997).

However, in this 'voluntary' phase, the pattern of school reform in UK in the name of gender equality was inevitably patchy. Initiatives and projects tended to be small scale and short lived, with consequent problems of under-financing and resourcing. They generally involved teachers at the lower end of the school hierarchy, and were more common in secondary rather than primary schools because gender differences in subject choice and examination results provided more tangible evidence of gender inequality. Critical to the development of such gender interventions was the sharing of information and strategies. In the UK context of a devolved curriculum, the existence of professional organisations and networks was vital for generating and sustaining innovation. Contact and communication networks (prevalent in the WLM) during this period played a key role in spreading ideas across diverse social communities, schools and phases of education (Weiner 1994a).

At the same time, in some mainly inner-city LEAs a more deliberate systematic approach to embed strategies in mainstream educational structures was adopted. In Brent and the Inner London Education Authority (ILEA), for example, in-service courses were designed around the concept of teacher–researcher to involve as wide a range of teachers as possible from the various sectors of education (Myers 2000). Equal opportunities advisers (and sometimes local inspectors) were used to promote gender networks through courses, projects and materials; in schools, special responsibility posts for equal opportunities and the development of school policies reflected LEA policy at the school level. In l983 a Women's National Commission's (1984) survey of LEAs found that although the majority had only briefed schools on the SDA, a substantial minority (about a third) had set up working parties or encouraged schools to 'take countering action', and 12 per cent had used or created special responsibility posts for gender.

By the 1980s, teacher unions who played a belated important role in supporting teachers' interests in gender equality also began to exert political pressure on local authorities and central government. In 1978 a group of women in the National Union of Teachers (NUT) had come together to respond to what they saw as the low priority given to women's rights issues in the union, the ghettoisation of women in the lowest-paid and poorest-funded areas of education, and the general domination of the union and its policy-making by men (Women in the NUT 1981). Such union activism highlighted the fact that gender issues in education could not easily be addressed without transforming male-dominated union hierarchies that kept women's issues at the bottom of the union agenda.

These diverse initiatives, however, also drew attention to the lack of political power within a devolved system of education. A strength of the English model of reform in this decade was that it encouraged a diversity of experiments on gender. The main weakness of this structure of education policy-making was its failure to encourage concerted government action and to achieve 'any ambitious and co-ordinated intervention' (Orr 1985). Equal opportunities in this period lacked political clout and was often only addressed at the rhetorical level by policy-makers.

At school level, initiatives to promote greater sex equality were characterised more by their diversity than their uniformity. That is not to say that the momentum generated by such initiatives did not have an impact. Educational feminism of this decade may not have infiltrated central government policy, but it deeply affected the climate and language of schooling in relation to girls' education, teachers' understandings about suitable curriculum content, the need to guard against preconceptions about femininity and women's role in society, and the necessity of responding to overt and covert incidences of sex discrimination. Well into the 1990s, teachers and headteachers who spoke with a commitment to gender equality still used a language which drew on feminism (Arnot *et al.* 1996).

Economic restructuring and family values: a new political context for education in the 1990s

Margaret Thatcher came to power in 1979 committed to reversing the welfare state, reorientating education and reinstating Victorian family values in order to revitalise an economy which was in crisis. Crises throughout the 1970s – in the economy, in employment and in international competitiveness – led to a breakdown in the political consensus about education in a social democracy (David 1980, 1993). By the end of the 1970s there were attacks on the welfare state, and education was particularly criticised as not having helped to sustain economic growth. The New Right targeted both for revision and reconstruction.

Conservative government policies, whether on the economy or welfare, had major gender effects. On the one hand, they encouraged economic restructuring, and on the other they initiated the destruction of communities based on industrial employment. Accompanying the growth in banking services and the re-emergence of the City of London as a global finance capital was a parallel decline in manufacturing industries and occupations, once central to the British economy. For example, in 1946, construction, mining and manufacturing industries provided 45 per cent of employment, and service industries 36 per cent of jobs. In 1989, these three great industrial sectors made up just 25 per cent of jobs in the country, while the service sector accounted for 15 million jobs – almost 70 per cent of total employment. By 1981, there were only 5.4 million working in manufacturing, compared with 8.6 million in 1966.

As Britain moved from industrialisation to post-industrialisation, gender relations in work and education for work changed. Complex economic, industrial and regional shifts in employment opportunities, particularly the growth of both public and private service sectors, had a clear impact upon gender relations, both within the family and in employment. Rather than being reduced by such transformations, the segregation of male and female work was aggravated. Traditionally the preserve of women workers, opportunities for service-sector work expanded, even if on a casual, temporary, part-time and/or low-paid basis. In contrast, opportunities for male employment, particularly for skilled or semi-skilled manual occupations, diminished. These kinds of shifts had a particular impact on working-class families and households.

Despite the social consequences, Conservative government policy concentrated upon redirecting public social services into the private (or privatised) sector, which included the family. The push to privatisation was both towards the implementation of business forms of organisation of the private or commercial sector and towards allotting to the private family, responsibility for social welfare and education. By the end of the 1980s a full programme of privatisation of public and welfare services, including health and education, was under way.

The 1980s and 1990s are also associated with new concerns about young people, and in particular their involvement in rising rates of crime, anti-social behaviour, exclusions from school, and youth unemployment. Young men were increasingly characterised as disadvantaged, and intimations appeared in the media that masculinity was in crisis and that boys were being 'lost' (Evans 1996). Those lower down the social scale were without jobs, and those higher up faced increasing job insecurity and competition from women. Education was viewed as partly responsible for this, as girls' raised examination performance at GCSE produced a reversal of previously male-dominated examination patterns and a closing of the gender gap (Arnot *et al.* 1999).

Whether Thatcherism made life excessively difficult for men is a moot point. Although there are extensive class and ethnic differences between men, some groups have clearly retained their dominance in the world of paid work and are pre-eminent in the worlds of power, politics, commerce, the civil services (Connell 1989). In contrast, the lack of job opportunities for young unskilled males offered little incentive for them to work hard at school or to gain qualifications (Mac an Ghaill 1994). Traditional male working-class jobs requiring physical strength disappeared in large numbers. With the decline of traditional apprenticeships that had eased the transition from school to work, young men needed to think imaginatively about how to achieve their aspirations.

Thus, when young men and women tried to anticipate their futures after full-time education in the 1990s, they received very different messages about male and female opportunities. Occupational opportunities and the youth labour market remained heavily structured by gender.

In the same period, the drift away from traditional family life to lone parents and the so-called 'parenting deficit' (Etzioni 1993) generated another set of moral discourses around the concept of Victorian virtues (Arnot *et al.* 1999). One response was to campaign for a return to traditional family values emphasising women's domestic responsibilities, especially in light of young male behaviour. Despite her own family and career, Margaret Thatcher was ideologically committed to the

Victorian family of paterfamilias and home-maker mother, and tried to reinvigorate the traditional family as the cornerstone and building block of community and society. She revived the term 'Victorian virtues' to distinguish between the 'deserving poor and the undeserving poor' (Thatcher 1993: 631). Both were to be helped, but in different ways. Thatcher's mission was to eliminate the dependency culture that sustained the 'undeserving poor'. Teenage single parents, one-parent families, absent fathers and divorced couples were all seen as highly problematic and dysfunctional. Because so much hung on how families operated, these groups became too important and central to the social order to remain outside the purview of the state.

The public spotlight was turned on teenage mothers, and questions were raised about their ability to raise a 'proper family'. They were vilified in the media and by politicians. Much of the attack on such families in the UK originated from the USA, using as an ideologue of the New Right, the ideas of Charles Murray (1994). But Durham (1991) argues that the influence of the 'moral majority' was not as fully developed in the UK, partly because government could not stem the tide of change. This it sought to do, for example, by restricting sex education and making teaching about homosexuality illegal (Kelly 1991). Moral campaigners could not but be disappointed by the lack of progress on the restriction of abortion and divorce and the continuing rise in illegitimacy rates, and their position in UK politics remained weak.

The attacks on single parents and attempts to develop moralistic family values appeared to have little effect on women's advancement. Early educational initiatives by Conservative governments to promote family life were also less than successful. Curricular reforms (e.g. school courses on parenthood) which encouraged traditional parenting roles were hard to implement within a decentralised educational system and were not the vehicle for a moral crusade, especially since they were not mandatory and occupied low status as non-examination subjects. Responsibility for sex education and parenthood education had been delegated to the new school governing bodies under the Education Act (1986), but children could be withdrawn from the classroom if their parents objected. The prohibition of teaching about gay and lesbian issues in schools in 1986 was symbolically and ideologically important but had little impact on practice, since few local authorities and schools had policies in place on teaching about sexuality.

New Right educational reforms, managerialism and gender inequalities

These various strands of Conservative educational policy between 1979 and 1997 were highly significant for gender. On the one hand, schools were expected to educate the majority of pupils in morality, respectful of authority, discipline and tradition. Education for parenthood, sex and moral education were building blocks of the programme to 'remoralise' the nation. On the other hand, individualism was encouraged through competitive, hierarchical structures and performance-focused services. Margaret Thatcher made it clear that the collectivist project which she felt had dominated wartime Britain and 'distorted' British society should be abandoned, along with the emphasis upon social equality (Thatcher 1995 : 46).

Thatcher saw high standards of education (defined in terms of qualifications) as increasingly important if Britain was to compete in the global economy. Deregulation was the only means of reversing what she saw as the worst aspects of post-war collectivist education policy. In this context, boys and girls were encouraged to turn their hopes and aspirations towards the world of work (rather than family or community) and abandon their outmoded identities and aspirations. Through schooling they were to engage with the technologically oriented global culture and the new individualistic spirit of the age. Schools were encouraged to modernise, to produce a work force that was not classed, sexed or racially classified. The future educated worker was to be mobile, flexible and qualified, well able to seize the opportunities made available.

In the event, economic benefits obtained by the removal of previous social barriers to the educational advancement of women seemed to outweigh other concerns about social order and family values. Indeed, the reform of the examination system in the mid 1980s, combining GCE/O levels with CSE examinations for secondary school pupils, marked the first steps towards a gender-neutral education. This approach was explicit, for example, in the funding criteria established for the Technical and Vocational Educational Initiative (TVEI) in 1983. In this key reform, 'liberal/progressive ideas concerning freedom for girls and women to move upwards in the educational and occupational hierarchies have become synonymous with "liberal", "laissez faire" ideas about labour market freedom' (Weiner 1989: 121).

The introduction of the GCSE in 1985 in retrospect seems to have been effective in encouraging students to study a balanced cluster of subjects, marking the beginnings of official change for girls. As a consequence, more girls were entered for science and mathematics than in previous decades, prompting the gradual shift in gender patterns of subject entry and performance.

This was followed by the reduction in subject choices which resulted from the introduction of the National Curriculum in the Education Reform Act 1988. This established ten subjects to be taught to children between 5 and 16 years old, national testing (SATs) and later the publication of performance league tables of schools' results for 16- and 18-year-olds (later widened to include 11-year-olds). The effect on girls' schooling was marked. While, in 1988, 42 per cent of girls who were entered for GCSE took home economics as one of their subjects, five years later, in 1993, this proportion had dropped to 15 per cent. The curricular reforms of the 1980s contributed to the restructuring of girls' subject choices (Arnot *et al.* 1996).

Notions of gender equality gave way to notions of individualism, the ideals of competition and the reward of performance. Significantly, Kenneth Baker (then Secretary of State for Education and Science) announced in 1988 that 'the age of egalitarianism is over'. As Phillips makes clear in Chapter 1 of this book, the Conservative reforms after 1988 can be summed up by the phrases 'standards' and 'choice'. By the time eighteen years of Conservative rule came to an end, the education landscape had shifted from one of minimal rhetorical commitment to social homogeneity to one of institutional variety and diversity, yet with an overriding centralism of policy steer, prescription of practice and inspection.

Feminist responses to Conservative education policies were generally not heard, nor were they represented in the new policy-making bodies. Their concerns about the traditional male orientation of the new curriculum were barely recognised. Thus, even though equal opportunities was listed as a cross-curriculum theme in 1988, it was viewed as too sensitive a subject to merit further development. There was no official commitment to monitoring sex (or race) bias in schools or in education more widely (Miles and Middleton 1990; Shah 1990).

Conservative educational reforms, however, became associated with greater participation of pupils in education beyond compulsory schooling. Indeed, far more pupils entered and passed GCSE and A levels than ever before. The publication of results (rather than government statistics) resulted in the gender analysis of students' performance at 16 and 18 which eventually heightened interest in gender once more, even if only to emphasise a 'crisis in masculinity' (Weiner *et al.* 1998; see also Epstein *et al.* 1998). Paradoxically, despite the alleged neutrality of New Right reforms on gender, the emphasis on results may have contributed to the development of what we termed a 'third wave' of feminist activity (Arnot *et al.* 1996), this time emphasising performance rather than social justice. Within this period, too, feminist teachers (the 'ordinary' classroom teacher) continued to inculcate in a new generation of girls a sense of what Whitty once called 'possibilitarianism' (Whitty 1974). As in the case of family change and the rise of female employment, so in the case of commitment to gender equality, the Conservative reformers were unable to reverse the tide of support for greater gender equality.

Education policy became more centralised and managerialist under the Conservatives, and the balance shifted away from interventions that depended on teachers and LEAs and towards government agencies such as the QCA and Ofsted. This shift from voluntarism to *managerialism* was part of the new economic/ educational structures. Previous informal, often idiosyncratic, models of school organisation were replaced by managerial regimes of 'line management', clearly defined job descriptions and boundaried responsibility, spheres of competence and expertise. Educational feminism itself had to change. Indeed, the new managerialism was viewed by some as a new set of male power relations located within a performance-oriented culture (Ball 1990; Maguire and Weiner 1994).

By the early 1990s, educational feminism had repositioned itself in relation to government policy-making in order to survive into the new managerial era (Weiner 1994b). Feminism, always 'a theory in the making' (hooks 1984), showed itself adept at meeting the need to change. Significantly, feminists who had been appointed to inspector and advisor posts in LEAs and who received training in new managerial techniques argued for feminist practitioners to 'manage' change more rationally and effectively. They aimed to treat gender initiatives like any other attempt at change, equivalent, say, to the adoption of a new reading scheme or alterations in staffing policy (see, for example, ILEA 1986). One of our most surprising findings in research carried out in the mid 1990s (Arnot *et al.* 1996) was the level of awareness of gender issues, given the lack of interest of UK governments towards gender equality since the 1980s. Rather than disappearing, as might have been anticipated due to their relative invisibility in the legislation, equal opportunities policies which included gender and were introduced after 1988 were claimed by most schools' respondents (81 per cent primary and 93 per cent secondary).

New Labour, new opportunities?

When the Labour government took power in 1997, the picture in terms of gender equality was complex. On the one hand, both boys and girls obtained far more qualifications than before, and in some cases the gender gaps in terms of subject choices and in terms of performance in a range of traditionally male or female subjects had closed. However, in 1998 only 80 boys to every 100 girls achieved five higher-grade GCSEs. Attention was drawn to the gender performance gap in literacy and language-related subjects (e.g. modern languages). In 1995, there was a 10 per cent gap in girls' and boys' achievement at age 7, and this gap continued through secondary schools. That year, 65 per cent of girls achieved A*–C grades in English GCSE compared with only 44 per cent of boys (Arnot *et al.* 1999).

After 16, the gender pattern was complex. On the one hand, girls matched boys' examination point scores at A/AS levels. In 1995, 75 per cent of girls were in full-time post-16 courses, compared with 69 per cent of boys. However, the performance data revealed an *increasing* 'masculinisation of science' and the continuing effects of a sex-segregated labour market on male and female post-school career choices (Arnot *et al.* 1996) An Ofsted-commissioned review on research findings which was published just after the 1997 election suggested that a wide range of economic, cultural and educational factors were involved, and that action was required to address the specific problems associated with boys and with girls, and those which had to do with social class and ethnicity (Arnot *et al.* 1998).

Since 1997, however, the New Labour government under Tony Blair has positioned itself within the performance debate in education rather than taking up the mantle of gender equality. The first initiatives on gender involved government ministers highlighting the importance of addressing the problems of disaffected boys and male underachievement as critical elements in improving school effectiveness (Weiner *et al.* 1998; Arnot and Millen 1998). LEAS and schools responded to the calls at various points from the Teacher Training Agency, the QCA, Ofsted and the DfEE for teacher research projects on boys' performance and for new examples of good practice in improving boys' achievement and literacy levels (Arnot 2000). Significantly, the patterns of male advantage in employment were not alluded to within this new official educational discourse, even though campaigns around improving women's maternity provision, tackling unequal pay and promotion prospects and the need to address the poverty of female single parents gathered force outside government (David 1999). New Labour has attempted to win women's vote by trying to 'meet the childcare challenge' (DfEE 1998) and by redirecting employment opportunities to single mothers (although these are not uncontroversial). The EOC, however, has urged that girls' educational needs continue to be recognised, not least because of the key relationship between employment opportunities and post-16 vocational and academic course choices. Encouraging schools to improve boys' performance but not 'at the expense of girls' is likely to be more problematic than officially conceived.

However, Moore (1996) argues that simple gender categories (such as those generated in the school performance tables) result in discussions about 'relative educational' achievements representing one group always as the 'problem' or, even worse, the 'victim' of the system. This tends to result in a failure to uncover the differences between those who are successful and those who fail to achieve within the current system of schooling. The extent to which one ethnic group, one social class or either sex is represented in the highest or lowest achieving educational group depends, to a large extent, on local context and conditions. As a review by Gillborn and Gipps (1996) of the achievements of ethnic minority pupils found, the effects of class and locality critically shape the patterns of performance of different groups of ethnic minority pupils.

Feminist and other commentators have expressed concern that the deeper social inequalities which had been aggravated by Conservative education policies have not yet been addressed by New Labour. The Social Exclusion Unit formed by New Labour in 1997 attempted to tackle the worst scenarios which resulted from the publication of results, namely the excessively high (and rising) number of school exclusions, many of whom were ethnic minority and white working-class male pupils. However, the National Commission on Education (1993) and the Dearing Report (GBNCIHE 1997) also highlighted major and continuing class differences in education and the severe disadvantages faced, for example, by 'the failing working-class girl' (Plummer 2000). Pressure on schools to perform in a competitive market have led to new organisational and cultural practices in schools which stress individualism and hierarchy. These have had major consequences for male and female pupils who historically did not achieve the benchmark grades. Recent evidence of the impact of school effectiveness discourses on the educational experiences and cultural responses of working-class or ethnic minority girls and boys has provided a challenging new agenda (Haw 1998; Mahony and Zmroczek 1997; Sewell 1997; Skeggs 1997; Walkerdine *et al.* 1996; Wright *et al.* 2000).

Conclusion

The elimination of sex discrimination and the promotion of gender equality have had a chequered history within government policy, since they have rarely taken centre stage. However, as ideals they have been deeply affected by, and influential on, mainstream educational policy. Any education policy, we have argued, cannot be divorced from welfare, not least economic and family policies.

As we have tried to show, the last twenty-five years of education policy-making has been extraordinarily complex for gender relations. The establishment of the welfare state with its attractions for female employees and the expansion of educational provision mainstreamed women's rights, albeit not always intentionally. The Sex Discrimination Act 1975 was the first official marker for this political movement of change. The break with Victorian family values was therefore well established before the Conservative Party came to power in 1979. It was exceptionally difficult for the New Right, despite its motivations, to 'put the genie back in the bottle' (Arnot *et al.* 1999). Paradoxically, a government which held little interest in gender equality oversaw many of the economic changes which were to undermine traditional gender patterns in family and community life. The destruction of manufacturing industry, the restructuring of the economy, the instability of many middle-class occupations and the destabilisation of family structures as a result of

New Right economic policies have had major unintended consequences for gender relations in schooling in the UK. At the same time, since the feminist movement had already found ways of using the educational system as the motor of gender change, Margaret Thatcher's educational reforms which introduced market competition in schools and colleges were unlikely to have equal gender effects.

The Conservative governments of the l980s and l990s thus put into place educational reforms which allowed some, particularly the most privileged, girls to seize more educational advantages. In contrast, at the other extreme, Campbell (1993) argued that Britain had became a more dangerous place to live in, and Wilkinson and Mulgan (1995) called a new form of alienated (often male) youth the 'under-wolves', while social commentators from the USA (Murray 1994) moralised about the rise of a new underclass.

The Conservative educational reforms from 1979 to 1997 were superimposed on a class-divided, sex-divided and racially divided education system. They did not aim to reduce gender inequalities or consolidate the school as an effective preparation for work but emphasised the accumulation of academic qualifications. They created the conditions in which young men and women in different social class and ethnic groups were faced with different sets of choices. The key issues for the government to address now are how such choices and conditions relate to the promotion of greater gender equality.

References

Arnot, M. (2000) 'Equal opportunities and educational performance', in J. Beck (ed.) *Key Issues in Secondary Education*, London: Cassell.

Arnot, M. and Millen, D., with Maton, K. (1998) *Current Innovative Practice in Schools in the United Kingdom*, Strasbourg: Council of Europe.

Arnot, M., David, M. and Weiner, G. (1996) *Educational Reforms and Gender Equality in Schools*, Research Series no. 17, Manchester: Equal Opportunities Commission.

Arnot, M., Gray, J., James, M. and Rudduck, J. (1998) *A Review of Recent Research on Gender and Educational Performance – Ofsted Research Series*, London: Stationery Office.

Arnot, M., David, M. and Weiner, G. (1999) *Closing the Gender Gap: Post-War Educational and Social Change*, Cambridge: Polity Press.

Ball, S.J. (1990) *Politics and Policy Making in Education: Explorations in Policy Sociology*, London: Routledge.

Byrne, E. (1978) *Women and Education*, London: Tavistock.

Campbell, B. (1993) *Goliath: Britain's Dangerous Places*, London: Methuen.

Committee on Higher Education (1963) *Higher Education* (The Robbins Report), London: HMSO.

Connell, R.W. (1989) 'Cool guys, swots and wimps: the inter-play of masculinity and education', *Oxford Review of Education*, 15(3): 291–303.

Coote, A. and Campbell, B. (1982) *Sweet Freedom: The Struggle for Women's Liberation*, London: Picador.

Coote, A., Harman, H. and Hewitt, P. (1990) *The Family Way: A New Approach to Policy-Making*, London: IPPR.

Crompton, R. (1992) 'Where did all the bright girls go?', in N. Abercrombie and A. Warde (eds) *Social Change in Modern Britain*, Cambridge: Polity Press.

Dale, R.R. (1969) *Mixed or Single Sex School? Vol. 1*, London: Routledge.

——(1971) *Mixed or Single Sex School? Vol. 2: Some Social Aspects*, London: Routledge.

——(1974) *Mixed or Single Sex School? Vol. 3: Attainment, Attitudes and Overview*, London: Routledge.

David, M.E. (1980) *The State, the Family and Education*, London: Routledge & Kegan Paul.

——(1993) *Parents, Gender and Education Reform*, Cambridge: Polity Press.

——(1999) 'Home, work, families and children: New Labour, new directions, new dilemmas', *International Studies in Sociology of Education*, 9(3): 209–29.

Deem, R. (ed.) (1984) *Co-education Reconsidered*, Milton Keynes: Open University Press.

DES (1975) *Curricular Differences for Boys and Girls. Education Survey*, London: HMSO.

DfEE (1998) *Meeting the Childcare Challenge*, London: Stationery Office.

Durham, M. (1991) *Sex and Politics: The Family and Morality in the Thatcher Years*, London: Macmillan.

Equal Opportunities Commission (EOC) (1975) *Do You Provide Equal Educational Opportunities?* Manchester: EOC.

Epstein, D., Elwood, J., Hey, V. and Maw, J. (1998) *Failing Boys? Issues in Gender and Achievement*, Buckingham: Open University Press.

Etzioni, A. (1993) *The Parenting Deficit*, London: Demos.

Evans, M. (1996) 'Perils of ignoring our lost boys', *Times Educational Supplement*, 28 June: 20.

Great Britain National Committee of Inquiry into Higher Education (GBNCIHE) (1997) *Higher Education in the Learning Society* (The Dearing Report), London: NCIHE.

Gillborn, D. and Gipps, C. (1996) *Recent Research on the Achievements of Ethnic Minority Pupils (Ofsted reviews of research)*, London: HMSO.

Haw, K. (1998) *Educating Muslim Girls: Shifting Discourses*, Buckingham: Open University Press.

hooks, b. (1984) *Feminist Theory: From Margin to Center*, Boston: Southend Press.

Hutchinson, G. (1997) 'The decline of a subject: the case of home economics', unpublished Ph.D. thesis, South Bank University, London.

Inner London Education Authority (ILEA) (1986) *Secondary Issues: Some Approaches to Equal Opportunities in Secondary Schools*, London: ILEA.

Kelly, L. (1991) 'Not in front of the children: responding to right-wing agendas on sexuality and education', in M. Arnot and L. Barton (eds) *Voicing Concerns: Sociological Perspectives on Contemporary Education Reforms*, Wallingford: Triangle Press.

Mac an Ghaill, M. (1994) *The Making of Men: Masculinities, Sexualities and Schooling*, Buckingham: Open University Press.

Maguire, M. and Weiner, G. (1994) 'The place of women in teacher education: discourses of power', *Educational Review*, 46(2): 121–39.

Mahony, P. and Zmroczek, C. (eds) (1997) *Class Matters: 'Working Class' Women's Perspectives on Social Class*, London: Taylor & Francis.

Meehan, E. (1982) 'Implementing equal opportunities policies: some British–American comparisons', *Politics: Journal of the PSA*, 2(1): 14–20.

Miles, S. and Middleton, C. (1990) 'Girls' education in the balance: the ERA and inequality', in M. Flude and M. Hammer (eds) *The Education Reform Act, 1988: Its Origins and Implications*, Basingstoke: Falmer.

Moore, R. (1996) 'Back to the future: the problem of change and the possibilities of advance in the sociology of education', *British Journal of Sociology of Education*, 17(2): 145–61.

Murray, C. (1994) *Underclass: The Crisis Deepens*, London: IEA Health and Welfare Unit.

Myers, K. (ed.) (2000) *Whatever Happened to Equal Opportunities in Schools? Gender Equality Initiatives in Education*, Buckingham: Open University Press.

National Commission on Education (1993) *Learning to Succeed: A Radical Look at Education Today and a Strategy for the Future*, London: Heinemann.

Oram, A. (1987) 'Sex antagonism in the teaching profession: equal pay and the marriage bar 1910–39', in M. Arnot and G. Weiner (eds) *Gender and the Politics of Schooling*, London: Hutchinson.

Orr, P. (1985) 'Sex bias in schools: national perspectives', in J. Whyte, R. Deem, L. Kant and M. Cruickshank (eds) *Girl Friendly Schooling*, London: Methuen.

Plowden Report (1966) *Children and their Primary Schools*, London: HMSO.

Plummer, G. (2000) *Failing Working Class Girls*, London: Trentham Books.

Pratt, J., Bloomfield, J. and Seale, C. (1984) *Option Choice: A Question of Equal Opportunity. A Study Sponsored by the Equal Opportunities Commission*, Windsor: NFER/Nelson.

Rendel, M. (1985) 'The winning of the Sex Discrimination Act', in M. Arnot (ed.) *Race and Gender: Equal Opportunities Policies in Education*, Oxford: Pergamon.

Sewell, T. (1997) *Black Masculinities and Schooling*, London: Trentham Books.

Shah, S. (1990) 'Equal opportunity issues in the context of the National Curriculum: a black perspective', *Gender and Education*, 2(3): 309–18.

Shaw, J. (1980) 'Education and the individual: schooling for girls, or mixed schooling; a mixed blessing?', in R. Deem (ed.) *Schooling for Women's Work*, London: Routledge.

Skeggs, B. (1997) *Formations of Class and Gender*, London: Sage.

Social Exclusion Unit (1998) *Truancy and School Exclusion*, London: Stationery Office.

Thatcher, M. (1993) *The Downing Street Years*, London: HarperCollins.

——(1995) *The Path to Power*, London: HarperCollins.

Walkerdine, V. (1981) 'Sex, power and pedagogy', *Screen Education*, 38 (spring): 14–25.

——(1983) 'It's only natural: rethinking child-centred pedagogy', in A.M. Wolpe and J. Donald (eds) *Is There Anyone Here from Education?* London: Pluto.

Walkerdine, V., Melody, J. and Lucey, H. (1996) Project 4:21 *Transition to Womanhood*, Swindon: ESRC.

Weiner, G. (1989) 'Feminism, equal opportunities and vocationalism: the changing context', in H. Burchell and V. Millman (eds) *Changing Perspectives on Gender: New Initiatives in Secondary Education*, Milton Keynes: Open University Press.

——(1994a) *Feminisms in Education: An Introduction*, Buckingham: Open University Press.

——(1994b) 'Equality and quality: approaches to changes in the management of issues of gender', in E. Burridge and P. Ribbens (eds) *Improving Education: Promoting Quality in Schools*, London: Cassell.

Weiner, G., Arnot, M. and David, M. (1998) 'Is the future female? Female success, male disadvantage and changing gender relations in education', in A. H. Halsey, H. Lauder, P. Brown and A. Stuart Wells (eds) *Education: Culture, Economy and Society*, Oxford: Oxford University Press.

Whitty, G. (1974) 'Sociology and the problem of radical educational change', in M. Flude and J. Ahier (eds) *Educability, Schools and Ideology*, London: Croom Helm.

Whyte, J., Deem, R., Kant, L. and Cruickshank, M. (1985) *Girl Friendly Schooling*, London: Methuen.

Wilkinson, H. and Mulgan, G. (1995) *Freedom's Children: Work, Relationships and Politics for 18–34 Year Olds in Britain Today*, London: Demos.

Women in the NUT (1981) *Newsletter*, London: NUT.

Women's National Commission (1984) *Report on Secondary Education*, London: Cabinet Office.

Wright, C., Weekes, D. and McGlaughlin, A. (2000) *'Race', Class and Gender in Exclusion from School*, London: Falmer.

Yates, L. (1985) 'Is girl-friendly schooling really what girls need?', in J. Whyte, R. Deem, L. Kant and M. Cruickshank (eds) *Girl Friendly Schooling*, London: Methuen.

15 Restructuring the education/social class relation

A class choice?

Susan Robertson and Hugh Lauder

Introduction

In the past twenty years there has been a fundamental restructuring of the economy and labour market. Concomitantly, education has also been restructured. This chapter addresses the ways in which economic and educational changes have led to a recasting of the social class structure in England and Wales. In doing so it also seeks to examine the question of whether the concept of social class is still of relevance. For as Reay (1997: 226) observes, 'understandings of class are products of specific historical and cultural locations ... and the 1990s has been a period when both politicians and academics have announced the demise of class and the advent of classlessness'. In order to answer these questions, we begin by outlining the key shifts within education policy and provision since Callaghan's Ruskin speech in 1976. As many of the chapters in this collection have made evident, 1976 signalled a sea change in state policy. In this chapter we argue that the educational reforms of this period had, at their heart, a reworking of the education/social class relation.

The chapter is in three sections. The first section documents the changes in education and the economy over the past twenty years. The second examines the nature of social class and its relevance to contemporary social and educational analysis, while the third section examines the evidence for the claim that, rather than social class disappearing, the recent changes in education, the economy and society have led to a reconfiguration of social class structures which have had profound implications for, and impacts upon, people's lives in England and Wales.

'The Great Moving Right Show'

'The Great Moving Right Show', as Hall (1983) so aptly named the various types of monetarist and authoritarian populist strategies of Margaret Thatcher and her New Right ideologues, can be read as a series of successful and strategically timed interventions in social and economic life following the 1970s oil crisis, stagflation and the consequent collapse of the post-war welfare state settlement. It was the New Right that established the view that the relationship between social democracy and moral, political and economic freedom could best be delivered not by a bureaucratically organised welfare system but through the unfettered market, an approach favoured by liberal capitalism (Pierson 1998: 38–9). The New Right argued that state intervention in welfare was administratively bureaucratic and hence stultifying; it was also paternalistic and failed to eliminate or eradicate unjust inequalities of opportunity (Gamble 1988: 27–60). As has often been pointed out, underlying these New Right or neo-liberal assessments of the relationship between capitalism, social democracy and the welfare state is a rehearsal of the sentiments of Adam Smith's advocacy of liberal capitalism, in particular the view that spontaneously arising market economies are the best means of securing both optimal individual and social welfare and the surest guarantee of individual liberty (Pierson 1998: 39).

The move to the 'right' signalled that a very different set of assumptions were being mobilised by the Conservative government in assessments about the nature and relationship of educational funding, provision and regulation within and between the public and the private sectors of education. In 1969, Margaret Thatcher, as Secretary for State of Education, issued Circular 10/70, which cancelled the requirement for local education authorities (LEAs) to proceed with comprehensive secondary schooling, an intervention that was intended to weaken the link between particular forms of schooling and social class. Kerckhoff *et al.* (1997: 23) show that in 1965 only 8.5 per cent of students in state-supported secondary schools were enrolled in comprehensive schools. By 1974, 57.4 per cent were, raising fears about the erosion of schooling structures that supported class differences. Despite the efforts of the Thatcher government to reverse this trend, 84.4 per cent were in comprehensive schools in 1983.

Throughout the 1980s the Thatcher government sought other mechanisms – in particular selection and specialisation – to weaken the effects of comprehensive schooling. The Education Act 1980 created a new publicly funded scholarship ladder, making it possible for 'able children to attend academically selective private schools which their families could not otherwise afford' (Edwards and Whitty 1997: 6). The introduction of school specialisation, in particular City Technology Colleges (CTCs) in 1986, also provided a different schooling route independent of LEAs, with selective admissions and programmes more likely to appeal to middle-class parents (Kerckhoff *et al.* 1997: 22). They also embraced the ethos of enterprise in their partnerships with business, technology and science. Unhindered by LEA control and selective in their intake (Gewirtz *et al.* 1991), CTCs were modern-day versions of grammar schools and an early register of the introduction of market principles in funding, providing and regulating educational provision.

The 1988 Education Reform Act (ERA) for England and Wales established the principle of the market as a mechanism for co-ordinating education. However, it was less a market than a quasi-market (Le Grand 1991), for it did little at this point to change the nature of supply (Walford 1997: 31). The ERA was entirely consistent with the New Right attack on comprehensive education and was seen as an attempt to undermine it. By giving families greater choice about the schools they wished to use, and by funding schools largely according to the number of students on the school roll, many schools – particularly at the secondary level – were placed in competitive relationships with each other, though for many schools this meant emulating the trappings and traditions of grammar schools, with their uniforms and highly managed *esprit de corps* (Fitz *et al.* 1993).

The move towards a market-like mode of governance of schooling was decried in leftist circles for fostering elitism and middle-class opportunity at the expense of the working class. The introduction of the Assisted Places Scheme in 1981 did little to ease misgivings. Conceived as a means of lifting 'working class embers from the ashes of failing inner city schools' (Edwards and Whitty 1997: 6), the Assisted Places Scheme rested upon an assumption that real academic opportunities could not be found in those comprehensive schools located in inner-city neighbourhoods. Rather, academic opportunities could only be found in those schools with high pass rates in public exams, high entry rates to universities, and a wide choice of academic subjects in the sixth form – in other words, typically middle-class schools. In any event, the 'embers' proved to be far less working class than the architects of the Scheme would want to acknowledge. As Edwards and Whitty (1997) point out, their study sample of students selected into the Assisted Places Scheme could be shown to come predominantly from homes with high levels of cultural and educational capital.

By 1992 the desirability of the market for organising schooling was more vigorously asserted by government around the maxims of choice, efficiency and democracy. For example, the 1992 White Paper *Choice and Diversity* argued that diversity would provide parents with the opportunity to choose the school they wanted for their child, while specialisation was presented as a consumer-driven response to the aspirations of parents for particular kinds of schooling (DfE 1992: 9–10). Following close in its wake, the 1993 Education Act further loosened the supply side, enabling groups of parents or their sponsors to set up their own grant-maintained schools (Walford 1997: 32).

The election of the Labour Party to government in 1997 did little to alter either the strength or direction of government policy regarding choice and markets, though it has, under the aegis of the 'Third Way', sought to develop the idea of a stakeholder society shaped by three concepts: 'real opportunity', 'civic responsibility' (White 1998: 18) and 'social inclusion' (Levitas 1998). In essence, Blair's 'Third Way' aims to reconcile a neo-liberal emphasis on economic efficiency with left concerns with equity and social cohesion, but where the state is now the guarantor of entitlements rather than necessarily a provider. Here the state is committed to the development of a regulatory framework where citizens are guaranteed access to opportunity goods, an approach Le Grand (1997) has called 'legal welfare'. Education can thus be seen as an opportunity good that enables access to work, and where work (not the state) is the primary means for participation in society, and therefore redistribution.

It could be argued, then, that choice and diversity policies in schooling, at least if the rhetoric were to be believed, would enable parents of whatever social class to select a school for their child that suited their social and learning needs: a shift that would break the hold of social class on schooling access in England and Wales. What, then, have been the social class outcomes of these initiatives? To answer this question, we need to examine transformations taking place within the economy and working- and middle-class labour markets which have had important consequences for schooling markets, principles of selection and occupational destinations.

New times and the restructuring of labour markets

A feature of organisational restructuring in response to the collapse of the post-war settlement (Brown and Lauder 2000) over the past two decades has been the move towards 'flexible', 'flatter' and 'leaner' organisational structures that would then enable greater responsiveness to demands in the marketplace. This was followed with a shift to privatisation and contractualisation of in-house services, together with a cutback in staffing to effect costs savings, leading to an overall reduction in the number of jobs offering long-term career opportunities (Burchell *et al.* 1999; Purcell and Purcell 1998). This has destabilised career structures in the public and private sectors, and, with them, guarantees of job security and advancement (Savage *et al.* 1992). It is also projected that the demands for managerial labour will rise, though as Brown (1995: 35) points out, it is unlikely these managerial positions will be lifelong. Rather, managers will require flexible skills and an enterprising demeanour in the search for a self-made career. It is argued such developments will result in an emphasis upon academic and professional credentials and may explain some of the expansion of post-school education. In Brown's (1995: 36) view, the expansion of post-school education:

> reflects the anxiety amongst parents concerning the education of their children, given that the populist appeal of the enterprise culture and personal improvement through the acquisition of material property is correctly understood by the middle classes to be a 'risky business'.

If middle-class career paths are being restructured, it should come as no surprise that the changes outlined above with regard to the higher education system (see Chapter 6) might create considerable anxiety among the middle and aspiring working class. The increasing competition for credentials – because of the growth of higher education – is occurring at a time when employers are finding it increasingly difficult to absorb the expanding number of higher-educated students. How, then, might universities and university credential holders differentiate themselves in the marketplace in the face of massification? Like the schooling marketplace, it would seem students are likely to seek those institutions that have higher relative social and academic worth, and that those students best able to realise this preference have the economic, cultural and social capital to do so.

One further point to be made with regard to middle-class labour markets concerns Brown's (1995: 40–1) view that flexible and entrepreneurial organisations in post-Fordist economies privilege and promote those individuals with a charismatic personality, a demeanour that is contrasted with the rule-following authority typical of bureaucratic organisations. In Brown's view, this results in a more explicit focus upon a new type of personality – based upon a combination of credentials, technical skills and charismatic qualities, which are then re-packaged and sold in the market for managerial and professional work. Without the appropriate 'social' education, applicants will find it increasingly difficult to 'decode' the rules by which the selection process is played. In essence, when individuals all hold approximately equivalent credentials, other ways are found to sort and select into positions within the labour market.

Restructuring labour markets has not been confined to the service or middle class in many Western nations. Starting in the early 1970s with the oil crisis and changes to the global economy, Britain has sought to realign its industries and labour markets in keeping with a competitive regional and global economy. This has resulted in the decline in manufacturing-based employment and the rise of low-paid 'junk jobs'. While unemployment figures have more recently been reduced by the combination of the expansion of the higher education sector, the limits on welfare entitlements, and the expansion of a casualised labour market, Britain still has the highest number of young people, irrespective of gender, in the 16–18 age bracket in poor-paying jobs.

Poor wages and the casualised labour market where most young people can be found is matched by growing poverty within the population in Britain in general. A recent OECD report (OECD 2000) estimates that approximately 55 per cent of the population experienced poverty at least once in six years between 1991 and 1997, and that this figure was only reduced to 40 per cent after tax and transfers. Poverty can also be shown to cycle through from one generation to the next. Johnson and Reed (1996), for example, show that 40 per cent of sons whose fathers experienced low income or periods of poverty in the 1970s are likely to experience a similar fate for themselves.

The links between systematic child poverty and educational performance are strong (Gregg *et al.* 1999), raising serious questions about the intergenerational entrenchment of inequality and the Labour government's ability to address this issue (Brown and Lauder 2000). Further, those who are poor not only show higher mortality rates but experience a series of health and other problems likely to impact upon their children's educational performance (Wilkinson 1996). There is a critically important relationship between poverty, education and labour markets which is central to understanding the nature of the social class/education relation within the context of the restructuring of the conditions of access.

Theory, social class and education

Throughout the period we are concerned with, class theory itself has come under fire and has been viewed as outmoded. On the one hand, the restructuring of the sphere of production and the decline of class-consciousness has raised questions concerning the usefulness of class as a category. Further, cultural theorists maintain that privileging social class ignores the multiplicity of positionings within contemporary social life based upon, for example, gender, ethnicity and sexuality.

Any attempt to defend the notion of class as being of significance to social and educational theory needs to acknowledge the latter point while seeing the emancipatory potential of class analysis in rather different terms from classical Marxism. The core insight on which such an analysis will rest is that the way work and income are distributed in society is of central relevance to the lives of those within it with respect to identity and life chances. Class in these terms is about understanding the way groups in society use their resources to generate privilege for themselves and exclude others in the process. Class is about the relatively stable structuring of these processes of inclusion and exclusion so that, in statistical terms, there is a high probability that from generation to generation a significant proportion of any specific social group will find themselves located in that group in terms of identity and life chances. The research on poverty by Johnson and Reed (1996) or on social class and higher education (Egerton and Halsey 1993) are good examples of how statistical analysis can be used to identify a relatively stable process of intergenerational reproduction of inequality, of the kind which suggests there are systematic processes of exclusion and inclusion involved.

It can be hypothesised that education has assumed even greater significance in determining who has power and privilege in England and Wales over the past thirty years than at any time since the Second World War. Inasmuch as education credentials provide a major resource in gaining an advantage in the labour market, so education has become increasingly significant as a determinant of life chances. This does not mean that the links between education, credentials and jobs are, or will become, more meritocratic (Goldthorpe 1996). Rather, it could be expected that the increased significance of a credential heralds an intensification of the struggle for advantage. As Halsey (1997: 814) notes, although education is 'increasingly the mediator of the transmission of status between generations and operates in important ways independently of the family', there is still no reduction within this intergenerational process in the influence that the family retains, or in the extent to which ascriptive forces find a way of expressing themselves as 'achievement'. The levels of basic education required in order to gain even a 'good' working-class job have been changed partly as a result of the introduction of new technology and work processes. Given these changes, it is perhaps not surprising that the competition for credentials has intensified, and there is a strong case for taking the view that many of the elements of change in the educational system in England and Wales reflect the outcomes to this struggle. If we look closely at the key changes that have occurred in the education system, we can see better the way class 'works'.

With respect to the introduction of markets in education, we can see this as a class strategy by which the rules of the game have been switched from a meritocracy in which, as Brown (1995) notes, the fundamental rules were based on the idea that:

individuals' abilities $+$ *effort* $=$ *merit*

to one in which:

parental resources $+$ *preferences* $=$ *choice*

It is those with the cultural and social capital who are most likely to be able to translate that capital into a market advantage by exercising the choices they consider most advantage their children. At the tertiary level, it is the case that many more now have the opportunity to participate, but it can be hypothesised that the relative class advantages remain. For as more individuals enter tertiary institutions, so the elite universities remain at the apex of the system providing entry into the most prestigious jobs.

Several writers have tried to elaborate on these general connections between social class and education, enabling us to better understand the changing nature of education provision and questions of access and outcome. Diane Reay (Reay 1997, 1998a, 1998b; Reay and Ball 1997; Reay and Lucey 2000) has written insightfully on this topic, seeking to develop an approach that takes into account class and other forms of difference, in particular gender, and which focuses upon class as a social process as it is played out in social relationships. Reay (1997: 226) argues that 'even when class is not overt and articulated in people's decoding of the social world, it is still there as part of the implicit, taken-for-granted understandings they bring to their relationship with others'.

The notion that the links between the structuring of exclusion and the social psychology of individuals may well be tacit or implicit is important. Much of the theorising about class is about the 'rational' judgements actors make in specific situations based on the resources they can draw upon. However, Lauder *et al.* (1999) refer to the 'wisdom of the class' in order to understand the origins and destinations of school leavers in New Zealand. They begin by noting that the concept of cultural capital is used to explain the success of middle-class students in terms of the informal education received at home through the language employed within the family, as well as through books and other cultural artefacts that they grow up with. Allied to this, studies have also shown that children raised in middle-class families have far higher educational aspirations and expectations of being able to act upon the world (Kohn and Schooler 1983). When these elements of class are taken together, they combine to create quite different frames of reference within which education is understood by the different classes. The 'wisdom of the class' thus describes these different frames.

Richard Hatcher (1998) takes up both the tacit 'wisdom' of the professional middle class and the calculation of risk involved for working-class students who consider transcending the limits of their class wisdom, seeking to explore, among other approaches, the value of Goldthorpe's (1996) 'rational action theory' for thinking about class and education. Goldthorpe's view is that education is an investment, that individuals calculate returns – particularly in higher education – and that class differences have remained, largely as there is little change in the relative cost–benefit balances for different classes (Hatcher 1998: 11). Hatcher's conclusion, after viewing some of the studies on choice and the working class, is to suggest that there would appear to be a range of working-class orientations to education, of which rational choice is only one.

Given the increased pressure on pathways and transition points arising from the restructuring of education and labour markets as we have outlined here, our interest is in whether the hypotheses raised above concerning the effects of the restructuring of education leads to an exacerbation or amelioration of the existing differentials in life chances. In other words, what does the evidence behind the rhetoric of 'choice', 'diversity', 'opportunity' and 'responsibility' tell us about the re-making of the links between education and social class over the past twenty-five years?

The evidence: class and the restructuring of education

In this section we concentrate on the class consequences of markets in education because, arguably, they are the single most significant innovation in educational policy over the past twenty years with the greatest implications for social class. In order to make sense of the empirical findings to date in the UK, we need to develop a model of the competing hypotheses concerning markets in education. On the one hand, proponents of markets argue that giving parents freedom to choose a school will produce two results. First, standards will rise as schools have to compete against one another for students, the assumption being that parents will choose the schools that are most successful in public examinations. Second, students in urban 'ghetto' schools will be able to escape the catchment areas that previously determined where they would go to school, and consequently schools will become more socially and ethnically mixed.

In contrast, critics view the introduction of markets as a class ploy in order that the middle class can sustain the privilege it enjoys for its children within a context in which credentials have assumed added significance with the decline of a career for life. In effect, it is an example of where the middle class determine the rules of the market, hence shifting the goal posts in their favour. The reasoning behind this view is that the middle class have the cultural capital and social networks to exploit the educational choices on offer in a way that working-class parents do not. Moreover, the logic of the situation is one in which middle-class parents will choose schools populated with similar middle-class students, because the latter provide the best proxy for successful school performance. Similarly, where schools are oversubscribed and are allowed to choose their students, they will choose white middle-class students for the same reason – they are the best guarantors of a school's success. The consequence for schools with a high proportion of working-class students is that they may go into a spiral of decline as middle-class students exit the school for others in the leafy suburbs.

One of the countries that has gone furthest in developing a market system of education is New Zealand, and here the predictions of the critics of markets in education have been accurate. There is now strong evidence to show that markets have caused spirals of decline in working-class schools, leaving students and teachers at risk of low morale, low funding and poor performance (Lauder *et al.* 1999; Fiske and Ladd 2000).

The question, then, is whether research in England and Wales has demonstrated the same kind of results as those found in New Zealand. Before looking at these results, we need to enter a caveat about the peculiarities of the situation here. There are several reasons why we might expect some contradictory evidence on the class effects of markets in education. No uniform system of market rules was imposed in England and Wales, and there are significant variations between LEAs as to their school admission policies. There have been other major changes in education during this period, especially in relation to the types of school that have developed (for example, CTCs and 'specialist' schools) and the introduction of the National Curriculum.

All these changes may 'muddy' the waters, since it is difficult to portion out the effects of one 'reform' from another. However, it is worth noting Brown's (1995) argument that – given the imposition of the National Curriculum – parental choice will largely be determined on the nature of the intake to a school. Finally, nearly all the macro studies of changes in enrolment as a result of the introduction of 'competition' have used official statistics which have required fairly heroic assumptions about which schools are determined as being in competition with each other (the LEA is usually taken as the unit of competition, but this is highly problematic), clearly a crucial factor in seeking to examine the effects of markets on, for example, flows of students. Finally, these data limit our understanding of markets in two further ways. Typically, they do not enable researchers to tease out demographic from market effects; in other words, where there are changes to the school roll, the data cannot help us determine whether this is because of changes in demography or changes in the choices people exercise. Further, the only data which can be used as a proxy for social class background is that of free school meal entitlement. However, while free school meals may be a rough proxy for some of the poorest students attending a school, such data can tell us very little about how the choices these families make relate to broader patterns of school attendance observed. Given these considerations, the data in England and Wales, in contrast say to Scotland or even New Zeland, are more difficult to interpret.

What is clear is that the predictions of market critics seemed to be borne out by the very early studies interested in the class-consequences of the restructuring of schooling focused upon the steps taken to diversify education funding and provision, such as the Assisted Places Scheme and CTCs. As we have already noted, the findings from these studies suggested that these initiatives favoured students from families with high levels of cultural and educational capital (Edwards *et al.* 1989). In other words, middle-class families were more likely to realise places in these types of educational settings.

This was followed by a series of qualitative research projects seeking to examine the relationship between parental choice and school markets. Arguably the most important and most widely cited study was reported by Stephen Ball, Richard Bowe and Sharon Gewirtz, based at King's College, London (hereafter referred to as the King's Study). The 'choice' reforms studied were those introduced from the early 1980s, and in particular the impact of the Education Reform Act 1988. As we have noted, these reforms allowed some parental choice of school, and schools are funded according to pupil numbers. Their sample was families selected from three local adjoining education authorities in London. Data were collected over a period of time through interviews with families and the local school community. The purpose of the study was to examine the relationship between choice, school markets and social class. A major conclusion is that 'choice is very directly and powerfully related to social class difference' (Gewirtz *et al.* 1995: 55) and also that 'choice emerges as a major new factor in maintaining and indeed reinforcing social class divisions and inequalities' (Ball *et al.* 1996: 110). So how does this work?

The King's Study argues that choice works through two factors: 'inclination' and 'capacity'. Inclination involves the extent to which families are engaged in the choice process, while capacity has *material* (money to pay for transport, after-school coaching, extra-curricular activities, for example) and *cultural* dimensions (self-confidence, familiarity with the education system). This produces the following categories: high-capacity/high-inclination families labelled 'privileged'; low-capacity/high-inclination families labelled 'semi-skilled' and 'frustrated'; and low-inclination families labelled 'disconnected'. Through this process, which takes the form of circuits of *localised, cosmopolitan* and *ruling-class* schooling facilitated by inclination and capacity, Ball and his colleagues argue that it is possible to see 'choice' as a central mechanism in the reproduction of social class relations.

Ball and his colleagues' conclusion that choice has reinforced social class divisions is lent some confirmation by other researchers. Gibson and Asthana (1999) produce interesting evidence to show that, according to their criteria for determining schools to be in competition, there has been a polarisation of GCSE results where schools with the lowest proportion of students with free school meals have extended their advantage over those with high proportions of free school meal students during the period between 1994 and 1998. While Gibson and Asthana provide evidence in support of Ball and his colleagues, Glatter *et al.* (1997) report that there is little evidence that choice has produced greater equality or indeed diversity; rather, there has been a tendency towards uniformity, and there has been no significant movement in the traditional hierarchy of schools. The strongest research evidence of the undesirable consequences of markets for working-class schools comes from Tomlinson (1997: 81), who shows that parents in communities with few social, cultural and educational resources are more likely to have 'failing schools'. It can be inferred from this that such students are likely to have a more uncertain educational experience, if not undesirable, as the school seeks to manage the conditions and consequences of its 'failing'.

The power of financial resources can also be reflected through choice exercised by house prices. That is, parents with economic resources may move to a particular locality pre-empting any 'obvious' choice decision about the school. Parsons *et al.*'s (2000) recent study on school catchments and pupil movements, where they examine the extent to which parents select out-of-catchment schools, shows that the hypothesis that middle-class parents will make more use of parental choice is not supported by their data. Rather, struggling and aspiring (working-class) families are more likely to seek other schools, while parents living in more prosperous areas are likely to stay put. If middle-class families are moving, it is either to a grammar school or because the middle-class family lives in an urban area where the social character of the neighbourhood is mixed and the middle-class population is a minority. Parents of high-status families in the main do not need to move, as they have already located themselves in areas where their local choice can be realised. The links between the housing and school markets are very important and in need of more systematic investigation. Parsons *et al.*'s study offers somewhat contradictory evidence to that of the King's Study. The virtue of this study is that it draws attention to the role of the housing market in the process of school choice. It also contradicts, to some extent, the hypothesis that it is largely middle-class families who are specifically advantaged by a market in education. The key theoretical point, however, is that middle-class families are likely to have greater resources as to how, where and when they exercise choices. If aspiring working-class families seek out schools other than the one closest to them, it is most unlikely that these will be private schools or indeed grammar schools.

Given that the hierarchy of schools approximates social class hierarchies, it could be argued that choice has not only reproduced social class inequalities but is implicated in increased disparities. Indeed, given this data, it would appear that middle-class parents seek out a segment of the market (including the private education market) that enables them to access the advantages that Brown alluded to earlier: educational settings that can be converted into a positional good in a more competitive labour market.

The conclusion that choice has reinforced social class hierarchies is not shared by all the research undertaken in this area. For example, Gorard and Fitz (1998a, 1998b) show that, by and large, students who are entitled to free school meals have benefited from the introduction of educational markets in so far as it has enabled them to gain admission to schools that previously were not open to them. However, their work so far is subject to the methodological problems identified above, in particular the inability to distinguish market from demographic effects. Similarly, Bradley *et al.*'s (1999) work on markets suggests that their introduction has been a success. While their work is in advance of that of Gorard and Fitz, they fail to examine the 'downside' to markets. More specifically, they do not consider the percentage of students entered for GCSEs in the schools in their sample, and hence the fortunes of those the market would consider inconvenient in relation to performance indicators such as the GCSE league tables. As with the other macro studies referred to, they assume that only schools within an LEA are in competition and it is on this basis that they judge the marketisation of education a success, for they seek to show that schools not in competition perform less well. This finding is in direct contradiction to that of Levacic *et al.* (1998), who did not use official statistics.

James Tooley (1997) is also keen to challenge the view that markets reinforce class inequalities. In a series of exchanges reported in the *British Journal of Sociology*, Tooley makes his claim, not on the basis of counter-evidence but on the grounds that the methodology of the King's Study – the most widely cited study on markets – was not able to deliver the level of generalisation it made. He also points out that there are errors of factual claim and omissions in the King's Study reporting which limit its ability to substantiate its choice/education/social class claims. While Tooley may be right in drawing attention to these findings, as Ball and his colleagues are concerned with understanding the mechanisms and processes of choice as they relate to social class, their insights are particularly helpful in focusing attention on the way the realisation of choices is likely to be shaped by cultural and material resources.

Overall, the jury is still out as regards findings from the macro studies that might help to throw light on the generalisability of the research of the King's Study. Nevertheless there is enough evidence of the difficulties encountered by schools, especially in inner-city areas, as a consequence of the introduction of educational markets, to make continued work in this area a priority. Qualitative studies continue to show the kinds of differences in class approaches to markets in education which suggest that well-designed macro and meso studies of markets might well show the kinds of class differences in outcomes that have been identified in New Zealand. For example, Reay and Ball in their more recent work argue that working-class parents view the child differently and have a different view of schools and status, and that schools are spaces where they feel out of place. Drawing upon data gathered through interviews, they theorise that working-class patterns of educational choice are characterised by ambivalence and appear to be as much about the avoidance of anxiety, failure and rejection as they are about 'choosing a good school for my child' (Reay and Ball 1997: 93). From the point of view of working-class families, choice – rather than being irrational – is motivated by a concern to 'fit in'. Looked at from this point of view, some working-class choices can be regarded as a very rational calculation.

'Fitting in' emerges in Power *et al.*'s (1998) study of the biographies of academically able students. In particular, they are able to show from data gathered over a period of years of academically able students from different social and cultural backgrounds in different schooling settings, that the cultural interplay between family, school and home continues to be an important factor in understanding the orientation towards school and academic achievement. While Power *et al.*'s data do not suggest a straightforward and unambiguous relationship between social class background and school culture – and suggest that it is also mediated by ability to do the work – they do call into question the claims that academically selective schools provide the best means for gaining commitment to education from academically able working-class children (1998: 173).

Reay (1997) explores this ambivalence and anxiety among mothers and their involvement in their children's schooling, in particular those mothers where education had clearly influenced their view of themselves. Her interest in mothers is well founded; considerable research has documented both the importance of mothers' role in social reproduction and where mothering work is generative of social class differences (Reay 1998a: 203; Reay and Lucey 2000). Reay pursues this idea of ambivalence about class identity, and in particular the way it is connected to what it means to accept being called 'working class'. She argues that to call oneself 'working class' is to accept inferiority; to resign oneself towards the inevitable. On the other hand, calling oneself 'middle class' is equally problematic, for to claim to be 'middle class' is to lose a sense of identity. The ambivalence is connected in a very powerful way to psychological and social rather than material resources, for social mobility has not bequeathed the certainty that middle-class women brought to their children's schooling. The outcome is to reproduce social class inequalities in a society that increasingly views such inequalities as the products of real choice rather than the outcome of situated agency.

The greater emphasis on parental involvement and partnership between home and school in the 1990s than at any time in the past can have perverse and often inequitable outcomes. Educational success has increasingly become a function of social, cultural and material advantages, in which mothers' caring within the family is transmuted by the operations of the wider marketplace to service the competitive self-interested individualistic ethos of the education market. One developing outcome is a culture of winners and losers within which one child's academic success is at the cost of other children's failure (Reay 1998: 197).

To what extent, then, has Blair's Labour administration, elected in 1997, altered the direction or mediated the effects of the class consequences of markets and managerialism in education. Education has been a key education portfolio, and Blair's famous utterance 'education, education, education' captures the centrality of education as a basis for social inclusion in an increasingly polarised society. Indeed, in delivering education, Labour is delivering a 'real opportunity' that provides access to the labour market. A key feature of the Labour government's 'Third Way' interventions to deliver equity is the multiplicity of social experiments that it is attempting, from text-based literacy to computer technology. It has also responded to the consequences of market polarisation and failing schools in inner-city areas in policies and initiatives such as *Excellence in Cities* (DfEE 1999) and the development of Education Action Zones. However, the problem with so many different 'experiments' is that they look as much a strategy of divide and rule as a genuine attempt to acknowledge the distinctiveness of different social and educational contexts and the ways in which these have been profoundly affected by the restructuring of access to economic, cultural and social resources since the mid 1970s.

Conclusion: a class choice?

In this chapter we have asked: what have been the likely effects of the restructuring of education on the link between origins and destinations, social class background and social futures? Second, to what extent do concepts such as social class and the way they are deployed give us some insight into these social processes, or are we facing the demise of class and a classless society? According to the political rhetoric, choice and diversity initiatives in schooling have enabled parents to select a school for their child that suits the child's social and learning needs. However, as this chapter has sought to show, what has been omitted from this equation is the possibility that choice operates as a social class process with social class consequences. We would hope that enough has been represented to indicate that it would take some considerable leap of the sociological imagination to suggest that we are facing the demise of class and a class society. Rather, the argument is that the restructuring and transformation of key elements of economic and social life have left education as a central site of contestation in the conflict over credentials and their links to the labour market.

References

Ball, S.J., Bowe, R. and Gewirtz, S. (1996) 'Circuits of schooling: a sociological exploration of parental choice of school in social class contexts', *Sociological Review*, 43: 53–78.

Bradley, S, Johnes, G. and Millington, J. (1999) *School Choice, Competition and the Efficiency of Secondary Schools in England*, mimeo, Lancaster: Management School, Lancaster University.

Brown, P. (1995) 'Cultural capital and social exclusion: some observations on recent employment trends in education, employment and the labour market', *Work Employment and Society*, 9(1): 29–51.

Brown, P. and Lauder, H. (2000) 'Education, child poverty and the politics of collective intelligence', in S. Ball (ed.) *Key Papers in the Sociology of Education*, London: Routledge.

Burchell, J., Day, D., Hudson, M., Ladipo, D., Mankelow, R., Nolan, P., Reed, H., Wichert, I. and Wilkinson, F. (1999) *Job Insecurity and Job Intensification*, York: Rowntree Foundation.

DfE (1992) *Choice and Diversity: A New Framework for School*, London: HMSO.

DfEE (1999) *Excellence in Cities*, London: Stationery Office.

Edwards, T. and Whitty, G. (1997) 'Specialisation and selection in secondary education', *Oxford Review of Education*, 23(1): 5–15.

Edwards, T., Fitz, J. and Whitty, G. (1989) *The State and Private Education: An Evaluation of the Assisted Places Scheme*, Lewes: Falmer.

Egerton, M. and Halsey, A.H. (1993) 'Trends by social class and gender in access to higher education in Britain', *Oxford Review of Education*, 19(2): 183–96.

Fiske, E. and Ladd, H. (2000) *When Schools Compete: A Cautionary Tale*, Washington DC: Brookings Institute.

Fitz, J., Halpin, D. and Power, S. (1993) *Grant Maintained Schools: Education in the Market Place*, London: Kogan Page.

Gamble, A. (1988) *The Free Economy and the Strong State: The Politics of Thatcherism*, London: Macmillan.

Gewirtz, S., Walford, G. and Miller, H. (1991) 'Parents' individualist and collectivist strategies', *International Studies in Sociology of Education*, 1: 173–92.

Gewirtz, S., Ball, S. and Bowe, R. (1995) *Markets, Choice and Equity*, Buckingham: Open University Press.

Gibson, A. and Asthana, S. (1999) 'Schools, markets and equity: access to secondary education in England and Wales', presentation at AERA, Montreal.

Glatter, R., Woods, P. and Bagley, C. (1997) 'Diversity, differentiation and hierarchy: school choice and parental preference', in R. Glatter, P. Woods and C. Bagley (eds) *Choice and Diversity in Schooling: Perspectives and Prospects*, London: Routledge.

Goldthorpe, J. (1996) 'Class analysis and the reorientation of class theory: the case of persisting differentials in educational attainment', *British Journal of Sociology*, 47(3): 481–505.

Gorard, S. and Fitz, J. (1998a) 'Under starter's orders: the established market, the Cardiff Study and the Smithfield project', *International Studies in the Sociology of Education*, 8(3): 299–314.

——(1998b) 'The more things change ... the missing impact of marketisation', *British Journal of Sociology of Education*, 19(3): 365–76.

Gregg, P., Harkness, S. and Machin, S. (1999) *Child Development and Family Income*, York: Rowntree Foundation.

Hall, S. (1983) 'The Great Moving Right Show', in S. Hall and M. Jacques (eds) *The Politics of Thatcherism*, London: Lawrence & Wishart.

Halsey, A. (1997) 'Trends in access and equity in higher education: Britain in international perspective', in A. Halsey, H. Lauder, P. Brown and A. Wells (eds) (1997) *Education, Culture, Economy and Society*, Oxford: Oxford University Press.

Hatcher, R. (1998) 'Class differentiation in education: rational choices', *British Journal of Sociology of Education*, 19(1): 5–24.

Johnson, P. and Reed, R. (1996) 'Intergenerational mobility among the rich and the poor: results from the national child development survey', *Oxford Review of Economic Policy*, 12(1): 127–42.

Kerckhoff, A., Fogelman, K. and Manlove, J. (1997) 'Staying ahead: the middle class and school reform in England and Wales', *Sociology of Education*, 70(1): 19–35.

Kohn, M. and Schooler, C. (1983) *Work and Personality: An Inquiry into the Impact of Social Stratification*, New Jersey: Ablex Publishing.

Lauder, H., Hughes, D., Watson, S., Waslander, S., Thrupp, M., Strathdee, R., Simiyu, I., Dupuis, A., McGlinn, J. and Hamlin, J. (1999) *Trading in Futures: Why Markets in Education Don't Work*, Buckingham: Open University Press.

Le Grand, J. (1991) 'Quasi-markets and social policy', *Economic Journal*, 101: 1256–67.

——(1997) 'Knights, knaves or pawns? Human behaviour and social policy', *Journal of Social Policy*, 26: 149–69.

Levacic, R., Hardman, J. and Woods, P. (1998) 'Competition as a spur to improvement? Differential involvement in GCSE exam results', paper presented to the International Congress for School Effectiveness and Improvement, Manchester, January.

Levitas, R. (1998) *The Inclusive Society? Social Exclusion and New Labour*, London: Macmillan.

OECD (2000) *Poverty Dynamics in Six OECD Countries*, Paris: OECD.

Parsons, E., Chalkley, B. and Jones, A. (2000) 'School catchments and pupil movements: a case study in parental choice', *Educational Studies*, 26(1): 33–48.

Pierson, C. (1998) *Beyond the Welfare State: The New Political Economy of Welfare*, Cambridge: Polity.

Power, S., Whitty, G., Edwards, T. and Wigfall, V. (1998) 'Schools, families and academically able students: contrasting modes of involvement in secondary education', *British Journal of Sociology of Education*, 19(2): 157–76.

Purcell, J. and Purcell. K. (1998) 'In-sourcing, out-sourcing and the growth of contingent labour as evidence of flexible employment strategies', *European Journal of Work and Organizational Psychology*, 7(1): 39–59.

Reay, D. (1997) 'Feminist theory, habitus, and social class: disrupting notions of classlessness', *Women's Studies International Forums*, 20(2): 225–33.

——(1998a) 'Engendering social reproduction: mothers in the educational marketplace', *British Journal of Sociology of Education*, 19(2): 195–209.

——(1998b) 'Rethinking social class: qualitative perspectives on class and gender', *Sociology*, 32(2): 259–75.

Reay, D. and Ball, S. (1997) 'Spoilt for choice: the working classes and educational markets', *Oxford Review of Education*, 25(1): 89–101.

Reay, D. and Lucey, H. (2000) 'Children, school choice and social differences', *Educational Studies*, 26(1): 83–100.

Savage, M., Barlow, J., Dickens, P. and Fielding, T. (1992) *Property, Bureaucracy and Culture: Middle Class Formation in Contemporary Britain*, London: Routledge.

Tomlinson, S. (1997) 'Sociological perspectives on failing schools', *International Studies in the Sociology of Education*, 7(1): 81–98.

Tooley, J. (1997) 'On school choice and social class: a response to Ball, Bowe and Gewirtz', *British Journal of Sociology of Education*, 18(2): 217–30.

Walford, G. (1997) 'Sponsored grant-maintained schools: extending the franchise?' *Oxford Review of Education*, 23(1): 31–44.

White, S. (1998) 'Interpreting the Third Way: not one road but many', *Renewal*, 6(2): 17–30.

Wilkinson, R. (1996) *Unhealthy Societies*, London: Routledge.

Part V

Conclusion

16 Educational performance, markets and the state

Present and future prospects

Tony Edwards

Introduction

It is now widely assumed that this country's economic future depends on a 'revolution' in skills and knowledge, to be driven forward by a suitably modernised education system closely monitored by the state. As this book has demonstrated, early moves in these directions were outlined by Callaghan at Ruskin, which is why his speech has kept its status as a memorable event. At the time, in October 1976, it was intended to steal Conservative clothes by aligning the Labour government with growing public concern about an education system which was apparently both failing to meet the needs of employment and self-protectively resistant to change. Yet while promising political initiatives, the prime minister indicated only a modest increase in direct government intervention. Despite persistent urging of much bolder measures by the radical Right, it was not until the Conservatives' 1987 election manifesto that the reform of schooling was given priority within a wholesale reconstruction of welfare provision on market principles. The Education Act of 1988 which followed a third successive Conservative election victory was acclaimed by two of the ministers responsible for implementing its innovations as the 'biggest single measure of social reform' of the Thatcher years, and the 'first real attempt since the Butler Act to revisit the basis of education policy' (Kenneth Baker and Kenneth Clarke, quoted in Ribbins and Sherratt 1997: 109, 149).

This final chapter focuses on some long-term outcomes of that 'revisiting' during a period of 'almost unprecedented government activism in education policy' (Pierson 1998: 140). Certainly, the education system which the New Labour government inherited in 1997 was very different from when the party had last left in office in 1979. The traditional providers' partnership, which Callaghan questioned quite mildly, had been so largely dissolved that LEAs appeared at risk of extinction except as monitoring agents for the achievement of national targets; teachers had become resigned to having their work closely prescribed, and so many new powers had accrued to the Secretary of State that the post had enough scope and visibility to attract several very ambitious politicians. If John Patten's story is true, the newly appointed Keith Joseph could be seen stalking his department's corridors in 1981 asking where were the 'levers' by which government could improve the system's performance (quoted in Ribbins and Sherratt 1997: 171). Powerful levers were soon in place. They were installed alongside privatising measures which are sometimes misleadingly described as 'stealthy' because their advocates made no secret of their wish to see public education opened up to market forces.

As Robertson and Lauder emphasize, however, what had been achieved by the late 1990s was only a quasi-market, heavily constrained by the strategy analysed by Broadfoot of state control through the setting of output targets and intrusive monitoring mechanisms. There was also continuing debate about how far market forces could be left alone to work in the 'national interest'. Improving human capital, a justification for educational expansion already familiar in 1976, raises big questions about how much of the population 'needs' to be educated and to what levels. Declaring 'investment in learning' to be the modern equivalent of the 'investment in the machinery and technical innovation that was essential to the first great industrial revolution', the incoming Labour government's first Education White Paper in July 1997 went on to identify the underlying (and 'easily stated') weakness of British education as a preoccupation with 'excellence at the top' while 'mass education' was neglected (DfEE 1997: 15). In attempting to reorder those priorities, the new government set education targets which would have seemed wholly unrealistic in 1976.

Particular policy changes are analysed in depth by other contributors, and it would be redundant to summarise their conclusions or to replicate Phillips' comprehensive introductory review. Instead, I concentrate on three main themes which run through, and will certainly run beyond, the period under review. First is the emerging agreement that 'Who shall be educated?' must be answered far more ambitiously than in the past if economic decline is to be avoided. Second is the undermining of traditional notions of education as a public service by belief in the greater effectiveness of market provision. Finally, and inseparable from both those issues, is uncertainty about the scope and direction of state intervention in public education after a period during which government control, institutional autonomy and consumer choice all markedly increased.

Educational performance and economic progress: the many, not the few

The merging in 1995 of the Departments of Education and Employment (DfEE) was a unique national solution to the complex relationships between those areas of government (Aldrich *et al.* 2000). It also looked back to Callaghan's apparent deference to the 'needs' of employment, with the new Department's first press release defining its mission as being 'to support economic growth and improve the quality of life by raising standards of educational achievement and skill and by promoting an efficient and flexible labour market'. Of course, justifying educational expenditure primarily as investment in human resources goes back at least to the 1960s, and the convenient political habit of attributing economic problems to the failings of schools much further back than that (Merson 1995). In the past, manufacturing industry (the main source of employment) and business seemed to work well enough with a small 'leadership' class and what H.G. Wells termed 'a conscript militia'. That view was still embodied in the Ministry of Education's post-war blueprint for *The Nation's Schools* (1945) which defined the new 'modern secondary' schools as providing for those children, assumed to be about three-quarters of their age group, whose future employment would not require 'any measure of technical skill or knowledge'. In sharp contrast, the new 'common sense', responding to the needs of a knowledge economy, is that a suitably modernised work force must be well educated at all levels of employment (Edwards 1997). Thus the White Papers on *Competitiveness* in 1994–6, exonerating or ignoring failures of management and capital investment, constructed the problem largely as an under-educated and inflexible labour force. The Labour government has retained much of that diagnosis while discarding more emphatically the traditional British (or, perhaps more accurately, English) preoccupations with a selected elite. For example, when John Major made explicit before the 1997 election his wish to see a grammar school in every town, Tony Blair dismissed it as 'a response to the needs of a vanished society' in which a huge supporting army of basically skilled and deferential workers were led by their educated 'betters' (Labour Party Education Bulletin 6, July/August 1996).

Neither in terms of practical politics nor of policy discourse, however, has the construction of an appropriately modernised response been straightforward. The priority still being given to the more obviously educable was very evident when James Callaghan expressed his concern for the under-educated majority. In the mid 1970s, more young people left school in England and Wales with no formal qualifications than did so with the two or more A-level passes normally required for entry to higher education (21 per cent compared with 14 per cent). And after over a decade of comprehensive reorganisation, only 23 per cent obtained the five or more 'good passes' at O level expected of pupils of 'grammar school ability' (Edwards and Whitty 1994). A generation later, the facts that over a third of the age group were 'qualified' for higher education and nearly half passed that traditional grammar school hurdle would seem to demonstrate a much wider definition of educability, and notably improved productivity by the system.

Although similar trends in comparable countries mean that Britain still has relatively low rates of participation in full-time education and training 16–18, and although there is also a wider attainment gap between the most and least educationally successful than in any of those countries except the USA (Robinson and Openheim 1998), it would have appeared absurdly ambitious in 1976 that, by 2002, 85 per cent of 19-year-olds should be expected to achieve five GCSE passes or their equivalent, or that ministers at the 1999 Labour Party Conference should have set the target participation rate in higher education at half the adult population. Nevertheless, such expansion has brought complaints about a consequent diluting of standards which reflect a continuing disbelief in the possibility of 'real' education for the many. The replacement in 1987 of previously restricted and divided 16-plus examinations by the inclusive GCSE is a case in point. Claimed by its defenders to be a main cause of higher staying-on rates because of its beneficial effects on young people's self-confidence as learners, it was persistently attacked by the New Right as a celebration of mediocrity typifying the egalitarian belief that none should fail. Revisiting the old theme that 'more means worse', a prominent curriculum adviser to the Conservative government doubted whether it was necessary for average standards to be high provided that about a fifth of the population were properly educated, a proportion too close to the pre-comprehensive grammar school intake to be coincidental. An education system which respected 'real distinctions between people', he argued, was rightly 'divisive, elitist and inegalitarian' (O'Hear 1991: 36).

From a New Labour perspective, that was the system which Conservative policies had promoted. In fact, those policies displayed a considerable tension between the traditional 'elitist' emphasis and a modernising recognition (documented in the Skills Audit carried out for the 1996 *Competitiveness* White Paper) that it was inadequate knowledge and skills at the middle and lower levels of academic ability which were now the main source of economic weakness. On the one hand, successive Conservative governments promoted the revival of grammar schools, and extolled independent schools as the embodiment of academic excellence, and therefore justified publicly assisted access to them as a restoration of real academic opportunities. These had been key points in the party's education policy in the late 1970s, intended to distance it from a Labour Party still locked into egalitarianism incompatible with high standards. Yet it was inadequate provision for the 'bottom 40 per cent' which Keith Joseph emphasised; the Technical and Vocational Education Initiative (TVEI) was introduced by the Secretary of State for Employment (David Young) as a more relevant curriculum for pupils below the top 15 per cent; and National Vocational Qualifications (NVQs) were created to provide a vocational route running all the way from basic skills to post-graduate-level credentials, with General NVQs added to challenge the unique prestige of A levels in post-compulsory education (Edwards 1997). In a particularly striking departure from 'elitist' traditions, the formal distinction between universities and polytechnics was removed in 1992 in response to the huge growth in higher education which preceded it.

Extensive marshalling and commissioning of evidence had supported the main recommendations of the Robbins Report in 1963 that higher education, then restricted to 5 per cent of the age group, should be available to 'all who can benefit'. That objective was accepted promptly by the Conservative Education Minister Edward Boyle. Yet in 1979, the model which Robbins had wished to expand was still recognisable. Initial Conservative priorities were not growth but the curbing of expenditure and a shift in student recruitment towards science and technology. After 1987, however, two very non-traditional objectives were quickly achieved by replacing a stratified (binary) with a formally undifferentiated system and by greatly increasing access to it. By 1992, the age-participation index had risen to 32 per cent from 12.4 per cent in 1979, and the subsequent Dearing Inquiry into higher education felt obliged to focus mainly on the funding and management of what had then become a relatively larger student population than in most comparable countries (Parry 1999). It was also a population very different in composition from a generation earlier. Over half were female, higher proportions were mature and part-time students, there was a proportional increase in students from working-class backgrounds, and rising postgraduate numbers were particularly significant in the context of political support for lifelong learning (Halsey 1993). But expansion also intensified competition for entry to the more prestigious universities because 'mere' possession of a degree no longer carried the promise of occupational advantage attached to it a generation earlier. This has had considerable marketing implications for schools conspicuously successful in that competition.

'Secondary education for all' has continued to be differentiated hierarchically.

Unlike France, for example, most elite schools are outside the public sector; indeed, their number rose sharply after the Callaghan government forced the direct grant schools to choose between remaining selective and continuing to receive public funding. At that time, the Labour Party still appeared to want the reduction and eventual abolition of private education, a threat which roused the sector to co-ordinate its defences more effectively and the Conservative Party to offer more consistently vigorous support (Edwards *et al.* 1989: 29–32). New Labour has posed no similar threat. It has promoted co-operation between the sectors, apparently maintaining the traditional assumption that this is a one-way process from which state schools learn how to 'stretch' their ablest pupils.

Within the public sector, the proportion of secondary pupils in England attending schools at least nominally comprehensive rose from two-thirds in 1976 to four-fifths in 1980, by which time the figures in Scotland and Wales were close to 100 per cent. That date may mark the high tide of comprehensive re-organisation. The incoming Thatcher government moved quickly to reassert the right of Local Authorities to return or restore academic selection, and introduced with the Assisted Places Scheme a thoroughly traditional scholarship ladder into 'academically excellent' independent schools. As Geoffrey Walford describes, the comprehensive ideal of 'common schooling' remained highly contested throughout the period under review. And although arguments have continued about relative performance of selective and non-selective systems and schools, with opposing positions able to draw on contradictory evidence (Crook *et al.* 1999), no government undertook or commissioned an evaluation either of the effects of reorganisation on standards overall or of the success of that minority of comprehensive schools not still competing directly with selective state or independent schools nearby (Benn and Chitty 1996: 12–13; Kerckhoff *et al.* 1996: 10). The Major government's last Education Bill in 1996 defended 'an element of selection' as an essential component of 'choice and diversity', and not only encouraged schools to restore or achieve grammar school status but would have enabled all comprehensives to select up to 15 per cent of their intake, and grant-maintained schools up to half of it.

It was the promise of a large-scale return to selection which Tony Blair then attacked as reflecting 'the needs of a vanished society'. In office, however, Labour policy has been more ambiguous (Edwards *et al.* 1999). A prohibition on returning to selection by general ability bore some resemblance to the position defined by an earlier Labour Secretary of State (Ted Short in 1970) – that 'if it is wrong to select and segregate children, it must be wrong everywhere' (cited in Kerckhoff *et al.* 1996: 34). Yet specialist secondary schools, their numbers rising rapidly after 1997, can select up to 10 per cent of their intake by 'aptitude for particular subjects', which is a criterion less easily distinguishable from 'general ability' at the early age of 11 than ministers have claimed. 'Fair and reasonable' admission policies are intended to limit the freedom of schools to manage their intakes without regard for possible effects on neighbouring schools, but allowing the remaining grammar schools to continue if local opinion supports them is a concession 'to reconcile the competing claims for school choice and educational equity' (Crook *et al.* 1999: 1). The new government's slogan of 'standards, not structures' was intended to reassure those who feared another burst of disruptive structural change or, worse still, a return to the bureaucratically imposed uniformity attributed to past Labour governments. It was not consistent, however, with the accompanying reference to a traditional preoccupation with 'excellence for a few', a structural bias which allocated children to types of schooling very unequal in resources, prospects and esteem.

The economic obsolescence of that preoccupation was where this section of the chapter began. Although the equation of 'better skills = jobs' is over-simplified because low-skill routes into employment persist, especially in some expanding service industries (Ashton and Green 1996), the gulf in earnings, security and prospects between 'qualified' and 'unqualified' labour appears to be growing, and with it the costs to future life chances of educational failure (Bynner *et al.* 1997; Bynner 1999). The very high proportion of those who leave school at 16 with few or no qualifications and poor basic skills who are unemployed or in low-paid and insecure jobs ten years later justifies the emphasis on raising educational standards 'for all', especially in those foundation skills which enhance chances of remaining employable in a fast-changing labour market. This is a necessary but insufficient economic policy (Coffield 1999). It is tempting for politicians to exaggerate the power of educational reform because it appears to offer unusual opportunities to act decisively. In doing so, I argue later, they may place unrealistically heavy responsibility on schools for remedying social ills, and expect too much direct economic benefit from better education and training.

Control, competition, standards and choice

The 'great' debate which followed the Ruskin speech illustrated how far confidence declined in the capacity of education reform to produce a society which was both fairer and more prosperous. And as confidence diminished, so controversy grew about how schools should be controlled and made accountable for their performance. Although the balance between public and private interests was hardly debated at all except as a matter of curbing 'excessive' professional autonomy, the mid-1970s appear with hindsight to mark the high tide of welfare ideology and the beginning of a 'retreat from collectivism' (Glennerster 1995: 169). Economic difficulties were then prompting most industrial countries to question the power of governments to remedy social ills, and consequently their right to spend heavily on trying to do so. Both Callaghan's government and its Conservative successor were therefore typical of their times in giving priority to raising economic productivity and in treating extravagant public expenditure as a root cause of economic weakness. Between 1975 and 1995, Britain's expenditure on education fell from 6.7 per cent to 5.2 per cent of its Gross Domestic Product (Glennerster and Hills 1998).

Beyond a shared wish to cut government spending, however, lay sharp differences of view about how far solutions to inadequate standards and runaway costs lay in empowering the consumers of welfare with choice, thereby compelling the providers of public services to compete for custom.

The Ruskin speech had suggested both a somewhat larger role for central government in managing the system in the national interest, and some amplifying of parental 'voice'. As the post-1988 reforms demonstrated, these objectives are not easily reconciled. The first reflected a growing political impatience with the constraints imposed on the Education Department by conventional obligations to work with its local authority and teacher union 'partners', and by a growing wish to see the national paymaster do more to call national tunes. Criticised in an OECD report in 1975 for maintaining a hands-off stance even when a clear policy lead was called for, the Department's response was that national education planning had to focus on inputs, because content was a matter for local authorities and schools and because it was impossible anyway to measure standards across the system (Aldrich *et al.*2000). Both disclaimers read oddly now.

Yet even in the mid 1970s, educational failure and the folly of simply trusting the government's partners to remedy it were already prominent themes in Conservative policy discourse (Knight 1990: 111–24). Rhodes Boyson (1975), for example, argued stridently for much tougher school inspection, for more parental choice, and for national tests (at the ages of 7, 11 and 14) which would enable parents to compare schools' performance and force failing schools either to improve or to go out of business. The first mechanism remained unattractive to the Right as long as it regarded Her Majesty's Inspectorate (HMI) as imbued with the 'progressive' softness about standards which had caused them to deteriorate, and until the creation of the Office for Standards in Education (Ofsted) in 1992 enabled the process of inspection to be devoted largely to securing schools' and LEAs' compliance with statutory requirements and to measuring progress towards national attainment targets. But compulsory publication by state secondary schools of their public examination results was included in the Thatcher government's first (1980) Education Act, annual schools performance tables soon becoming the largest exercise in public information organised by any government department. That the National Curriculum greatly extended the scope of such surveillance after 1989 was some consolation for those on the Right who regarded it otherwise as incompatible with market principles. Indeed, as Broadfoot describes, it made the English/Welsh school system the most tested in the world. That left the prime mechanism of consumer choice, which its advocates regarded as the certain route to improved educational performance.

Although education reform was given little attention by the first two Thatcher administrations, a concern that her government was 'stale and running out of ideas' led to hectic activity by the Downing Street Policy Unit and by independent think-tanks which produced the 'best ever Conservative manifesto' (Thatcher 1997: 572). That manifesto placed the empowering of consumers at the centre of a radical reshaping of welfare which appeared to some foreign observers to be a 'defining expression of international neo-liberal reform' (Seddon 1997: 167; Chubb and Moe 1992; Elliott and MacLennan 1994).

The ground for it was prepared by a systematic campaign against the so-called producers' monopoly, maintained at the consumers' expense and supported by allies in local government and the Civil Service. Kenneth Baker's claims to have masterminded the 'great' reforms of 1988 largely ignored this preparatory work, both the destructive 'discourse of derision' directed at the old system and the constructive zeal with which market alternatives were advocated (Ball 1990). For example, when a lament that the state had ever become involved in schooling was published by the Institute of Economic Affairs, a pressure group founded in 1957 to assert the superiority of the market 'as a device for registering individual preferences and allocating resources to satisfy them', both the general proposition and its application to state education were presented as defiantly heretical (West 1970). By the late 1980s, however, similar arguments could be advanced (for example, by the Hillgate Group 1987; Sexton 1987) with confidence that the 'unthinkable' had become familiar and that erstwhile 'extremist' positions had accumulated friends in high places. Whereas the traditional Conservative approach to policy-making had been to carry through 'necessary' reforms with due regard for traditional interests, rather than 'in obedience to abstract principles and arbitrary general doctrines' (Disraeli in 1867, quoted in Lawton 1994: 3), faith in market principles now appeared to override warnings from inside the party against 'the politics of simple answer' and 'the theory that tells all' (Patten 1983: vi, 104).

Even at the height of its influence, however, market theory was more conspicuous in rhetoric than in practice, because no government was willing to trust market forces to do its work (Pierson 1998). The theoretically perfect mechanism of the education voucher continued to be avoided as impractical. And although the 1988 Act's combination of 'open' enrolment with delegated school budgets determined largely by pupil numbers was welcomed by market enthusiasts as constituting virtual vouchers without arousing the political objections attached to the real thing, they deeply regretted that the effects were so limited by the statutory obligations of the National Curriculum. It was illogical, they argued, to free schools to compete for custom and to be rewarded directly for increasing their intake while denying them scope to be different and thereby to secure a distinctive market niche. From that perspective, there had been 'no need to set a National Curriculum, or control examinations or testing, or in any other way control content; the market of parents, children, employers and universities will do that better, more flexibly and more effectively' (Sexton 1999: 170; for a similar view, see Tooley 2000: 178).

Not only were 'unnecessary' restraints on trade constructed, they were on a scale and with a detailed prescriptiveness not found in any other country. This has been deplored as a last-ditch victory by the DES over right-thinking efforts to make its role residual (Sexton 1987), and welcomed as a sensible Civil Service strategy for curbing the excesses of free market extremism while also responding to public demand for higher standards (Graham 1993). Such personalised explanations ignore the widespread agreement by the late 1980s that some form of national curriculum was desirable. They also ignore the perceived value of standardised assessments of nationally prescribed school knowledge, both as a necessary condition for devolving more powers to schools by holding them to account for poor 'measured' performance, and as a means of informing consumers about the 'best' schools in their locality. These were the functions which Baker's successors, vigorously prompted by their prime minister, were determined should largely replace the initial complex, formative and teacher-centred approaches with externally imposed 'simple pen-and-paper' tests (Daugherty 1995).

That the initial 'broad and balanced' National Curriculum went so far beyond the 'basics' favoured by Thatcher herself also reflected very different policy strands within the Conservative Party. To the neo-liberal Right, anything more than a core curriculum was too bureaucratic, and a huge obstacle to giving consumers what they wanted. Modernisers criticised both its scope and its academic character as an obstacle to meeting the needs of a 'new knowledge'-driven economy, as inhibiting innovation, and as inappropriate in a society too diverse to fit into any single educational mould. Similar views were later apparent on the Left as part of its own modernising agenda (Barber 1994; DfEE 1999). But to the conservative Right, committed to 'restoring' traditional educational values and standards, its construction from academic subjects was seen as countering the narrowing effects of a utilitarian obsession with relevance. Strong components of national history and English literature would also contribute to social cohesion. From that perspective, market forces had to be restrained in the interests of continuity and community, and the claims of 'the sovereign market give way to the sovereign state' (Marquand 1988: 172; Johnson 1989). Finally, from an egalitarian (or at least one-nation) position sometimes adopted by Baker himself, the first broad version of the National Curriculum meant discarding divisive notions of a curriculum suitable for keeping different kinds of learner in their places in favour of a high common threshold of knowledge, skills and understandings, to which all children were entitled 'wherever they live and go to school'. In that form, at least in principle, it embodied the comprehensive ideal.

State power and the limits of state responsibility

What role the state should take in the provision of education, and for what predominant purposes, are questions which Callaghan raised rather cautiously. In 1976, despite the mounting attacks on egalitarian social engineering, it was still largely assumed that public education should be provided by democratically accountable bodies and be shaped towards making society less unequal (Finch 1984; Timmins 1996). The extent of this surviving social-democratic consensus can be exaggerated by ignoring the commitments to parental choice and market accountability already conspicuous in Conservative education policies, and emerging arguments about how much the state should do and pay for. Indeed, what remained of it rested on assumptions about the provision of social welfare which the neo-liberal Right wished to discard entirely. When approximations to what they wanted instead were implemented after 1987, their basis in market principles presented a familiar dilemma in policy studies. Should a master plan be looked for beneath the surface of particular initiatives, or is it safer, without solid evidence to the contrary, to expect the more usual mixture of ad hoc initiatives and pragmatic responses to problems and pressures?

The Conservatives' White Paper *Choice and Diversity* (1992) constructed policy coherence retrospectively. John Major's foreword claimed a steadily developing strategy based around the five great 'themes' of choice, diversity, freedom, standards and accountability. Assisted places and the creation of City Technology Colleges were then identified in the opening chapter as first steps towards a system of self-governing schools responsive to consumer wishes which the forthcoming Education Act would bring close to completion. Certainly, whatever reservations the New Labour government might have had about the quasi-market it was inheriting and despite the return to 'vigorous and assertive leadership' by the state predicted earlier by a principal author of its own (1997) White Paper (Barber 1994), there was no going back to bureaucratically allocated school places, or to LEAs making decisions on behalf of 'their' schools, or to hiding school performance from public scrutiny, or to discouraging diversity of provision. In these policy areas, even the less obviously doctrinaire Secretaries of State (John MacGregor and Gillian Shephard) took it for granted that the Conservatives had won the battle for ideas (Ribbins and Sherratt 1997). As Phillips argues in his introductory chapter, remarkable transformations 1987–97 have been followed by substantial continuity since (see also Power and Whitty 1999).

Assessing the prospects for further marketisation, in conditions where 'at least for the moment conservatism is in retreat' (Giddens 2000: vi), requires a distinction to be made between choice as a recognition of consumer rights, and choice as an appropriate response to increasing social and cultural diversity (Hirsch 1997). The first line of advocacy sometimes treats private education as exemplifying the benefits of direct accountability to the market. The example is unconvincing. In this country, unlike (for example) Denmark or the Netherlands, the sector provides for a very small, predominantly advantaged, minority of the school population, and its leading schools have responded to rising demand by becoming more selective rather than larger. In general, there has been no bold transfer of schooling to private providers, but a progressive blurring of boundaries between public and private through the state's purchase of education outside the public sector, the creation of schools which do not charge fees but are outside local authority 'control', and increasing encouragement of parental and business contributions to school resources. Although the incoming Labour government immediately announced the phasing out of assisted places and some consequent redistribution of public funding, it welcomed their partial replacement by privately and school-funded scholarships. It has also considerably expanded the specialist schools programme, an essential component of which is the matching of business sponsorship with government grants. Potentially even more significant has been its willingness to experiment with replacing publicly 'owned' and democratically accountable educational provision by public–private partnerships, and to allow private take-overs of 'failing' schools and LEAs.

In these respects, New Labour's 'third way' appears to resemble neo-liberal preferences for 'recasting' public services on market principles more closely than it does 'old' Labour priorities (Ball 1999; Power and Whitty 1999). Yet there is also a political commitment to securing a 'better balance' than in the recent past between public and private interests, specifically between fairness and co-operation on one side and 'the power of schools to decide their own affairs' (DfEE 1997: 66). The government's approach (for example) to specialist secondary schools resists the market logic of unrestrained institutional self-interest by insisting that their 'distinctive strengths', rewarded with additional funding, should be made available to 'local people and neighbouring schools', and not used to secure competitive advantage. And whereas Conservative governments promoted diversity of supply largely as a necessary correlate of different consumer demands, the Labour government has done so largely as a modernising acceptance of social heterogeneity.

From that perspective, promoting 'choice and diversity' in educational provision is an appropriate response to profound global changes which have apparently taken most industrial countries in broadly similar directions. Yet their different histories and cultures have produced large national variations in what powers the state has delegated to whom, and how far the school curriculum has continued to be politically managed in the interests of social cohesion or economic competitiveness (Green 1997: 23–6; Whitty *et al.* 1998). In Britain, the Labour government's interventions in the quasi-market have included a substantial targeting of additional resources on areas of social disadvantage (DfEE 1999). This indicates some turning back to 'old' social-democratic policies of positive discrimination, the apparent failure of which to achieve more equal outcomes should be set in the context of widening inequalities during the 1980s, when those policies were reversed (Glennerster 1995: 11; Edwards and Whitty 1994). Recognising the interaction of multiple social disadvantage, low expectations and a 'culture of fatalism' (DfEE 1999: 5), as the government has done in its creation of Education Action Zones and its measure to counter social exclusion, offsets a tendency to trivialise the problems created by the increasing concentration of children from poor families in a minority of schools by treating them as excuses rather than as partial but powerful explanations for educational failure.

'How much diversity is consistent with equality?' was identified by Michael Barber (1994: 359) as a key question for a future Labour government. Creating 'diversity without hierarchy', which is what the Conservatives claimed to be doing, requires that schools in a competitive quasi-market are regarded as different in kind but broadly equivalent in quality and esteem. This is why Hirsch (1997), drawing on the cross-national survey he had carried out for the OECD, concluded that where schools are judged to be 'good' by the same criteria, then demand is concentrated on the market leaders rather than being dispersed around a variety of suppliers. In those conditions, the likely outcomes are very unequal chances of being admitted to the most popular schools and the differentiation of schools more by intake than by what or how they teach (see also Whitty 1997). These polarising effects have been the main factor against 'free' parental choice. The evidence pointing one way or the other is highly contested, as Walford's chapter shows. Most of it, however, indicates an increasing middle-class advantage in entry to the 'best' schools and a widening gap in performance between those winning or losing in competition for pupils 'with whom it is easier to display effective schooling' (Green 1997: 106). Such inequitable effects justify limiting, in the public interests, the various forms of direct and indirect selection by favoured schools which a competitive market encourages (West and Pennell 1997).

Looking ahead

This chapter has identified questions about the structure of educational provision, particularly about the state's role in raising standards, which were being asked in 1976 and which remain unresolved. During my training as a history teacher, I was warned away from contemporary history because it lacked that vertical perspective from which the significance of past events can be understood from knowing what happened next. Looking ahead will obviously appear much more hazardous except to those whose ideology tells them that what 'must' be will be.

Whether the state should be involved at all in providing education is a question which market enthusiasts were beginning to raise in 1976, and which they have answered since with confidence that the times are on their side. They appear certain that what has been achieved already, although a very imperfect market, is both a point of no return and no more than an interim stage. What they see are those 'utopian uplands' in which a consumer-led competitive market will be 'independent of political control' (Sexton 1999: 169–71). There would be no state provision, no state funding except as a last resort, minimal state regulation and easy entry to the market for new education suppliers; in short, what is properly required of the state is that it should 'leave education well alone' (Tooley 2000: 1). In contrast, and although the contours of the 'third way' remain somewhat misty, it rejects the 'excesses' both of market individualism and of state enforced collectivism (Giddens 2000).

Both my historical training and a deep dislike of 'theories that tell all' rule out confident alternative prediction, and the brief 'conclusions' which follow are therefore hopes rather than firm expectations. I hope to see the balance sought by 'third way' politicians still weighted towards a publicly accountable public service and well away from the market view that the public good is nothing more than the aggregate of private choices. I question whether old social democracy was as committed to 'egalitarianism at all costs' as Giddens claims, or whether the 'dynamic life chances approach' which he advocates in its place can continue to underestimate the impact of socio-economic factors on school-level performance or fail to encourage rigorous investigation of the effects of consumer choice.

From my perspective, I would like to think that 'the limits of the quasi-market have nearly been reached' (Gordon and Whitty 1997: 46). I welcome the Labour government's commitment to 'high-quality education for the many rather than excellence for the few'. But as Robertson and Lauder point out in their chapter, there have been so many 'experimental' initiatives in educational provision that even the most fervent believers in evaluating their effects would be hard pushed to identify what caused what. What is certain is that, while educational success has become more critical in shaping life chances, and for a very much higher proportion of the age group than in 1976, educational opportunities have not become less unequal. At the same time, I hope that current efforts to raise standards 'for all' avoid treating educational improvement mainly as a requirement for economic competitiveness, and complement that objective with the broader benefits of good education to citizenship and quality of life. I also hope that the abandonment of notions of common schooling will come to seem a less obvious consequence of the heterogeneity of modern society. To an extent which probably reflects my continuing interest in 'old' sociology, I reject the view of education as the individualised consumption of differentiated products and retain some belief in the potential power of schooling to develop a sense of attachment to collective life across widening social and cultural divisions.

Acknowledgement

I am grateful for constructive comments on an earlier version of this chapter from Frank Coffield.

References

Aldrich, R., Crook, D. and Watson, D. (2000) *Education and Employment: The Department for Education and Employment and its Place in History*, London: Institute of Education.

Ashton, D. and Green, F. (1996) *Education, Training and the Global Economy*, Cheltenham: Edward Elgar.

Ball, S. (1990) *Politics and Policy Making in Education: Explorations in Policy Sociology*, London: Routledge.

——(1999) 'Labour, learning and the economy: a "policy sociology" perspective', *Cambridge Journal of Education*, 29(2): 195–206.

Barber, M. (1994) 'Power and control in education 1944–2004', *British Journal of Educational Studies*, 42(4): 348–62.

Benn, C. and Chitty, C. (1996) *Thirty Years On: Is Comprehensive Education Alive and Well, or Struggling to Survive?* London: David Fulton.

Boyson, R. (1975) *The Crisis in Education*, London: Woburn.

Bynner, J. (1999) 'New routes to employment: integration and exclusion', in W. Heinz (ed.) *From Education to Work: Cross-National Perspectives*, Cambridge: Cambridge University Press.

Bynner, J., Ferri, E. and Shephard, P. (eds) (1997) *Twenty-Something in the 1990s: Getting On, Getting By, and Getting Nowhere*, Aldershot: Ashgate Press.

Chubb, J. and Moe, T. (1992) 'The classroom revolution: how to get the best from British schools', *Sunday Times*, 9 February: 18–36.

Coffield, F. (1999) 'Breaking the consensus: lifelong learning as social control', *British Educational Research Journal*, 25(4): 479–99.

Crook, D., Power, S. and Whitty, G. (1999) *The Grammar School Question: A Review of Research on Comprehensive and Selective Education*, London: Institute of Education.

Daugherty, R. (1995) *National Curriculum Assessment: A Review of Policy 1987–1994*, London: Falmer.

DfEE (1997) *Excellence in Schools*, London: Stationery Office.

——(1999) *Excellence in Cities*, London: Stationery Office.

Edwards, T. (1997) 'Educating leaders and training followers', in T. Edwards, C. Fitz-Gibbon, F. Hardman, R. Haywood and N. Meagher (eds) *Separate but Equal? A-levels and GNVQs*, London: Routledge.

Edwards, T. and Whitty, G. (1994) 'Education: opportunity, equality and efficiency', in A. Glyn and D. Miliband (eds) *Paying for Inequality: The Economic Cost of Social Injustice*, London: Rivers Oram Press.

Edwards, T., Fitz, J. and Whitty, G. (1989) *The State and Private Education: An Evaluation of the Assisted Places Scheme*, Lewes: Falmer.

Edwards, T., Power, S. and Whitty, G. (1999) 'Moving back from comprehensive education?' in J. Demaine (ed.) *Education Policy and Contemporary Politics*, London: Macmillan.

Elliott, B. and MacLennan, D. (1994) 'Education, modernity and neo-conservative school reform in Canada, Britain and the United States', *British Journal of Sociology of Education*, 15(2): 165–85.

Finch, J. (1984) *Education as Social Policy*, London: Longman.

Giddens, A. (2000) *The Third Way and its Critics*, Cambridge: Polity Press.

Glennerster, H. (1995) *British Social Policy Since 1945*, Oxford: Blackwell.

Glennerster, H. and Hills, J. (1998) *The State of Welfare*, 2nd edition, Oxford: Oxford University Press.

Gordon, L. and Whitty, G. (1997) 'Giving the "hidden hand" a helping hand? The rhetoric and reality of neo-liberal education reform in England and New Zealand', *Comparative Education*, 33(3): 453–67.

Graham, D. with Tytler, D. (1993) *A Lesson for Us All: The Making of the National Curriculum*, London: Routledge.

Green, A. (1997) *Education, Globalization and the Nation State*, Basingstoke: Macmillan.

Halsey, A. (1993) 'Trends in access and equity in higher education: Britain in international perspective', *Oxford Review of Education*, 19(2): 129–40.

Halsey, A., Lauder, H., Brown, P. and Wells, A. (1997) 'The transformation of education and society', in A. Halsey, H. Lauder, P. Brown and A. Wells (eds) *Education, Culture, Economy, Society*, Oxford: Oxford University Press.

Hillgate Group (1987) *The Reform of British Education*, London: Claridge Press.

Hirsch, D. (1997) 'Policies for school choice: what can Britain learn from abroad?' in R. Glatter, P. Woods and C. Bagley (eds) *Choice and Diversity in Schooling*, London: Routledge.

Johnson, R. (1989) 'Thatcherism and English education: breaking the mould or confirming the pattern?' *History of Education*, 8(2): 91–121.

Kerckhoff, A., Fogelman, K., Crook, D. and Reeder, D. (1996) *Going Comprehensive in England and Wales*, London: Woburn.

Knight, C. (1990) *The Making of Tory Education Policy in Post-War Britain 1950–1986*, Barcombe: Falmer.

Lawton, D. (1994) *The Tory Mind on Education 1979–1994*, London: Falmer.

Marquand, D. (1988) 'The paradoxes of Thatcherism', in R. Skidelsky (ed.) *Thatcherism*, London: Chatto & Windus.

Merson, M. (1995) 'Political explanations for economic decline in Britain and their relationship to policies for education and training', *Journal of Education Policy*, 30(3): 304–15.

O'Hear, A. (1991) *Education and Democracy: Against the Educational Establishment*, London: Claridge.

Parry, G. (1999) 'Education research and policy making in higher education', *Journal of Education Policy*, 14(3): 225–42.

Patten, C. (1983) *The Tory Case*, London: Longman.

Pierson, C. (1998) 'The new governance of education: the Conservatives and education 1988–1997', *Oxford Review of Education*, 24(1): 134–42.

Power, S. and Whitty, G. (1999) 'New Labour's education policy: first, second or third way?' *Journal of Education Policy*, 14(5): 533–46.

Ribbins, P. and Sherratt, B. (1997) *Radical Education Policies and Conservative Secretaries of State*, London: Cassell.

Robinson, P. and Openheim, C. (1998) *Social Exclusion Indicators*, London: Institute for Public Policy Research.

Seddon, T. (1997) 'Markets and the English: rethinking educational restructuring as institutional design', *British Journal of Sociology of Education*, 18(2): 165–86.

Sexton, S. (1987) *Our Schools – A Radical Policy*, London: Institute for Economic Affairs Education Unit.

——(1999) 'Education policy: the next ten years', in J. Demaine (ed.) *Education Policy and Contemporary Politics*, Basingstoke: Macmillan.

Thatcher, M. (1997) *The Downing Street Years*, 2nd edition, London: HarperCollins.

Timmins, N. (1996) *The Five Giants: A Biography of the Welfare State*, London: Fontana.

Tooley, J. (2000) *Reclaiming Education*, London: Cassell.

West, A. and Pennell, H. (1997) 'Educational reform and school choice in England and Wales', *Education Economics*, 5(3): 285–305.

West, E.G. (1970) *Education and the State*, 2nd edition, London: Institute of Economic Affairs.

Whitty, G. (1997) 'Creating quasi-markets in education: a review of recent research on parental choice and school autonomy in three countries', *Review of Research in Education*, 22: 3–47.

Whitty, G., Power, S. and Halpin, D. (1998) *Devolution and Choice in Education*, Buckingham: Open University Press.

Index